GW01372960

First published April 2013 in Great Britain by InfoDial Ltd
PO Box 195
Prenton
CH26 9DF

www.roydutton.co.uk

Copyright © 2013 by Roy Dutton

Every effort has been made to locate and contact the holders of copyright material reproduced in this book.

All rights reserved. No part of this book may be reproduced or transmitted in any form or by any means, electronic or mechanical, including photocopying, recording, or by any information storage and retrieval system, without the written permission of the Publisher, except where permitted by law.

Ships in the Mersey

This book is dedicated to my family who proceded me and those that will follow.

Acknowledgements

I would like to thank Mr Ken Clark and for allowing me to use of his photographs. Also thanks to the late Stewart Bale for some spectacular photographs taken in the period between the wars and later.
Special thanks to Carla Bird for permission to reproduce Bob Bird's photographs used in the *Wallasey News*.
Moe Koltuniak for photographs and information concerning Lilian & Bill Jones, and New Brighton RLNI.
I would like to thank Gary Dutton for information in connection with the Dutton Ancestry, together with some interesting photographs.
Maureen Peers for some fantastic photographs of family members.
Also Mr Robert Bailey for our wonderful informative conversations, both verbal and by email.
Chris Middlemiss for his M.T.C photographs and news sheets.
Mr Steven Sharp for access to Mr Brian Foster's Archive and for his foresight in saving the same from a skip.
Mr Martin Pugh and Mr David Hepkie for permission to use their New Brighton photographs.
The many photographers who had the foresight to record our glorious past whose names we will never know.
Members of the Library staff at Elston library for their help and assistant.
Several photographs of special interest including the Horror House photo thanks to the National Fairground Archive, held at University of Sheffield.
Local Newspapers, *Liverpool Mercury*, *Cheshire Observer*, and *Wallasey News*, and *National Illustrated London News* and *The Graphic*. And finally the wealth of information to be found on the internet, including Paul's History of Wallasey web site and Group on facebook.

"OLDEN TIMES."

Though the coachmen of old are dead,
Though the guards are turned to clay,
There are those who remember the "yard of tin,"
And the Mail of the olden day.

The good old Coach of days gone by,
Why should thy wheels now idle lie?
The pleasant road—the vale and hill,
Are England's treasured pictures still.

Contents

CHAPTER 1 - The Dutton Family
Introduction p 4 - Dutton Family History 1631-1860 p 5
Setting the scene p 10 -Ham and Egg Parade p 11 - Promenade p13
New Brighton Pier p 14 - Field Road p15 - Old Wallasey p16
Hunts Guide to New Brighton 1877 p17 - Inspector Dutton p 34
John Dutton 1841-1910 p 36 - Liscard Village p 43 - Doctor Crippen p 44
May Day 1901 p 46 - Margaret Dutton 1840 - 1911 p 47
John & Margaret's children p 48 - Mary Dutton p 49 - Shara Dutton p 50
Harriet Dutton p 51 - Thomas Dutton 1867 - 1939 p 52
John Dutton 1869 - 1937 p 55 - Margaret Dutton p 57
Edward W. Dutton p 58 - Liscard Model Farm p 59 - William Dutton p 60
Wallasey Carnival p 62 - James H.Dutton p 64 - Dutton gravestone p 67
Liscard p 64 - Thomas Dutton's children p 69 - Emily E. Dutton p 70
Edward Dutton p 72 - Thomas Dutton 1897 - 1976 p76 - Edith Dutton p 80
Alfred Dutton p 82 - Yoxall Wedding p 95

CHAPTER 2 - The Hammond Family
Peter Hammond 1838 - 1896 p 96 - Julia M. Hammond p 97
Dorothy Hammond p 99 - George Hammond p 101
Sidney Hammond p 102 - A mysterious relative p 104
Family photographs p 105 - Joyce's story p 106 - Eve's story p 119

CHAPTER 3 - My Autobiography
The early years p 130 - New Brighton Baths p149
My Neighbourhood p 150 - New Brighton in the 1960s p 158
The Tivoli p 160 - Birkenhead Market p 161
School years p 162 - The Big Bang p 183
Buried Treasure p 186 - Wirral Astronomical Society p 194
Smugglers Cave p 197 - Civil Defence p 198
New Brighton Tower p 199 - Tommy Mann's MIniature Railway p 211
Palace Indoor Fairgrounds 215 - Tenpin Bowling p 219
Wilkies Circus p 220 - Captains Pit p 222

CHAPTER 4 - My Working Career
Sunderland Forge p 225 - Tate & Lyles p 229 - T&J Harrison p 239
Cadbury p 259 - Octel p 262 - Bidston Steel p 263 - Costain p 276

CHAPTER 5 - Pop Groups
Pop Groups p 291 - Clubs and Pubs p 301 - Buy a Pet p 308
Richard & Jenny p 309 - Liverpool F.C p 310 - Strange goings on p 311
Mountaineering & Touring Club p 312 - Family photographs p 315

Appendix -317

Introduction

Introduction
The famous opening words in Dickens novel *A Tale of Two Cities - It was the best of times it was the worst of times* - also apply to my tenure on the planet. My life has been a magical experience with many people helping me along the way. It all took part in the "Playground of the North" my Disneyland New Brighton.
For over sixteen decades my family has been woven into the very fabric of Wallasey life. The book, with many original photographs and information, was originally intended for members of our family, but it may be of interest to a wider audience. Many of the places described no longer exist and have been wiped off the map. Life is an adventure and I have tried to aspire to certain objectives for myself and family in my progress through this maze of reality and dreams. Within these pages I try to explain my life, my thoughts, my passions and my philosophy to the generations that follow me. This is a real indulgence for me as I can write whatever I like because I am the publisher. I don't need sales of 1,000s of copies - I only need to satisfy a burning desire to record our family history. I have been very fortunate to have met many interesting characters; some have had an influence on me, some have persecuted me and others have been my inspiration. The book starts with the history of the Dutton's on my fathers side and the Hammond's on my mothers side of the family.
Most peoples lives are like a footprint in the sand. No one is immortal but I honestly believe that, just like DNA has mapped the genome and the very essence of our humanity, so in the future every single thought that has passed through your mind can be revealed to future generations.
Science will tap into your brains DNA, but just in case I am wrong and to entertain a generation or two in the future, I have penned this book. We live in the heads of those who remember us; it could be said that your very existence exists in the eyes and ears of others. So if the memory becomes distorted, this book could help set the record straight.

My academic limitations have been a draw back to expressing my observations of the world so with this in mind I have gifted my offspring the best education that money can buy. My next most important mission in life is to indulgence in travel, especially visits to ancient monuments to try and understand the origins of humanity with the ultimate goal of visiting 100 countries. My other passion to write books about my heroes that are seldom acknowledged in our politically correct society.
I make no excuse for the liberal use of photographs throughout this work. My mother was the proud owner of a Kodak Brownie Camera and would take photographs whenever the opportunity arose. When the shutter clicks, the picture is well and truly frozen in time, and every picture tells a story. Welcome to my life and my ancestors, I hope you have as much enjoyment reading this book as much as I have had in writing it.

Dutton Family History 1631-1860

Beginning my Research with the 1861 Census

My starting point was my uncle Edward's article in the *Wallasey News* dated 22 November 1952 which clearly stated that John and Margaret Dutton had lived in Saighton, Chester before they moved to the Wirral in the 1860s. I enquired at the local post office to try and locate the village church, and was informed that the church of St. Mary The Virgin Bruera was the nearest to Saighton. I had hoped to locate the church records, but having spoken to the vicar, found that all the records had been placed in the Chester Archives. Enquiring into the possibility of a Dutton being buried in the churchyard, I was informed that there were indeed a large number. That weekend I travelled down to the church, and to my amazement, on entering the churchyard, I found the grave of my great-great- grandfather Thomas Dutton located only a short distance on the right- hand side of the path leading to the church. The inscription on the stone read as follows:

"In memory of Mary, Daughter of Thomas and Jane Dutton of Churton Heath, who died March 4th 1842 aged 17 months. For of such is the kingdom of heaven. Also the above Jane Dutton who died December 11th 1874 aged 68 years. Also the above Thomas Dutton died February 1st 1888 aged 83 years."

Searching through the numerous Dutton tombstones, I was unable to make any other connections. Taking the search further, I visited the Chester archives where I discovered the marriage of John and Margaret. I had hoped they might have been married shortly before they moved to the Wirral. Saighton is in the parish of Chester St. Oswald, and I was fortunate enough to find the marriage records quite easily.

25th December 1859 (Record of John Dutton's marriage) St. Mary's Church

John Dutton, 20	Bachelor Labourer	Saighton	Thomas Dutton	Labourer
Margaret Roberts	Full Spinster	Saighton	Edward Roberts	Labourer

Witnesses
John Dutton, X (his mark)   Samuel Fleet, X   (his mark)
Margaret Roberts   Mary Baker, X   (her mark)

I then checked the 1861 Census of Saighton and found:
Bruera   Place of Birth
Thomas Dutton   Head   55   Labourer   Tattenhall   Cheshire
Jane Dutton   Wife   55   Malpas   Cheshire
Mary Dutton   Daughter 17   Housemaid Churton Heath Cheshire
Elizabeth Dutton   Daughter 14   Housemaid Churton Heath Cheshire

Dutton Family History 1631-1860

I did not find John and Margaret Dutton and feel they might have moved immediately after their marriage. I then checked the 1851 Census and found;

Bruera Chapelry	(1851 Census)			Place of Birth	
Thomas Dutton	Head	46	Agricultural Labourer	Tattenhall	Cheshire
Jane Dutton	Wife	46		Malpas	Cheshire
John Dutton	Son	9	Scholar	Saighton	Cheshire
Mary Ann Dutton	Daughter	7	Scholar	Saighton	Cheshire
Elizabeth Dutton	Daughter	5	Scholar	Saighton	Cheshire

I also found the Roberts family;

Saighton Village	(1851 Census)			Place of Birth	
Edward Roberts	Head	49	Farm Labourer	Denbighshire	N. Wales
Ann Roberts	Wife	52		Huntington	Cheshire
Margaret Roberts	Daughter	11		Saighton	Cheshire
James Roberts	Son	10		Saighton	Cheshire
Harriet Roberts	Daughter	5		Saighton	Cheshire

Churton Heath (or Bruera Chapelry) in the Parish of St. Mary-on-the-Hill. (Chester is 5 miles south-by-east). It has a small church, called St Mary's (commonly called the church on the heath), consisting of nave and chancel with a small turret containing one bell. The acreage of the township was 129, the population in 1861 was 44.

The next step was to trace the marriage of Thomas and Jane.

I then found the birth of Thomas:

Nov 6th 1804 Thomas Dutton, son of Richard Dutton of Tattenhall, farmer and Rachel Dutton, daughter of Samuel Wright.
Sept 2nd 1803   ? Dutton, daughter of Richard Dutton and Rachel.
June 14th 1806 Mary Dutton, daughter of Richard Dutton and Rachel.
Marriage 15th August 1802

Richard Dutton of the parish of Bunbury to Rachael Wright of this parish by license.

Richard's baptism in 1781 was quickly found. The bond relating to his marriage in 1802 showed that he was at least aged 21 at the time and therefore must have been born in 1781 or earlier. Entry for his older brother Thomas, son of Joseph Dutton, is recorded at Burwardsley in September

> Banns of Marriage
>
> N° 176 Richard Dutton of the Parish of Bunbury and Rachel Wright of this Parish were Married in this ____ by Licence ____ this ____ Day of August in the Year One Thousand eight Hundred and two by me Charles ____ Minister
> This Marriage was solemnized between Us { Richard Dutton / Rachel Wright }

> KNOW all Men by these Presents, That we Richard Dutton of Burwardsley in the Parish of Bunbury Farmer and John Hough of Beeston in the Parish of Bunbury aforesaid Farmer are held and firmly bound unto the Right Reverend Father in God Henry William by Divine Permission, Lord Bishop of Chester — in the Sum of Five hundred Pounds, of good and lawful Money of the united Kingdom of Great Britain and Ireland, current in that Part of the said Kingdom called England, to be paid unto the said Right Reverend Father, his lawful Attorney, Executors, Administrators, or Assigns; to which Payment well and truly to be made, we bind ourselves and each of us severally for and in the whole, our Heirs, Executors, and Administrators, and the Heirs, Executors, and Administrators, of each of us firmly by these Presents. Sealed with our Seals, and dated the fourteenth Day of August in the forty Second Year of the Reign our Sovereign Lord GEORGE the Third, by the Grace of God of the United Kingdom of Great Britain and Ireland King, Defender of the Faith, and in the Year of our Lord God, One Thousand Eight Hundred and two —

> THE Condition of this Obligation is such, that if the above-bounden Richard Dutton and Rachel Wright — now licensed to be married together, be neither of Consanguinity, or Affinity, the one to the other, within the Degrees prohibited for Marriage: It also there be no Let or Impediment, by Reason of any Precontract, entered into before the Twenty-fifth Day of March, One Thousand Seven Hundred and Fifty Four, or any other lawful Cause whatsoever, but that they may be lawfully married together, both by the Laws of GOD, and this Land: Moreover, if the Persons, whose Consent is required by Law in this Behalf, be thereunto agreeing: And lastly, if the said Marriage be done and solemnized in such Manner, as in the Licence to them granted is limited: Then this Obligation to be void, or else to remain in full Force and Virtue.
>
> Sealed and delivered in the Presence of   Richard Dutton

1754, but Joseph was not among the marriages recorded there, nor was he married at Bunbury. A check of Malpas baptisms, however, revealed a Joseph, son of Mary Dutton, baptised on the 13th June 1722, also a Benjamin Dutton of Farndon, 30th August 1722, and that both were 30 years old at the time. I feel sure that this Joseph must be 'ours' especially as he named his first son Benjamin (Burwardsley, 8th January 1748/9. The children of Benjamin and Mary we have are Robert (Harthill, 15th July 1723, Thomas (Malpas, 20th September 1725, and there is also a Martha baptised at Harthill on the 17th June, but can only be dated between

Chapter 1 - Dutton Family History 1631-1860

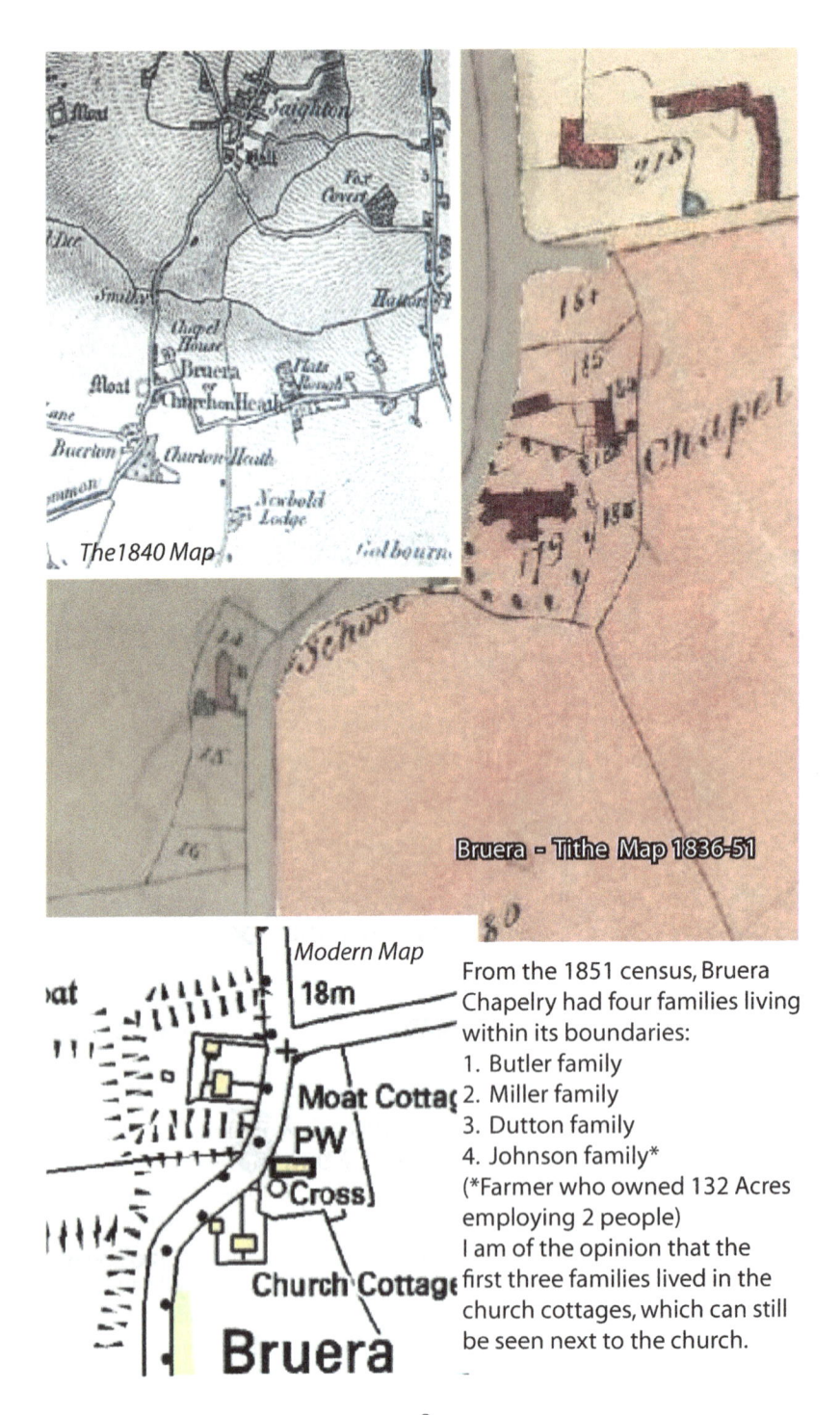

The 1840 Map

Bruera - Tithe Map 1836-51

Modern Map

From the 1851 census, Bruera Chapelry had four families living within its boundaries:
1. Butler family
2. Miller family
3. Dutton family
4. Johnson family*
(*Farmer who owned 132 Acres employing 2 people)
I am of the opinion that the first three families lived in the church cottages, which can still be seen next to the church.

8

Chapter 1 - Dutton Family History 1631-1860

1729 and 1733, as these years have not yet been searched. What is not clear is whether Benjamin was actually the father of Joseph, or whether the marriage of Benjamin and Mary was a marriage of convenience, he possibly being a relation outside the prohibited degrees of marriage who was willing to provide for Mary and her illegitimate child. I looked at the will of John Dutton of Broxton 1722, thinking that it might give some indication. It mentions a daughter Mary and a granddaughter, Mary, but there is no reference to either being married or having an illegitimate child. A search of Farndon baptisms 1665-95 revealed the baptism of Benjamin, son of Thomas on the 1st January 1690/1. I found other children of Thomas in earlier years. Although there were entries going back from 1682, I felt that these must be children of either a different Thomas or a previous marriage. There is a record of a marriage license issued to a Thomas of Farndon on the 6th August 1687 which would fit with the entries from 1688 onwards. The marriage did not take place at Farndon, and the Holt register has not yet been checked.

Malpas baptisms 1688-92 and Harthill baptisms 1688-92 did not contain any Dutton entries, but I found an entry for Mary, son of John of Haughton in Bunbury on the 1st November 1692. From the records, there was more than one John in the parish, but I think Mary's father was the John of Haughton who was licensed to marry Mary Ferman on the 3rd April 1684. The marriage is recorded on the 5th April 1684 in the typed version of Nantwich registers, where Mary's surname is given as Fennah.

Searches of Malpas 1670-40, Farndon 1670-40 and Bunbury 1670-53 have revealed the baptism of only one Thomas who could be Benjamin's father, at Bunbury on the 22nd June 1658. More research would be needed to try to settle this. It becomes increasingly difficult to identify the lines this early because of the limited detail given, as well as the physical condition of some of the records. In another search earlier I happened to notice the burial of Mary, wife, of Benjamin Dutton, at Farndon on the 23rd April 1762. We may have Benjamin's line back to Thomas who married Margaret Lewis in 1627. I knew it was not going to be easy to work out, and so it proved. First I thought that Benjamin's father was Thomas who married Sarah Bankes in 1687, and that he was the son of Thomas who married Elizabeth Edge in 1656/7. However, this latter Thomas left a will proved in 1692, in which he refers to his wife Sarah. This prompted me to search further for another Thomas as a father to Benjamin. I searched Tattenhall registers, which was very time consuming, as the registers are badly faded I did find a Thomas baptised in 1665, the son of Peter Dutton. Peter had another son, Benjamin baptised in 1668. I pursued this line for a while, but in the end rejected it. Peter's Christian name does not recur in our line, and I think it would have done had there been a direct link. Going back to Thomas's, I think the answer is probably that Thomas (1631-2/92) married twice, firstly to Elizabeth, and secondly to Sarah. This is not proved.

Chapter 1 - Setting the scene

To set the scene for the arrival of my ancestors in Wallasey I have started this section with the very first official Hunt's guide to New Brighton produced in 1877, together with some of the oldest photographs and illustrations in my collection.

Chapter 1 - Ham and Egg Parade

New Brighton's Palace Theatre, opened in 1882, and was part of a small-scale covered amusement park, a theatre, a skating rink and an aquarium. It was demolished in 1933.

The photograph above shows the sea wall extension. The foundation stone was laid by the late Lord Leverhulme, then William Hesketh Lever, Esq., M.P on 22nd June, 1907, and stands opposite the new Floral Pavilion.

Chapter 1 - Ham and Egg Parade

New Brighton had a skeleton and it wasn't in the cupboard! The 'Ham and Egg Parade' was big, brash, and vulgar, with cheap lodging houses and eating houses. It was not only a thorn in the side of Victorian and Edwardian respectability, but a total embarrassment to the council who in 1905 bought the property and pulled the lot down. It had been a hawkers' paradise, with shooting galleries and fortune-tellers. There were wooden steps down to the soft white sands; the walkway outside was so narrow that quite often people fell off. The sands opposite were disfigured by tawdry sideshows. Degeneration had set in.
There were fights. There were it was said "goings on." It was certainly rich with life and colour. It cost the Wallasey Urban District Council the princely sum of £41,500 to buy it and then knock it down. The town applauded its removal. A eyesore had gone.

The notorious "Ham and Egg Parade." displaced by Victoria Gardens below.

Chapter 1 - Promenade

Until 1891 the River Mersey was open to the shore, with the exception of small areas adjoining the Seacombe and Egremont Ferries and the 'Ham and Egg' Parade near the New Brighton Ferry. The first length of promenade to be constructed extended from the bottom of Sandon Road to Egremont Ferry, this was extended to just south of Holland Road in 1891 and some eight years later to beyond New Brighton pier.

New Brighton Pier

The pier is supported upon 120 stone columns, firmly fixed in the rocky foundations. Four lines of longitudinal main girders run throughout the entire length of the pier, braced diagonally and transversely with wrought-iron beams fixed to the main girders and upon these are laid planks, wedged and bolted and covered with close planking, to afford an even and comfortable promenade. Along the entire length of the pier sitting accommodation is provided. The area of the pier is between 50,000 and 60,000 superficial feet. There is a handsome saloon, with ornamental houses available for shelter; there is also a refreshment room.
From the bazaars in the centre tower and the galleries over the saloon there are magnificent views of the shipping in the River Mersey.
There is a splendid area provided for the band, and there are weather screens similar to those erected at Brighton New Pier for the first time, which have been highly appreciated by the public. Entrance to the pier is by a flight of steps, 30ft, in width, from the gangway of the landing pontoon recently erected by the Wallasey Commissioners.
(*Illustrated London News 1867*)

13

Chapter 1 - New Brighton Pier

Don't Forget the Diver - Recollections of a holidaymaker.
Most years we spent our Wakes-Week holiday at Egremont, on the Wirral peninsula. It was a poor relation of the grander seaside resort of New Brighton. We could not afford the fleshpots of New Brighton but several times a week we could taste its heady delights, for it was within walking distance. As a special treat we sometimes made the short trip by boat, catching one of the fussy, black and white, round-rumped ferry boats. Two of these boats had earned the prefix 'Royal' because of their part in the raid on Zeebrugge in 1918. They were the *Royal Daffodil* and the *Royal Iris*.

When we did go by boat one of the exciting things to look out for was the famous diver. He was a daring, one-legged man who made death defying dives from the height of New Brighton pier into the murky waters of the Mersey. He timed his spectacular plunges with the arrival of the ferry-boat full of trippers, and his wife collected pennies from them by means of a bag on a long stick. She would cry, 'Come on now. Don't forget the diver. Every penny makes the water warmer,' and, 'If you don't put a penny in the bag it'll rain before you go home tonight.' After each dive he had to climb back up a narrow, iron companion ladder, his one leg making him hump up like a sea lion. This impressed me almost as much as the dive.

The Liverpool comedian Tommy Handley, in the ITMA broadcasts during the last war, used the catchphrase "Don't forget the diver."

Chapter 1 - Field Road

Tram shown at the top of Field Road / Rowson Street. Wallasey United Tramway & Omnibus Co Ltd.

Horse Tram Depot, opposite my house at 33 Field Road.

15

Chapter 1 - Old Wallasey

The Smithy, School Lane, Wallasey. Resident in 1881 William Peacock blacksmith, wife Ellen and two daughters Mary and Margaret.

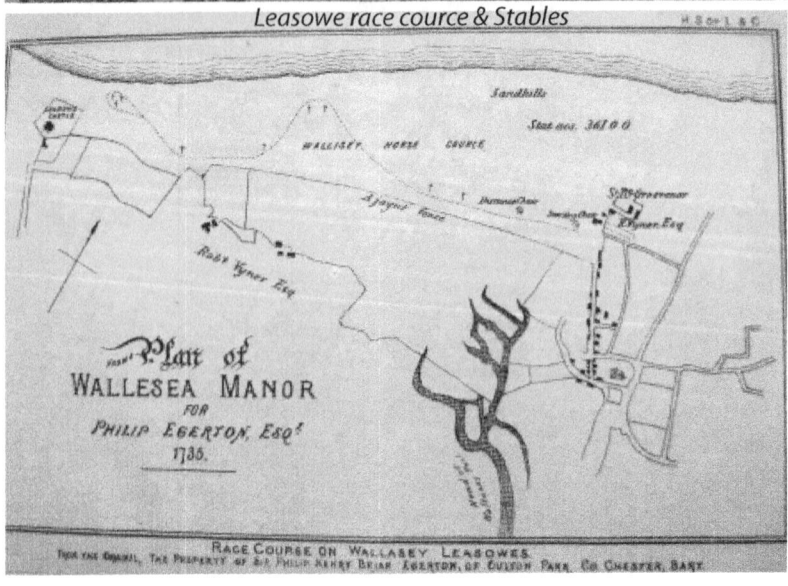

Leasowe race cource & Stables

Chapter 1 - Hunt's Guide to New Brighton 1877

HUNT'S
ILLUSTRATED GUIDE
TO
NEW BRIGHTON,

(With Six Finely Engraved Views,)

AND

List of Cab and Boat Fares, Horse-hire, and Charges to Places of Amusement and Refreshment.

PUBLISHED BY
J. HUNT, THE LIBRARY, NEW BRIGHTON.
1877.
Entered at Stationers' Hall.

Chapter 1 - Hunt's Guide to New Brighton 1877

These old town guides make for delightful reading and there follow some extracts from The 1877 Hunt's Guide to New Brighton.
The want of a Guide to New Brighton has been so long felt, that last summer our librarian determined that before another season came round one should be supplied at any risk, and that the guide should be

PROMENADE PIER NEW BRIGHTON

published in a cheap form, so as to place it within the reach of all classes of visitors. In giving this little work to the public, we have endeavoured not only to point out to the visitor where he can go, and what is best worthy of his attention, but also to give in full the carriage fares, boat fares, charges for horse hire, and the prices of admission to the different places of amusement and refreshment in and around New Brighton, so that the reader may at once decide what places he would most like to see, and how much he requires to spend, without wasting the too fleeting hours of his brief holiday in endless discussions, which have hitherto too often resulted in his doing nothing but strolling over the sands under a scorching sun, to the intense fatigue of his wife and children, if not his own.

New Brighton was first brought into existence by Mr James Atherton, an eminent Liverpool merchant, who, in 1830, purchased 170 acres of sand hills. Our visitors can hardly realize that just 47 years ago this lovely little spot, now so full of interest and life, was but a desert waste of endless sand hills. So fast do we move on that now it is the most numerously attended of all our local watering places.

At the Liverpool Landing Stage our visitor will find a steamer ready to start for New Brighton every half hour 7.45am until 11 pm. The first boat leaves New Brighton at 7.50 am and every ten minutes before and twenty minutes past the hour till 10.20 pm for Liverpool. In summer the New Brighton boatmen will gladly row visitors all the way back to Liverpool for a very low charge; and for those who are fond of the sea this will be found a pleasanter mode of transit than the overcrowded steamer. The following are the boat fares:-

    Rowing Boat, one hour ... 2s
    Rowing Boat, two hour ... 3s
    Sailing Boat, per hour ... 2s
    For the whole day, 1s per hour,

When the boat leaves the Liverpool Stage, she steams across the river to Egremont ferry. After a delay of a few moments, to land and embark passengers, the steamer turns her head seaward, and soon comes in sight of the beautiful wood-clad hill on her left. Through the dense foliage we catch here and there glimpses of the old stone gables of Rock Point, the beautiful residence of the Molyneux family. A little further on, nestling modestly in a very bower of green, as if ashamed of its close proximity to the large mansion, is the charming little villa called West Bank, while the hill itself is fitly crowned by the tapering spire of New Brighton church. We must call the visitors attention to a large boat moored to the south end of the stage. It is conspicuous for its gay painting of pink, white and blue. This is the New Brighton life boat. As she lies there dancing so peacefully in the sunshine, one can hardly realize that her brave crew have nobly encountered many a fearful storm, and carried life and hope to perished souls, shipwrecked on our coast. Not less than 160 were saved by the *Willie and Arthur* during the last three years, under the command of Captain Thomas. Is it not, we ask, a standing disgrace to the largest maritime town in England, that these brave men are so poorly recompensed for the terrible risks they run to save human life. It has been truly said no amount of money could repay them, and that many volunteer their services for nothing. This is quite true. Still, money would enable them to make provision for the helpless ones depending on them at home. A moment more and the steamer is alongside the landing-stage, and the visitor finds himself on New Brighton Pier. This new pier was opened in 1867. On the right is the Promenade, 550 feet long, 70 to 130 feet wide at the back is a covered saloon 180 feet long, 28 to 34 feet wide above it is a similar promenade with a Byzantine tower in the centre. From this pier there is a splendid view of the whole line of Liverpool docks which now reach as far as New Brighton on the opposite side of the river These docks are seven miles long and cost over £9,000,000. There is also an uninterrupted view down channel Formby and Crosby Lightships, Waterloo, Bootle all lying before us, with Welsh hills on the left. Here our large ocean going steamers may be seen to the greatest advantage, passing in and out. There is a yearly Regatta, which take place at the

Chapter 1 - Hunt's Guide to New Brighton 1877

end of August or early in September. The flagship is generally anchored close to the pier. There are also constant sailing matches throughout the summer.

Admission to the Promenade pier...2d
Admission upper Promenade……...1d

The Pier & Promenade New Brighton

It would be a vast improvement if that part of the pier leading to and from the steamers could be covered, for it is no easy matter to get along when there is a strong north-west wind blowing. Having reached the end of the pier a sharp turn to the right leads to the foreshore along which we now take our reader. On the left an upper and lower terrace has been erected within the last few years. The upper terrace consist of good sized houses, chiefly let as lodging houses. The lower terrace consists entirely of refreshment rooms very neatly got up in the French style. Here the holiday maker can procure a substantial dinner or tea at most moderate chargers, Standing in front of these terraces the stranger might fancy a fair was being held, for crowded together are swings of every kind, merry-go-rounds, shooting galleries, ice stands, weighting chairs, cheap photographers as well as an almost endless number of donkeys and ponies for hire. Here thousands are content to spend their day, and think they have seen New Brighton. A new Hotel Baths and Aquarium are being erected at the end of the Marine Parade.

The Fort or Battery, built on Perch Rock, forms a conspicuous object. This Fort was commenced 1826, and opened 1829, the total cost amounted to £26,965. It contains barrack rooms for 100 men, with officer's apartments. It mounts several large guns, and it's completely surround by water at high tide. It was erected under the superintendence of Capt. Kitson.

Chapter 1 - Hunt's Guide to New Brighton 1877

Esplanade, New Brighton

Visitors are allowed to go over the fort free of charges. About two hundred yards further on is the Rock Lighthouse, erected in 1830, on the same principle as the Eddystone, each stone being dovetailed into the others, and each course attached by iron braces, forming a solid piece of masonry up to 85 feet, above which are the keeper's room and the lantern. The lighthouse rises 90 feet above the level of the rock. Visitors can see the inside for a trifling gratuity. Between the Fort and Lighthouse there is a fresh water spring. It rises among the salt sea sand and it's buried twice a day below the waves, yet its water is fresh and sweet. Dr. Guthrie thus beautifully describes it *"Image of the Grace which, rising in a Christian heart a well of water springing up into everlasting life casts out impurities".* It is called the Widow's Well. A gentleman, taking pity on a woman who had been left destitute by the death of her husband, turned this spring into her means of living, by sinking a barrel over it, and installed the window there with a table and glasses to supply the travellers and earn their halfpence.

We pass the Marine Hotel and the principal Bathing ground, about which we must say a few words of warning to the stranger unacquainted with our shore. It is most unsafe to bathe on this side of the shore when the tide is going out, as there is a strong current and numerous quicksands. A large Flagstaff points out the Coast Guard Station. A little further on we come in sight of some of the prettiest villas in New Brighton hill all commanding a splendid sea view. Immediately in front of these villas are some curious red sandstones rocks, (commonly called "Red Noses") and caves, about which various legends are told. A very old man told us that here in ages past wicked sprites held high revel on stormy nights, luring the unwary mariners to destruction by waving their tiny torches. We are bound to say that our informant, though firmly believing in the wicked sprites when pressed hard was forced to confess he had never seen them, nor did he know any man who had.

The visitors can walk all the way to Leasowe along this shore, but we advise him to choose the road, as he will find the sand very fatiguing. Having seen all that there is to attract notice on the foreshore we invite our visitor to take a walk up our main street, called in honour of our good Queen, Victoria Road. It is no uncommon thing to hear both our residents and visitors remark "Oh, there is nothing to be got in New Brighton." Now experience has taught us this is far from true, and must be made in ignorance of the capabilities of our little town, or merely to serve as an excuse for a visit to Liverpool, as at the same prices the shops are numerous and well supplied.

The Victoria Hall

This hall has been finished during the last year, and is now open to the public. It is a fine hall, where concert and meeting are held.
It accommodates about 600 people. The Young Men's Christian Association meet here every week.

The New Brighton Skating Rink

This is situated halfway up Victoria Road, on the right, and approached by Wellington Road. There is a covered and open skating space of 4,000 square yards, open to the public daily, - Sunday excepted -

Morning	from	10 am to 1 pm
Afternoon	from	2.30 pm to 6.30 pm
Evening	from	6.30 pm to 9.30 pm.

Admission One Shilling. Sixpence is charged for hire of skates.

The Church

The Church, which was erected in 1855, is a handsome building, in the early English style, dedicated to St James. The Vicar is the Rev. Richard Drake Fowell. The Wesleyans have also a fine place of worship in Rowson Sreet. There is a small Welsh Chapel in Egerton Street.

The Lending Library

Mr Hunt, the librarian, is in charge of a large collection of standard works, besides a regular supply of new books every month. Any book not in the library can be readily procured on order. All the magazines and reviews are also to be had in this library. There is a first-class stationer's shop attached to the library, where most costly and elegant trifles of all kinds, suitable for birthday and Christmas gifts maybe be had. The visitor will here find rare specimens of art and literature, selected with much taste and care.

The Assembly Rooms

This building is on the summit of the hill, command a lovely view.
Six subscription balls are held here every year. The rooms are let for public and private use. They adjoin the Victoria Hotel, one of the oldest established here. Proprietor, Mr John Garrant,

Chapter 1 - Hunt's Guide to New Brighton 1877

Victoria Hotel

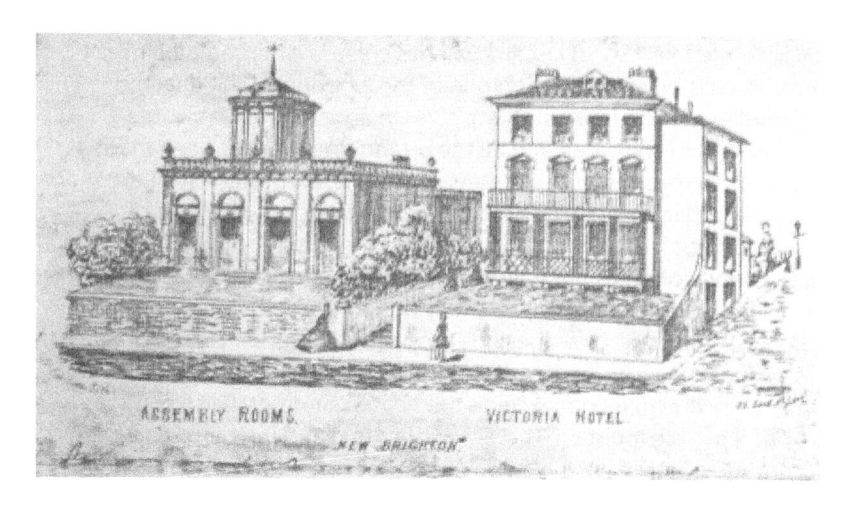

The Nursery Gardens
There are two excellent gardens of this kind in New Brighton, one at the top of Victoria Road, kept by Mr Turner, the other on St George's Mount, kept by Mr Langley. In these gardens the visitors can procure an ample supply of flowers during the summer, cut or in pots, grown for the table, at very moderate prices.
There is also another public garden, more exclusively for the sale of fruits and vegetables, in Egerton Street. Mr.Dawkins, Proprietor.
There is a Convalescent Institution for women, supported by subscription in Rowson Street.

Little Brighton
This is a small village between New Brighton and Liscard, and contains a handsome Congregational Church, of which the Minister is the Rev. John H, Gwyther, R.A.

Liscard
Liscard is a small village which has made very considerable progress in that century. The Church is a doric edifice, without tower or spire, and dedicated to St John. It was erected in 1833 to seat 2,000. The Reverend T P. Ball is the perpetual Curate. A new church, to be called St Mary's, is being erected in Within's Lane. There is a fine Roman Catholic Chapel, dedicated to St, Alban. The Primitive Methodists and the Society of Friends have also places of worship here. A fine Public Hall has been built in the last few years also handsome Free Grammar Schools.
In no place can the triumph of art and industry over the sterility of nature be more apparent than in this neighbourhood, where many of the mansions, now surrounded with almost luxuriant foliage, occupy a site which only a few years ago was but a waste of barren sand hills.

Chapter 1 - Hunt's Guide to New Brighton 1877

We cannot leave Liscard without calling the attention of our visitors to one who has created a garden where a wilderness formerly existed. Harold Littledale Esq of Liscard Hall has created a garden and model farm which is beyond question one of the wonders of the day, and is visited by all who interest themselves in agriculture. No trouble or expense has been spared and all the arrangements have been made by one of the best practical farmers of the day; the result has been everything that could be desired. The farm consist of 440 acres of arable land, with several model buildings. There is a comfortable and picturesque house for the bailiff, a dairy, labourers' cottages, stabling and cowsheds, rick yard, and indeed every possible convenience. There are stalls for a hundreds cows, besides proper buildings for calves. Great care has been taken to make the ventilation as a perfect as possible. The walls of the dairy are hollow to exclude the heat in summer it also contains a beautiful marble fountain. There is a room for smoking hams and curing bacon, a slaughter house, a smithy, manure tanks. A large pond feeds a tank which extends over the whole of one of the buildings and supplies the cattle with water. There is a huge steam engine, which does nearly everything from thrashing the corn to churning the butter.

Leaving the village of Liscard, the drive down hill to the Great Float (where, alas, so many of our large vessels and yachts now lie idle) is very pretty. We pass over the Halfpenny Bridge, leaving the Docks Cottages and St James Church on our left. Taking the road to the right we soon arrive at another interesting feature of the area.

Rhododendron Gardens.

These gardens, which are well worth a visit in the Spring when trees are literally covered with blossom, belong to Mr Vyner, who kindly opens them to the public free of charge for the summer months.

A narrow road on the West side of the gardens leads to the Bidston Observatory, on the top of the hill; and though the ascent is very fatiguing, the visitor will be amply repaid by the splendour of the view. The whole of the surrounding country for miles lying spread out as it were at his feet, like some magic picture framed by the mighty sea. Half a mile further on we come to the old village of

Bidston

The village is thus graphically described by poor Albert Smith in his *Christopher Tadpoles* - *"It is a little quite grey village - as very grey, indeed, and venerable and quaint that no flaunting red brick had dared to show itself and break the uniform tint of its gabled antiquity. The houses were grey, the wall fencings were grey, and so was the church tower, so also was the pedestal of the sundial is the graveyard, that so mutely spoke its lesson on corroding time to all who cared to heed it. And the old Grange, with its mullioned windows and ivy-covered gateway was the greyest of all. There was scarcely any surmising as to when it had been a green, damp, level, young house.*

Chapter 1 - Hunt's Guide to New Brighton 1877

The Ring a Bells, so celebrated for its consumption of ham and eggs in mighty quantities. You would have had bad luck through the year if you did not eat of both to something beyond repletion in the more or less Elizabethan parlour of the hostel. Whether the bells rang out too noisy chimes or not we cannot tell - they are silent now - no cheery sign invites the weary traveller to walk in and taste the beer and liquor, though our driver informed as we still could get tea with ham and eggs within the grey old walls.

Leaving Bidston, further on to the left is Upton Hall, the seat of William Inman Esq. of the celebrated Inman Line of Steamer sailing weekly from Liverpool to New York. Below lie the Convent and village of Woodchurch.

Leasowe Castle,

The seat of General Sir Edward Cust K.C.H was built is 1593 by Ferdinando, Earl of Derby, for a hunting lodge. It is situated two miles from the village of Wallasey. The Castle was for many years called "Mock Beggar Hall" which is a very ancient sailor's nickname for a large lone house and it is a name found along the entire shore of the kingdom.

The Egertons of Oulton held the Castle until 1784. It was afterwards sold to the widow of Lewis William Boode, Esq., who considerablely enlarged and improved it This lady was killed by a fall from her pony carriage in 1526. An elegant gothic cross marks the spot where the accident occurred, at the turn of the road from Poulton to Wallasey. This lady left the Castle to its present proprietor, the wife of Sir Edward Cust.

It is a fine stone building, containing several handsome apartments, one of which is fitted up with the chimney-place and oak panelling that once covered the walls of the famous Star Chamber, at Westminster. Wallasey Leasowe was the oldest gentlemen's race course in the kingdom. It is said the Duke of Monmouth, son of Charles the Second, rode his own horse at one of these races, and won the cup, which he presented to his goddaughter, the Mayor of Chester.

The last of these races occurred in 1782; they were then removed to Newmarket, where for many years the Wallasey Stake was the leading prize. An old building in the village, said to have been the Grosvenor Stables, yet exists.

About fifteen years since a number of guineas, apparently fresh from the mint, some coins and ornaments were found on a part of the shore now known as the golden sands; they were supposed to have come out of the strongbox of some unfortunate ship that must have foundered as far back as the reign of Charles the Second, as the few other coins found were also of that time. It is probable that the chest at length gave way, as this money was only found for a few days.

In 1844 Lady Cust established in a small building near the shore, Dennet's Rocket Apparatus for saving lives from shipwreck, many having been lost within a few yards of assistance for want of means of rendering it. In 1889 the *Pennsylvania, St Andrew, Lookwoods,* and other vessels were lost on this coast. Many of the poor sufferers were taken to Leasowe Castle, and every exertion used to restore them. Several were buried in this church yard.

The parish is particularly bare of timber, though on both side of the Berkin large trees are found. Whenever the plough or spade invades the soil to any depth, horns, bones, and other forest remains are found. The shore of both counties especially those in the vicinity of the River Mersey, on either side contain to this day numberless trunks and roots of large forest trees, chiefly oak, and many of them are discovered standing erect as they grew while large tracts of peat are observable in many places. Starting out among the sand large lumps of this peat are constantly washed up on the shores by the high tides. Remains of these woods or forests are frequently found below the range of the tides around Mockbeggar, now Leasowe Castle. In these submarine forests have been found fossils remains of the hippopotamus of the South Seas, The Irish Elk with horns of stags of all ages and sizes and also those of the Bos-Taurus, a native of the old British forests. Some horns have been found in the bed of Wallasey Pools not in a fossil state retaining their animal matter.

In 1828 a cemetery was found opposite the present lighthouse at Leasowe about 150 yards below the flow of the tide.

Leasowe Lighthouse

It is about 110 years since the present lighthouse was erected near Leasowe Castle to supply the place of one that had previously existed. Nearer to the sea by half a mile occupying a site which at the time of its erection appeared to be firm dry land yet the waters not only flowed over it, but threatened to involve the present fabric in a similar ruin, until measures were taken for its preservation and that of the neighbouring country, by raising the Leasowe embankments.

The Village of Wallasey,

Wallasey Village consist of one street on the summit of an elevated ridge that commands a beautiful view of Bidston and the Leasowe, a level tract which commences immediately under the village and reaches to the sea. In 1820 an embankment was erected which extends westward from the Castle for nearly two miles. It was constructed at an expense of £20,000. Wallasey extends north to the sea it contains 12,470 acres of land of which the greater portion is covered with water.

The old church was burned down in 1857, the tower of which is still standing and presents a fair specimen of the architectural style that prevailed in the time of Henry the Eight when it is stated to have been rebuilt; the date 1530 appears on the tower.

A new church, built to seat 900, was opened 1859. The Rev Thomas Espinal Espin, Chancellor of the Diocese is the Rector. The singing in this church is a very good there is full choral service every Sunday morning.

The view from the churchyard of the surrounding country with the Irish channel in the distance are splendid.
There is a free Grammar School also a National School.
A most picturesque old windmill stands close to the church on the hill above the village. In 1696 the troops of William III were encamped in the village and neighbourhood previous to their embarkation for Ireland accompanied by his Majesty in person and his staff, the Duke of Monmouth the Marquis of Ormonde, the Earls of Manchester, Oxford, Portland and Scarborough and many others. The host of the *Cheshire Cheese* still takes pleasure in showing the kitchen, which is said to have been once the royal dormitory.

General Remarks

Of the vast number of our manufacturing population who yearly visit our little watering place we can hardly speak too highly. These holidaymakers spread in thousand over our sands and amuse themselves in the most innocent manners, enjoying fully the many (and to them novel) wonders of the deep, creating no disturbances whatever". It is even a rare thing to see a incapable drunkenness. For those visitors who come with their families to remain a few days or months there are many attraction to be found In the beautiful walks and drives round and about New Brighton, Wallasey, Leasowe, Bidston, Hoylake, West Kirby, and numerous old English villages all being within reach by carriage, drive or rail.
One of our resident Physicians in a pamphlet recently published, describe New Brighton as the "Elysium of English watering places" He writes. "It is particularly valuables as a residence for young children the more so if they are suffering from any family defect of constitution."

The Shore Missions

Much good has been done by means of these Missions. Several of our resident gentleman spare neither time nor trouble in their efforts to further this Christian work. Many a wanderer who could never be induced to enter a church, seeking bodily rest in the cool tent has by its simple means been led to a knowledge of that *Peace and rest that passeth all understanding.* Even the little children who crowd our shore gladly for sake their sand castles and joke in the glad hymn of praise that float so sweetly on the listeners ear.

Thus evermore shall rise to Thee
Glad hymns of praise by land and sea.

Horse and Car Fares

Donkeys per hour 6d, Short Rides as may be agreed on - the Donkey Proprietors are not obliged to hire by the hour; Ponies per hour on the shore 2s, ; good saddle Horses may be hired at P. Belshaw's, Tolomache Street, charges 2s. 6d per hour; also at Clark's, Rowson Street, and T.Lucas's, Mount Road. Car hire, 1s, per mile going and 6d, returning.

WALLASEY LOCAL BOARD CAB FARES.

	Miles	s	d
To the West,			
To Mount Road, Bouches' Gates	1	1	0
To the South West,			
.. Mount Pleasant Road, Mount Pleasant	1	1	0
.. Grove Road, Rose Mount	1 $\frac{1}{2}$	1	0
.. Wallasey, Sandheys	2	2	0
.. Wallasey	2 $\frac{1}{2}$	2	6
.. Rake Lane, Fairfield House	1	1	0
.. Liscard Village Thornville House	1 $\frac{1}{2}$	1	6
.. Wallasey Road, Newlands	2	2	0
.. Poolton Road, 70 yards South of Mosslands	2 $\frac{1}{2}$	2	6
.. Mill Lane, Pinfold	2	2	0
.. Poolton Road, The Slopes	2 $\frac{1}{2}$	2	6
.. Poolton Road 50 yards beyond Elm Cottage	2 $\frac{1}{2}$	2	6
.. Poolton Road Somerville, opposite stile	3	3	0
.. Liscard Road, Liscard Hall, North gates	2	2	0
To the South			
.. Penkett Road, Mr, Walter Pritt's House	1	1	0
.. Old Public Offices	2	2	0
.. Seacombe, corner of Brighton Street and Victoria Road	2 $\frac{1}{2}$	2	6
.. Liscard Road, Brougham House	2 $\frac{1}{2}$	2	6
.. Somerville	3	3	0

REFRESHMENT CHARGES

	s.	d.
Lunch, Meat and Potatoes	1	3
.. Chops or Steaks	1	3
Cup of Tea or Coffee	0	2
Large ditto	0	3
Plain Tea	0	8
Ditto with ham and Eggs	1	3
Ditto with boiled ham	1	2
Dinner Chops or Steaks	1	6
Tea, with Eggs	0	10
Ditto with Shrimps	1	2
Ditto with Jam	1	0

Chapter 1 - Hunt's Guide to New Brighton 1877

ADVERTISEMENTS.

CONFECTIONERY.

IMPORTANT TO VISITORS.

THE MISSES RAWLINSON,

14, VICTORIA ROAD, NEW BRIGHTON,

Have always on hand a First-class Stock of

CHOICE CONFECTIONERY,

Not to be equalled.

JELLIES, CUSTARDS, BLANC-MANGE, &c.

A great variety of

HOME-MADE JAMS AND MARMALADE

Always on hand.

SPECIAL ATTENTION IS CALLED TO THEIR COMFORTABLE AND WELL VENTILATED

TEA AND LUNCHEON ROOMS,

Replete for the accommodation of private parties and others visiting this favorite resort.

First-class Refreshments, Chops, Steaks, &c.,

On the most moderate terms.

BALLS, PARTIES, & PIC-NICS SUPPLIED.

Chapter 1 - Hunt's Guide to New Brighton 1877

ADVERTISEMENTS.

VICTORIA HOTEL,
NEW BRIGHTON.

Established 1837.

On the Hill next to the Assembly Rooms.
Commanding a fine view of the Sea.

Moderate terms for Families and others.

PROPRIETOR—
JOHN GARRATT.

CHARLES ROSE,
DISPENSING & FAMILY CHEMIST,

(Opposite the New Brighton Hotel,)

VICTORIA ROAD,
NEW BRIGHTON.

All Prescriptions and Family Recipes are Dispensed with the greatest care by the Principal who has had great experience in that department of the business.

Agent for British and Foreign Mineral Waters.

Proprietor of ROSE'S CELEBRATED BOUQUET DELICES.

Chapter 1 - Hunt's Guide to New Brighton 1877

ADVERTISEMENTS.

NATIONAL LINE TO NEW YORK.
LARGEST STEAMERS AFLOAT.

Consisting of the undermentioned magnificent, full-powered Iron Screw Steamers—

	TONS.		TONS.		TONS.
EGYPT	5,064	THE QUEEN	4,441	HELVETIA	3,974
SPAIN	4,900	CANADA	3,500	HOLLAND	3,847
ENGLAND	4,600	GREECE	3,500	DENMARK	3,723
ITALY	4,302	ERIN	3,956	FRANCE	3,571

FROM LIVERPOOL TO NEW YORK EVERY WEDNESDAY,
Calling at Queenstown (Co. Cork) on Thursdays, and
FROM LONDON TO NEW YORK EVERY TEN DAYS.

Saloon Passage to New York, 10, 12, and 15 Guineas, according to position of State Room, all having equal privileges in the Saloon. Return Tickets 22 and 24 Guineas.

Steerage Passage to New York, Boston, Philadelphia, and Baltimore, £6, including an abundance of fresh provisions, cooked and served up by the Company's Stewards.

The Steamers of the National Line have all been built for strength and durability, combined with all modern improvements. They are justly celebrated for their safe and regular passages across the Atlantic, having, in the course of the past eleven years, carried upwards of 400,000 passengers, without loss to a single life by accident at sea. Owing to the large size of the steamers great steadiness at sea is maintained, thereby considerably reducing the liability to sea-sickness.

The Saloons are replete with every convenience and luxury, the State Rooms being unusually large and entering directly off the Saloons.

The Steerages are very spacious, well warmed and ventilated, and passengers in this class will find their comfort and convenience carefully studied. The deck space arrangements for exercise and amusement, in both wet and fine weather, are unsurpassed by any line afloat.

Stewardesses carried by each Steamer, to wait upon female steerage passengers; and medical attendance and medicine is dispensed, free of charge, to all passengers when required.

Passengers booked through to San Francisco and all parts of the United States and Canada at low rates.

For particulars apply to

THE NATIONAL STEAM SHIP CO., LIMITED,
23, WATER STREET, LIVERPOOL,
or to their Agents in all towns.

Chapter 1 - Hunt's Guide to New Brighton 1877

ADVERTISEMENTS

THE LATEST NOVELTY!

LARGE
Life-like Portraits

(14 inches by 12 inches),

Beautifully colored in Oil, Mounted & Framed complete, with 1 doz. highly-finished Cartes,

FOR £1 6s. 0d.

LIST OF PRICES FOR CARTE DE VISITES—
HIGHLY-FINISHED.

| 1 Carte | ... ... | 1s. | 1 Carte | ... ... | 1s. 6d. |
| 10 ,, | ... ... | 3s. | 13 ,, | ... ... | 5s. 0d. |

Splendid Berlin Cameos... ... 7s. 6d. per doz.
Beautiful Cameo Vignettes... 10s. 6d. ,, ,,

—o—

THE ABOVE ARE ACKNOWLEDGED TO BE

THE PORTRAITS OF THE DAY.

—o—

Visitors to New Brighton should not fail to view the Studio of the

Liverpool & London Photographic Co.,
12, LORD STREET,
LIVERPOOL.

Chapter 1 - Hunt's Guide to New Brighton 1877

ADVERTISEMENTS.

MASON'S ROYAL FERRY HOTEL,
ADJOINING THE PIER & PROMENADE,

NEW BRIGHTON.

RICHARDSON & KERSHAW,
CRYSTAL PALACE STUDIO
VICTORIA ROAD,

NEW BRIGHTON.

EASTHAM ZOOLOGICAL GARDENS.

LIONS, BEARS, LEOPARDS, SEALS, WOLVES, FOXES, EMUS, CHEETAHS.

Aviary, Lion House, Seal Tank.

SPLENDID ZOOLOGICAL COLLECTION,
And every variety of Holiday Entertainment.

Steamers from Liverpool Landing Stage constantly throughout the day.

GARDENS 3d.; BOAT 4d.

Chapter 1 - Inspector Dutton and the Mysterious Affair

Romantic Tragedy at the Tower - Cowboy Shoots Himself
Considerable excitement was caused in the Tower Grounds, New Brighton, on Wednesday afternoon, when it was announced that that one of the cowboys connected with Colonel Fred T. Cummins' Wild West Show had died under dramatic circumstances. So far as could be ascertained, the unfortunate fellow, George Price, aged 22, of Oklahoma, had blown his brains out with a rifle. It seems he was engaged to a young lady named Margaret Riley, of Duke Street, Everton, and was shortly to have married her. For some reason or other he appeared to be rather despondent, and a rumour was current that he lost a sum of money which he had saved with which to enter upon his matrimonial career.
Yesterday afternoon, in the Egerton Hall, New Brighton, the Coroner (Mr J C Bate) conducted an inquest on the remains.
Mr Arthur Ellis, manager for the Tower Company, was in attendance, as was also Mr F A Small. Addressing the jury, Mr Bates said the deceased, a young man of 22 years of age, was a native of the United States. He had been employed for some months in connection with a show at the Tower Grounds as a gunsmith. On Wednesday last he was found lying at the back of the show with a gunshot wound in his head. From the evidence that would be given he thought there would be no doubt that the deceased committed suicide, and it would be for them the jury, to say what the state of the man's mind was at the time he committed the act.
Frederick Ross, secretary to Colonel Cummins, stated that the deceased lodged with him at 52, Tollemache Street, New Brighton. Price was a native of Pownee, in the state of Oklahoma, and came over with the Colonel's show in May last. At times he was a little eccentric and he had "got the reputation among the boys of being a little soft at times." He was all right when witness saw him last at 8p.m on Tuesday. He had never complained of any trouble. The rifle produced was known as an old Springfield, a portion of the barrel of which was cut to fit the stage coach exhibition.
At the Coroner's inquest Inspector Dutton was involved in the investigation of the death of George Price. "He must have stood with the rifle muzzle facing him and shot himself in his mouth. Margaret Riley, waitress in Victoria Road, New Brighton, stated that she had known the deceased for two months and had been keeping company with him: they were to have been married on Thursday morning at 11 o clock. She saw him at a quarter past ten on Wednesday morning, and went with him to Birkenhead, whence they travelled to the office of the registrar in Brougham Terrace, West

Chapter 1 - Inspector Dutton and the Mysterious Affair

Derby Road, Liverpool, and procured a marriage license. They made an appointment, arranging to meet at New Brighton Pier between one and half-past on the following afternoon. She turned up to time, and a girl sent by Mrs. Carver came and told her that George was taken ill. She accompanied the girl and then learnt that her fiance was dead.

The verdict returned was that the deceased committed suicide, but there was no evidence to show the state of his mind at the time he committed the act.

The funeral will take place at Rake-Lane Cemetery at noon today, and will be attended by the Cowboy Band and members of the Wild West Show.

Wild West Show. *Wallasey News* 5th September 1908

The greatest show at the Tower Stadium was the Cummins-Brown "Wild West" and Indian Congress which was staged for the summer season, starting on 23rd May 1908, running to the autumn. The Manager-Director at the Tower was Mr. J. Calvin Brown, and together with Colonel Frederick T. Cummins, was in charge of the performance on the Athletic Ground while, in the theatre, the Millican's Minstrels and Old Plantation Show was staged. A parade of Cowboys and Indians, Horses and Stage Coach from Lime Street in Liverpool to the Landing Stage to meet the ferry was arranged to publicise the Congress. The Wild West Show had a six months season. 500 men and horses took part, including many cowboys and cowgirls, U.S. Artillery, Crackshot Rifle Displays, U.S. Cavalry men, Cossacks, Indian Warriors, Chariot Drivers, Acrobats and Contortionists. The poster portrayed Anna Shaffer on her horse. It advertised "lady bronco riders, Indian Warriors, Squaws and papoose". They claimed "Educated Wild Beasts" performing. The horsemanship was superb with Colonel Cummins taking part. The Redskins called him "Chief Lakota" and there are many stories about him. Wild Highland Cattle were brought from Scotland for the cowboys to lasso as American animals were not allowed into the country.

While the show was at New Brighton, one of the show people died and a large procession was arranged for the funeral at Rake Lane Cemetery. It was led by cowboys and cowgirls, followed by a large number of fully dressed Indians and squaws with headdresses, along with their "Chief", with his beautifully feathered headdress. There was also a small band. At the rear was the cortege on a sort of gun carriage pulled by piebald horses. They made their way from Molyneux Drive to Rake Lane in a slow procession mourning their loved one.

Gun Firing at the Tower *Wallasey News* 15th **June 1908**

Complaints were received from members of the public concerning the noise from the gun firing at the Tower Grounds, and the practice rounds fired off at the Battery. Eighty-three residents signed a petition, including one whose baby went into convulsions.

Chapter 1 - John Dutton 1841-1910

John Dutton - 1841 to 1910
On the 25th December 1859 John Dutton married Margaret Roberts daughter of Edward and Ann. The wedding took place in a small church called the Church of St Mary the Virgin in the parish of St. Mary-on-the-Hill, Bruera. (Chester is 5 miles to the south-east.)

It is interesting to note in the marriage register that John was unable to read or write and signed by using X (his mark). His age shown on the marriage certificate does not tie up with the ages on the respective censuses. Margaret, however, was able to sign, and from all accounts was educated in domestic service. John worked on the land as an agricultural labourer and lived with his family in Saighton, with his two younger sisters Mary Ann and Elizabeth.

Their first child Mary was born in Saighton the following year.
Mary was christened in the same church where the couple had married. The family chose the name Mary in memory of John's little sister who died age 17 months in 1842; her red sandstone tombstone stood opposite the entrance to the church. The baptism of Mary took place on the 19th February 1860. Shortly afterwards, the family decided to leave the village and move to Roscoe Heath in School Lane, Lower Bebbington. This move was to be short-lived; opportunities for work had been scarce.
John eventually obtained a job working for the Local Board in Wallasey.

Chapter 1 - John Dutton 1841-1910

John and Margaret went to stay with their aunt Ellen Roberts at No 9 Wallasey Terrace, (Twenty Row) on Leasowe Road; she had a spare room which she let them use. Ellen was a short likable lady, but the elements had taken their toll. With a reddish complexion and matching hands from washing other people's clothes, she had aged beyond her years.

Wallasey Terrace - showing the Twenty Row pub

Let me take you on a journey back in time to when John Dutton my great-grandfather arrived in Leasowe. If we move from the village along Leasowe Road on the left-hand side at No1 lives Richard Spragg; just behind his house stands the brewery. Richard was a Brewer a complicated task in those days. The sixpenny beers sold at the *Twenty Row* came from Richard Spragg's Wallasey Vale Brewery.

Leasowe Road, railway bridge in the distance and Spraggs Vale Brewery on the right.

Chapter 1 - John Dutton 1841-1910

The 1861 census records Emma, brewer's wife, living with three daughters and three sons.

On the right-hand side, No 2 Leasowe Road is occupied by William Webster, living there with his wife, three sons and four daughters. Walking past Cross Lane we see no more property until we reach the *Twenty Row*, or Wallasey Terrace. The public house was at the end of a row of nineteen terraced dwellings. According to the *Wallasey Chronicle* it was opened in 1835. Excluding the public house, access to which was gained via Leasowe Road, the nineteen terraced houses were reached by an unmade track and one approached the dwellings by a long garden. The houses were very tiny and built in bricks, obtained from the local brickworks. At the rear was a small yard opening on to a very narrow entry "jigger" which was only two feet wide. Thomas Joyce at number seven, at the age of 70, would challenge all newcomers to a 100-yard race providing he could have a yard start. This agreed he chose the jigger to race down! Its narrow width made overtaking impossible and thus his victory was ensured.

On the left hand side there is a small deep ditch which contained clear water. Thomas Westcott observed: *The first time I noticed the place, an old person named Mrs Roberts who took in washing was ladling out the water into a large can. Being a bit inquisitive I asked her if they had to use this water for washing at the Twenty Row, 'Aye lad', she answered, and eating too. When I got home I told my father what I had seen and the answer I got, he told me that the old folk about here used the word eating instead of drinking; be that as it may, it was the first time that I had heard of anyone eating water. You will see by this where the tenants of the Twenty Row got their water for domestic purposes.*

The *Twenty Row* consisted of twenty small terraced houses the last one being a pub; the landlord was William Ledsham the local blacksmith, who kept the smithy at the corner of Folly Gutter. In the 1861 census the terrace was numbered 3 - 22 Leasowe Road.

Chapter 1 - John Dutton 1841-1910

It comes as no surprise that John and Margaret moved to 18 Russell Place, off Liscard Road. During this period John joined the local fire brigade. Records indicate that the Brigade came into being in the early 1880s. The picture shows the following members, from left to right: John Fellowes, James Lea, Robert Carson, John Dutton, James Leather (captain), Thomas Somerville and John Bleakley, with Harold Gibbons, driver. The cottage behind the carriage stood at that time opposite the water tower in Mill Lane, the occupier at one time being John Pemberton and afterwards

Harry Keenan. Branches of the Brigade were formed, one at Seacombe, under Mr John Howarth, a tobacconist in Brighton Street, and another in Wallasey Village, under Abraham Halewood, one of the water inspectors. Until about 1900, the Wallasey Fire Brigade was 'voluntary', the men drawing a small retaining fee with the water dept. In 1890 it was decided that the original Liscard Fire Station in Mill Lane would be demolished and moved to Manor Road. The alarm bell, which was stationed at the water tower ever since the brigade was formed, was also moved to the new station. The central fire station consisted of an old stabling area and a yard at the top of Manor Road, Liscard. The equipment was a manual fire-engine, ladders etc. with horse carts in sheds at Seacombe and Wallasey Village. When the fire took place at New Brighton Tower, one man (Shone) lost his life by falling from the top of the tower, being instantly killed. He fell to his death carrying water across a partially burned plank. The fire started on a workers' scaffold 172ft from the ground, which in turn set fire to woodwork below. Fire originated from a riveter's furnace. The firemen clambered about the burning part of the tower with buckets served from casks of water raised by the crane. This was arduous and highly dangerous work; fanned by the breeze, the scaffolding timbers

Chapter 1 - John Dutton 1841-1910

blazed furiously, and every minute saw new dangers. John Dutton was a breeder of horses and some of his animals were used by the Volunteer Fire Brigade, of which he and three of his sons, Thomas, Edward and Walter were all members, and the sons were, in fact, in attendance during the fire at New Brighton Tower, when Fireman Shone met such a tragic fate. On one occasion a fire took place on a ship in the dock, and one of the firemen fell in the water. Dutton saw him fall, but did not know who it was. He cried out, 'There's someone in the water.' Suddenly a bald head was seen beneath the surface, and it was at once recognised as that of the Captain Leather, and he was saved from drowning through his lack of hair. His brass helmet fell off, and is still at the bottom of the dock.

Wallasey Fire Brigade Open Day at Central Fire Station, Manor Road 1915.

Wallasey Fire Brigade official photograph taken outside Cliff House, Mariners' Park, Egremont. All wearing brass helmets and axes in their belts.

Chapter 1 - John Dutton 1841-1910

Wallasey Fire Brigade May Day 1901

Margaret Dutton worked for Gravesons of Liscard, milking and caring for their cows. With the surplus milk she bought from Mr. Graveson, she worked up a small milk round in Liscard, which grew so rapidly that she bought a horse and float and John eventually left the Local Board to drive for her. This was the beginning of the business which expanded to great dimensions and was carried on from 244 Liscard Road (Downes & Roberts) and milk was supplied by E. T. Evans of Bidston Hall Farm, Parkinsons, Wilkinsons and Lambs, all being Bidston farmers.

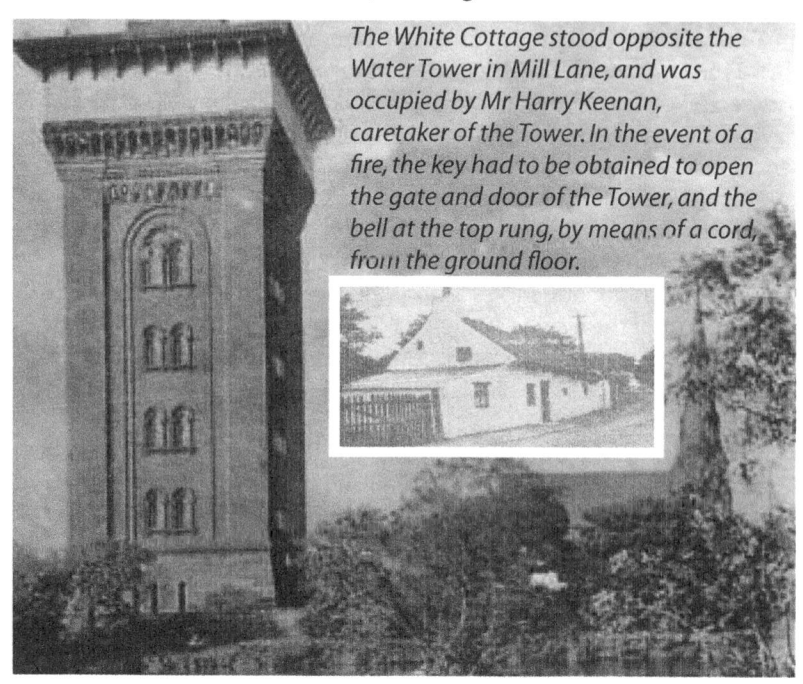

The White Cottage stood opposite the Water Tower in Mill Lane, and was occupied by Mr Harry Keenan, caretaker of the Tower. In the event of a fire, the key had to be obtained to open the gate and door of the Tower, and the bell at the top rung, by means of a cord, from the ground floor.

Chapter 1 - John Dutton 1841-1910

Heart Failure. Liscard Resident's Sudden death.
Wallasey News, Saturday, 30th July1910.
Mr J C Bate (Coroner for West Cheshire), held an inquest on Wednesday at the Presbyterian Schools, Seacombe, as to the death of John Dutton, aged 69, of 244, Liscard Road, Liscard, who was found dead in bed on Monday evening.
Margaret Dutton, wife of deceased, explained that her husband had recently been complaining of being tired and poorly. He did not see a doctor and carried on his usual work. On Monday night he went to bed at eleven o'clock, and did not complain more than usual. He commenced the breathe very heavily.
She asked him what was the matter, but he did not reply. She called her daughter and sent her for the doctor, and before the arrival of the Dr Davies, the deceased expired.
Dr Seymour Whitney Davies stated that at half-past eleven on Monday evening Miss Dutton called and told him that they thought Mr Dutton was dying. He found the deceased lying in bed quite dead. He had been dead a few minutes, and from the the appearance of the body, death was due to failure of the heart or haemorrhage of the brain.
A verdict in accordance with the medical evidence was returned.

          ***   ***   ***

Funeral of an Old Fireman
The funeral took place at the Wallasey Cemetery, yesterday afternoon, of Mr John Dutton, milk dealer, of Liscard, who died suddenly of heart disease. The deceased was an old fireman, and his coffin was borne to the grave by five members of the Liscard Brigade. The funeral ceremony was performed by the Rev. R. Ellwood.

          ***   ***   ***

A Dead Man Summoned - For "Having His Lights Out"
Major D.A.S. Nesbitt and Mr C.J Woodroffe were on the Bench at the Second Court of the Liscard Petty Sessions on Wednesday, when John Dutton, Liscard, was summoned for driving a vehicle without a light. When Dutton's name was called it was explained that he had been dead four weeks.
John Nicholls was the driver of the vehicle without a light on 16th August. He explained that he was driving the milk float with John Dutton's name inscribed upon it, and he had given his late master's name. The reason why he had no light attached was that he expected to be home before lighting-up time. The train bringing the milk was late.
The Bench remarked that it was no fault of his own; they would only fine him 1s.

Chapter 1 - Liscard Village

In the early 1900s William and his brothers Harold and James Gibbons lived at No1 Liscard VIllage. They were carriage proprietors and they hired out horses and carriages for weddings and funerals. Known locally as Gibbon's Stables. My great-grandfather was in direct competition for the contract of supplying horses to the fire brigade. The Duttons being members of the volunteer brigade. Dutton's farm in Mill Lane also bred horses. Gibbons eventually evolved into John W. Griffin and Son, one of the leading wedding and funeral directors in the area.

The stables were later demolished and The Capitol Picture House was built in its place. One of my best friends Charles from school had an uncle who worked at the funeral directors. Uncle Jack Fielding was the MD until his retirement whereupon the sole owner Mrs Gibbons stopped trading and sold the land. Charles took great delight in explaining how they went about embalming some of their customers. At the time I used to sneak into the Royal Cinema to watch such classics as *The bride of Frankenstein* and *Count Dracula*. So this additional knowledge just helped to reinforce the existence of such creatures, which made going to bed just a little more dIfficult. Unbeknown to Charlie's Uncle he was to change the fortunes of the Dutton family, but more of that later.

Chapter 1 - Doctor Crippen and Liscard Road

You may well ask what does 224 Liscard Road has to do with the Crippen murders. Dr Hawley Harvey Crippen was married to Cora, who preferred her stage name 'Belle Elmore.' A lady of dominating ways, 'Belle' was a mediocre theatrical singer and she was described as being overbearing in their marriage, with a fondness of collecting diamonds and frilly pink clothes. Belle had acquired a taste for alcohol and liked flirting with men; she was persistent in henpecking and nagging her husband and he eventually turned his interests to his 28-year-old secretary, Ethel Clara Le Neve. Belle had apparently become aware of her husband's philandering and threatened to leave him with nothing. He lied about his wife's disappearance and paraded his mistress, Ethel le Neve, in his spouse's jewellery and sailed off into the sunset on an ocean liner bound for Quebec with his lover dressed as a boy.

He stumbled into legend by becoming the very first person to be caught by telegraph in 1910. The inevitable happened: he killed his wife and buried her in the basement.

This covert picture was taken at Crippen's trial with a camera concealed under a bowler hat by none other than Madame Tussaud's grandson Jack, so that a wax model could be made of the accused for her wax works, before the trial was even over.

Chapter 1 - Doctor Crippen and Liscard Road

Crippen gave Ethel a set of four diamond and ruby rings and what Belle used to refer to as her "rising-sun brooch," a gorgeous pendant with inlaid diamonds. He was planning to pawn the remainder of the jewels. (The jewels he pawned netted him, according to the Holloway North London Police website, £3,195.) Inspector Walter Dew took a faster ship, the *S.S Laurentic* and arrested Crippen before he could land in Canada.

In 1911 part of Cora Crippen's jewellery was sold at auction in London. Mr Charles Fry a well known pawnbroker and jeweller had a shop next door to our dairy. He purchased the "rising-sun brooch," probably the most famous of the Cora's jewellery pieces. It was a truly spectacular broach with a black centre stone cut with a cluster of diamonds from which extended a ray-beam design of smaller diamonds. My great-grandfathers shop was next door to Fry's pawnbrokers. The commotion caused by the display in Fry's window ground the traffic to a halt in Liscard Road. Hundreds of people came to view the spectacle, and prevented customers getting to John Dutton's shop.

Dr Crippen the homeopath was found guilty and executed, while his alleged accomplice Ethel was acquitted.

Another connection with New Brighton, in 1907 he gave a lecture concerning one of his supposed medical cures "The Aural Remedies Coy." a treatment for deafness.

CRIPPEN WILTS AS DOOM APPROACHES

Wife Murderer Hanged in London This Morning Collapses Miserably and is Helped to Gallows

OFFICIAL DENIAL THAT HE CONFESSED

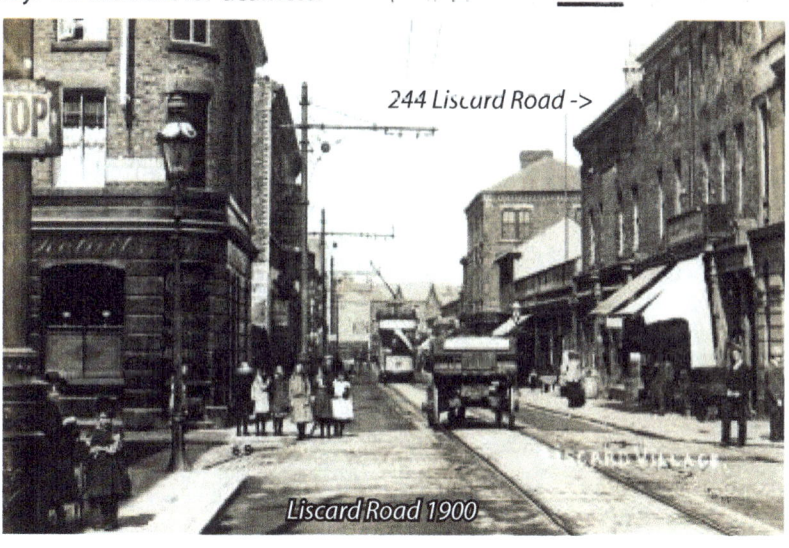

244 Liscard Road ->

Liscard Road 1900

Chapter 1 - May Day Parade 1901

May Day 1901 Life Boat Crew Collecting for Charity

May Day 1901 Volunteer Fire Brigade

Chapter 1 - Margaret Dutton 1840-1911

This is the last Will and Testament of me Margaret Dutton of 244 Liscard Road Liscard in the County of Cheshire widow I give devise and bequeath all my property of whatsoever kind and nature equally between my son Thomas and my daughter Mary subject to them allowing to my son James a sufficient part of the Milk round attached to my business so that his own present milk round may be increased by Forty Gallons a day. And I appoint my said son Thomas and daughter Mary Executors of this my will In Witness whereof I have hereunto set my hand the eleventh day of February one thousand nine hundred and seven - M Dutton.

Proved 19 June 1911 to Thomas Dutton and Mary Hughes the Executors.
Margaret drew up her will on the 11th February 1911, some four years before she died. The only benifactors were Thomas, James Dutton and her widowed daughter Mary Hughes. Margaret had started the business and intended for it to continue. Milk churns were used to carry milk in the days before tankers. Half pint and pint milk ladles would be hung inside the milk churn so that the milkman could measure out milk on his rounds, often into a jug left on the doorstep. Without home refrigeration, milkmen deliverd three times a day for breakfast, lunch-time pudding and afternoon tea. Milk deliveries drop to two a day during the First World War. Horse-drawn milk carts were still a common sight until the 1950s. but were gradually overtaken by electric vehicles.

Chapter 1 - John & Margaret's Children

John Dutton 1840-1910

John Dutton b 1840 d.1910 Churton Heath

Margaret Roberts b 1840 d.1911 Saighton

- **Mary Dutton** b 1860 d 1948 Saighton — Mary married Joseph W. Hughes
- **Sarah Ann Dutton** b 1861 d.1950 Bebington — Name on grave stone Sarah Ann Wilkinson.
- **Harriet Dutton** b 1865 d 1937 Liscard — Harriet married Nathan Bird in 1887.
- **Thomas Dutton** b 1867 d.1939 Liscard — Thomas my Grandfather, married twice.
- **John Dutton** b 1869 d 1937 Liscard — John married Elizabeth Hicks
- **James Dutton** b 1871 d.1871 Liscard
- **Magaret Dutton** b 1872 d.1939 Liscard — Magaret married Frank Piper in 1896
- **Edward W Dutton** b 1874 d.1956 Liscard — Edward married Alice Samples in 1897.
- **William Dutton** b 1877 d.1951 Liscard — William married Elizabeth Buckley in 1899.
- **Emily E Dutton** b 1879 d.1895 Liscard — Emily Elizabeth Dutton died aged 16 in 1895.
- **James H Dutton** b1882 d.1945 Liscard — James Herbert Dutton married Hannah Bexon in 1901.

Chapter 1 - Mary Dutton 1860 - 1948

Mary Dutton 1860-1948

Mary Dutton (aunt Polly) was born in 1860, and was the first-born child of John and Margaret. In early summer 1882 Mary married Joseph William Hughes at the Church of Our Lady in Liverpool. The marriage was to be short-lived with Joseph dying the following year.

In 1891 Mary is living with the Dutton family at 36 Leopold Street in Liscard, occupation assistant housekeeper. Leapold Street was later changed to Tower Street. After the death of Frances in 1909, my father was looked after by auntie Polly who lived for a time at 11 Merton Road in Liscard.

Mary was to remarry Edward Irish, at one time a postman in Liscard, who served in the Cheshire Regiment. My father was to have a happy childhood with aunt Polly and always talked kindly of her. When aunt Polly lived at the farm, in her younger days she had a dog called Toby which she was very fond of; when the dog died it was stuffed and later took up residency in Merton Road. It would appear from the records that Mary produced no offspring. She also lived for a time in Queen Street where she looked after Thomas's other children.

In 1911 she was still a widow living and working at 244 Liscard Road, in the Dutton's dairy business and shown on the census as an assistant in the business.

From left ro right my father Alfred Dutton, aunt Polly and Ivy Dean. Together with an old friend who was 100 years. old.

49

Chapter 1 - Sarah Dutton 1861 - 1950

Sarah Dutton 1861-1950
Sarah Ann Dutton was born in Bebington, Cheshire in 1861, after the family had moved from Saighton.
When Sarah was 20 years old she was working as a cook/servant for the Rumsey family on Rake Lane. In the late spring of 1889 she married David Wilkinson a tailor, and they went to live in Bradford, Yorkshire.
Eventually she must have returned to Wallasey because she is buried in the family grave in Rake Lane Cemetery. The photograph below shows Sarah standing outside the shop that they owned at 32 Barkerend Road, Bradford. They also owned the property next door and took in boarders. They had no children of their own, and decided to employ young William Piper the son of Sarah's sister Margaret.

From left ro right my father Alfred Dutton, my mother Dorothy, aunt Polly and Sarah. The photograph was taken outside their newsagent's shop in Bradford. Shown below shops in Barkerend Road, in the1980s.

50

Chapter 1 - Harriet Dutton 1865-1937

Harriet Dutton 1865-1937
Harriet Dutton was born in Liscard in early 1865, and was baptised at St Hillary's Church, Wallasey on the 12th March 1865, see below:

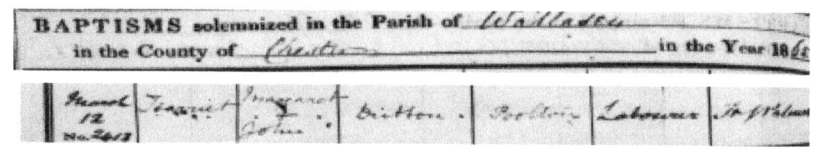

Harriet's mother already had a job working for Gravesons, and was able to get her a job as a general servant working for the same firm in Liscard.
In 1887 Harriet married Nathan Bird a dock labourer at St Mary's Church, Liscard. They went on to have 15* offspring, with eight still living in 1911.

(1) Emily Bird	b 1888	Liscard	m. 1915 Ben. Humphreys
(2) Mary Bird	b 1890	Seacombe	m. 1912 William Faulkner
(3) Margaret Bird	b 1892	Seacombe	m. 1913 Harry Carter
(4) George Bird	b 1894 d.1894	Seacombe	
(5) Nathan Bird	b 1895	Seacombe	
(6) Harriet Bird	b 1896 d 1896	Seacombe	
(7) John Bird	b.1897 d.1897	Seacombe	
(8) Annie Bird	b 1898	Seacombe	m. 1926 John Brady
(9) William Bird	b 1900	Seacombe	m. 1927 Doris Cooke
(10) Sarah Bird	b 1902	Seacombe	m. 1921 James Jones
(11) Eileen Bird	b.1904 d1904	Seacombe	
(12) Fred. Bird	b.1906 d.1906	Seacombe	
(13) Edith Bird	b 1908	Seacombe	m. 1935 Thom. Humphreys
(14) James Bird	b.1910 d.1910	Seacombe	

(2) Mary Bird had three sons, William, Frank & Eric
(3) Margaret three daughters, Margaret, Emily, Edith, and two sons William and Arthur.
(8) Annie Bird one daughter Margaret, and four sons John, Francis, Charles & James.
(9) William Bird one daughter Marjorie, and a son Edward.
(10) Sarah Bird four sons, George, James, Edward & Ronald.
Next to the grave of John & Margaret is the Bird family grave: *In loving memory of my dear husband Nathan Bird died 5th Dec. 1933, aged 68 years. Also* Eleanor, his daughter died 29th Dec. 1898, aged 9 years 4 months. Also Harriet, dearly loved wife of above, died 12th Nov, 1937, aged 72 years. Also Edith beloved daughter of above who died 8th March 1947. Aged 39.*

St Hillary's Church

51

Chapter 1 - Thomas Dutton 1867-1939

From the census of 1901 both Thomas and James are working as milk van drivers. Milk was the family business and produced a good livelyhood for the family. After the unexpected death of Margaret Dutton in 1911, Thomas, the eldest son, returned home and he and his sister Mary inherited the business with the two eldest children Emily and Edward all working in the business, together with John Nicholls who was Thomas's adopted son.

Two Articles from the *Wallasey News*. Below " family Lives" dated 1935. And opposite Ted Dutton's "old Families of Wallasey" dated 23rd November 1952.

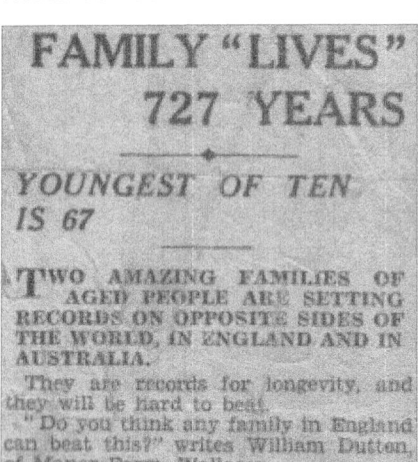

FAMILY "LIVES" 727 YEARS

YOUNGEST OF TEN IS 67

TWO AMAZING FAMILIES OF AGED PEOPLE ARE SETTING RECORDS ON OPPOSITE SIDES OF THE WORLD, IN ENGLAND AND IN AUSTRALIA.

They are records for longevity, and they will be hard to beat.

"Do you think any family in England can beat this?" writes William Dutton, of Manor Farm, Wallasey.

"I have eight brothers and sisters, all living, and their combined ages total 591 years. The youngest is fifty-three and the oldest seventy-five. All had the same mother and father."

Well, from Wingham, New South Wales, came news yesterday of a family named Joyce. There are ten "children," the eldest is eighty-seven and the youngest sixty-seven.

Their combined ages total 727 years and their average age is 72.7.

Four of them are sisters who have all celebrated their golden weddings. Their parents, Mr. and Mrs. B. Joyce, were pioneers who pitched camp on the Bopo Creek. Can that be beaten?

FURTHER details of old families of Wallasey, have been supplied by "News" readers, whose contributions are given below.

From Mr. Edward R. Dutton: The Dutton family first came to Wallasey from Saighton, Chester, in the early 1860's, when my grandparents, John and Margaret Dutton, came to Twenty Row, Leasowe Road. John Dutton working for the Local Board as teamsman and helping in the construction of Leasowe embankment. Margaret worked for Graveson's of Liscard, milking and caring for their cows. With the surplus milk she bought from Mr. Graveson she worked up a small milk round in Liscard, which grew so rapidly that she bought a horse and float and my grandfather eventually left the Local Board to drive for her.

This was the beginning of the business which expanded to such great dimensions and was carried on from 244 Liscard Road (now Downes & Roberts) and milk was supplied by H. T. Evans of Bidston Hall Farm, Parkinsons, Wilkinsons and Laines, all being Bidston farmers.

The farm known as Dutton's Farm in Mill Lane, situated between Love Lane and the maternity Hospital and stretching back to Central Park, was also part of the enterprising development in the business. John Dutton was a breeder of horses some of which were used by the Volunteer Fire Brigade of which he and two of his sons, Thomas (my father), Edward and Walter, were members; the two latter being in attendance at the fire at New Brighton Tower in 1898 when Fireman Shone met such a tragic fate.

There were nine children who survived them. Thomas, Mary (Auntie Pollie), Sarah, Harriet, John, Edward Walter, William (the farmer of Gorser Lane), Margaret and James Herbert known as "Farmer Dutton" and who played for Tranmere Social A.F.C.

Of these only one is at present living, Edward Walter, who was timekeeper for the Highways Dept. of the Corporation for many years and now in retirement living at 10 Sea View Ave., Liscard. The following generations form a great network in Wallasey and must by now represent quite a large part of the community.

One never looks back to the days of the hospital carnival without remembering the efforts of my grandfather and uncle Bill with their very fine turnouts of horseflesh and decorated milk floats which won many first prizes.

52

Chapter 1 - Thomas Dutton 1867-1939

Thomas Dutton, with his son also called Thomas,

1911 Census details- 244 Liscard Road, Wallasey

Thomas	Head	44 Widower	dairyman	Employer	Liscard
Mary Hughes	Sister	51 Widow	Assistant	Worker	Saighton
Emily Eliz.Dutton	Daug.	16 Single	ditto	Worker	Liscard
Edward Robert Dutton		15	ditto	Worker	Liscard
Thomas Dutton	Son	13 School boy			Liscard
Edith Maud Dutton		6 at school			Llanidloes
Alfred Rhayder Dutton		2 baby			Rhayader
John Nicholls	Adopted	19 Single	Assistant	Worker	Birkenhead
John Roberts	Uncle	76 Widower		Gentleman	Saighton

Thomas Dutton fathered a total of 9 children born alive, and in 1911 five children are still living and 4 children have died.

53

Chapter 1 - Thomas Dutton 1867-1939

From the *Wallasey News* dated 7th January 1939
The Late Mr T Dutton - Death of old Wallaseyan
A Fireman's tragic death recalled.
The death occurred on Friday of last week of Mr Thomas Dutton of 47, Mill Lane, Liscard, following a painful illness patiently borne.
Mr Dutton who was in his 73rd year was born in Liscard and lived in Wallasey all his life.
He was the eldest surviving son of the late John and Margaret Dutton, cow keepers and dairymen of 244 Liscard Road.
In his youth Mr Dutton was a keen Rugby Player and played for West Kirby. He was a member of the Cheshire Volunteer Corps and the St. John's Ambulance Brigade.
Some of his proudest memories were connected with his service in the Wallasey Auxiliary Fire Brigade of which he was a member prior to 1908. During his service as a fireman he assisted in a fire which broke out at the top of the New Brighton Tower in 1898 when a fireman met a terrible death by falling from the top of the tower.
The interment took place on Tuesday at Rake Lane cemetery, being preceded by a service at St. Thomas's church, Seaview Road, Liscard the vicar the Rev. Evelyn White officiating.
The chief mourners were Messrs Edward R Dutton, Thomas Dutton, and Alfred Dutton (sons) Mrs J.A. Dean and Mrs R. Dean (daughters). Mrs Irish and Mrs Piper (sisters) Mr J.H. Dutton and
Mr W Dutton (brothers) Mrs G.R.Dutton (daughter-in-law) Mr J.A.Dean and
Mr R.Dean (sons-in-laws)
Mrs J.H Dutton (sister- in- law) and
Mr Nicholls.
The Wallasey Fire Brigade were represented by Mr H.Winstanley a member of the brigade.
The funeral arrangements were in the hands of Messrs John Kenna, Brighton Street.

Note correction
***Wallasey News* 21st January 1939**
In reference to the report of the death and funeral of the late Mr Thomas Dutton we are asked to state that the deceased died at his daughter's residence, 8 Devonshire Road, and not at 47 Mill Lane, as reported in our issue of the 7th inst.
The report of the funeral was a contributed one.

Chapter 1 - John Dutton 1869-1937

At the young age of 12, John started his working career as a druggist's shop boy. He later tried his hand as a plumber, but eventually settled on a job as a house painter. In Gore's Directories his occupation was a painter. John married Elizabeth Hicks in 1891. Shortly after their marriage they went to live in Wigan. By 1894 they where living in Seacombe before eventually settling down in Liscard The family lived at both No 2 and No 6 Pear Tree Grove in Liscard.

The couple went on to have eight children

Margaret Dutton	b 1892	m.1915 Albert Spalding
John Dutton	b 1894	m.1919 Elizabeth Winder
Elsie Dutton	b 1897	m 1920 James Birnie
William R Dutton	b 1898	m 1919 Agnes Kelly
Mary E Dutton	b 1901	m.1926 David Corbett
George E Dutton	b.1902	d. 1918
Millicent B Dutton	b.1905	d. 1908
Gwen Dutton	b.1909	m. 1931 Gerald Artell

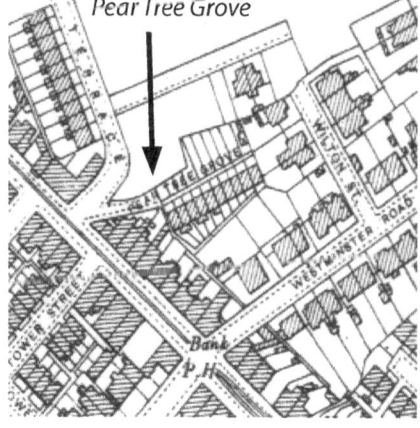

John Dutton lived at No 2 Pear Tree Grove 1896-1905

Pear Tree Grove

Chapter 1 - John Dutton 1869-1937

Wallasey News 2nd **November 1918**
Lost at Sea
Much sympathy is extended to Mr and Mrs J. Dutton, of 2 Peartree Grove whose third son George Edward was lost at sea, on September 9th last, through the torpedoing of the vessel on which he was serving. Hopes were fondly entertained that he might have been picked up by some passing vessel, but unfortunately they have not been realised and death has been presumed. Deceased was only sixteen-and-a-half years old. He used to be a regular attendee at Wesley Hall, when at home.
On the 9th September 1918, *SS Missanabie*, defensively armed, built in 1914 was torpedoed and sunk by German U-boat UB 87, fifty-two miles from Daunts Rock, Ireland. Owned by Canadian Pacific Ocean Services Ltd.
A total of 45 lives lost, this relates to crew members and/or civilian passengers only, not troops. Military personnel were aboard.
The US destroyer McCall assisted the survivors and some of her crew were awarded the Silver Cross.
"We sailed from an Irish port on Sept. 8 at 11.30 in the morning." said a passenger. "We were in convoy, and the *Missanabie* was the only ship carrying passengers and mails. We proceeded in fairly choppy weather, at about eight knots, with the Missanabie the last ship in line. She had had engine trouble, and had been forced to drop behind the main body of the convoy. When the stricken steamship was almost perpendicular, with her bow pointing skyward, her engines, anchors, and other heavy material crashed toward the stern, and this and the blowing up of the magazine undoubtedly caused her to sink so rapidly." She sank in seven minutes.
The New York Times 20th September 1918

Chapter 1 - Margaret Dutton (Piper) 1872-1939

Margaret was born in the spring of 1872 in 18 Rossett Place in Liscard, and was baptised on the 12th May 1872. Margaret married Frank Garfield Piper in 1896 at Birkenhead, shortly afterwards the couple moved to Fleetwood where Frank found work as a ship's steward.

Mrs Piper moved back to Liscard and attended her brother's funeral in January 1939. Margaret was to pass away a few months later.

By 1913 the family had grown to eight children.

Frank Piper	b 1896	Fleetwood
William Piper	b 1897	Fleetwood
James H Piper	b 1899	Fleetwood
Margaret Piper	b 1901	Fleetwood
John Piper	b 1907	Fleetwood
Alfred Piper	b.1909	Fleetwood
Alice Piper	b.1910	Fleetwood
Edith Piper	b.1913	Fleetwood

Shown on the 1901 census are ten people all resident in a little two-up two-down terraced house at 11, Rhyl Street, Fleetwood, Lancashire. With four boarders it must have been very crowded. No wonder Frank went to sea, and the family was to grow even bigger.

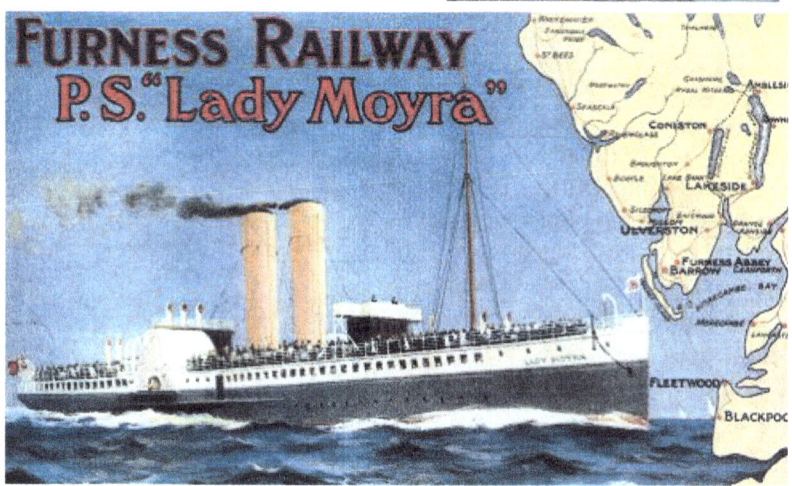

57

Chapter 1 - Edward W. Dutton 1874-1956

Edward Walter Dutton was born in the summer of 1874 at Rossett Place. He married Alice Samples in 1897 and they went on to have twin boys Edward and Robert born in 1899 and a daughter Alice born in 1903. He was probably the best educated in the family and went on to become a time keeper in the Borough Engineer and Survey dept. When Edward Dutton wrote the original article on the Dutton family in 1952 he records that Edward for many years was in retirement living at 10 Sea View Ave. In Rake Lane Cemetery (2C-58) a white memorial stone reads as follows: *In loving memory of Alice beloved wife of Edward W. Dutton died 19th November 1923 aged 52 years. Also Edward Walter Dutton beloved husband of the above died 25th September 1956, aged 82 years.*

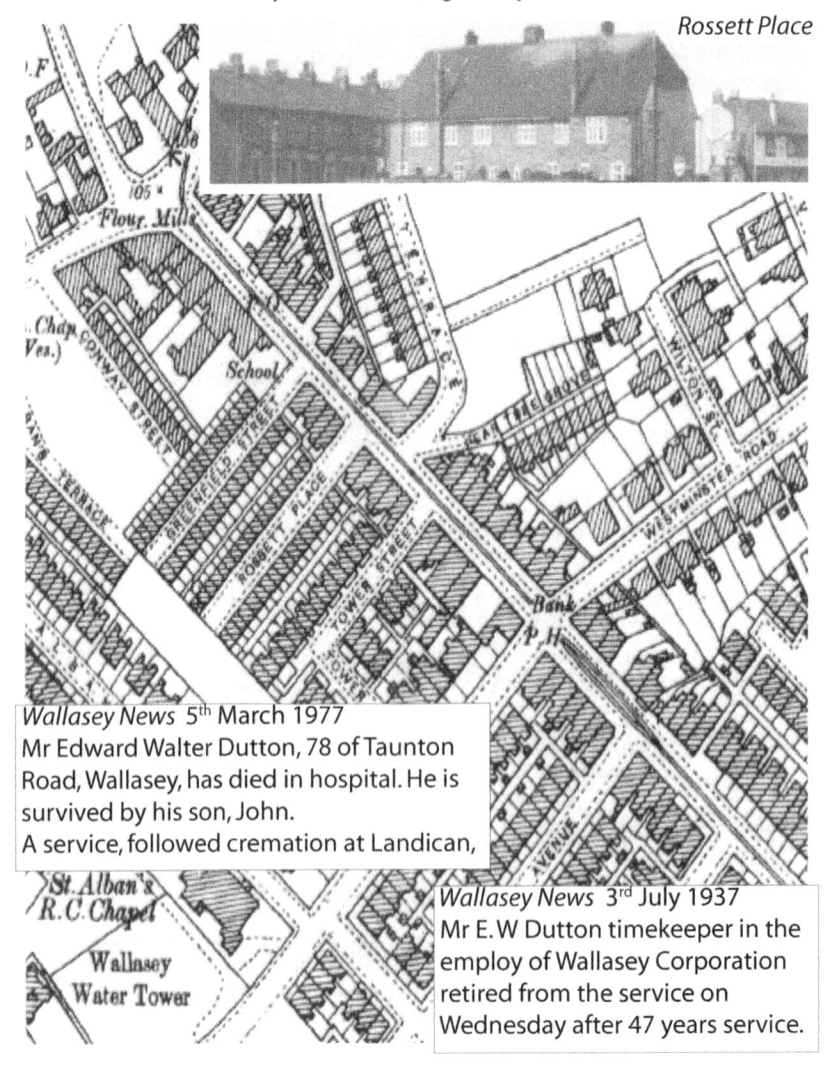

Rossett Place

Wallasey News 5th March 1977
Mr Edward Walter Dutton, 78 of Taunton Road, Wallasey, has died in hospital. He is survived by his son, John.
A service, followed cremation at Landican,

Wallasey News 3rd July 1937
Mr E.W Dutton timekeeper in the employ of Wallasey Corporation retired from the service on Wednesday after 47 years service.

58

Chapter 1 - Liscard Model Farm

The first mention of the settlement was circa 1260 as Lisnekarke. Liscard Hall was built in 1835 by a Liverpool merchant, Sir John Tobin one-time Lord Mayor of Liverpool. He died on 27th February 1851 and is buried in St. John's churchyard. His tomb can still be seen on the north side of the church. Liscard Hall was passed down to his son-in-law Harold Littledale. It was not until 1845 with the establishment of a model farm, conceived and established by Mr Harold Littledale, that Liscard was put truly on the map, and played a part in the history of Wallasey. With the help of a Mr Torr from Lincoln, one of the best practical farmers of the time, who directed the layout and established the various working practices, the farm was brought to fruition.

To quote from the *History of Wirral* by Mortimer, *The model farm of this Gentleman is unquestionably one of the greatest lions of the day, as is proved by its being almost daily visited by everyone who takes an interest in agriculture....There are one hundred stalls for cows, as well ventilated as Her Majesty's stables at Buckingham Palace.......The dairy contains a marble fountain, which would put to shame those exquisite specimens of national taste recently erected in Trafalgar Square......*

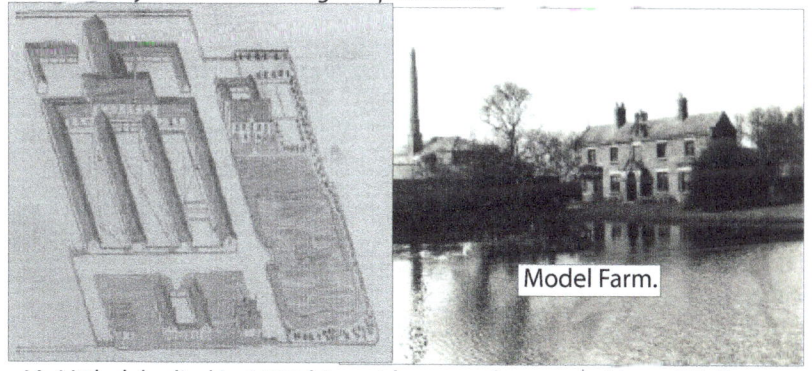

Model Farm.

Mr Littledale died in 1889, his residence and grounds, Liscard Hall, were acquired by the local board, and converted into the Central park and the building itself later became an art college. The former Grade II listed building was destroyed by fire on 7th July 2008, and eventually demolished. Another sad day for our heritage (See below).

Chapter 1 - William Dutton 1877-1951

The farm known as Dutton's Farm in Mill Lane, was situated between Love Lane and the maternity hospital and stretched back to Central Park. It was also part of the enterprising development in the Dutton business.
William Dutton had two daughters Emily and Mabel. One of the girls is probably standing in the doorway and William's wife Elizabeth is working in the garden. On the above photograph the Water Tower in Mill Lane is just visible top right. Joe Dean worked on the farm; it was here that he met Emily and married her.
From the *Wallasey News* dated 24th January 1949
William Dutton celebrated his Golden Wedding Anniversary. He married Elizabeth Buckley on Christmas Day 1899.
In Rake Lane cemetery Section 22c G37: The grave of William Dutton who died 6th September 1951 aged 74 years. also his beloved wife Elizabeth Dutton who died 8th May 1963 aged 83 years. also Mabel Wall dearly loved daughter of above who died 14th July 1982 aged 77 years. Emily Wray daughter of above 1902-1991.

William Dutton standing between the horses

60

Chapter 1 - William Dutton 1877-1951

MANOR FARM DAIRY,
Norwood Road, Poulton.

Established for the Sale of Absolutely Pure Home Produced Milk.

WM. DUTTON, Proprietor.

Hotels, Institutions, etc., supplied on Special Terms.

DELIVERIES TWICE DAILY.   The ONLY COWKEEPER in the District.

The photographs of Dutton's farm form part of a collection held in the Central Library in Wallasey, and are dated 1913. In the postal directory of 1914-15 William Dutton is shown living at 37 Mill Lane. Occupation Dairyman.

Chapter 1 - Wallasey Carnival to Wirral Show

From Wallasey Carnival to Wirral Show
The Wallasey Carnival was an annual event which took place in June each year to collect donations for local hospitals. This was a spectacle of horse-drawn floats covered with flowers and people. The floats were interspersed with bands and dancers.

From the *Wallasey News* of 10th June 1922. Once again the premier award for best decorated turnout went to Mr Dutton, of Dutton's Farm.

This was Mr Dutton's seventh success at the Wallasey Carnival, and he has also taken prizes in other districts. Everywhere along the route there were large crowds of spectators, the foot walks along King Street, Egremont, especially, almost being impassable. It took over half an hour to pass a given point.

In June 1924 the event was carried out under the auspices of the Committee of Wallasey Gentlemen who, as the result of their activities last year in connection with the carnival and Horse Show which succeeded it later in the season, were able to hand over £1,000 to the fund for Victoria Central Hospital Memorial Scheme.

At the conclusion of the Carnival a fancy dress ball was held at the Tower. With prizes and awards for the best displays: Best decorated light two-wheel turnouts: W. Dutton. Wallasey (Indian pagoda)

The Annual Wirral Show which started in 1977 as a Community project aimed to resurrect the 'Wallasey Carnival' with decorated floats parading through the town and finishing on the promenade in New Brighton. As it became more difficult to arrange the floats, the stalls erected at the end of the parade took greater prominence.

Prior to the outbreak of war in 1939, Wallasey had always prided itself in producing the "Wallasey Village Carnival". The major float carried the Carnival Princess and her court, whilst the whole event was led with great aplomb by the Wallasey Village Silver Band (which used the *Lighthouse Pub* in Wallasey Village as its unofficial headquarters). The whole event was so big for a small town, school children had the day off to help celebrate. Clowns, morris dancers, singers, soldiers, scouts, fire engines, police as well as the entire population of Wallasey Village turned out for this grand day in the calendar. Inexplicably, this grand tradition lapsed for some years.

In 1977, the Rotary Club of Wallasey were considering an event to mark the 25th anniversary of HM The Queen's ascension to the throne. It was put to the Rotary Club the suggestion of celebrating the event by reviving the lapsed Wallasey Carnival. It proved to be a successful event and the historic day of 1st September 1977 became known as the Great Wallasey

Chapter 1 - Wallasey Carnival to Wirral Show

Carnival of 1977, with over 80,000 people lining the one-mile route from Central Park to New Brighton Promenade.

From the *Liverpool Echo* dated 9th December 2009

Organisers have pulled the plug on the Wirral Show after 33 years.
The annual two-day event started life in 1977 as a revival of the Wallasey Carnival. It has since become one of the UK's biggest free attractions, drawing thousands of visitors each year to New Brighton Dips. Volunteers from Wallasey Lions Club and the Rotary Club of Wallasey, together with Wallasey Round Table, have run the Wirral Show for many years with support from Wirral Council.

The Dips

The Dips on King's Parade

Before they built the promenade if you went down Portland Street you could jump straight on to the sand. The construction resulted in the golden sand being lost for many years. The Council had to pay a lot of money to try to bring it back and we ended up with a prom with nothing but grass dips. The Dips are popular with people and for many years the Wirral Show was held on the site; there was motorcycle racing at full speed around the promenade. And now we have the Annual Kite Festival. As a child I played football but if there was a breeze, it was out with the kite, which would sail over the multi-coloured tents, full of holidaymakers enjoying the sunshine. In the winter the Dips are a very different place; they can be bleak and windswept. Sometimes strong winds and high tides combine to produce massive waves which lash against and over the sea wall, flooding the summer playgrounds which in turn change into mini marine lakes. Step in the E.U with a load of cash to construct new sea defences. It is hoped this will prevent flooding: as for the sand lets hope that it hangs around for another millennium or two.

Chapter 1 - James H. Dutton 1882-1945

James Herbert Dutton was the youngest child born in 1882; he was the second James born to John Dutton. The first James born in 1871 died within 6 months. Herbert known as 'Farmer Dutton' played for Egremont Social A.F.C. Margaret (James' mother) in her will, arranged for her son James to receive *"a sufficient part of the milk round attached to my business so that his own present milk round may be increased by Forty Gallons a day."* The family connection with horses started by James Herbert's father who was a breeder of horses some of which were used by the Volunteer Fire Brigade. James married Hannah Bexon in 1901 and the couple went on to have three boys, James Herbert born in 1903, William Richard born in 1905 and Frank born in 1907.

Chapter 1 - James H. Dutton 1882-1945

James   Hannah   James   William Frank

The above photograph was taken at 39 Ashburton Road in 1911 and shows the family in the yard of the property. The younger couple with their daughter in the centre of the photograph have not been identified.

The two-up two-down terraced house, is very close to Dutton's farm and the water tower can be seen in the background. James lived at 244 Liscard Road working in the family business until he branched out on his own.

Asburton Road. With Water Tower top left

James   James   Frank   Hannah   William

65

Chapter 1 - James H. Dutton 1882-1945

Mabel *Frank*

The photograph opposite is of Hannah's youngest son Frank with Mabel Dutton the daughter of James' older brother William.

The school formerly known as Dutton's Dancing School, was started in 1916 in Birkenhead by James Herbert Dutton and his wife Hannah. The school was continued by their granddaughter Jean Dutton in the 1940s.

The school was then taken over by Jean's cousin, June.

Jean moved to Australia in 1964 and then opened a school (still known as Dutton's Dancing School) in the eastern suburbs of Melbourne, moving later to Chelsea in 1978, which was then run by Jean and her daughter Jeanette.

Since 2007, the school has been known as Art Evolutions Dance School and is now run by Jeanette's daughter, Jessica.

Jessica started dancing at the age of 3, not surprising due to her family's history in dance. Jessica has studied under the teaching of her mother and grandmother and has achieved her teaching qualifications with the Australian Academy of Theatrical and Ballet Dancing Inc. Jessica has experience in competitions, concerts and academy recitals and also has widened her experience with hip-hop, salsa and swing dancing.

James *Hannah*

Duttons Dancing School 1916

This photo was taken at a World War I hospital in Chester, England, where the dance troupe entertained injured soldiers.

Chapter 1 - Dutton gravestone

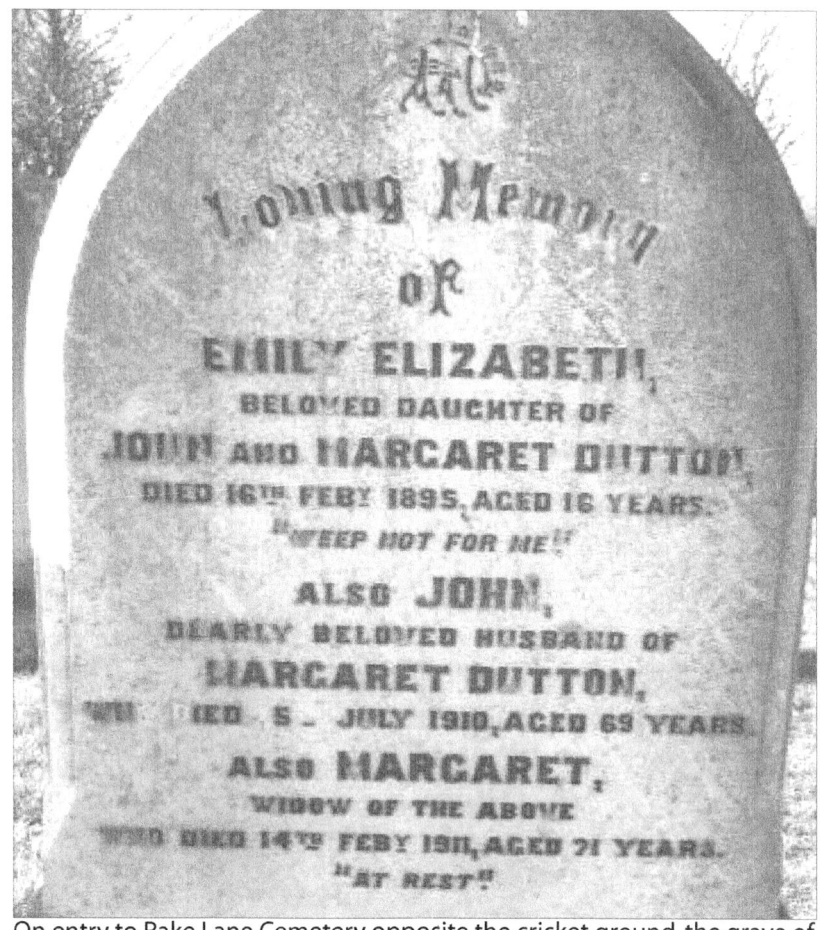

In Loving Memory of
EMILY ELIZABETH,
BELOVED DAUGHTER OF
JOHN AND MARGARET DUTTON
DIED 16TH FEBY 1895, AGED 16 YEARS.
"WEEP NOT FOR ME"
ALSO JOHN,
DEARLY BELOVED HUSBAND OF
MARGARET DUTTON,
WHO DIED 5 - JULY 1910, AGED 69 YEARS.
ALSO MARGARET,
WIDOW OF THE ABOVE
WHO DIED 14TH FEBY 1911, AGED 71 YEARS.
"AT REST"

On entry to Rake Lane Cemetery opposite the cricket ground, the grave of Thomas Dutton my grandfather can be found on the left-hand side of the second plot of graves, third row plot No. 8c - 187. There is no headstone; originally it was fitted with a wooden memorial which has been removed.

1899 Margaret Dutton	Aged 26
1939 Thomas Dutton	Aged 72 (Died 3.1.39)
1945 James Herbert Dutton	Aged 62
1959 Hannah Dutton	Aged 77 (James Herbert's wife)

Just behind this plot No 8c - 185 is the grave of my great grandfather John Dutton. Headstone shown above.

1895 Emily Elizabeth Dutton	Aged 16
1906 Millicent Beatrice Dutton	Aged 2 years 11 months
1910 John Dutton	Aged 69
1911 Margaret Dutton	Aged 71
1950 Sarah Ann Wilkinson	Aged 88 (John's daughter)

Chapter 1 - Liscard

Liscard 1902

Liscard Cresent Co-Op

Chapter 1 - Thomas Dutton's children

Thomas Dutton 1867-1939

- Margaret Sherlock b1872 d1899 Hoylake
  - *John Dutton b 1893 Wallasey — John married Mary Houligan in 1917
  - Emily Dutton b 1895 Wallasey — Emily married Joseph Dean in 1914
  - Edward Dutton b 1896 Wallasey — Edward married Gladys Harrison in 1917
  - Thomas Dutton b 1898 Wallasey — Thomas married Alice Whetnall in 1920
  - Mary S. Dutton b.1899 d.1899 Wallasey — Mary Sherlock Dutton

- Thomas Dutton b1867 d 1939 Liscard

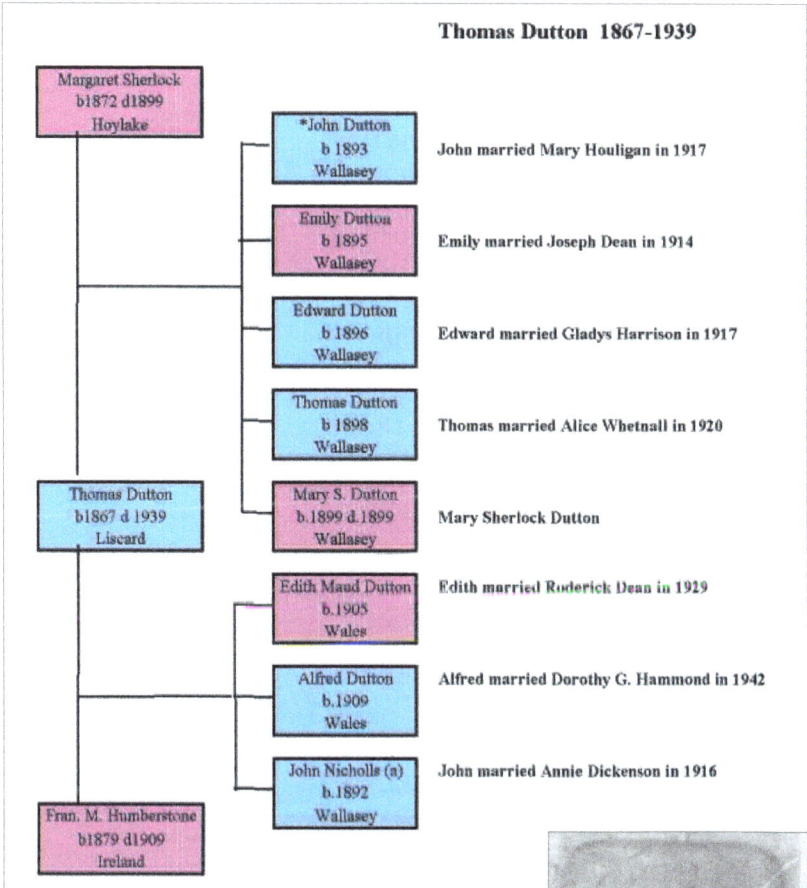

- Edith Maud Dutton b.1905 Wales — Edith married Roderick Dean in 1929
- Alfred Dutton b.1909 Wales — Alfred married Dorothy G. Hammond in 1942
- John Nicholls (a) b.1892 Wallasey — John married Annie Dickenson in 1916

- Fran. M. Humberstone b1879 d1909 Ireland

Notes:

* I have been unable to research John Dutton. The 1901 census has him living at 244 Liscard Road with his grandfather and widowed father. I could not find any record of him on the 1911 census; nor has the marriage been confirmed. An interesting observation from *Wood's Wallasey Directory* 1904-5.
  John Dutton dairyman 101 Poulton Road.
  John Dutton 6 Peartree Grove.
  John Dutton dairyman 244, Liscard Road.
On the 1911 census Thomas Dutton Head of the family living at 244 Liscard Road. Records a total of nine children born alive with four having died. On the family tree produced by Gary Dutton he records an additional two children William R. Dutton & Albert E. Dutton.

Margaret Sherlock

Chapter 1 - Emily E. Dutton 1895 - 1972

After their marriage Thomas and Margaret moved to 42 Burnaby Street. It was not until they moved into a cottage in Egerton Grove opposite the general post office also in Liscard, that they brought Edward, Thomas and Emily into the world. The cottage was in a group of three cottages dating back to the late sixteenth century. It was a long, low, thatched building made of sandstone and whitewashed walls. With distinctive seashell decoration embedded in plaster around the window openings. This charming bit of old Wallasey was demolished in 1924 and Hebron Hall was built on the site. Emily Elizabeth Dutton was born in 1895 in Liscard. She was named after Emily Elizabeth Dutton

Emily & Iris

the daughter who died in 1895 aged 16. And is buried with her parents in Rake Lane Cemetery. When Thomas lost his wife in 1899, the family moved into 244 Liscard Road, so that the young children could be looked after by their grandparents. Thomas was a plumber by trade and would need to travel around the country to find work.

Emily married Joseph Arthur Dean in 1914, at St Hilary's Church in Wallasey. Ivy S Dean was born on the 9th February 1914, followed by Iris M Dean in 1917. The young family lived in Secombe before moving to 3 Queens Road in Liscard. An amazing coincidence is the fact that two half-sisters on the Dutton side of the family married two brothers on the Dean side. Joseph in later life became a spiritualist, and had a chapel in the attic of his home.

Joe Dean

Chapter 1 - Emily Dutton's Children Ivy & Iris

Ivy S. Dean married William H. Griffiths in Wallasey in the winter of 1938. Ivy took her middle name from her mother's maiden name Sherlock.

From the *Wallasey News* dated 31st January 1942
Married at Liscard O'Neill - Dean

St. Alban's Church, Liscard was the scene of a pretty wedding on Saturday, when Miss Iris Margaret Dean, youngest daughter of Mr and Mrs J.Dean, of Queen Street, was married to Mr James A. O'Neill, R.A.F., younger son of the late Mr James O'Neill of Devonshire Road. The ceremony was conducted by Father McNally.

The bride's parents are well known in local Civil Defence, Mr Dean being a Fire Guard and his wife an Air Raid Warden.

The bride was very charmingly attired in a grey and maroon ensemble. In attendance were her sister, Mrs H. Griffiths, and Miss Dorothy O'Neill sister of the bridegroom. Mrs Griffiths chose a pretty dusty pink dress with a brown and green coat and hat, and Miss O'Neill wore a pleasing silk floral dress under her wine-coloured coat.

Mr. McDonald, a comrade of the bridegroom, served him as best man, and Mr Bert Newnes and Mr Lamont were ushers at the Church.

Following the ceremony a reception was held at a local cafe, about thirty guests attending. The bride's mother wore a handsome gown of black silk Moroccan, with fur-trimmed coat and velvet hat to match, and a becoming navy silk dress, with black coat and hat was worn by the bridegroom's mother.

The happy couple who were the recipients of many handsome and useful presents, later left for Southport, where they will spend their honeymoon.

Ivy Dean

Ivy & Iris

Joe ran an entertainment show, with his daughters putting on shows locally.
In a letter from Ronald Dean dated 9th Jan 1999, he records that Ivy was resident in a nursing home in Penkett Road, Wallasey. Ivy was to pass away the following year in June 2000.

Chapter 1 - Edward R. Dutton 1896 - 1972

Edward Robert Dutton was born on the 25th March 1896 in Liscard the son of Thomas Dutton. His very first job was in the family dairy business at 244 Liscard Road, not only serving customers but helping with the book work.

He was to marry Gladys Harrison in St Hilary's Church Wallasey on the 5th January 1917.

Ted was the family historian, and took the research of our family firmly on his shoulders. He was a close friend and confidant of my father his half-brother, and would offer his counsel on various issues. I will always be grateful for his help in sorting out my fathers estate and helping my mother, in her time of need. My father passed away while I was floating around the Atlantic Ocean, and Ted came to our rescue. He was an intelligent and charming person to meet and always had time for you. Their first child was born in 1918 and was named after her mother Gladys M Dutton. Eric E Dutton was born in 1920, followed by Joan S Dutton born 1925, Sidney J Dutton born 1928, Kenneth J Dutton born 1930 and finally Audrey E Dutton born in 1932. All born in Birkenhead.

Wallasey News dated 7th January 1967

Celebrating their golden wedding anniversary tomorrow (Sunday) will be Mr and Mrs E. R. Dutton, of Withens Lane, Wallasey. They were married at St. Hilary's Church, Wallasey on January 5th, 1917. Mr and Mrs Dutton have three daughters and one son, and 20 grandchildren.

Sharing their celebration will be the Mayor and Mayoress (Alderman and Mrs. T. Garnett), who will visit their home.

GOLDEN DAY FOR RAKERS' MAN

Wallasey News dated 8th July 1972

Ted Dutton, secretary of New Brighton FC for 20 years until his retirement two years ago, died suddenly in hospital on Thursday.

He was aged 76 and lived at 165 Withens Lane, Wallasey.

Chapter 1 - Edward R. Dutton 1896 - 1972

Edward Dutton Secretary of New Brighton Football Club (The Rakers)
The club had reached the 4th round of the FA Cup on three occasions; in the 1927–28 season when they lost to Port Vale, in the 1937–38 season when they lost to Tottenham Hotspur in a replay, and most impressively in the 1956–57 season, when as a non-League club, they beat three League clubs before losing to Burnley.

Ted helped organise the match of the decade on the 29th October 1962 to commemorate the first match to be played under the new floodlights. Liverpool sent a strong team and New Brighton featured guest appearances by Tom Finney, Nat Lofthouse and the big Bill Liddell.
Liverpool side: Lawrence in goal, fullbacks Ferns and Moran,
halfbacks Milne, Yeats, Stevenson,
forwards Callaghan, Hunt, Lewis, Melia, and Wallace.

But all this investment was to prove fruitless-with falling gate receipts it spelt the beginning of the end for the Rakers. On the 29th January 1969 the proposed 10-million-pound scheme to transform New Brighton Tower grounds into a giant sports centre was cancelled.

Ted Dutton had battled on to try and save the deal, but as reported in an earlier edition of the *Wallasey News* "Some members of the board are beginning to lose faith in the whole thing," said secretary Mr Ted Dutton, "But I am very optimistic." Councillor Baker said the club was fighting for its very existence. "We intend to keep going and will honour our obligations to the players' contracts this season. But next season we will have a largely amateur side." Ted Dutton refuses to look on the black side. "There is room for a wonderful development here. If we get these things advanced there is every chance we will get into a higher grade of soccer. I have made application for re-election to the Football League every year since 1961.

Murch Leftwich & Co.
Estate Agents, Auctioneers, Valuers, Surveyors
ERIC J MURCH, FRICS, FSVA   DAVID R LEFTWICH

BY ORDER OF WIRRAL BOROUGH COUNCIL
Residential Building Land to be offered at Auction by Murch, Leftwich & Company at the Town Hall, Wallasey, on Wednesday, June 24th, 1981, at 2.30 p.m.

TOWER GROUNDS, NEW BRIGHTON

10.62 acres suitable for high density residential development. Gently sloping site with open views over River Mersey towards Liverpool.
Freehold.
Main services.
Full particulars on application.

Chapter 1 - Edward R. Dutton 1896 - 1972

FOOTBALL UNDER FLOODLIGHTS

MONDAY, 29th OCTOBER, 1962
kick-off 7-30 p.m.

New Brighton
Versus
Liverpool

TOWER GROUND
NEW BRIGHTON

OFFICIAL PROGRAMME — PRICE 6d.

Ted Dutton, veteran secretary of New Brighton A.F.C who retires from office at the end of the season, was presented with a fine tankard by the Rakers number one supporter and team mascot Robert Wooley before last Thursday's floodlit cup-tie. Also in the picture is player-manager Roy Lorenson who thanked Ted for his services on behalf of the team.

Chapter 1 - Edward R. Dutton 1896 - 1972

Wallasey News dated 1st October 1949
Mr Eric Ashworth and Miss Joan S. Dutton
The wedding took place on Saturday of Miss Joan Sherlock Dutton, of 28 Trinity Road, Wallasey, and Mr Eric Ashworth, son of Mrs, and the late Mr. S Ashworth, of 86 Egerton Street, New Brighton. The second daughter of Mr and Mrs E.R. Dutton, Miss Dutton was given in marriage by her brother, Eric, at the Egremont Presbyterian Church ceremony, her father being unable to be present owing to illness.

Wearing a gown of heavy white brocade satin with full skirt, heart-shaped neckline and with a full-length veil secured by an orange blossom headdress, the bride carried a bouquet of pink roses.

The bride's sister, Mrs Cotterall was the matron of honour and Miss Phyllis Sutton was the bridesmaid. Mrs Cotterall wore blue floral silk and Phyllis chose pink floral with full skirt and heart shaped neckline. Both wore pearl necklaces (gifts of the bridegroom), and carried pink carnation bouquets. Linda Jolly (cousin of the groom) and Norman Cotterall (niece of the bride) made two charming little attendants in pale blue crepe and shell pink respectively. On leaving the church the bride was presented with a silver horseshoe by Beryl Dutton, her small niece.

Mr Harry Jolly, uncle of the bridegroom was best man and Messrs W.C. Cotterall and Harry Ashworth were stewards. Following a New Brighton reception, the happy pair left for a Lake District honeymoon, the bride travelling in a donkey-brown coat, pale blue dress and brown hat trimmed with pale blue.

Everton
NORMAN ERIC DUTTON
June 21st 2012
Peacefully at home.
Aged 69 years
Devoted husband to Hazel, much loved dad to Gary and Christine and loving grandad to Sammie, Michael, Molly and Ellie.

A special smile,
A special face,
In our hearts a special place.

Funeral service at St Hildeburgh's Church, Hoylake on Monday 2nd July at 1.30pm, followed by cremation at Landican at 2.30pm. Enquiries, flowers and donations in aid of the R.N.L.I., Hoylake to Quinn's Funeral Service, Hoylake.
Tel: 0151 632 2205

DUTTON NORMAN
21.06.2012
Aged 69 years.
Peacefully after a bravely fought illness. Dearly loved son of the late Eric and Peggy, and much loved brother of Brian, Beryl, Les, Mavis, Joyce (dec'd), Jean, Steve, Ron, John, Bobby, Eddie, Anne and Julie, also all in-laws, nephews and nieces. Will be greatly missed.
(Gone fishing)
x x x x x

Chapter 1 - Thomas Dutton 1897-1976

Thomas Dutton was born on the 17 June 1897 in Wallasey.
In 1920 Thomas married Alice Whetnall in St Mary's Church Liscard. The couple went on to have two children; Alice Dutton born 1921 and Thomas Frederick Dutton born 1st September 1927.
My father would take my mother out for a drink on a Saturday night, and quite often meet Tommy in the *Traveller's Rest*. They had both worked together in the painting trade, before Tommy decided to go it alone. Tommy could not read a word of music, but by all accounts was a spectacular pianist, and would entertain the regulars with a sing-song in the pub.

The above photograph shows Tom and Alice with John their grandson.
The photograph on the right was taken during a fishing trip to New Brighton. From left to right Alice Dutton (Thomas' sister), John (son of Alice Dutton), Alice Dutton (Nan) Jane (Sheila's daugther b 1956), Thomas (Sheila's husband) and Fred. (Sheila's eldest son b 1958). With a lucky catch each.

The above photograph was taken during the storms in the 1950s Tommy Dutton is removing a fallen tree from his Bedford van. Dutton's Contractors eventually became T.F Dutton Ltd and had their office and workshops at the top of Sandfield Road until Mr Dutton died in 1993 and the company closed down. With many fine buildings built in and around Wallasey including the spectacular villa at 46 Warren Drive, they have left an indelible mark on the landscape.

Chapter 1 - Thomas Dutton 1897-1976

From the Wallasey News dated 2nd March 1946
Miss Alice Dutton, daughter of Mr and Mrs Thomas Dutton, 48 Grosvenor Road, Wallasey, was on Saturday, 16th February, married to Mr George Chalder-Royle (ex-R.A.F), of Croydon, Surrey, son of the late Mr and Mrs George Chalder-Royle.
The wedding took place at St James's Church, New Brighton, the Rev. W.L.Beckies Goodwin, Vicar, officiating.
The bride, who was given in marriage by her father, was attired in a gown of white figured satin, with dainty embroidered dress of orange blossom. Her bouquet consisted of pink carnations.
Miss Betty Rimmer was in attendance as bridesmaid in a gown of pink figured satin, with pink net headdress and accessories, and carried a bouquet of white carnations.
The best man was Corporal Arthur J. Border, R.A.F, of London, the ushers being Mr V.Howe and Mr A.R. Dutton.
A reception was held at the bride's home, after which the married couple left for their honeymoon, in North Wales. The bride travelled in a blue tweed suit and camel hair travelling coat, gloves and shoes to match. Cars were provided by J.Kenna and Sons, of Wallasey.

Next to Alice left to right is Thomas Dutton, Alice Dutton (Tom's wife) Miss Betty Rimmer. Between Alice and Betty my father Alfred R Dutton. Centre on the back row is my mother on her right Betty and standing in front of her Joyce Hammond.

Chapter 1 - Thomas Dutton 1897-1976

Top: Painting by Alice Chandler-Royle The *Magazine Pu*b, New Brighton.
Middle Left: Nan Dutton with daughter Alice.
Middle Right: Nan Dutton with Thomas Fredrick Dutton
Bottom: L to R: Nick Carter, Keith Elliott, Steven Hill and *Fred Dutton.
* Eldest son of Thomas F. Dutton. Owner of Medkoi a Koi fish farm in
Cyprus.   Fred's background being in the construction industry.

Chapter 1 - Thomas Dutton 1897-1976

It was in the early 1970s that I called upon the expertise of Thomas Fredrick Dutton; his knowledge of the building industry was to prove invaluable in our quest to become property developers. A few months earlier we had formed a consortium with Peter Turnbull, Roy Dutton, Tom McCullock and Robin Jackson of W.T Jackson and Sons solicitors.

Our first major project was going to be the purchase of just over three acres of building land outside Amlwch, at a place called Rhos-y-bol. Mrs Parry had obtained outline planning permission. Her family even had a mountain named after them. At the time property was booming; people were buying property 'off plan'. How could we possibly loose?. Peter had developed a real rapport with Mrs Parry even to the point of befriending her pet pig, Dulce. We negotiated a spectacular deal including a longer than normal completion period, to give us time to kick start the project. Wait for it… then bang! The property crash of 1974! By this time we had already paid the 10% deposit and we were locked into the deal. We could stand to loose a small fortune, if the land was put back on the market. The bank had pulled the rug from under us so there was no way that we could finalise this project even if we wanted to.

Thomas advised an alternative strategy to help us salvage something from the deal, and along with Robin Jackson we managed to escape by the skin of our teeth. It transpired that even before the deal collapsed, the builder had approached Mrs Parry's solicitors with a view to taking over the project. Without a similar surname Williams or Jones and a Welsh pedigree to match, we were doomed. Courtesy of a satellite photograph via Goggle we can all view our unfulfilled dreams, which came to fruition using our plans and ideas, such is life. We did have some success with property; one in Pensby Road which was a profitable venture. I did manage to get my original investment in the company back. Luckily I decided not to continue; the company went on to purchase property in Chester, which ended up with litigation and a massive fall-out between the partners.

Chapter 1 - Edith Maud Dutton 1897-1995

Edith was born in the winter of 1904, in Llanidloes mid-Wales. I remember Ronald telling me he took his parents on a nostalgic journey and Edith recognised the street that she had lived in as a child.
In 1929 Edith married Roderick J Dean.
Ronald was born in 1930, their only child. They lived for many years in the Fireman's Cottages in Manor Road. Roderick worked on the buses.

Whenever my Mom and I went shopping in Liscard we would call in to see aunty Edith. A warm welcome and a cup of tea and biscuits were always forthcoming. I have correspondence from Ronald, Edith's son telling me of the visit to try and find his grandmother's grave in Rhayder.

My dad, mother & Roderick Dean
Photo taken 20th Sep 1943

Edith

80

Chapter 1 - Edith Maud Dutton 1897-1995

Standing next to the bride is Edith, Mamie Dean, Josie Dean then Ted's wife Gladys and my mother.

From the ***Wallasey News*** dated 14th January 1956

Wearing a gown of nylon lace over satin with trailing veil and carrying a bouquet of pink carnations, lily of the valley and white heather, Miss Norma Mary Parsons was married on Saturday at St Luke's church to Mr. Ronald James Dean. The Rev. A.E.Lockley officiated.

The bride is the daughter of Mr and Mrs J.W. Parsons of Dinmore Road; the bridegroom is the son of Mr and Mrs D.Dean of Manor Road. Given away by her father, the bride was attended by Miss Margaret Tebbet and Miss Carol Dodds. The first two were in turquoise gowns with flowered headdresses and carried daffodils. Miss Dodds wore a similar gown and carried a muff with a spray of anemones. Mr Stanley Pickles was the best man and the steward was Mr Bill Owens. After a reception at the home of the bride, the couple left for their honeymoon, the bride in a kingfisher blue coat with tan accessories. J.Pritchard, Wallasey Road supplied the cars.

A keen mountaineer, he first met Norma through their joint interest in rock climbing. Unfortunately the marriage was not to last and they divorced several years later. They got married quite late on in life and both were set in their ways. Aunt Edie was devastated by the news as they had always appeared to be a loving couple.

Ronald worked for many years in the Midland Bank eventually being promoted to the manager of the Wallasey Village branch. He moved to Church Stretton were he took up a post with the National Trust. My last communication with Ronald was in April 2010, I have since tried to make contact without any success.

81

Chapter 1 - Alfred R. Dutton 1909-1969

Frances

When Thomas Dutton met Frances M. Humberstone she was working as a domestic servant in the employment of the Bozman family of "Hillside" St George's Road. On the 1901 census her age is recorded as 22. Frances was the second wife of Thomas. After their marriage they went to live in Llanidloes, where in 1904 Edith was born. Thomas had served an apprenticeship as a plumber. In the days before the arrival of water 'on tap' to houses, the village water pump was a vital facility for the community. The plumbing skills of Thomas helped to connect the houses and businesses to a water supply. The photograph shown was taken around 1895, and shows the pump which was then located in Long Bridge Street at the very centre of the town, next to the Market Hall in Llanidloes in Montgomeryshire. Thomas eventually travelled down to Rhayader in Powys, mid-Wales to obtain work as a plumber.

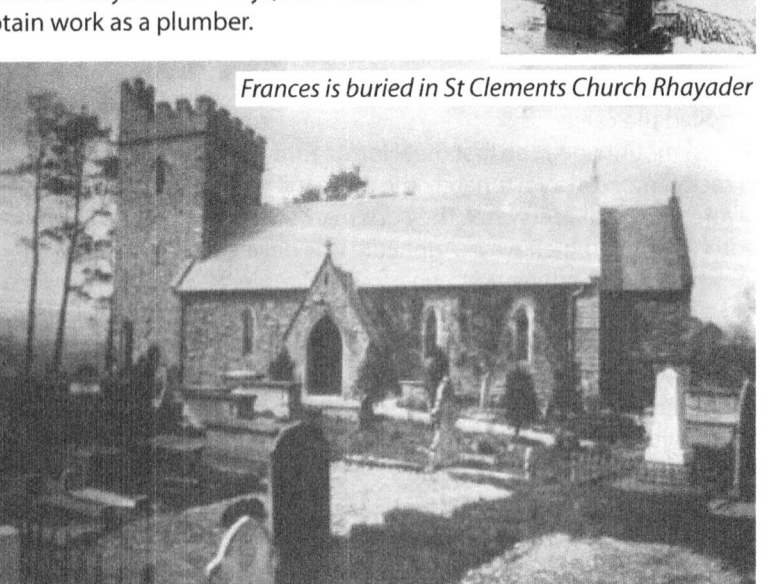

Frances is buried in St Clements Church Rhayader

82

Chapter 1 - Alfred R. Dutton 1909-1969

Old Swan Inn, West Street
My father was born in Old Swan, Rhayader in Montgomeryshire. Frances died giving birth to my father on 6th April 1909. Francis was only 31years old, and is buried in an unmarked grave in the village church yard. My father was christened Alfred Rhayader Dutton in remembrance of this tragic event.

The photograph below was taken in West Street, looking east towards

Old Swan Inn - Now Tea Rooms

the old Market Hall at the main crossroads in the centre of town. The picture is captioned 'Old Swan', which was the white-fronted inn on the right. The original building was mentioned in 1676 as being one of the two inns in Rhayader at that date. During the 1860s the Old Swan stopped trading as an inn, and it was used in later years as a hardware shop, a saddlers, a butcher's shop, and is now Tea Rooms and Cake Shop. Frances' death certificate records died in child birth at *The Old Swan* on the 6th April 1909.

83

Chapter 1 - Alfred R. Dutton 1909-1969

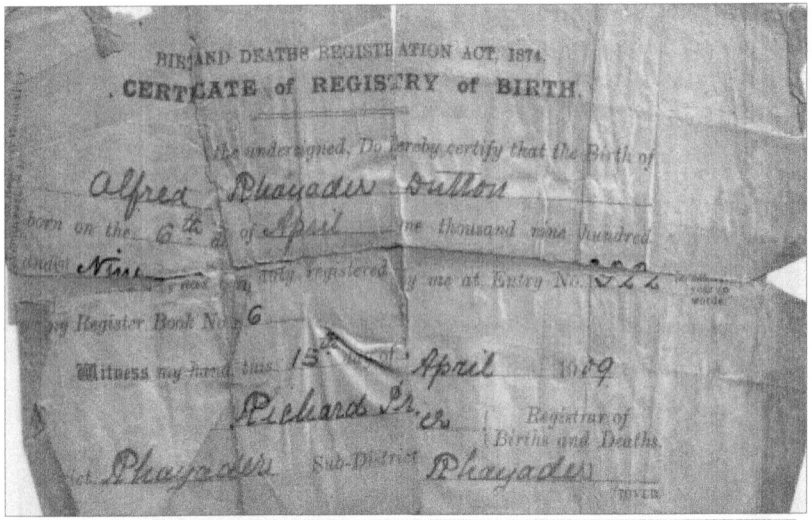

The above photograph taken circa 1911 shows my father Alfred R Dutton holding hands with one of his uncles and Thomas, his brother with whip in hand. Many photographs up to the early twentieth century show boys wearing dresses, made by doting mothers as they were the ones caring for small children. It was done across class barriers for centuries. This was not exclusively a Victorian custom; rather it was the norm in European cultures for centuries. We only see the popularity of this fashion waning after about 1900 and by the First World War it was no longer a major fashion convention. I have heard that it was to confuse gypsies who would take young male children and leave a sickly changeling in their place. And this was believed in the twentieth century!
How this photograph survived I will never know; if my father had found it, I am sure it would have gone in the bin.

Chapter 1 - Alfred R. Dutton 1909-1969

After leaving school at the age of 14, my father served an apprenticeship as a painter and decorator with Winstanly a Wallasey company. At the time this occupation was regarded as a highly skilled trade. He would be responsible for mixing the paint with pigments, oils and driers. I remember all of the doors in our house had been expertly painted with a fine brush to depict the grain of the wood. We probably had the best decorated terraced house in Field Road. My father always took a pride in this appearance. The photograph opposite has Thomas Dutton with a Hat, John Dean seated and my father as a young man.

Standing at the back Mr Ernest Ball who lived at 9 Bushy Cottages, married to Polly. I went to school with his daughter Norma, the eldest daughter was called Delma. The boy in the centre of the photograph is Derek Hammond my dad's apprentice. My dad is sitting to the left of the lady. At the time he was working for Henry Dodd a Wallasey firm of painting and decorating contractors. (Dodds Flying Squad)

Chapter 1 - Alfred R. Dutton 1909-1969

My father enlisted in the Royal Artillery on the 16th September 1940, Army Number 1657105, and was immediately posted to the 25th Light Anti-Aircraft Regiment RA (TA), which had been formed in Liverpool on the 23rd June 1939. On the outbreak of war the Regiment was deployed around the Mersey, on both the Liverpool and Birkenhead coastline. Liverpool was the most heavily bombed British city outside London. Ships would arrive daily bringing supplies of food and other cargoes from America and Canada. Without these supplies Britain would have starved and lost the war. Between August 1940 and January 1942 the German Luftwaffe made over eighty air raids on Merseyside. On the nights of the 12th, 13th and 14th of March 1941, the Luftwaffe used hundreds of bombers, to drop thousands of high explosives including tens of thousands of incendiary bombs, which fell on Bebington, Birkenhead and Wallasey.

Ironically, my dad must have missed shooting down the actual bomber that destroyed his future brother-in-law's home (Sidney Hammond). The bombing was aimed mainly at the docks, railways and factories, but large populated areas were also destroyed on both sides of the Mersey. Decoy fires were lit on the golf course to try and fool the Germans, but this probably directed their efforts towards Wallasey. Using Bofors, 3", and 2 pr Vickers Guns they had to protect the docks and city. By October 1940, they were stationed on the Wirral side. It must have been a very strange experience knowing that if you missed shooting down these bombers, they could possibly go on to kill your family and friends. Wallasey alone had 320 killed and 275 seriously injured, with many thousands killed and injured in Liverpool and Birkenhead. On the 1st October 1943 my dad was appointed Lance Bombardier. My father's nick name was "Spotter Dutton," He had an uncanny knack of spotting the enemy planes faster than anyone else.

In April 1945, the regiment received orders to proceed overseas. The 108th Light Anti-Aircraft Regiment joined the 52nd Division in Europe. As the war progressed the air threat decreased and both heavy and light AA units were used in the field role. My father was very reluctant to discuss the war. His medals lay unopened, in the very envelopes that the post man had delivered them in. On the couple of times I tried to broach the subject of what he did in the war, it was met with "A bloody waste of time" or "Your mother made the shells and I shot them at the hun" or "What do you want to know that for" or some other short one-liner to fob me off. So all the information within these pages are from his army records and discussions with my relatives. On the 10th October 1942 my father Alfred Rhayader Dutton married Dorothy Gladys Hammond. He was granted 9 days leave. Because of the scarcity of any camera film we do not have any photographs of the wedding. They held their reception in the Sandrock Hotel.

Chapter 1 - Alfred R. Dutton 1909-1969

Out in the Mersey in E-Boat Alley are situated warships that will never ever move, but stay to face the elements. The strange-looking objects are sea forts, structures of steel and concrete commissioned as a deterrent to prevent minelaying aircraft from reeking havoc on the approaches to the Port of Liverpool. With observation towers, living quarters, magazines and ammunition stores they could be almost self-contained.

My father spent a couple of months walking between the catwalks to man the anti-aircraft guns. In bad weather, if the supply ship was delayed they were expected to make their own bread and do a spot of fishing. There were between 60- 80 officers and men on board.

One of the forts is shown in the picture below, with a map showing their location. In all three installations Formby, Queens and Burbo A.A Towers.

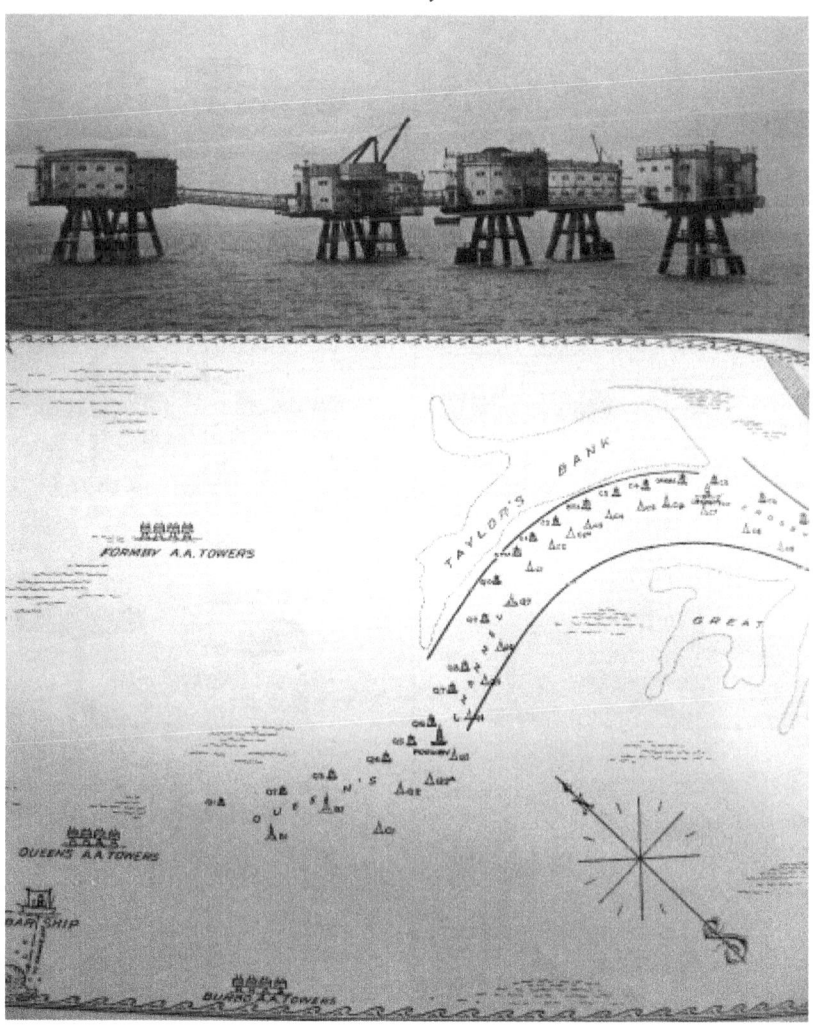

Chapter 1 - Alfred R. Dutton 1909-1939

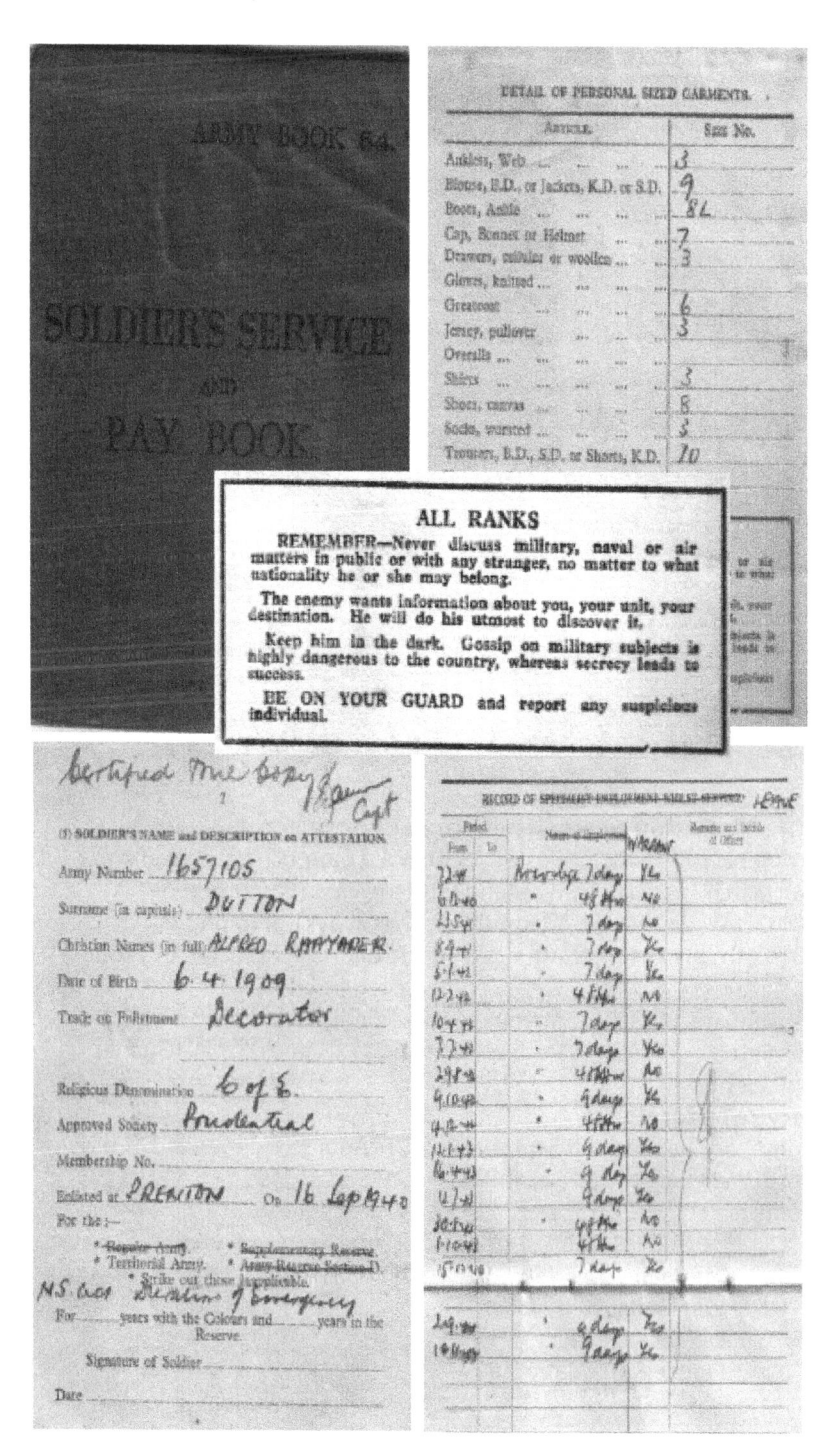

Chapter 1 - Alfred R. Dutton 1909-1969

Chapter 1 - Alfred R. Dutton 1909-1969

My father seated on the right front row

EXEMPLARY.   1657105 Gnr. Dutton A.R.

Gnr. Dutton is a steady and willing worker. He applies himself conscientiously to his duties and has always been found honest and trustworthy. He can be depended upon to do his best at all times.

Major. R.A.
Commanding 356/108 L.A.A. Regt. R.A.

Alfred R. Dutton Summary of War Service:

16th Sept.	1940	Posted 138th A.A.Z Battery (Anti-Aircraft)
16th March	1941	Weekend Privilege Pass. (Barret Green)
10th Oct.	1942	Married Dorothy Gladys Hammond.
10th-26th July 1944		Attended course of instruction at 4 AA Group TNG Centre (Recognition Wing)
31st January	1945	Attached 98 LAA Regt. R.A pending posting.
1st Feb	1945	Reclassified to Class 1A rates of pay. Gunner.

Service history
Home	6th Sept. 1940 - 27th April 1945	4 years 224 days
North West Europe	28th April 1945 - 2nd Dec. 1945	219 days
Home	3rd Dec. 1945 - 4th Feb. 1946	64 days

Total Service 5 years 142 days

Medals:
War Medal 1939/45
Defence Medal,
France & Germany Star,

Chapter 1 - Alfred R. Dutton 1909-1969

The destruction of No2 & No4 Field Road by the Luftwaffe occurred on the 12th March 1941. March was the worst month for Wallasey, with the most brutal bombing attack of the war.
Eleanor and Norah Craig died in No2 and Lucy Clewett died in No 4. During the war the school at the top of Field Road was occupied by a barrage balloon squad; they had the top floor and the basement was used by the A.R.P warden service. My mom told me that The Sandrock Hotel, now demolished, on the corner of Molyneux Drive and Rowson Street, had its large basement reinforced and made into a public air raid shelter.

The property was later to house GIs waiting for the D-Day landings. But the largest air raid shelter in the area was in the basement of The Tower in New Brighton. The old tram sheds in Field Road were used as temporary mortuaries for victims of bombing, which unfortunately were to include some residents of Field Road. Geraldine Craig, a friend of my mother's, lived at 2 Field Road and died aged 29 at David Lewis Northern Hospital, Taggart Avenue, on the 18 March 1941.
The names of some 67,092 are commemorated in the Civilian War Dead Roll of Honour, located near St. George's Chapel in Westminster Abbey London.

No 2 Field Road

91

Chapter 1 - Alfred R. Dutton 1909-1939

In the spring of 1943 the Americans Yanks or GIs (Government Issue as they were called) landed in England. These young men had quite an influence on the local people, especially the girls. They had plenty of money, cigarettes, sweets and "candy" and the ever-popular chewing gum, stockings and all sorts of things that were rare in England. With smart uniforms, lots of medals and the confidence that "they were going to kick butt" why wouldn't a young girl not be impressed?

Whilst serving in England, my father was able to get leave to visit home. During one of his visits he was introduced to Larry, a GI who was dating Joyce my older sister. By all accounts they hit it off. My father had always been the type who would stand no messing. He was always direct, and to the point. So on a trip to the *Sandridge pub* in Rowson Street, a couple of punters decided to vent their feelings. Bloody Yanks! Overpaid, over sexed and over here!

The UK had been fighting since 1939 and the consequent shortage of food and other essentials aroused some jealousy which then caused resentment towards the GIs. A few more derogatory comments followed. When my dad had heard enough, he suggested to one of the fraternity that it may be a good idea to step outside while we discuss this further. From all accounts a couple of left hooks sorted out the problem. He then returned to the pub to continue his drink as if nothing had happened.

The last time the bombs fell on Merseyside was on the 10th January 1942. Let's hope that they never fall again.

I remember my mother telling me that Larry (Keith's nickname) could not understand why the beer was always warm; in the US it was ice-cold. He also thought England was tiny compared to the huge prairies in Nebraska.

The local kids would shout to the Americans "got any gum chum?" and the servicemen would give them a stick of gum each. Keith was to return to the States at the end of 1945.

At long last the suffering and anxiety was over. On the 14th November my dad was given his 'Notification of Impending Release' whilst stationed in Germany with the 108 LAA regiment of the Royal Artillery. With a date of disembarkation set for the 12th December 1945 he could be home for Christmas! And just in time for Joyce's wedding. What a Christmas present. With his exemplary record and a first-class reference signed by Major Fawcett, it was back to civvy street. It had lasted 5 years and 24 days a big chunk out of his life.

During his time in the army, he had married, shot down enemy planes, and chased the hun back into Germany. Now he was the proud owner of a demob suit and waterproof overcoat courtesy of the government.

From living at 11 Merton Road he now took up residence at 33 Field Road with his wife to start his life all over again.

Chapter 1 - Alfred R. Dutton 1909-1969

One last twist in his military career was a return for training on the 24th June 1952 where he joined 493 HAA Regt. RATA. He completed training on the 31st August 1952. So he was now re-trained for the next political adventure, luckily he was too old to fight in Korea.

One of his favourite saying - *Bloody War! It's just legalised killing.*

My dad back row 3rd from the left.

My father's best friend was Norman Evans who lived in Pasture Road, Moreton. Norman went away to sea; the highlight for me was when he arrived back on leave. He would always bring me a present, something so unusual as to make me the talk at school. I had a stuffed alligator, a blowfish and other exotic animals. He would hire a taxi from the company in New Brighton Station. It was always the same driver - a red-haired six footer and he would chauffeur them around the clubs and pubs.

I would eagerly look in the *Liverpool Echo* to find when his ship was next due in to Liverpool, either the *Reina del Pacifico* or its sister ship the *Reina del Mar*.

Norman passed away in 1960 at the young age of 51. The photograph was taken in the *Travellers' Rest* with Norman, his wife Nancy (Nann) and my mom. My dad had just gone to buy some cigarettes.

93

Chapter 1 - Alfred R. Dutton 1909-1969

During the school holidays I would be deposited with Nan's sister Etty, in Llangollon; this allowed my parents together with Norman and Nan to take a holiday. This was always a big adventure for me, playing in the mountains and woods that surrounded her home. The countryside surrounding Llangollen is steeped in myth and legend. Dinas Bran Castle is the legendary hiding place for the Holy Grail. To the north of the town is Caer Drewyn, a mysterious hill fort.

Etty & Nann

My father was a regular type of person who never squandered his money. He always paid my mother her housekeeping on time. His only indulgence was a small bet each Saturday on the horses, and smoking those full strength cancer sticks.

My biggest grievance was the lack of communication. It was probably a generation thing we had no interest to share. He was from the old school where weekends were for total relation. He would say
'I've worked all week; I'm having a relax !'

My inspiration came from other directions. Uncle Joe started me off collecting and Brian Foster got me interested in the outdoors. My uncle Frank took me fishing and to interesting places. Dad was the first in the street to buy a television, and a tape recorder to send messages to America. Where we lived in Field Road it was partly surrounded by big posh houses, but people didn't seem to be envious. It was only much later in life that the penny dropped, we had nothing but it really did not seem to matter at the time. I lost my father before I even knew him, I was just too busy in the swinging sixties and he was the man behind the paper. My mother would say,
'Alf, you're always reading the paper. Why don't you do so and so' the rely;
'The paper won't read itself'.

My father died in April 1969 so he never shared in my success.

This is the very last photo of my father taken six months before he died. Here he is at a wedding with my mother, and one of the guests.

94

Chapter 1 - Wedding Theresa Lilliott to Robert Yoxall

Tessa   Robert   Dorothy   Alfred

Robert C. Yoxall married Theresa Lilliott in the summer of 1936. The photograph shows the bride and groom with my father as best man and mother as bridesmaid. The couple lived in Manor Road for a number of years. My mother was to lose her best friend in February 1988, when she passed away. The small photograph was taken in Liscard House, Mill Lane in the 70s and shows Tessa, my Mom and Mercie.

95

Chapter 2 - Peter Hammond 1838 - 1896

The Hammond Branch of the Family.
Peter Hammond was born in 1838 in Ludlow, Shropshire. In 1841 he was living with his mother Margaret in The *Fox Inn* at Upper Gaolford, St Lawrence, Ludlow. Esther Davies who was a widow is shown on the census as the innkeeper and Margaret's mother. In 1851 they are both still living in *The Fox Inn*, and Peter Hammond, grandson 13 years is shown as a scholar. Margaret does not appear on the 1861 census.

By 1861 Peter had moved away and was living and working in Kew. It was during this period that the gardens at Kew were extensively restructured. With the arrival of the railway, Kew's role as a public attraction grew. Many hundreds of gardeners including Peter were gamefully employed in the Royal Botanic Gardens. It was in Kew where he met and married Emily. Shortly after their marriage they moved to Bishop's Castle a market town located eight-and-a- half miles from Shrewsbury. They are shown on the 1871 census living at 94 Union Street, Bishop's Castle. Peter Hammond Head aged 33, nurseryman. Emily wife aged 36, Julia daughter aged 3, Jessie daughter aged 2 and Sarah aged 6 months. Also living in the same house Julia Bond sister-in-law, and Harriet Jukes servant. Peter's other two children George William Hammond aged 7 and Emily Mary Ann Hammonds aged 4 are shown living with their grandparents George and Mary Ann Bond at Walcot Garden House, North Lydbury, Shropshire.

Slater's 1880 Directory shows Peter's occupation as a nurseryman living at Prospect Place in Bishop's Castle. In 1881, the family were living at 2 Blundells Hall Cottage, Bishop's Castle. The building was Elizabethan and had been converted into three cottages. There were 4 daughters recorded on the census Emily14, Julia13, Sarah 11 and Lucy aged 6.

The 1891 census shows only Lucy living at home, and she is shown working as a servant.

In 1901 Emily aged 64 is recorded as a widow living at 1 Apsbey Avenue off Rake Lane, Liscard with daughters Julia 29 and Lucy 26 all working from home; occupation laundress. Emily the other daughter was working as a domestic servant but living in at 87 Osbourne Road in Liscard. She is shown on the census as being single and 34 years old.

Generally, laundresses were seen as unskilled, poorly paid and at the mercy of seasonal fluctuations in demand. In the morning they would collect laundry from local houses and churches to wash at home. One big

Chapter 2 - Julia M. Hammond 1869 - 1947

problem, was getting paid by their customers. The greatest asset was the labour of Emily's children, women who took in lodgers could also provide a laundry service.

The early twentieth century Liberal MP John Burns, whose own mother was a washerwoman and his sisters, ironers, acknowledged that laundry work was back-breaking work, but that without it many women would have had to taste the 'crumb of charity'. The heat of washing and ironing created a breeding den of germs, and most succumbed to sicknesses such as bronchitis and tuberculosis. Women who could not rent or buy a mangle would take their washed clothes to the mangle owner to have them wrung. Eventually they bought their own mangle and this became the only family heirloom. I remember it was still around in my teens. The Wood's Directory of 1904/5 shows no Hammonds living in Apsley Avenue. In the 1911 census we have five people living at 33 Field Road. Julia Margaret Hammond the head of the family shown as single and 42 years old, born in 1869 occupation laundress. Lucy Elizabeth Hammond her sister and single 35 years old born in 1876 occupation daily domestic help. Living with them was Sidney George Hammond nephew, age 9 born in 1902 in Liscard. Sidney was the son of Emily, who died at child birth. (On the death certificate it records: Emily Mary Ann Hammond. Died on the 2nd April 1902, at 3 Apsley Avenue, Liscard).

Julia Margaret Hammond my grandmother on my mothers side

Also living in Field Road my Mother Dorothy Gladys Hammond, daughter age 1 born on 21st May 1909.

Also in the same small terraced house a lodger Rose McDemott, age 27 born in Orkney Isles also a daily domestic help.

Times were very hard, and to make ends meet Julia took in washing; she also cleaned the *Sandridge* pub, which in the days of spittoons and saw dust floors was no easy task. Whenever possible they took in lodgers from Liverpool. Sidney would take the pram down to the pier in New Brighton to collect their luggage, then the big push up the hill to home.

Then it was over the road to Kennas, the Funeral Directors the stables were opposite our house in Field Road. In those days the hearse was drawn by black horses with black feather plumes; the cortege consisted of horse drawn carriages, the men with long coats, and black top hats and

Chapter 2 - Julia M. Hammond 1869 - 1947

each with a black crepe sash across their chest. The women all in black from head to toe and black veils covering their faces. It was Sidney's job to brush and comb the horses to make them immaculate for their next melancholy task. With so much pressure on him as a young boy to try and support the family, it was no wonder that he developed a serious stutter. It was within this poor spinster family that my mother grew up; most things were pawned and money was borrowed from day to day to try and make ends meet. My mother's first love was a young man of the same age, whom she met when she was 16 years old. We can never be certain of his name but from certain clues, to be revealed later, we think his name was Joseph Brammall. The scandal in those days of having two children out of wedlock was truly horrendous. The first birth at home was Joyce, born on the 29th October 1927. Then my mother gave birth to Grace (Eve) on the 24th March 1929. At the time the family were destitute and unable to afford a midwife, so Eve was born in the infirmary at Tranmere. It was in February 1913 when the Tranmere Workhouse was separated from the infirmary. When the authorities discovered the plight of my mother, pressure was applied to have Eve adopted; infact according to Sid's account of events, he had difficulty in getting my mother released from the hospital. Eve's birth certificate records her birth place as 56 Church Road, Tranmere, the location of the Birkenhead Workhouse.

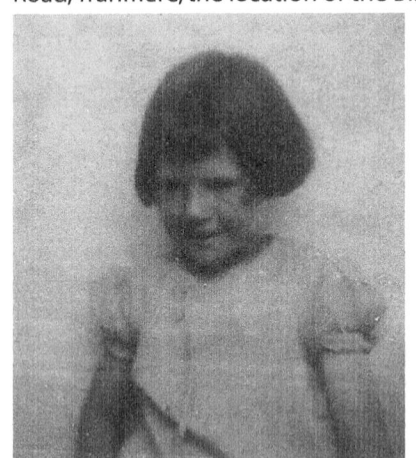

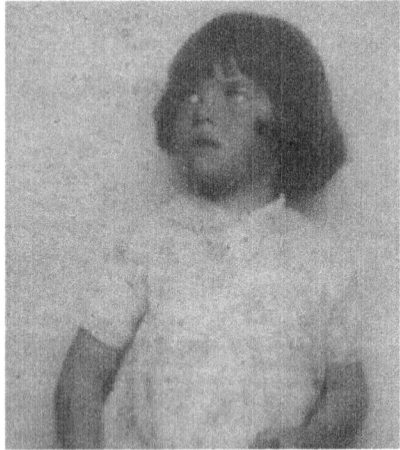

On the left Joyce born 29 October 1927.
On the right Grace (Eve) born 24 March 1929

Unmarried pregnant women were often disowned by their families or their families were just too poor to support them and the workhouse was the only place they could go during and after the birth of their child. From 1904 onwards, the place of birth for those born in the workhouse was just given as 56 Church Road, Tranmere in order to help protect them from disadvantages in later life. The workhouse later became Birkenhead

Chapter 2 - Dorothy G. Hammond 1909 - 1999

Municipal Hospital then, in recent times, was known as St Catherine's Community Hospital. The main building was demolished in 2010. The National Health Service Act came into force on 5th July 1948. Institutions now came under the control of Regional Hospital Boards but many still carried the stigma from their workhouse days. It was Sidney who managed to persuade them to allow her out. Various documents were signed and certain undertakings had to be given, including that the children would be put up for adoption. Because the family were in no position to feed and support both girls, adoption was the only option. My mother resolutely refused to force her lover to take any real responsibility for the children. True love is an amazing thing, with all logic going out of the window. For a time they lived together as man and wife, without the permission of his parents. By all accounts he had a job of responsibility, and when the family found out that they wanted to marry, they were completely against it. The fact that the occupants of Field Road consisted of spinsters whom they considered as undesirable future in-laws, continuous pressure was applied for him to finish the relationship. This was not the place for their upwardly mobile son; eventually, they had their way, but only after he had fathered two baby girls.

George William Hammond.

If you were under the age of 21 you had to have your parent's permission to marry. I think my mother always thought that they could get together again and marry and live happily ever after. For a while after the birth of Eve they continued to see each other. But eventually his parents had their way and the relationship ended. From all accounts they were madly in love. Eve was put up for adoption on the 1st April 1931.

This broke my mother's heart and all the arrangements had to be organised by Julia. The events had played on Julia's mind; she was my mother's legal guardian. It was Julia shouting out in her sleep that Joyce became aware of having a little sister. The adoption weighed heavily on all the family, with Julia having nightmares, and the haunting belief that she was to blame. Sidney had been the main breadwinner in the family. It

Chapter 2 - Dorothy G. Hammond 1909 - 1999

It is very easy to be judgemental but these events were common in those days. Today with social security benefits and a more liberal attitude to promiscuity, no one would bat an eyelid.
Sidney married Margaret Mc Donald on Valentine's Day 1925.
They went on to have three children Margorie, Derek, and Ronald. The property must have been crowed, with even the front room being used as a bedroom, infact Margorie was born in the room.
A few years later they were able to leave Field Road for a council house in Goredale Road.
IMy mother was a live wire and loved to dance; the Tower ballroom was a magnet to her. Her best friend was Vera, who by all accounts was a little on the wild side. Vera was married but was trying to get a divorce. Her husband a Roman catholic refused. He would not even allow her to visit her daughter. Uncle George would visit Field Road regularly and help the family when he could; he seemed to be the only one with any money. Some years later he asked my mother if she would be his housekeeper, and help him in his old age. It was eventually agreed that my mother would work part-time, and he promised he would leave the house in Magazine Lane to her. I remember as a child going with my mother to clean the house and do the washing and shopping this went on for years. Eventually the inevitable happened and Uncle George passed away.
"You're a bloody fool, Dot, you've been taken for a ride" were the words shouted angrily by my father.
"I told you it was a waste of time. Did he ever show you his will?" For weeks on end the arguing went on.
"He had a daughter she'll get the house, not you. How could you be so stupid".
My poor mother had been taken in, the daughter got the house and all we ended up with was a bag of washing.
Uncle George did help finance the purchase of a grave in Rake Lane Cemetery. George William Hammond and Lucy Elizabeth Hammond have a right of burial in section 13 plot No 222. The document was dated 1st October 1903. The plot had been purchased for the burial of Lucy's mother Emily Mary Ann Hammond who was interred on the 16th Sept. 1903. The document records George and Lucy living at 24 Merton Road.

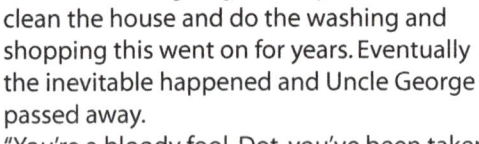

Chapter 2 - George W. Hammond 1864 - 1950

George W. Hammond, elbow on side of charabanc, off to a day at the races.

On the 1891 census the couple are living in Wistanstow in Shropshire. Her name recorded on the census Mary

From the 1901 census details for: 394, Dickenson Road, South Manchester.
```
Name                           Sex Age  Birth Year  Occupation
Hammond, George. W  Head  Married  M   37   1864        Gardener
Hammond, Marie. E          Wife   Married  F   38   1863
Hammond, Julia.E.M        Daughter         F   10   1891
Hammond, Jessie.G         Daughter         F    8   1893
```
Both children were born in Wistanstow.
After the family moved to Wallasey, they seem to vanish from the records I have been unable to locate them on the 1911 census.

Longsight, Dickinson Road

Chapter 2 - Sidney G. Hammond 1902 - 1988

The War Years
On the 12th March 1941 in trying to bomb the docks the Luftwaffe missed their target and bombed large parts of Wallasey including Sid's house. The attack on the Borough covered three nights, the heaviest part of the attack started at Wallasey Village and stretched down to the docks; decoy fires had been lit on the Golf Links at Bidston Moss, to try and confuse the enemy, but this only resulted in bombs being dropped on populated areas .
A rescue party, working in Lancaster Avenue, heard the faint cry of a child. Frantically they worked to unearth the child and this was some three days after the raid. The baby had been protected by the bodies of its parents both killed in the blitz. The baby was taken to Victoria Central Hospital and recovered from its ordeal. They were forced out of their home and went to live in a temporary asbestos bungalow in Arrowe Avenue in Moreton - if the Germans didn't get you with bombs then asbestosis would finish you off. Ronald and Derek were evacuated they went to live on a farm in Wales where they had a torrid time not allowed to attend school but had to work long hours on the farm. Sidney in his 40s received his call-up papers. Originally only 18 to 41- year-olds were called up but as things got more desperate by 1942, the top age limit was increased to 51.

Goredale Road after the Luftwaffe had destroyed Sids house.

During the war Marjorie joined the Land Army driving a horse and cart around the farm, getting in the harvest, which was a massive physical effort. She was knocked unconscious while helping a cow to deliver its calf. She swears now in old age that most of her aches and pains were caused by these exertions. Marjorie went on to marry James Newton in 1944 and have two children David and Gillian. A little later Joyce got married at the tender age of 19, using the same wedding dress. Jimmy was the best man and Betty Rice from next-door, the bridesmaid.
Derek can remember it well. "It was during the rationing and food was scarce. At the wedding reception the main meal was a large mixed salad with spam."
The Hammond side of the family were sworn to secrecy concerning my mother's offspring, and it all worked for a while until the skeletons fell out of the cupboard.
Joyce had a good idea that she had a younger sister, and managed to lever the truth out of my mother, during her visit to America in 1965, but she too was sworn to secrecy, so I carried on oblivious to the fact that I

Chapter 2 - Sidney G. Hammond 1909 - 1988

had a sister Eve. It was not until years later that Denice (Joyce's daughter) told me the truth.

Derek had a daughter Janet and a son Michael. Later after the war Sidney and Margaret managed to move into a more normal house built by the Corporation in Woodstock Road.

Marjorie remarried and has now become a Hurst. Derek while on National Service in 1954 met a beautiful young lady called Suzy, so at the tender age of 16 years she married our gallant soldier.

The photograph shows the best man a sergeant who also had a German bride together with Suzy's mother. After the war Derek spent many happy years working in Germany.

left to right Marjorie Hurst, my mother Dorothy, Roy Dutton, Jennifer and Richard Dutton my children. Celebrating my mom's 86th birthday.

A Mysterious Relative.
I have been asked by various members of our family to try and find out the identity of my mother's lover, the father of Joyce and Eve. The only clues available:
1. My mother always referred to him as Joe.
2. Eve had spotted the name Bramall on some documents early on in her life.
3. He lived somewhere in Birkenhead, possibly near Corporation Road.
4. Had some German connection.
5. That he died sometime in the 1980s
6. He was the same age as my mother.
7. He was possibly a policeman or a railway worker.

We can never be 100% sure but a likely candidate that satisfies all of the above conditions is a Joseph Garside Brammall who was born on Christmas Day 1908, at 97 Cleveland Street. His father's name was Lawrence Brammall, occupation licensed victualler, and his mother's name was Lena, formally Hertwick, born in Germany. This information was taken from his birth certificate BXCF 306863. Just to confuse matters a different surname is recorded on the 1911 census. A Joseph Bramwall aged 3 living at 97 Cleveland Street with his parents and two older bothers and a sister. Cleveland Street is a short distance from Corporation Road in Birkenhead. In Gore's 1912 Directory , Lawrence Brammall is recorded as being the proprietor of the Wirral Hotel at 97 Cleveland Street. It is possible that the numbers in the road have changed because this property is now a small terraced house.
From the *London Gazette* dated 22nd August 1941.
Joseph Garside Brammall, London and Midland and Scottish Railway. When incendiary bombs fell on a siding, Brammall, who was aware that ammunition trucks were stabled there, at once made his way to the spot and found a sheeted wagon of ammunition on fire. He removed an incendiary bomb from the top and then uncoupled and levered the wagon away. He helped to isolate other burning wagons and remained on duty in the siding until all the fires were extinguished. Brammall showed courage and devotion to duty in very dangerous circumstances. He was awarded the British Empire Medal.
Kelly's Directory dated 1946 records Lawrence Brammall, butcher, living at 228 Cleveland Street. In Kelly's 1952 Directory he is recorded living at 3 Downham Road, Higher Tranmere. Returning to Joseph, he married Annie Brand in 1930 and died in April 1985. I can only conclude that if the original clues are correct, then Mr Joseph Garside Brammall was my mother's lover and the father of both girls.
I have my mother's photograph opposite looking at this very page and the question I must ask, "Was this him?"

Family photographs

16 April 1946. Joyce & friend. Before travelling out to the U.S. Outside 33 Field Road.

My mom in 1932

Sidney my uncle, mother and me.

Marjorie with her mom Margaret and yours truly.

Chapter 2 - Joyce's Story 1927 - 1974

Left to right: Derek Hammond, Betty Rice, Margery Rice, Keith, Joyce, Ted Dutton, Gladys Dutton (Ted's wife) Alfred and Dorothy Dutton, with Tommy Dutton looking over my dad's soulder.

The wedding of Joyce Hammond to Keith Menefee on the 25th December 1945. Held at Emmanuel Church in Seabank Road. From left to right: Betty Rice bridesmaid, Marjorie and James Newton best man, Keith, Joyce, Alfred and Dorothy Dutton, Sidney Hammond my Mom's half brother.

Chapter 2 - Joyce's Story 1927 - 1974

On the outbreak of the Second World War in September 1939, a plan by the British Government for evacuating children was put into place called Operation Pied Piper because of the fear that the German Air Force would bomb our cities and factories. The evacuation meant children swapped one life for a completely new life in the country.

Both Joyce and Eve where evacuated. Joyce travelled out to Farndon outside Chester and Eve to Ormskirk outside Liverpool. Children were told to bring their belongings to their departure point in a pillowcase - many came from poor families so had very little. Each child was sent with a brown paper bag containing things like corned beef, evaporated milk, biscuits, fruit, their gas masks and a label showing their party number, name, home address and school. Schoolchildren were usually evacuated with their school. Joyce attended Vaughan Road School, in New Brighton. Eve was only 10 and Joyce 12 years old. Here are their stories:

Joyce arrived at Broxton Railway Station with other children from her school accompanied by their teacher. The group was transported to Farndon Memorial Hall. The bewildered children, all plainly labelled, were distributed among anxious foster parents. Finally after an hour the hall was deserted and the settling-in period began. Joyce was taken by Mr and Mrs Payton. He was the head gardener of Sibbersfield Hall. But although the name is ancient, the present Sibbersfield Hall was only built in 1875 for the Parker family of Farndon and in the early 1900s it was occupied by the Holts of shipping fame.

Understandably my mother did not want to let Joyce go, but decided it was for the best. Life was difficult for all concerned; my mother had to deal with bombings, rationing, and trying to support her aging mother. It was also a requirement to pay what she could towards Joyce's upkeep. Parents could visit their children but were encouraged not to go too often as this could upset and unsettle them.

With the influx of additional children, Farndon Village School became overcrowded and education had to organised around a shift pattern, with lessons interrupted by air raid drills as the children practised assembling in their air raid shelters. When the alert sounded it was on with their gas masks, and then an orderly walk to the shelter. Happily the threatened bombing never materialized. Joyce was to lean many new skills in her new home, from being a townie she was now expected to help grow food for the war effort. Every available space was turned over to grow vegetables which had to be tended. Lots of chickens and a couple of pigs were also resident on their smallholding. The family living in the big house on the estate had to change their ways with the land being turned over for more productive endeavours, the horses taking on a lesser roll. The 30 acres surrounding the Hall have produced some well-known racehorses, the most famous being 'Our Mary Ann' which won the Chester Cup in 1870. To commemorate the event a gilded model of the horse was

Chapter 2 - Joyce's Story 1927 - 1974

mounted on top of the clock tower. Life was to change dramatically for all concerned. Householders who billeted (housed) city children were given money by the government. They got 10s. 6d. a week (53p) for the first child they housed and 8s. 6d. (43p) for any other evacuees they billeted.

The village was a hive of activity with some army huts, once used by strawberry pickers, being converted into a hostel for the Women's Land Army, and occupied by these girls working on farms in the surrounding district. Their choices were limited; it was either munitions work or join the ATS or the Land Army.

Early photograph of the Sandrock Hotel

Joyce was able to return home before the war ended, because the threat from bombing decreased. So in early 1944 Joyce returned to Field Road. She was able to get a job in C&A in Liverpool. But with very limited supplies and strict rationing, the store had very little to sell. The government rather rashly announced the end of official evacuation on 7th September 1944, the day before the first V.2 rocket fell on London. It was now that her world was to change yet again. In early 1944 after America had entered the war, large convoys of liberty boats sailed from New York to Liverpool to deliver troops and materials. Private Keith Meneffee managed to dodge the Nazi menace and arrive safely on our shores. As fate would dictate his army unit was billeted a short distance from Field Road were my sister lived. Private First Class RA- 37452939 Lawrence (Keith) Menefee's unit were responsible for the trucks and transports that now occupied New Brighton Tower Car Park and Football pitch. The unit called the Wallasey Camp Depot 0616 was under the command of Col. Earl Zwingle. The Sandrock Hotel on Rowson Street/Molyneux Drive was the US Kitchen. With troops billeted in the hotel and the Sandringham Road area. The 347th officially moved into Wallasey in December 1943. The Palace was used to assemble and

War Brides on their way to New York

108

Chapter 2 - Joyce's Story 1927 - 1974

VE-DAY—IT'S ALL OVER

waterproof the machines for the D Day landings; the equipment arrived in kits from the U.S. On the 28th of January orders were received assigning the 347th to the First Army but with instructions to remain at New Brighton. Keith was later to join the 82nd Airbourne. The equipment had to be ready and maintained in preparation for the D-Day invasion. The Sandrock hotel was a very popular dance venue which held regular weekend dances. It was here that Joyce was to meet her future husband. Joyce would dance away the hours with her best friend. "We thought they were lovely. But we found the Americans couldn't dance. They just shuffled," remarked Betty Rice. Joyce's friend.

After several months of dating, Joyce and Keith's relationship became serious. The courtship was not without challenges. Preparations involved interviews with military personnel, medical and psychological examinations, and plenty of paperwork. Joyce received a letter requesting that she present herself at the American Embassy in London to be interviewed and receive the necessary documents.

Emmanuel Church

Keith's parents had to send a statement of their finances, whether they owned their home, and that they were willing to sponsor and guarantee to look after Joyce and support her, as long as necessary, as their own daughter. A smallpox vaccination was required and a couple more medical examinations. Eventually all of the obstacles were overcome and the marriage date was fixed. Cars were used for emergencies only and a wedding car was just too difficult to obtain so all of the venues had been selected because they were in walking distance. Someone Joyce knew managed to get a film for his camera to record the big event.

4602 St Paul Ave. Lincoln, Nebraska
Keith's parent's house.

Everything was strictly rationed but

109

Chapter 2 - Joyce's Story 1927 - 1974

friends came to the rescue with precious rations of ingredients to make a wedding cake and this was put on display. The family saved up their food coupons to buy extra food and a contact in the black market arranged the supply of some alcoholic drink. An uncle with some contacts managed to get his hands on a few tins of spam. No questions asked; it was beginning to look as if a wedding feast was imminent. Derek recalls that the banquet was held at the Sandrock Hotel, and consisted mostly of salad. Keith and Joyce were married at the Emmanual Church on 29th December 1945. The Second World War in Europe was now truly behind them and they could look forward to a life of peace and prosperity away from bankrupt Britain and rationing.

Keith returned to the US in September 1946. Joyce, meanwhile, remained in England waiting for an assignment to a transport ship. The letter arrived with only days to spare before her departure date. Before Joyce left England she wrote out her favourite English recipes for roasts and stuffing, puddings, cakes, biscuits, and scones. Her mother insisted on her taking family photographs, so with a few pounds she had saved up and the few clothes she had managed to acquire during the austere years, she filled her suitcase for the adventure of a lifetime. Her name was painted on the outside of the suitcase in large letters, as per instructions.

It was a typical cold miserable day when she crossed the Mersey for the last time, arriving at Lime Street Station in time to catch her train to Southampton. It was with tears in their eyes that the little party of well wishers waved goodbye wondering if they ever see her again? As the train disappeared into the distance my mother was consoled by her friend Ann Davis.

Joyce had to report to the orientation meeting in Southampton. Then she boarded the *General George W. Goethals*, a US Army Transport, and sailed for New York.

Joyce shared the eight-day journey with other war brides and their children. Seasick and weary, the women gratefully disembarked in New York, only to be delayed by protestors angry that American soldiers had married foreign women. Luckily the military had organised accommodation and buses to take the brides to the train station.

First came romance. Then came marriage. Then came life in a strange and faraway land. Most GI brides wouldn't have traded it for the world. All the passengers lined the rails to see the Statue of Liberty at 5 am. It was alight and such a wonderful sight to see in the early hours after so many years of blackout.

Joyce with her Grandmother

Chapter 2 - Joyce's Story 1927 - 1974

People's thoughts were mixed; happiness and sadness combined with anticipation at a new life ahead of them. Many a tear was shed; no one knew when they would see England or their families again.

It was almost 20 years before my mother was to see her daughter again. The long journey to America began with a train journey from Liverpool to London where there was an eleven-hour wait before boarding the BOAC 707 for New York. Arriving there on 2nd June 1965, with another journey just as long from New York to Lincoln in Nebraska.

My mother had saved for years to make the trip and when her employer Mrs Leary-Shaw found out, she agreed to help, and apart from allowing my mom to be off work for three months, she helped with the fare. She had a fantastic time and met all the family and even met some Hollywood stars including Mickey Rooney. It was with a tear in her eye that she had to return home on the 4th September 1965.

Chapter 2 - Joyce's Story 1927 - 1974

The next time my mother visited Joyce was during much sadder times, arriving in Nebraska in July 1974. A letter my mother received from Joyce was dated the 11th December 1973, shortly after she had surgery. She was very positive about her operation and was looking forward to getting back to normal. Unfortunatly this was not to be the case the cancer had spread.
I quote extracts from a letter sent by Keith on the 14th September 1974.
"We have Joyce home now and she is doing better... I have a nurse 5 days a week so that helps a lot. Loise came up from Oklahoma; she is a nurse so she has helped out a lot...Barry came home to visit Joyce...the girls are back in school now and they are doing very well.....Ray and Collette send their love and Denice and Bruce and the little ones."
"Mother Joyce has not much pain but her time to be with us is very short and every day is a very very happy day.....we talk a lot and laugh and cry together, our lives have been so dear and loving and always will be.
Dear Mother I have a hard time expressing myself but my feeling for Joyce are so deep it is hard for me to put into words....."
Joyce was to pass away on the 7th October 1974.

Chapter 2 - Joyce's Story 1927 - 1974

The Wallasey News
AND WIRRAL GENERAL ADVERTISER.
Vol. XLII No. 2948   SATURDAY, OCTOBER 10, 1942.   Two Pence.

AMERICAN TROOPS AT EGREMONT.
Great Crowds Give Welcome In Church And Streets.

About three thousand people attended at Egremont Presbyterian Church on Sunday afternoon for the Anglo-American Friendship Service, a number probably unique in the history of Wallasey, and a striking evidence of the goodwill of local residents towards those who come from the other side of the Atlantic to join in the struggle for freedom.

Arrival of the Americans in Wallasey on the 10th October 1942

About three thousand people attended at the Egremont Presbyterian Church on Sunday afternoon for the Anglo-American Friendship Service ....striking evidence of the goodwill of local residents towards those who come from the other side of the Atlantic to join the struggle for freedom. Every available seat was filled, with an overflow service in the Church Hall. The American Chaplin Rev. Frank O. Taafel (Major of the American Chaplin's Corps) gave his address to the hall as well as in the church.

Following the singing, the Mayor (Ald. P.G.Davies) welcomed our friends from across the water "You have come here" said the Mayor "to fight with us against that which I suppose is the strongest military power the world has ever known, and probably the most ruthless and cruel enemy that we can imagine".

Chapter 2 - Joyce's Story 1927 - 1974

BRIDE ARRIVES FROM ENGLAND

MRS. KEITH MENEFEE

Arriving a week or two ago from Cheshire, England, was Mrs. Keith Menefee who came to join her husband, Pvt. Keith Menefee, at the home of his parents, Mr. and Mrs. S. N. Menefee.

Pvt. Menefee, who returned to the States two months ago, and who now is stationed at Lowry field, Denver, Colo., received a thirty days furlough which enabled him to be in Lincoln to welcome his wife, who came in time to celebrate their first wedding anniversary which is on December 29. The wedding took place in England in 194

Keith & Joyce at a card party March 1957

114

Chapter 2 - Joyce's Story 1927 - 1974

Lawrence (Keith) Menefee was born on the 12th November 1921.
His father was Shirley Norton Menefee, and he married Juna Clare Kirkland. They had 4 children, Alan Menefee, Lauence (Keith) Menefee, Harlen Wayne Menefee and Beverly Jean Menefee.
Keith married my sister Joyce Maureen Hammond on the Christmas Day 1945.
They had 6 children:
Barry R. Menefee, – one daughter and 2 grandchildren
Denice Maureen (Menefee)Zenger (Deceased) – two children and four grandchildren
Raymond Anthony Menefee - one son and two grandchildren
Laurie Kathlene Menefee – two children and two grandchildren
Jennifer Joyce (Menefee) Sacca– three children and three grandchildren
Gillian Michelle (Menefee) Roach(Deceased) - four children and three grandchildren
Barry is married to Jackie and they have one daughter Chelsea who is married and has two children. Barry is a successful racehorse owner and trainer.
Denice married Gary Zenger this was her second marriage. She had two children from her first marriage to Bruce, Jeffery and Michelle. Gary and Denice were involved in a fatal accident on the 20th May 2012.
Raymond married Melissa the couple had one child Tony but later divorced. Following a severe disability Ray is being looked after in a living care facility. Tony is also divorced and has two boys, Nicholas and Luke. Ray was a boxer, gym owner and a successful fight promoter.
Laurie lives in Denver Colorado, along with her son Eric and his wife Kendra, they had two sons, Ronen and Samson. Samson was 3 months old and passed away last year due to down's syndrome complications. Their daughter Leyla was killed last year by a drunk driver. She was 34 years old and leaves behind a 17-year-old son, Shane Ray Menefee. He currently resides with his dad.
Jennifer married Bradley Lynn Sacca in March 1978 in Manitou Springs. Brad was in the Army for 22 years which took the family all over the world and back. The couple went on to have three children Joshua Owen Sacca born 27/11/78. Dominic Isaiah Sacca born 07/11/06; and a daughter Lindsey Marie Sacca Martinez born in Lincoln Nebraska 13/4/1981.
Their youngest son Justin Bradley Sacca was born in Frankfurt, Germany On the 27/12/1982 he was killed in a car accident at the age of 23 27th November 2006 on his way to work (Josh's birthday also) He left behind 1 daughter, Breanna Michelle Gamboa- Sacca, she was born 11/05/2002.
Gillian Joyce's youngest daughter married Damon Roach, and went to live in Plainview, Nebraska. Tragedy was to hit the family when in May 1994 Gillian had just dropped off the children with a baby sitter, when she was involved in a fatal road accident.

Chapter 2 - Joyce's Story 1927 - 1974

The male side of the family have been dominated by sports, with Barry racing horses and both Ray and Tony, boxing in title fights. Raymond Menefee was a former WAA Lightweight Champion. Last year the Amateur Boxing Association for Golden Gloves in Lincoln, Nebraska honoured Keith, Ray, Barry and Tony, for all of their accomplishments in boxing. Ray was big in sponsoring young kids in boxing at the towns youth centres. Tony has his own gym now.

Keith was to enjoy a prosperous and awarding life and passed away at the age of 83 on the 8th August 2005, to be reunited with his dear wife.

Laurie   Jennifer   Gillian
Photograph taken in August 1965

Mrs Menefee   Denice   My Mom

Barry & Harlan, Raymond is walking away in the background. photograph taken in Colorado

116

Chapter 2 - Joyce's Story 1927 - 1974

Midlands News

Plainview, Neb - Damon Roach has learned how to laugh. It helps him through the hard times, he said, now that he's left alone with four young children to raise. "I never thought I'd be sitting here -a widower with four children to raise myself." he said. "It's tough, "The hard times came last May, when Roach's wife, Jill, was killed in a two-vehicle accident near Foster, Nebraska, just after she'd left the children with a babysitter. After six months, Roach, said, he still hasn't gotten over his wife's death. The children keep him going, he said.
"It's there," he said, "It's always close at hand. I don't know how long grief lasts. I've wrapped my life around the children. The're my security blanket." Roach said Gabriel 6, twins Adam and Elliot 4, and Shelby 3 have come to understand, in their own way, their mother's death. They know she's in heaven," Roach said.
A neighbour, Shirley Bemecker, said that shortly after the accident she overhead Gabriel talking about his mother's death.
Gabriel said, "She's not coming back. She's always going to be happy and she's never going to be sad", Mrs Bernecker said. "I thought that was a neat way for Damon to tell them. It made tears come to my eyes."
Roach, 33 said he never considered having someone else raise his children. But, he said, he soon learned how difficult it is for a single parent with young children. A babysitter watches the children during the day while Roach works for Burlington Northern Railroad, He cares for them at night and on weekends. Two months after his wife's death, Roach said, he became depressed. "I was really wondering if I was going to have the strength to get through," he said. Lately, Roach said his emotional strengh has returned, along with a positive outlook.
"That's when you get your life back together", he said. Roach said he plans for now to remain in this Northwest Nebraska town where he grew up. I'm real comfortable here," he said.
His home needs some attention Roach said. Before the accident, he always tried to fix one thing every night after work. "I've got four months of one thing a night to do," he said. "My goal was Christmas; now, I'll settle for May." Roach said he appreciates his neighbour's patience while he gets his life back together. He said he knows he hasn't been the perfect neighbour. Roach said he's looking forward to summer, when he can spend more time with his children. He said he enjoys taking them to a lake near Tilden, Neb. "We're going to be OK."

Chapter 2 - Joyce's Story 1927 - 1974

Gary & Denice

19th May 2013 Two people were killed in a multiple-vehicle accident today in West Springfield, police on the scene said.
Police Sgt. Tom Luellen; said a white van and a dark SUV were both northbound on the West Bypass just south of Grand Street when the two vehicles collided at about 1:14 p.m. The SUV was forced into the southbound lanes of the West Bypass, where it hit a pickup and three motorcycles. Police have released the names of two people killed in a west Springfield accident Saturday afternoon.
Gary Zenger, 56, and Denice Zenger, 62, were killed when their Harley-Davidson motorcycle, driven by Gary, was struck head-on by an SUV at about 1:14 p.m., according to a news release from police.

MEMORIAL RIDE

In Honor Of Gary and Denice Zenger
Plus All Others Involved
In The Accident On West By Pass And Grand
May 19th 2012

When:

June 9th 2012

Where:

Remington's Parking Lot
1655 West Republic Road Springfield,
MO 65807
Meeting at 1:00PM
Starting Ride at 2:00PM
ALL BIKES WELCOME
Any Questions Call: (417) 522-3830 or
Contact Us On Our Facebook Event Page:
Gary and Denice Zenger Memorial Ride

Chapter 2 - Eve's Story

Eve's Story

Evelyn aged ten in 1939 recalls a charmed world that was suddenly to change for ever. This is her story.

At that time, I lived in the Fire Salvage Station on Derby Road, Bootle with my parents. My father was a fire officer and our home was one of the apartments in the building. There were about half a dozen other firemen and their families living there too. The Liverpool Docks were within walking distance and very vulnerable to attack in wartime.

Looking back, life was quite idyllic, inasmuch as I was part of a circle of childhood friends living in our own little world. We all played together in one of the big yards at the back of the station, not getting in the way of the hard-working men who were very tolerant of us children. Yes, it was a special kind of existence living with the day-to-day running of the Fire Station. The sounds of the fire alarm, the clanging of the engine bell, the hosing down of the appliances, the polishing of all the brasses, and keeping the yards spick and span were all part of the firemen's daily routine. They even arranged Christmas parties for us all with a big tree and presents. That took place in the 'Engine Room' minus the fire engine, which would be moved out, of course.

Left to right: Evelyn Davies with Audrey Jump and Pamela Fletcher in the Fire Station yard. The families lived in flats around the yard.

It was the wireless that gave us news of war breaking out and the atmosphere was sombre in my home. Although I was an only child I don't remember feeling too frightened at the prospect of having to be evacuated, even though I had never been away from home. I was glad that some of my friends would be coming with me to wherever that would be, which turned out to be Ormskirk, and I didn't even know where it was!

The journey, by train from Sandhills Station, did not take long and we alighted at Ormskirk railway station. We were then formed into a 'crocodile' and walked in twos down Derby Street. I remember some of us commenting on the little terraced houses and comparing them to the bigger 'posh' houses. Some of us said we hoped we did not go to this or that house feeling a bit particular, I suppose! There would be one or two people, mainly housewives, outside each house, probably weighing us all up, and seeming to make an instant decision on which children to take.

Chapter 2 - Eve's Story

So one or two of us children would vanish from the 'crocodile' as we trudged along Derby Street, carrying bags or haversacks on our backs, and with our gas masks dangling from a cord over our shoulders. We must have all felt nervous as we had no choice who would take us.

My friend, Audrey Jump, and I walked along with the others and we felt delighted when Mr and Mrs Pope, who had a sweet shop in Derby Street, took the two of us. We had stuck together, as friends do, but Audrey's sister, Pat, had to go to another couple round the corner from us. When Audrey's mother found out, of course, she said 'Why didn't you stay with your sister?'

Mr and Mrs Pope, whose son was in the Air Force, also had their daughter-in-law from down south, with her baby, who had come

Evelyn Courtman (right) in her first job, aged fourteen, at Brighton le Sands Post Office, near Waterloo.

to escape the London Blitz. This led to my first lesson in ironing. I was allowed to iron the baby's clothes and to take it for short walks in its pram. So I felt really grown up. Evelyn Davies left school during the war. Her first job was in the Post Office at Brighton-le-Sands, near Waterloo. 'I certainly needed my times tables for that job!' Later, I took a job with the solicitor, Marcus Davies, in Dale Street, Liverpool. Clothes were a problem for all those growing up during the war years and Evelyn was no exception. At that time, clothes and shoes were still scarce and I needed new foot-wear. I had to order the only ones available a pair of clogs, and then waited months for them. The uppers were of navy blue leather with red laces, but I think the soles and heels must have been wood! I wore them to go to work and every step I took resounded loudly as I walked round the office. Marcus Davies would say `I hear Miss Courtman is wearing her clogs today.' So I tried not to wear them too often. Yes, being a teenager in wartime was very different from now.

Evelyn Davies returned to her home at the Fire Station in Bootle from evacuation in Ormskirk when there was a lull in the bombing attacks; she remembers the courage of the adults in the Fire Station community in the presence of the children, and the undaunted spirit of the firemen who fought to save their city from the flames that threatened to engulf it. After some weeks (the raids) started again but much worse than

Chapter 2 - Eve's Story

ever. Luckily we had our own underground air raid shelter at the Fire Station. Quite often it was about 6pm at night when the noise of the siren would start. On hearing it, mothers and children would make their way down the flights of stone steps. It was like an exodus. Each family would be ready with blankets, cushions, a hot drink in a thermos flask, maybe a book or two or some knitting. If the siren went later in the evening, mothers and children would be in their nightwear with a warm coat on top. We could hear the almost monotonous drone of the German planes flying overhead and got used to their particular sound.

John and Henrietta Courtman. Eve's foster parents.

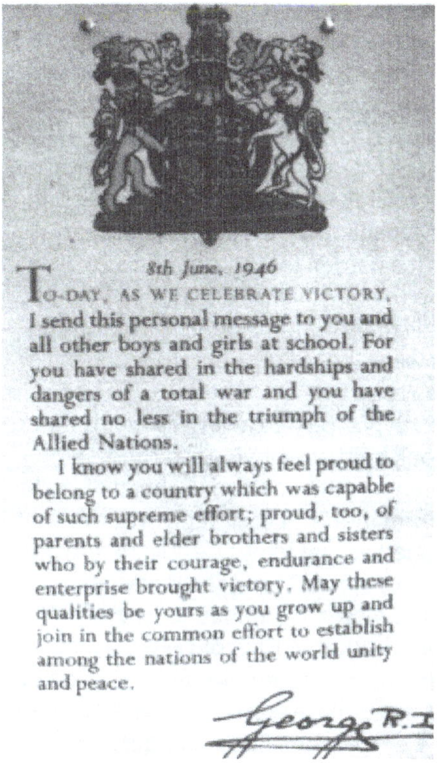

I think people held their breath, praying they would go away. You could also hear and feel the blast of a bomb exploding in the surrounding areas and the dockside. News would filter down to the shelter that fires could be seen glowing in the distance. We knew Liverpool had been hit badly. If our parents were frightened, they managed not to show it for our sakes. The firemen would return from their duties with blackened faces from the smoke and fires they had dealt with, all looking weary but with no time to sleep.

8th June, 1946

To-day, as we celebrate victory, I send this personal message to you and all other boys and girls at school. For you have shared in the hardships and dangers of a total war and you have shared no less in the triumph of the Allied Nations.

I know you will always feel proud to belong to a country which was capable of such supreme effort; proud, too, of parents and elder brothers and sisters who by their courage, endurance and enterprise brought victory. May these qualities be yours as you grow up and join in the common effort to establish among the nations of the world unity and peace.

George R.I

121

Chapter 2 - Eve's Story

Eve went on to marry Robert (Bob) Hulme on the 2nd Jan. 1950, at St Nicholas church. Blundellsands. They went on honeymoon to London. Bob's mother Phoebe, reminded them by sending them a letter! "You are only supposed to be away for four days" and must be back for the weekend; As she helped out an odd day or two. They met when Eve was 18 and Bob was 23 years old. They had three children- Derek, John, and Janet. They worked well together and their greengrocer's business was to flourish but it was continuous hard work, with very little spare time to themselves; even the children had to fit around the business, from early morning market to fetch the fresh products, to deliveries and bookwork into the late evening. Eve thought up the name "Fresh Farm Produce." A professional sign writer was employed to paint the name over the frontage, and it helped create the idea of fresh and healthy food, with the customers thinking that they actually owned a farm. It certainly put a strain on the relationship, but they managed. Eve's biggest regret was having to live over the shop, without a garden for the children to play in; the business and the customers had to come first as it was their living. When time permitted an occasional family outing would be organised; the Van would be cleaned, and out went the sacks of potatoes and in went wooden boxes for the children to sit on.

Marrage of Bob Hume to Evelyn Courtman

It was only after Eve's adopted parents had passed away that her burning desire to find her natural parents took hold. The obvious starting point was a letter to Somerset House in London, the Registrar General of Births, Marriages and Deaths to ask for information, but their reply was not helpful; they said it could not be done. Eve would not be able to find out her original name or the names of her parents. This was a devastating blow, and if anything made Eve all the more determined to find her origins. Many years before, her adoptive mother had told Eve that she came from Birkenhead and had been born in Tranmere. It had only been some two years earlier in 1927 that a national register of adopted children was introduced in England. Bob had encouraged Eve in her quest to find her mother. Eve managed to persuade Vincent a friend to take her over to Birkenhead Town Hall. When she arrived at the enquiry desk, the clerk was busy dealing with other enquires. When it was Eve's turn, she walked up to the desk and lowered her voice to pose the question.

"Excuse me sir," Have I come to the right place to inquire into past adoptions; I wish to locate my birth mother. I think I was born in Birkenhead."

"Yes Madam, but I will need your date of birth and adoptive name, and some proof of your identity." was his official and passive reply.

I suppose working in the births, deaths and marriage registry tends to be a drain on the emotions. Passing a piece of paper and pen across, he said, " Please write down your details".

Eve was caught a little off guard; she fumbled for her spectacles and wrote in block capitals and passed the paper back.

The clerk glanced at the paper and nodded.

"Please take a seat and I will see what I can be done."

He immediately disappeared into the back room.

It was now that the enormity of the situation dawned on her, with butterflies in her stomach; could this be the moment after 42 years that the truth could be revealed. They sat in silence, deep in their respective thoughts. Vincent had slipped off to use the toilet when this elderly chap, sat opposite them with his companion, seemed to be struck by divine intervention. Walking straight up to Eve he enquired.

"Could you please do me a big favour and be a witness to my wedding," without even thinking Eve agreed. He then went outside to ask a young man passing by to be a witness too.

Eve had now been totally distracted, and was now part of a marriage ceremony. In her winter coat and woolly hat and the young man in open-necked shirt and scruffy jacket, they all trooped into the registry office and joined the couple while they got on with their nuptials. The Superintendent Registrar asked for their signatures after the wedding to witness the proceeding. All she needed was a photographer to appear. It had certainly been an informal ceremony. With her mind still in orbit, she returned to the waiting room.

Eventually the clerk appeared with a ledger and beckoned Eve over to his desk. A piece of paper had been inserted in the relevant page.

As he opened the page her heart sank. The clerk pointed to an entry. "This is your adoption record." And then he stopped abruptly.

Eve looked intensely at the neat handwriting taking in every detail. It read Adoption of Grace Hammond and date then mother Dorothy Gladys Hammond then the address 33 Field Road, New Brighton. Her heart started to pound! At long last she had found her mother.

When Grace was adopted her name was changed to Evelyn Courtman. It was there in black and white. My mothers name and where she lived in

Chapter 2 - Eve's Story

1931 when Eve was adopted.
"Can I write down the details please". Of course was the courteous reply. The day had been overwhelming. Eve needed space and time to think, Finding her long lost mother, a wedding, a trip into the unknown.
"Vincent please take me home!"
It was with a sense of satisfaction, and shock, that they returned to the car. On the journey home she went through every possibility in her mind. What if she doesn't want to see me? Could I face the rejection. Will she look like me? What do I say? Will she have a husband and family? Do they know about me. What if she don't live there anymore, and more 'what if's'. Eve had plenty of time to reflect on things before she finally took the plunge to visit 33 Field Road. Vincent was recruited for this delicate task, and using his A to Z he quickly found the road. They decided to park their car by Busby Cottages and walk the length of the road. It all looked a bit bleak and run down. A row of terraced houses met their gaze all with odd numbers, so it had to be on the left-hand side. The numbers started to get higher then the numbers ran out- it was waste ground. The house was missing; no number 33 or 35 for that matter. What was going on? Her mind was racing; could there be another Field Road? No, this has to be the one. Looking around to see if she could find someone to ask, she noticed a shop on the corner. The door to the shop was open and Eve went in.
"Hello, can you tell me what has happened to number 33 Field Road?"
The middle-aged lady looked up from her newspaper.
"It's been demolished. They've knocked them all down on that side of the road."
"Oh, well do you known if a Dorothy lived at number 33? I'm not too sure of her surname.
"That'll be Dot Dutton came the instant reply.
"Yes, that'll be her - Dorothy Dutton".
Eve repeated the name to make sure she heard it correctly.
"She's moved to 71 Liscard House, in Mill Lane. A few others residents have moved there too. Some went to Moreton and others to Seacombe, but Dot chose Liscard."
"Thanks. You've been most helpful".
Eve made a note of the details on a scrap of paper and left, a little confused. "What now," said Vince?
"I'll go home and look in the telephone directory."
The number was ex-directory so no luck on that score.
It was a sunny winter's day when Eve approached Liscard House. The property had been built for the corporation some three years earlier in 1967/8. It was a tall imposing 14-storey block of flats situated in the centre of Liscard, with an adjacent shopping centre and car park in the front. It certainly looked new and modern.
Just as Eve was trying to figure out how the intercom worked, a lady

appeared and held the door open. Eve entered and thanked the lady and the door shut abruptly behind her. In the entrance there were two lifts, one going to the even floors and the other to all the floors.
A sign next to the lift told Eve number 71 was on the 7th floor. Pressing the call button for the lift, she could hear in the distance the grinding engine noise gradually getting closer. There was no turning back as the doors opened swiftly. She entered quickly and pressed the 7th floor button, with a sudden claustrophobia of fear, and expectations; the aluminium doors quickly closed and with a shudder the lift started its journey. It just gave Eve another moment to rehearse in her mind what she would say when her mother or whoever opened the door. Too late it had arrived. The elevator lights flickered and then the lift ground to an abrupt halt. Eve stepped out of the lift and there were four doors facing her. She quickly discovered number 71. Nervously she pressed the bell; in the distance she could hear it ring and then footsteps.
Mother opened the door with a smile, and after a few words asked Eve in. "Come in. We can't stand chatting here. Excuse the place I'm getting the lounge painted."
Derek was up a ladder putting the finishing touches to the ceiling. They went In her bedroom to talk. It did not take long before mother told her she had a sister Joyce, and a brother Roy. That was the start of Eve getting to know her mother. The day had gone better then Eve had expected. Dot was easy to talk to and there were so many things to catch up on. They chatted over a cup of tea, and a photograph album was produced to show Eve her unknown relatives. They exchanged telephone numbers, and agreed to meet again.
Eve was told to keep her identity secret, for the time being at least. So with a kiss on the cheek they parted company, their first meeting in over 40 years.
They kept in contact by telephone and exchanged birthday and Christmas cards. The next visit was to be the first time that I would cast eyes on Eve, be it very fleeting. My mother had taken Eve around to visit my pet shop; my mom was very proud of my modest achievements, and would tell everyone, to my total embarrassment. At the time I was working at Cadburys in Moreton, and had returned from work to collect something from the flat. As I entered the lounge my mom was chatting to a lady sat opposite. She looked up just as I shot into the kitchen. And that was it - our very first sight of each other. Eve knew who I was, but I did not even know I had a sister apart from Joyce.
That was not until I went on a trip to America with Mercie and the family. After we had returned from a trip to Denver in Colorado. Denice, Joyce's daughter, was to break the news to me.
We were sat around relaxing watching the television.
Denice took me to one side and speaking in a quite voice told me.

Chapter 2 - Eve's Story

"I have something to tell you,"
and then taking a deep breath continued,
"I think you should know, that apart from my mother you have another sister called Eve."
The shocked look on my face must have said it all.
"Are you sure? How do you know?" was my immediate response.
Before I could say anything else, Denice interrupted,
"It's for real!, Your mother had two daughters with the same guy, but Eve was adopted."
I was stunned. I went into question mode. I discovered she was living in Southport, had three children, and that she had even seen me, and that she had been in contact with the family for years.
I had so many mixed emotions I didn't know what to think or do.
I suddenly felt out of place. Why had no one told me before?
It does cause me sadness to think that my mother felt she had to hide that part of her life from me. When I returned home I went around to see my mother and we talked it over, but she was still quite guarded about the whole affair. I did not want to upset her so I didn't ask any searching questions; in hindsight, I wish I had. I decided to send Eve a letter as a short of introduction to break the ice. I think everyone was happy that it was now all out in the open. It was a couple of months later that I took my mother over to meet Eve and David, and after some more contacts we developed a friendship.
Bob her first husband was to pass away in the prime of his life.
She eventually married David; this in her own words was a big mistake. They were not really compatible. They both lived and worked in Manchester for a couple of years before returning to Merseyside. It was around this time that David started to develop MS which was yet another major problem for the family to overcome. Multiple Sclerosis is a terrible wasting disease that destroys the body and dampens the spirit, a truly terrible affliction. I remember quite vividly when I attended Janet's wedding that David could hardly walk, it took a real effort for him to get into the church. I helped to support his weight, but even on two walking sticks it was difficult. His condition gradually deteriorated to the point that he required the intervention of specialised nurses for treatments; it was then that he went into a nursing home. Eventually his suffering was brought to an end.
The children were all grown up by then; it was only a matter of time before Eve was to meet Fred Davies and they hit it off almost immediately. The couple went to live in Southport. Soon after meeting, Fred told Eve that he felt like Rip Van Winkle waking up and coming to life again. He had had years of looking after his sick wife who had eventually died. This was to be a very happy union, and lasted until he passed away about 17 years ago.   Eventually Eve was to find happiness with Donald Bishop.

Chapter 2 - Eve's Story

They had met, of all places, in a Littlewood's restaurant, having to share a table. He had travelled the world in his profession and she found him an educated interesting man, and very sensible. He sorted out problems, even before they happened which she thought a bonus. They went to live in Southport to take in the sea air; they both had a need to share the rest of their lives together. He too had lost his wife and needed company. After twelve years of an enjoyable life and both learning to cope with old age, fate dealt a terrible blow, when Donald developed cancer. By the time it had been detected it had progressed too far for anything to be done. He passed away in 2008.

Eve has now moved to the place she grew up in, Waterloo on Liverpools' coast to be closer to her family and four grandchildren. The two eldest study at Sheffield university and are due to get their degrees this year. She will be kept busy.

John was to graduate with a BSc. with honours in stats. & computing at The John Moores University Liverpool. The bank he worked for offered a lot of their employees redundancy. So now retired he can enjoy his great love of music, guitar and piano playing and also entertains with his pals at local pubs.

Gary (At rear), Ray, Eve & Denice (L-R).

John married Ann in 1988. Ann was a staff nurse and they have a son Stephen almost 21yrs and daughter Emma 17yrs.

Janet married Paul and moved to Sheffield. They married a year before John & Ann. Janet is a qualified hairdresser, but she always wanted to become a librarian. She eventually passed all her qualifications and has now fulfilled her ambitions. They have a son Richard aged 17 and Gemma 21, not forgetting Arnold, Gemma's hamster who had to stay

Chapter 2 - Eve's Story

behind when Gemma went to university.

Derek is Eve's eldest son and is still a bachelor and keeps himself busy, which keeps him happy, but he never reached his full potential, getting side-tracked along life's weary way.

Eve's adopted dad John Courtman fought in the First World War in the Scots Guards Reserve and was one of the first to be called up. He was in battle of the Somme, taken prisoner and sent to Wittenberg Camp Germany. "He was one of the old contemptibles."

Everything seems to go around full circle in Eve's life. Vincent was Eve's very first love, and she spurned him, of course being stupid. They both married, but somehow they always kept in touch. He lost his wife about the time that Don died, and so now they are able to share some time together.

John, Ann, Eve & Janet. (L-R)

The photograph above shows John with his wife Ann, then Eve and Janet Eve's, only daughter. Bottom photograph was taken in 71 Liscard House, with Margery my mom's best friend, my Mom in the centre and Eve.

Chapter 2 - Eve's Story

Eve with Mrs Wivell her assistant in "Fresh Farm Produce" the name of the shop in Bridge Road.

Derek, Bob, and John at New Brighton riding on the donkeys and motor boat on Tower lake.

Derek, John and Eve at Southport

129

Chapter 3 - The early years

The early years.
I was born on the 6th February 1947 during the hardest winter in living memory; with 20-foot-high snowdrifts in the countryside, many villages and towns were cut off. My father was unable to visit the hospital as there was no transport running. In desperation he tried to walk to the hospital but the blizzard conditions forced him back. He had to wait until the following day before a limited bus service was in operation.

After six years of war, rationing was still in operation even though the war had ended in 1945. Meat, butter, lard, margarine, sugar, tea, cheese, soap, clothing, petrol, sweets- the list was endless. The weekly ration of meat from the butcher had been reduced to one shilling's worth. Worse still, potatoes were on the restricted list for the first time. Power stations closed for lack of coal, millions were on short-time working, and we still had to pay off the huge debts amassed during the war. Britain had emerged from the war, bombed out, exhausted and now bankrupt. My parents must have thought what will the future hold for their little bundle of joy? The harsh winter was followed by a warm and pleasant summer which was a cause for the Box Brownie to appear. My delighted parents took many photographs of their son accompanied by our friends and relatives. The picture below shows my Mum and Dad in Vale Park.

I was a quiet child; an observer, skinny, and pale, I was always daydreaming. Thankfully this was to change over the years as I gained in size and confidence. To make sure I would become a budding genius in later life, every child under the age of three received daily milk, orange juice and cod liver oil to help keep them healthy. This was all well and good but the Minister for Health did not have to swallow a spoonful of cod liver oil every morning. My mother devised a plan; a sweetened version of Malt extract would follow which was shovelled down my throat to take the taste away. I don't think the project worked too well judging by some of the comments on my school reports. "Must try harder", "He has an overdeveloped unawareness.""This boy does not need a scripture teacher. He needs a missionary".

My earliest memories of the house, the one in which my mother grew up, date back to the early fifties. Over the years, air pollution had coated the original red bricks with grime, and harsh weather had raked out their

Chapter 3 - The early years

mortar, giving them a ragged appearance. Grey Welsh slates covered the roofs and the chimneys bellowed out dark black smoke; even the lace curtains at the windows were dingy yellow.

The terraced houses were squashed together; every front door was painted black all in regimental lines; the other side contained business premises. On entering our house in Field Road you would step over the doorstep, which was regularly honed to perfection with a pumice stone. Every week my Mum would get down on her hands and knees to clean the soft sandstone and a clean step was a matter of public pride. On entering the narrow hallway, there was a hall stand in the centre, upon which hung my father's raincoat, which also contained a jacket. The two were inseparable. Both had seen better days. My duffle coat with its four wooden fastenings with rope loops to attach to the toggles, hung to the side. It really made a fashion statement; an elastic string ran through the arms with a mitten attached to each end. The large pockets contained a balaclava and a scarf. During the winter, a musty smell would prevail from the wet clothes. Just like the knights of old wearing armour, my father's outer garments could stand up on their own. My mother's coat hung in between. We still had traces of blackout paint around the windows which had not helped the poor souls at No2 Field Road when the house was hit by Luftwaffe bombs. The maze of cellars in the basement became our playground. Originally there was no electricity in our house and the lights were powered by gas. The landlord eventually installed electricity and automatically increased the rent. Oh the delights of capitalism. Mrs Hough would call to collect the rent each week; my parents were paranoid about the prospect of being in arrears and then thrown out onto the streets. So if we missed her visit I was dispatched to St George's Park to pay the rent in person. This was a daunting task; I could hear all the bolts being slipped across in strict order. The door then timidly opened. "Who is that," I heard as a weathered hand would search and grope for human contact. Mrs Hough's elder sister was totally

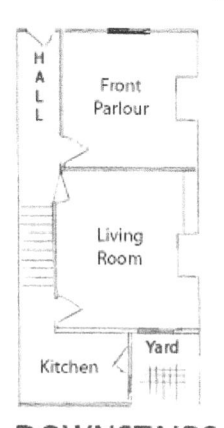

DOWNSTAIRS

UPSTAIRS

131

Chapter 3 - The early years

blind; she wore dark glasses and always appeared to be staring straight ahead. The power of her imagined gaze just cut through me. "I've come to pay the rent," I would say in a sheepish voice placing the envelope in her outstretched hand. "Wait here!" The door shut in my face and it always took ages. But the relief in getting the rent book back from this witch's cauldron was well worth the wait.

The dingiest room in our Victorian terrace was the front parlour used for funerals and the like. On the wall a set of three plaster flying ducks took centre stage. It was a damp and miserable place and contained our electric and gas meters both operated on a shilling coin. I can remember the meter man coming to empty the shillings out on the kitchen table. When we didn't have a shilling, we used washers or foreign coins; it was ridiculous. In our house my parents would have a row about whose turn it was to put a shilling in the meter. The power always went out when you were listening to something interesting on the radio and then later the television. When the meter was emptied there was always a refund; the meter man always put the washers back into the discount pile before he took the payment and never said a word!

Our family would use the back parlour (Living Room) for everyday living. Just like animals entering the ark, the chairs, all second hand, had arrived in the house two by two. There were two black Edwardian painted side chairs, two spindle-back, and two ladder-back chairs. In those days you thought yourself well off if the floors were linoleum-covered and scattered with the odd rug or two. My father always sat in his easy chair beside the fire reading the *Daily Chronicle* and fumigating the room with smoke from his full-strength Senior Service cigarettes. With the slogan on the packet: Satisfaction in every packet - Senior Service Satisfy - Tobacco at its best. There was no nandy pandy health warning, so we all inhaled the stuff. My mother did not smoke, but we were all probably addicted to the nicotine anyway. The grate with its coal fire provided a focal point around which the family would gather. On the mantelpiece above sat two imitation Chinese vases, in the centre a clock, on one side a spill holder, and on the other a penny-swallowing negro's head money box. Above them an oval mirror hanging on a chain which provided the room's only concession to vanity. My dad's easy chair located on one side of the fireplace matched the one opposite. A small two-seater settee completed the seating arrangements. Space was at a premium; for our meals my mother would remove the card table from under the stairs, the legs were hinged. Once in position the table would be laid and the chairs

132

Chapter 3 - The early years

from the front parlour put in place. We had a small writing bureau, which was the home of all the important family documents such as the rent book, the life assurance "penny policy" collected weekly by the Prudential Man and our tontine club book in which we would save up for Christmas. The Milk tokens were also in the bureau. They were purchased from the Co-op and they were put out with your empties to pay your Co-op Milkman. There were also some old family photographs, my old school reports which I managed to destroy and Dad's medals which were still in the envelopes that they arrived in and never opened. I remember asking why don't you wear them and getting the reply.
"It was all a bloody waste of time".
The most important object in the room was the radio. Dad and I would listen to *Journey into Space* on a Friday night. It was on the BBC Light Programme and after a bit of careful tuning and a few hisses, we were ready. The year is 1965 in the future, and Jet's father (Sir William Morgan) launches his A.24 rocket from the Rocket Research Station at Poker Flats. But something goes wrong, and the rocket heads towards Las Vegas, out of control. The music and sound effects were second to none. As a little boy I was quite frightened when it came to bedtime. Things would jump out of the shadows on my way up the steep staircase to bed. Then after my head hit the pillow, I too would depart on a journey into space. Another radio favourite at Sunday dinner was *Billy Cotton's Band Show* with his "Wakey Wakey". If the hissing persisted, my dad would instruct me to go outside and pour some water on the earth wire, and this seemed to do the trick. The earth from the radio went all the way down the wall and into the ground, and according to my dad should be kept damp or wet at all times to get good reception. We had a very small kitchen, with an Ascot 'geyser' which was the only supply of hot water. Underneath was an enamel basin that had seen better times. With a gas cooker in the opposite corner and a kitchen cabinet, our gastronomic equipment was complete. A couple of steps and you were outside in the yard. In the summer flies were everywhere and we always had a roll of sticky orange flypaper hanging from the kitchen ceiling.
Upstairs had two bedrooms and a small box room, later to become my laboratory. My bedroom was at the rear of the house with spectacular views of the narrow entries and the back of the terraced houses in Eleanor and Catherine Street and the houses opposite in Sandridge Road.
In the centre of the room a cast-iron fireplace that was never used it had

Chapter 3 - The early years

identical alcoves on either side of the chimney breast. One side housed a cupboard with two drawers above, and on the other side an old dressing table with tilting mirror which did not lend themselves to any form of symmetry. With an ordinary sized double bed up against the wall, and an ottoman under the window, it just left sufficient space to fit a small school type desk in the corner, and that was my bedroom. In the winter the bed was always cold even with a couple of hot water bottles. I had numerous blankets and a thick eiderdown on top, but it was still cold. I would wake up in the morning with ice on the windows.
With no central heating the secret was to keep moving; all the bedrooms were like the inside of a fridge.

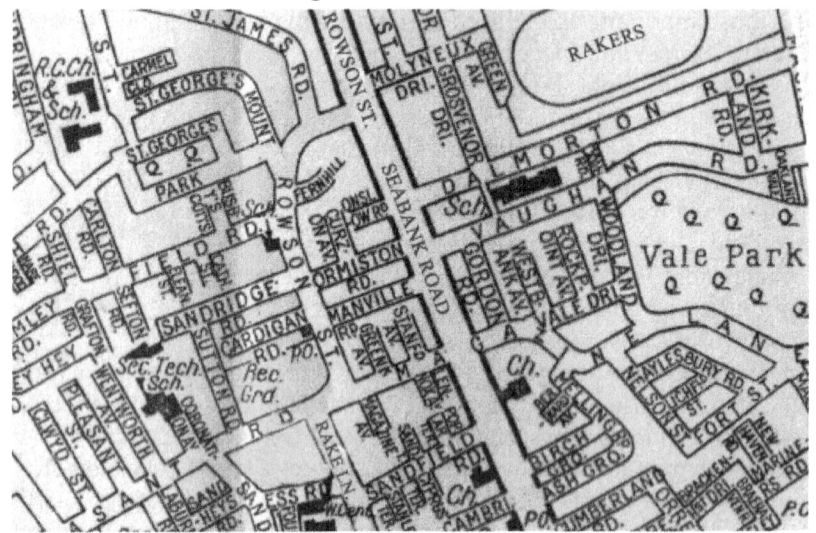

Street map showing some of the places mentioned in the text
When I was eventually allowed out to play, the side streets of Eleanor and Catherine Street were my regular haunts. In those days the roads belonged to the kids as very few cars were around. The hopscotch numbers drawn on the pavement, and the goal posts and cricket stumps drawn on the walls all set the scene for lots of fun. Make holes in two tin cans, put string through them - instant stilts! Handstands against the wall, hula hoops and yo-yos, skipping with a rope, rounders, clenched fists - One potato, two potato, three potato four...... five potato, six potato more! The Girls would reply:

> *1,2 Tie my shoe*
> *3,4 Shut the door*
> *5,6 Pick up sticks*
> *7,8 Lay them straight*
> *9, 10 A big fat hen.*
> *Let's get up and count again!*

Chapter 3 - The early years

Trentham Gardens, Stoke, 11ᵗʰ August 1956
People from my local area on a coach trip organised by Maggie Glover, from Catherine Street, Wallasey. In this photo:
Front row Left to Right : 1-Peter Glover, 2?, 3-Eric Black, 4-Lenny Black, 5-Gary Evans, 6?, 7-Trevor Waghorne, Robert Bailey, John Glover, Malcolm Waghorne, 11-Annie Glover holding Margaret Glover
Next Row : 1?, 2?, 3-Kenny Black, 4-Cathy Plant, 5-Paul Plant, 6-Pat Plant, 7- Pat Banks, 8? 9- Peter Jenkins, 10?
Next Row : 1?, 2-Tommy Quinlan, 3-Joan Black, 4-Mary Evans Joan's Mum, 5-Maggie Glover, (wearing the hat) 6?, 7-Peter Banks, 8?, 9?
Back:1?,2- Mrs Garnett, 3?, 4?,5-Mrs Waghorne,6-Ethel's Mum, 7-Ethel Plant.

Maggie had four sons, the youngest was John. Her husband was a cook on one of the big passenger liners. A short man of large statue, cunning eyes and a protruding chin, whose performances with traditional dishes of local gastronomy were renowned; namely tripe and onions!
He was the very person who ignited my interest in science and travel. I was playing outside their house when a loud bellowing voice shouted out.
"Roy come in here".
I thought, I'm in for it this time. I picked up my ball and entered the two-up two-down house, with the front door opening onto the street, expecting to be greeted by a complaint about kicking the ball against his wall. The smell of stale beer hit me almost at once and it took a moment for my eyes to adjust to the gloom. The old white ceiling was yellowing under the bombardment of nicotine, the cracked ceilings being the only interlude to the dark stain. A couple of large leather suitcases were on the floor with some of the contents hanging over the sides. The family all sat around the

Chapter 3 - The early years

room admiring their presents from his latest circumnavigation.
It was a hot summer's evening and Mr Glover was wearing a singlet, which struggled to cover his stomach.
"Here lad. Take this book. John doesn't want it. I brought it all the way from New York. Here take it."
He thrust it into my hand. It was the The Reader's Digest Great World Atlas First Edition 1963. It was the best and biggest book I had ever seen. I ran home to show my Mum. With pictures of the world's treasures (rocks/stones), explorers' routes, space, and the solar system. And not forgetting all the countries and cities shown on the maps whose locations fired up my imagination. My dreams did come true, as in later life I would be lucky enough to visit many of them. Communities were close-knit with people going through life in a way very similar to everyone else. It was everyone's dream to have their offspring do better than themselves. How any of us survived we will never know! Our toys were covered with brightly coloured lead-based paint which we chewed and licked. We would call at stranger's houses and ask for a drink of water. We ate food that actually had living things on it, lettuce with caterpillars. We would leave home in the morning and play all day, as long as we were back before it got dark. We had no childproof lids on medicine bottles. We ate dripping sandwiches, bread and butter pudding and drank fizzy pop made from sugar, but we were never overweight because we were always outside playing. We walked to friends' homes. I shared a drink between my mates, from one bottle and no one actually caught anything or died. We wore no helmets when we rode our bikes. I spent hours building go-carts out of bits and pieces and then went top speed down the hill, only to find I had forgotten the brakes. The risks some of us took hitchhiking, and all this before the lawyers and the government regulated our lives for our own good. We played doctors and nurses and did not get tried at the Old Bailey. Our parents didn't invent stupid names for their kids like "Trixi" and "Blade". Common sense and the knowledge of right and wrong with respect for authority were distilled into your very soul. We did not have to worry about knives, drugs and strange men, and I'd walk home by myself at night and my mother didn't have to worry. If you wanted to buy something you just saved and got a paper round and didn't expect "owt fer nowt".
We were real kids, snotty noses, lots of mates, lean and mean and we made our own fun. Bath night was usually on a Friday. Our house did not have a bathroom. My Mum brought the large zinc bath that hung on an outside wall and placed it in front of the fire. The hot water

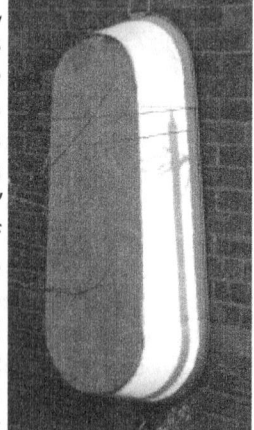

Chapter 3 - The early years

arrived via a kettle and several pots that had been boiling on the gas stove. We took turns to bathe in the same water keeping it warm with fresh additions from the kettle. My Dad was always first. It was a relief when I started my apprenticeship, I could take a shower every day.

My Mum tried her best to keep the house clean but it was a thankless task. The back-kitchen floor was made of red quarry tiles. The living room had lino. All the rugs were taken outside and banged against the wall to dislodge the dust. Then the mop with disinfectant was applied. I can still remember the smell.

Every household kept a mangle outside the back door. After boiling the washing, wooden tongs were used to ladle it into a zinc tub and then pounded it with a 'dolly' to release the dirt. I would sometimes help my Mum to put the sheets and clothes through the mangle's clanking rollers to squeeze out the excess water. My mother's enthusiasm quite often left my dad with broken buttons on his shirts, which would produce another row. My Mum's hands were always chapped and red because of the washing and cleaning that she did. Even in bad weather, my mother would always try to put the washing out to dry. On a frosty day the washing would come in stiff like boards, and her fingers would be white with cold.

The loo was a small brick building at the bottom of the yard next to the coal bunker it's wooden door was half-hanging from its hinges. I hated the place and avoided using it for as long as I could. The enamel bowl of the lavatory was in a box-like container which went the width of the cubicle. The lavatory seat consisted of planks of wood across the whole width of the lavatory which my mother scrubbed every other day. There was no toilet paper so we used newspaper cut into squares, threaded with string and hung on a hook. At least there was something to read; the other bonus of course was having the headlines printed on your backside.

In the winter a paraffin lamp was put in the hovel to prevent the pipes from freezing. We used chamber pots when the weather was bad and during the night.

Next door to the toilet was the coal shed. The coal merchant arrived every Monday shouting "Any Coal; Any Coal". With a hessian sack draped over his head and shoulders, he weaved his way through the entry at the back of the house and left a trail of coal dust in his wake. Mum ordered. "Watch him, count how many bags he puts in that coal shed. I'll swear he never put three bags in there last time".

Sometimes the quality of the coal left a lot to be desired. If it contained a lot of slate, the grate in the morning would be a mass of grey ash. But worst of all, the slate would spit out, and the red-hot embers could set the place

Chapter 3 - The early years

on fire. With good quality coal, a fire would look wonderfully welcoming and cheerful. We only put the fire on in the evenings or at the weekend. I could gaze into the fire for hours looking at the volcanoes formed on the coal as the tar inside melted an ever-changing scene. When my mother wanted to build the fire up quickly she would hold a newspaper in front of the grate to get the fire to draw. Then as the newspaper started to change colour and turn brown and burn, she would grab it just as it was about to burst into flames and throw it onto the fire. My mum always liked to have a blazing fire when my dad came home from work. My father's full name was Alfred Rhayader Dutton he was born in Rhayader, a small historic market town in mid- Wales, the son of Thomas and Frances who died giving birth to my father on the 6th April 1909. My father's middle name is in remembrance of my grandfathers beloved wife who had passed away.

Dad had been brought up by Aunt Polly and from all accounts had been waited on hand and foot. My parents' authority was absolute. "Don't ask where babies come from." "Don't show your nakedness"; appearances meant everything; hands, outer clothing, doorsteps and entrances were always kept spotless, as were reputations. Rules to govern behaviour and thought were intended to stifle curiosity, to suffocate desires. But the 60s were to drive a bus through the old beliefs. Rather than silence -be seen and not heard and old wives' tales -the music, the pill, and the barmy wars were to change society forever. Instead of children being exact clones of their parents, a new generation was growing up fast, with a totally different outlook on life. Welcome to the swinging sixties.

If my father's slippers were not warming gently by the fire, there would be another row. He was in love with racing, with the world of fixed odds, Canadian and Yankee bets but to make a living he was forced to spend his days trapped in a world of test tubes and Petri dishes.

It was in later years I came to realise that it was these qualities that made my father special. My dad was the perfect gentleman, a local husband and a caring father in his own way. I quite often, at the time, could not understand his strict ways. No paper rounds.

"You will spend your whole life working so concentrate on your studies." When I needed a drum kit, he said,

"Save up, son! Don't borrow anything from anyone, and no hire purchase" And on the subject of a career, he said,

"Get a trade; no matter what you do, you can always fall back on it".

The Jones next door had been fishermen all their lives and had a long tradition of service with the R.N.L.I. Both father and son had made many

Chapter 3 - The early years

life-saving rescues. The 23rd November 1938 was a very stormy day, with some of strongest gales ever recorded. Coxswain William Jones and his crew braved the elements to rescue three men from the fishing boat *Progress* and then four men from the schooner *Loch Ranza Castle*. The crew had been forced to climb up into the rigging. The lifeboat manoeuvred over the submerged deck and then two of the crew jumped and were dragged aboard the lifeboat. The other two in the port rigging were too exhausted to move. The situation was desperate! William managed to get the lifeboat under the rigging, and with the last man barely conscious the lifeboatmen with great difficulty managed to get him on aboard. The lifeboat was seriously damaged while going over the deck of the schooner, yet with flooded compartments she limped home, and was found to have three large holes in her hull. William was awarded a Silver Medal for his heroic deeds on the day. Coxswain 'Pinky' Jones retired in December 1938. The stress of the rescue and loss of Joe Stonall a fellow lifeboatman who died whilst out fishing the day after the rescue, was the right time to call it a day. William, the son of 'Pinky' Jones, took his father's place and in 1947 was awarded a Bronze Medal for evacuating the crew of six from a fort in the River Mersey. Tommy Jones the brother of Pinky also joined the R.N.L.I and was to witness his father drown on his fishing boat in the Mersey. They were truly remarkable people. My mum would send me next door to find out if Tommy had landed his catch. If the back door was wide open, Lil Jones, would be standing behind a wooden table with some scales and weights and a couple of large trays full of ice and fish.

Bill's boat called the *Sheila May*

Billy

Tommy

139

Chapter 3 - The early years

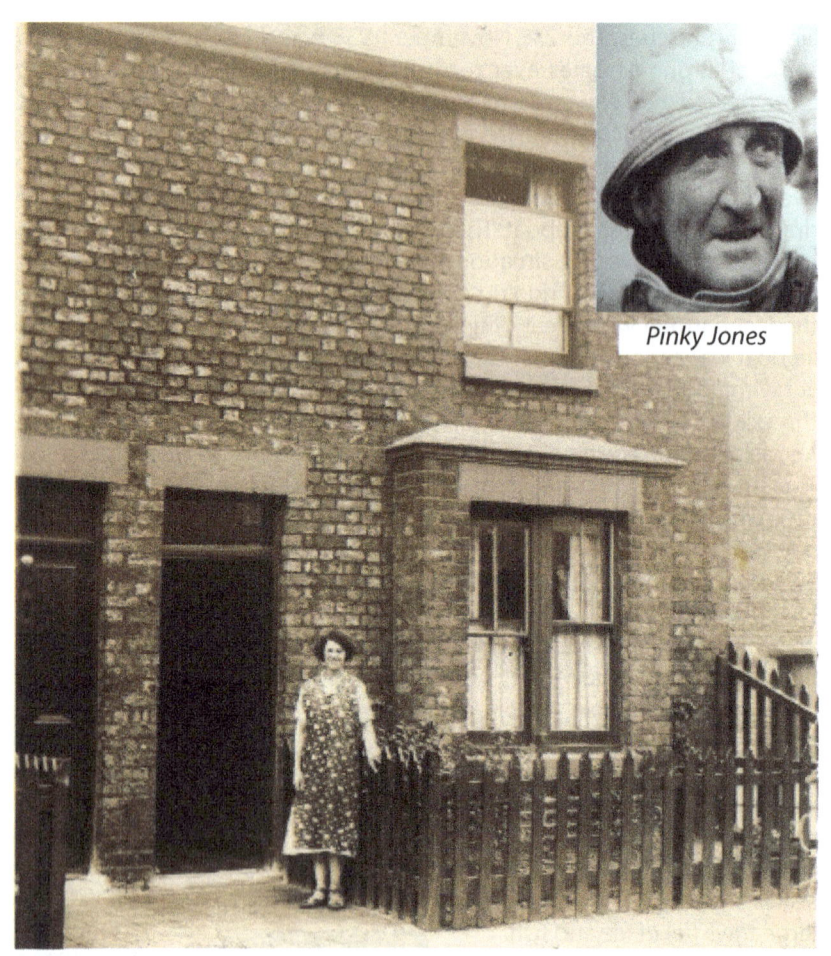

Pinky Jones

Periwinkles cost two pennies for a cupful; shrimp cost five pennies a cup. Lilly was a slim lady in her late 50s, always laughing and full of fun.
After a short rest, Tommy would proceed to the pub with the takings. His favourite tipple was Guinness. He was a very popular guy and well liked. He always had a tale to tell when he had an audience. The above photograph of Lillian Jones shows her standing outside her house at 35 Field Road, which was next door to our house at 33. Lil, as she was known, lived with her brother Tommy. Their parents were Jane and William from Constantine Terrace. Moe Koltuniak recalls; "Auntie Lil was quite a character....she used to light a fire in the back bedroom when it was very cold...or throw another coat on the bed. Nana had the licence to sell the fish......from the back yard!! Mum says the neighbours used to queue up in the entry.
Whilst the 'posh folk' would come to the front door."
In those days most people were poor but Lil had time for everyone.

Chapter 3 - The early years

"Roy, tell your mum we've got some really nice fresh plaice", she whispered. Returning with the necessary funds, the plaice would be wrapped up in newspapers and slapped down on the table.
"There you go!"
We could not wait for the weekend to come around fast enough. Every Saturday morning it was off to the Winter Gardens Cinema for the Children's Matinee. You could sit where ever you liked, which meant as close to the screen as possible. As soon as the doors opened you were overtaken by a tidal surge of kids who all had exactly the same idea.
Roy Rogers, Flash Gordon, a singalong, and talent shows would be our entertainment. In those days you bought a bag of Smith's Crisps with a little bag of salt contained within a blue packet. For the sing-along, the words would appear on the cinema screen with a dot bouncing across the top of the word as you sang.

> *And we pushed the damper in and we pulled the damper out*
> *and the smoke went up the chimney just the same.*
> *And we pushed the damper in and we pulled the damper out*
> *and the smoke went up the chimney just the same.*
> *and the smoke went up the chimney.*
> *und the smoke went up the chimney.*
> *and the smoke went up the chimney.*
> *and the smoke went up the chimney just the same.*

The whole audience would participate in the sing-along with the necessary hand signals mimicking the smoke going up the chimney. The compere, Cecil on stage with the microphone, would lead the kids in these activities. He had a slight lisp extenuated by his ill-fitting teeth which slide around his palette, especially when using any word containing an S. He had a voice like a foghorn, and kept the children in order, and he also sold pop and ice-cream during the interval. When there was a film on with cowboys chasing Indians, the noise of the stamping feet and the yelling was deafening! Cecile did a wonderful job of controlling the children (and the fleas), by going around and squirting 'Jeyes Fluid' everywhere. We loved that place, especially if the film broke down the booing would start.
"Why are we waiting?"
It would almost develop into a full-blown riot. The uproar never subsided until the cartoons and current serial started - Flash Gordon, Zorro, Rin Tin Tin. How our imaginations were ignited. My friend Norma Ball had a potential brother-in-law in the shape of Alan who was going out with Norma's sister Delma. He would appear from time to time during the talent shows to accompany any budding singers using my guitar, which my mum had bought for me. He would borrow the guitar and bring it back months later to my annoyance.
After the matinee we dispersed into the local woods and fields to re-enact the heroic deeds we had just witnessed which usually ended with us being

Chapter 3 - The early years

chased off someone's property. I remember the old joke was that you would go into the Winter Gardens wearing a pullover and come out with a ball of wool. But to us kids it was fantastic; our heroes came to life for two hours every Saturday.

A favourite pastime was to collect empty bottles and return them to shops and collect the 2d for each one. Some of our enterprising friends could get at the empties in the yard behind the shop and recycle them once again.

Our shopping was done locally except for our weekly trip to the Co-op which stood for Cooperative Wholesale Society. Customers had a Co-op number. Ours was 131154. Every quarter of the year the Co-op gave its customers what was called a divvy (dividend), which was a certain amount back for every pound spent.

Christmas in our house was a time of great expectations. Would I get the present I'd asked Santa for? Each year, my mum would take me to Blackler's Winter Wonderland Grotto in Liverpool. Over 10,000 visitors a week went to see the magical scenes, to tell Santa Claus what they'd like for Christmas and of course to ride Blackie the wooden rocking horse. Blackler's sadly closed their doors for the last time in April 1988 after 80 years and Santa was made redundant.

We always hung decorations around the house. I would help my mum to lick the glue on the multicoloured paper chains that would be attached to the light fitting and then attached to each corner of the room. We would save up bottles of lemonade and beer under the stairs ready for the festive season. Our get-together with friends was one of the highlights of the festive season. Betty and Wally, accompanied by Doreen and Frank, would visit our house over the holiday. They would sing and chat all night long. Betty had a fantastic voice - her Welsh ancestry helped to underline her credentials and she would sing lovely ballads in the Welsh tongue. Frank had been a baritone in a choir at some time or other and after a few whiskeys would insist on singing *The Yeomen of England* or *The Fishermen of England*. He seemed to extenuate the bass notes which took him down a vocal path of no return. We had to make our own entertainment and it always proved to be good fun.

It was customary for the postman to call on Boxing Day for his Christmas present called a Christmas Box which would be just a few coppers. We also gave the bin men a tip if they had been user-friendly during the year.

We were probably the first family in the road to buy one of those new fangled dangled things called a television. My mum was of the opinion that if you sat too close, the harmful rays would damage your eyes. My dad discovered an advertisement in the newspaper that guaranteed to increase the viewing area, and supply colour to the screen. So off went the postal order, and a week or two later a box arrived. It was from the same company that supplied x-ray glasses that enabled the user to see under the clothes of the opposite sex. This fact we discovered a little later, so our

Chapter 3 - The early years

enthusiasm was a little dampened in case the same technology was being used. We eagerly opened the parcel and read the instructions; this giant magnifying glass fitted over the screen. We switched on the television. I was sat to one side, and as if by magic we could see colour for the first time. But wait a minute, everyone on the screen was the colour of a rainbow. If you sat directly in front of the thing it did magnify the screen. But moving slightly to one side their heads became elongated, like one of those crazy mirrors in the fairground. The thing was full of oil which created the false colour. Just another worthless purchase to collect dust under the stairs. In the early 50s, television was only broadcast for a few hours a day.

The very first programme I can remember seeing on our television was Michael Bentine's *Bumblies*. At the start of every programme 'Professor' Bentine would order: "Bumbly One, come on down; Bumbly Two, come on down; Bumbly Three, come on down", and all because the Bumblies slept on the ceiling.

Then there was *Watch with Mother*, *Picture Book* on a Monday, *Andy Pandy* on a Tuesday, *The Flowerpot Men* on a Wednesday with Little Weed. Or rather, Little Weeeeeeeed. *Rag, Tag, and Bobtail* on a Thursday, and the *Woodentops* on a Friday and don't forget *Muffin the Mule*. Oh happy days! I would even watch the test card and loved that disappearing dot after the epilogue!!!

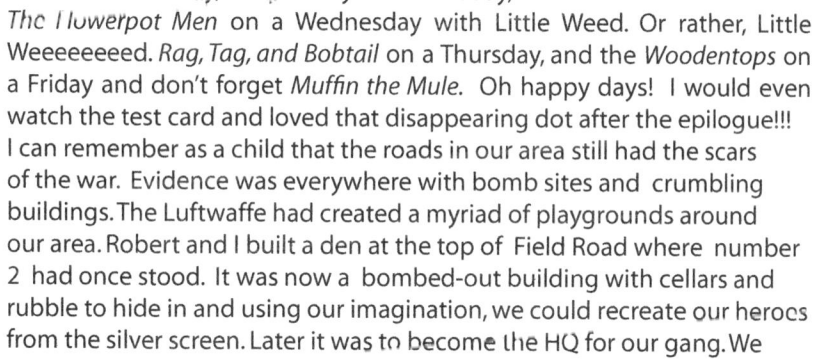

I can remember as a child that the roads in our area still had the scars of the war. Evidence was everywhere with bomb sites and crumbling buildings. The Luftwaffe had created a myriad of playgrounds around our area. Robert and I built a den at the top of Field Road where number 2 had once stood. It was now a bombed-out building with cellars and rubble to hide in and using our imagination, we could recreate our heroes from the silver screen. Later it was to become the HQ for our gang. We moulded our team around Enid Blyton's Famous Five which would help fuel our imagination. Sometimes we had battles with Peter Banks and his gang from the next street. My earliest recollection of a

143

Chapter 3 - The early years

Christmas present was a clockwork train my dad bought me; it consisted of a circular track, an engine and some wagons. All it did was go round and round in circles, but to me it was still fantastic. At least it went in the opposite direction to the goldfish, a present from the rag and bone man. He would arrive with his horse and cart shouting "Any old Iron" followed by "any old mangle handles". Don't ask me why. Joe was from gipsy stock, a big hard-looking man. He wore mismatched jackets, shirts, and trousers. He always had about an 1/8th of an inch of cigarette stuck permanently on his lip. Wearing his flat oily cap, a scruffy old muffler round his neck, and three days growth and a slight limp from a war wound, he certainly looked the part. He was popular with the gardening fraternity who would follow the horse to use the manure on their rhubarb. With a very long rein on the pony he used to sit on the back of the trap with his legs swinging. The pony had got cheesed off at being pulled from side to side by the bit in its mouth as it responded to his shouts and calls to turn left and right. The reins were covered in small bells and a loud jingling sound accompanied the clip-clop of the pony's hooves. He could be smelt some distance away probably due to the bag of bones he had on his cart. It was during the school holidays when no one was at home that I gave Joe some old clothes, and in return I received a goldfish.

The goldfish had to have a name, so in a sudden bolt of inspiration I named him or her Goldie. It was after about a month when out of the blue he jumped out of his bowl onto my dad's *Sporting Chronicle*, making a wet mark over the runners in the 2:30 at Newmarket. My dad carefully put him back, and noticed a horse called Goldie Boy in the 2:30. This had to be divine intervention.

"Dot, go around to the bookies and put a bet on."

My Mum's name was Dorothy but dad always called her Dot.

Picking up his Indelible Ink pencil and wetting the end on his tongue, he duly wrote out the bet. My dad often sucked on Rennies to help with his indigestion. This produced a short of white deposit around his mouth, so along with a purple tongue, I am sure anyone visiting would find it a little odd. Bet placed, we listened intently to the radio, at the same time looking at the goldfish in its bowl. The announcer certainly seemed to take his time, but at last the racing results. "and the winner of the 2:30 at Newmarket... Goldie Boy 8-1 with the favourite Blue Lagoon coming second followed by......" We had won! It was going to be ant eggs all around. I could see my father looking at the goldfish bowl and I was just hoping he was not trying to devise a way to get the goldfish to jump out of its bowl again. My dad said, with a look of contentment in his eye," Dot, when Joe comes around give him the old rusty bike in the yard. One good turn deserves another." Goldie lived for ages after his sporting ordeal, and retired from the field of acrobatics. What became of our rag and bone man, Mr Joseph Nolan. He was still in operation in the early 80s. His horse and cart were stabled in

Chapter 3 - The early years

Borough Road, Seacombe.
The next man to arrive in the road on a regular basis was the knife sharpener with his cart and foot-operated grinding stone. The sparks would fly and the kids would gather to see the spectacle. On reflection this was probably the start of my fascination with pyrotechnics.
Gypsies would arrive from time to time. They were very spiritual people, who believe that you are always surrounded by spirits, good and bad' and the use of charms and spells are needed to protect you from harm and bring you luck. If my mum noticed a gypsy in the road we would lock the doors and hide. They arrived selling clothes pegs and telling fortunes. If you didn't buy anything then a curse would follow. My mum was very superstitious, walking under ladders, black cats, spilling salt and the likes. So gypsies were a definite no no. Nowadays Tesco value pegs are a good buy but the checkout girls are obviously not gypsies and would have a different way of cursing ! I did chance providence in my early teens by having my palm read by a gypsy in the Tivoli Building, New Brighton. Looking deeply into my palm, and then looking into a crystal ball, I was informed that I would be going away on a long trip, and I would be away a long time. She looked up to see my reaction; I just shrugged my shoulders, and looked blank. You have to remember they are good at dropping key words and noticing tiny reactions from the person getting the reading. Vague statements and lots of total dribble was the order of the day, and my faith in the occult was severely dented. I remember the gypsy telling me that she felt I did not believe her predictions
"Few possess the all-seeing eye",
she said as she gazed once again into her crystal ball,
"You are going to have huge money problems" (true, but could it have anything to do with the fee she was going to charge me?). Even good ones get it wrong sometimes!
But the highlight for me was the phrenologist who would predict the future by the bumps on your head. She would run her fingertips and palms over your head feeling the enlargements or indentations. And then proceed to map out your entire existence as it appeared from your nut. The modifications to my skull had in the main been carried out by other people. Elisa Birket had hit me over the head with a plank that contained a rusty nail, and just for calling her names. Then the head that flew off the hammer shaft produced a direct hit on my skull, and last but not least the home-made go-cart that went out of control going down Rowson Street. In my ignorance I

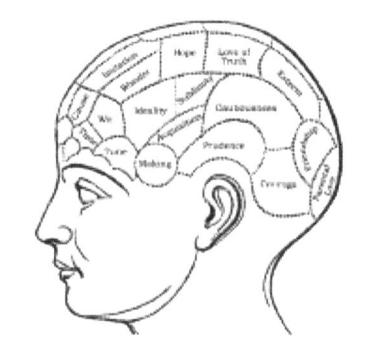

Chapter 3 - The early years

thought that the phrenologist would be able to relate all these incidents from the scars and bumps on my head. But no it was just the same old stuff; you will get married, have two children, and have a long and worthwhile career. So from that day to this, my belief in the occult has been a little sceptical.

Bonfire night was a children's festival, when boys and girls built their own bonfires and set off fireworks, and friendly fire was something we'd all gather round on bonfire night to enjoy our baked potatoes. Weeks before the 5th of November we would all be out collecting inflammable rubbish. We could reduce a sagging old sofa to a bundle of wood, springs and stuffing in no time. Each street would have at least one bonfire. It was every kid's aim to have the biggest bonfire in the area. Rival gangs of children would steal wood from each other's piles. Over-enthusiastic children would quite often acquire garden gates from disgruntled home owners. Jobsons, the newsagent, had an unlimited supply of penny bangers, sparklers, catherine wheels, rockets, and golden rain fountains. You had to be quick lighting the fireworks as the blue touch-papers were not very long and they would go off within seconds of being lit.

Another highlight of the festivities was making a guy make from old clothes stuffed with screwed up newspapers. "A penny for the guy?" was the chant used to entice passers-by to contribute a few coppers to the cause. We would sit our guy on the pavement outside a pub or by a bus stop, we used to say 'Remember Remember the 5th of November' when asking for a penny for the Guy.

> *Please to remember*
> *The fifth of November*
> *Gunpowder, treason and plot.*
> *I see no reason*
> *Why gunpowder treason*
> *Should ever be forgot.*

The pennies collected were used to buy bangers which were small in size and cheap to buy. You would light the blue touch-paper and throw the thing behind someone. The guy was supposed to depict Guy Fawkes, and would sit on the top of the bonfire. It's a shame because he was probably the only person to go into the House of Parliament with good intentions. My father found out what I was up to and was not very happy with my entrepreneurial activities.

"It's just bloody begging. Stop it at once." So the operation had to take

Chapter 3 - The early years

on a more distant perspective. I can remember the bonfire blazing away; the sparks flying and the sky turning a lovely orange colour just as the fire brigade arrived to put it out. Luckily for all concerned the Fireworks Act of 2003 prohibited people under the age of 18 from carrying fireworks in public.

I always wanted a tortoise. I had seen them in the pet shop and this was my burning ambition. My mother at first was not too keen; she said dad was allergic to animals! He evidently wasn't allergic to betting on horses!

It took quite a bit of moaning and persuasion to get my own way. Then when I had saved up enough pocket money, it was off to the Pet Shop by Strodes Corner. All the tortoises were in the bottom window walking around in sawdust. Which one should I pick? Unlike dogs none of them took any interest in me peering through the glass, not an inkling of recognition, not even when I tapped the glass, nothing! Eventually I decided on Timmy, a medium-sized specimen that looked very active for a tortoise. I was to find out a little later that the local cat was of the opinion that this was a toy ball with four legs attached, and would insist on rolling it over on its back. Luckily for all concerned the government has now got involved so a DEFRA License is required with each tortoise sold.

I was 8 years old when my mother took me to see The Tree Walk Illuminations in Vale Park. The novelty of walking through the trees with hundreds of fascinating illuminated animals and birds peeping through the branches, was a truly wonderful experience with the birds singing and the animals chattering. The "Aladdin's Cave" and "Teddy Bears Roundabout" being my favourite displays. It was a special treat being able to stay up until after dusk to see this wounderland.

The Tree Walk was 15 feet high with the visitors walking through the trees, with the animated models, some illuminated in 3-D, and all this before Disneyland was even thought of.

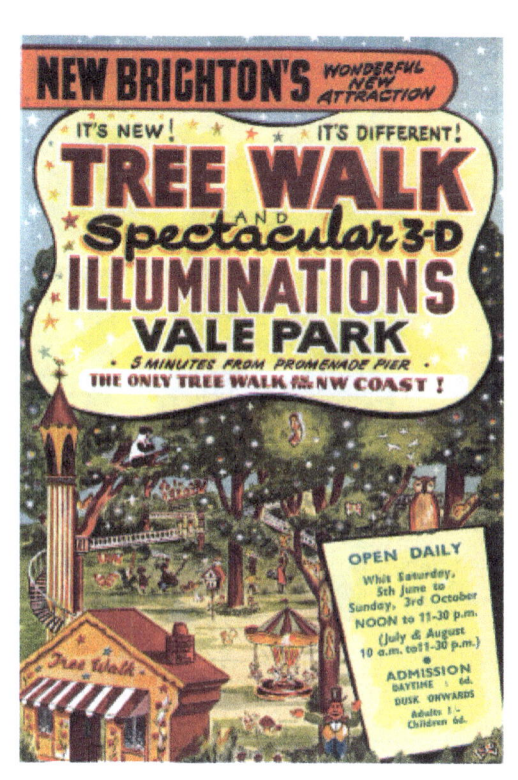

147

Chapter 3 - The early years

Chapter 3 - New Brighton Baths

Opened in June 1934 it was the largest aquatic stadium in the world, with 1,376,000 gallons of pure sea water which was constantly cleaned and filtered. I would spend many a happy hour in New Brighton Baths; in those days we had long hot summers. If I close my eyes I can still hear the splashing of water and the sound of excited children, the tannoy announcement of a lost child and the smell of the water mixed with suntan creams. The end came in February 1990 with hurricane force winds causing irreparable damage to the structure.

The *end*

My Neighbourhood

Taking a look back on my childhood in the late 1940s and into the 1950s so many things have changed, it seems as if it all happened in another world. If I were magically plucked up from that time and brought here to 2013 it would be easy to imagine that I had been transported by aliens to another planet rather than just another time. So let's travel back in time and I'll take you on a trip down memory lane. On leaving my house, number 33 Field Road, you would walk past a block of terraced houses before arriving at Catherine Street which was 'Dickensian' to say the least, with rows of neat two-up two-down houses on both sides of the street. The only interruption to their regularity was a long narrow passage which led to our back yards. Opposite Catherine Street was Kennas, the Funeral Directors. We all used to play in the garage there and one of the chaps used to show us the coffins and sometimes tell us which ones were occupied. There was a swivel chair in the office and he would sit us in it and spin us around until we were dizzy. His main tasks were to clean the limousines and look miserable at the funerals, but I think he was bored, so our company was much appreciated.

The old tram sheds opposite our house at 33 Field Road.

Returning to the other side of the road we passed Field Road Mission. I attended the coronation party there in 1953 and was given a crown (five shillings). Next was Mables the sweet shop, a regular port of call for liquorice sticks, Uncle Joe's mint balls, flying saucers, pear drops, and tiger nuts all

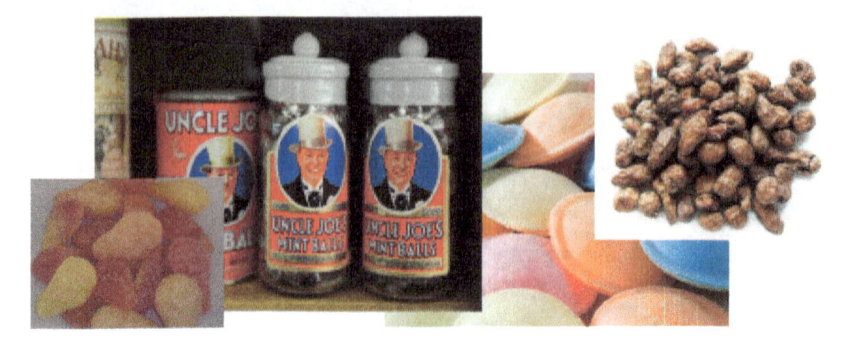

Chapter 3 - My Neighborhood

in nicely labelled jars. We bought sweeties normally an ounce at a time. My all-time favourite was lemon sherbet which made your finger yellow. A little later in life, I graduated to buying loose cigarettes! (one cigarette at a time, irrespective of age).

Mable was a small oval-shaped lady in her mid-sixties; she spent most of her time knitting while waiting for customers to pop in. You could buy vinegar, but you had to bring your own bottle. She also sold Carter's little liver pills which were to be a slight problem to me in later life.

I can remember Robert and myself coming from the matinee at the Winter Gardens having seen *Roy Rogers*. Roping steers and shooting Indians was thirsty work so it was into Mables for a shot of the hard stuff. She sold brightly coloured carbonised water under the exotic titles of orange, strawberry and raspberry pop, the latter two tasting the same. They were cheap at a penny a shot and were popular with the kids. I downed mine in one and Robert copied one of his cowboy heroes and bit on the glass and it broke! "Stupid Bugger! That'll cost you three pence for the glass," was her swift retort. There was no consideration if the boy was injured; just the bottom line mattered! No harm done we saddled up and rode out of the shop seeking more adventures.

Past the technical college on the corner, I did not know at the time but this would be the venue of my woodwork classes with Mr Bradshaw. Turn right at the top of Field Road into Rowson Street, past the magic phone box that sometimes delivered pennies by pressing button B. Past Jobsons the newsagents, my order of the Eagle was picked up every Friday after school. Mr Jobson's son also went to Vaughan Road School, but was not allowed to work in the shop. My mates Robert Bailey and Alan Jackson both had paper rounds. Everything about Mr Jobson can best be described as stubby. He was a short stubby chap with stubby hands that had large fat fingers attached; he used to have trouble picking up the small change that customers would

151

Chapter 3 - My Neighborhood

throw down for the papers in the morning, as they were in a rush to get the bus to work. The No 10 would wait for nobody; its driver and conductor had a schedule to follow. Upstairs to the gas chamber or downstairs no smoking; the choice was that simple. They should have put a health warning on the bus tickets. A conductor in a dark blue uniform supervised us as we boarded the vehicle. Slung over one shoulder he wore a leather satchel on a broad strap; over the other shoulder was a little printing machine. When I tendered my fare, he placed the money in the satchel, dialled the fare on the printer, turned a handle and tore off my ticket as it emerged from a slot at the front. A regular conductor on the number ten was Les, what a name! The name can linger on the tongue Lesssss…. hissing the "s" like a snake. He was in his fifties and his face was craggy and deeply etched. He had suffered at some stage from acne. The volcanoes had subsided to form craters, which had aged his appearance. He wore a smart blue uniform, with a mirror effect on the seat of his pants, the crease being highlighted by the use of braces. I don't think his legs actually made contact with the material. His hand was always black from handling the large number of copper coins. In the good old days the coins actually had a value in the copper or silver contained within them. None of this quantative easing or casino banking, just real money. A regular word that seemed to spring from his lips, which you no longer hear nowadays was "twerp" meaning bumptious little prat. The bus would actually wait a few additional seconds if he saw you running up the Road. "Come on lad get a move on" then ding, ding, and away we would speed off towards the ferry. He would call out the stops in rhyming slang! Most conductors were funny and always ready to offer an opinion on the topics of the day to any passenger who would listen.

Next door to Jobsons was Armitage, the butcher. I can still vaguely remember my Mum going there for her meat, using her ration books. Customers had to register with a particular shop and exchange the coupons for their rations. During the war families had meat to the value of 1s. 2d. and jam at 1lb in weight every two months. In 1951 people could still buy only 10d. (4p) worth of meat each week. My focus was on sweets, the allowance being 12oz every four weeks. Two new commodities were rationed after the war, bread from 1946 to 1948 and potatoes for a year from 1947. Fruit was a luxury, chicken or sweets a rarity. Queues outside butchers lined the streets. The points system ended in 1950, but things did improve with time. Farthings were still in circulation up to 1956; they were mainly used to buy bread at ninepence-farthing, the price being fixed by the government. Our kitchen sometimes took on the appearance of a scene from *The Texas Chain Saw Massacre* with pigs trotters (Feet), tripe (cows stomachs) and other indescribable delicacies hanging out of pans on the stove. The cheap cuts from the butchers made our ration last longer, so on a good day boiled tripe and onions, cow heel soup or oxtail with stale crusts. My poor old mum's favourite was roll mops (pickled herring). The smell was awful. Nothing was

Chapter 3 - My Neighborhood

ever wasted; when the cheese grew a green coat, it was cut off. Anything left from Sunday dinner was warmed up and used for Monday tea. A little further down Rowson Street you arrived at Halsall's fish and chip shop where a massive heap of old newspapers decorated the counter, whilst in the queue you could hone in on your talent for reading the *Daily Sketch* upside down. Who can forget the sound of newly-peeled -and-chopped potatoes being thrust into the boiling fat, the sight of catching the chips in wire baskets for a pinch test and then closing of the hood like a metal piano or the smell of the vinegar and fat. Every Friday I was dispatched to the chippy to buy three fish and three bags of chips. Handing over the 3/6d, the bundle of goodies were quickly wrapped in layers of newspaper. Everything was saturated in salt and vinegar and on the way home I used to try and encourage a chip out of the wrappings.

A few more shops down and we eventually arrive at the male boudoir of Mr Snuffy Glover the proprietor of the Barber's Shop. Bill Glover's pole didn't turn round. His red and white helix just stayed static, a sign of the excitement that was to reveal itself on entry. The origin of the red and white barber pole is associated with the service of bloodletting and was historically a representation of bloody bandages wrapped around a pole. Sweeney Todd made meat pies of his customers; Snuffy just bored them. Bill was a man of infinite local knowledge; middle aged with black centre-parted brylcreemed hair. He had a distinctive voice that whistled through his teeth and bounced off the walls, which made his whispers audible to all and sundry. His announcement at the conclusion of each scalping-"Anything for the weekend Sir," made it all the more embarrassing.

His sharp nose, the overall buttons he wore and central parting were all in line, as if a spirit level had been used. Unusually for a barber he was allergic to hair; his sentences were punctuated with short intakes of breath followed by periodic bursts of sniffing, with a longer sniff at the conclusion of his riveting dialogue.

He had several leather straps attached to the back of the chair, to sharpen his cut-throat razor. Sweeping backwards and forwards a few times, the blade would be honed to perfection. Then with a flick of the wrist a small sliver of paper would fall to the floor, another couple of satisfied sniffs would follow, and all was ready for the customers shave. Another twenty or thirty sniffs and another satisfied closely shaven customer would hit the road. It was now my turn for a hair cut. Unfortunately I was generally accompanied by my father, who would take charge of the proceedings. "Bill, give him a short back and sides" was the order before my backside even landed in the chair. My dad, being used to the standard army haircut, was not in the least invigorated by The Beatles' mop top style which I was trying to copy, so the lot would be lopped off. It was not until later in life that I was lucky enough to escape the wrath of the clippers. Memories of basin-cuts and strange goings-on kept me as far away from that revolving red and white

Chapter 3 - My Neighborhood

pole as possible.

We were woken up in the early hours by a commotion, the sound of fire engines and men shouting. A rancid smell drifted through the house and I jumped out of bed to investigate. My father shouted, "I've got work in the morning, get back to bed." I thought a good night's sleep is not going to be much use if the house burnt down. I listened more intensely, and looking out of the window could catch some bellowing smoke which appeared to be coming from the top of Field Road. It was not until the following morning on my way to school that I passed the Chocolate Cup Factory, which had taken over the old Mission building opposite Busby Cottages that i could see the whole right-hand side of the factory was badly damaged. It was more like Willy Wonka's chocolate factory, where the chocolate had melted in the fire and covered the road outside.

I did contemplate getting a piece, but a fireman spotted me looking at the floor and shook his head. I was to find out later that 15,000 Easter eggs, plus chocolate cups, and thousands of chocolate novelties had all melted and become victims of the fire.

What a waste, I told my mates at school, and we decided it must be worth a visit after school had finished.

My mum did not have any hobbies; it was only later in life that she enjoyed the TV and writing poetry. Relaxation was simply the bits in between work. My mum would buy the *Wallasey News* so she could read the obituary columns, and wonder why everyone on the Wirral died in alphabetical order. Every Friday night my dad would take my mum out for a drink, normally it was to the *Traveller's Rest* in New Brighton, where they would meet up with friends and family. Tommy Dutton would play on the piano. He could not read a word of music but could play almost anything if he had heard it before, and by all accounts he was very good.

Dad's hobby was studying the form on the horses and he regularly bought the Sporting Chronicle, and proceeded to study form with numerous notes and underlines to indicate his choices.

When going to the pub, dad always looked as smart as possible and was never seen unkempt outside of our house or in his working clothes. It was always a worry to me when I was left in the house on my own. If I went to sleep and was good I would be promised a War Cry and a packet of crisps. His favourite programmes on the TV were Bootsie and Snudge in the *Army Game*, *Rawhide* and the *Pondersa*, my Dad loved westerns.

He was like clockwork getting up at six-thirty every working day. The alarm clock bell went ballistic until he whacked the thing with his fist. The reserve alarm clock was also cancelled. Winter mornings were the coldest with ice on the inside of the windows, with no morning sunlight to help him out of bed. He removed his teeth from the glass tumbler by the side of the bed, walks from the front bedroom where he slept, down the stairs to the kitchen. Washed and shaved over the enamel wash basin; same routine

Chapter 3 - My Neighborhood

day in day out. He slept in late on Saturdays and Sundays. Forty-odd years starting at six-thirty have taken their toll. He is starting to look older than his age, and his health is starting to deteriorate. He would periodically calculate if he worked another year how much pension he would receive. Then another three or four months would pass and he would do the calculations again. He was looking forward to his retirement and a lapse in the routine. Needless to say he did not make it and died before he could retire. I vowed that no matter what, I would not steer the same path in life working 7.30am to 4.00pm every day with three week's paid holiday, this was not for me. My poor dad never had the opportunity to enjoy his retirement, so I was going to make sure my retirement started much earlier than the prescribed 65 years.

Family outing with our best friends. Left to right:
Doreen, Betty, Dad, Mum, Roy and Wally 7th Aug 1962 taken at Blackpool
Doreen, Betty's daughter from a previous marriage was married to Frank Cox, Walter Ward (Betty's Husband) was a gardener at the Mariners Home. Frank worked as a fitter at Tate & Lyle. I remember Uncle Frank taking me around lots of the side shows, including the museum of freaks with the two-headed giant, winged cats, the man with eight fingers. In the 60s Blackpool was wild a real adventure for a teenager.

The poem below taken from the internet, author unknown.
Remember those days of Azetec bars,
Matchbox, Corgi and dinky cars,
Four Feather Falls and Supercar,
Collecting caterpillars in a jam jar,
And summer holidays that were actually sunny,
The Sunday School treat, that was a joy,
Those glorious days when I was a boy.

Chapter 3 - My Neighborhood

View from the top of New Brighton Tower. Rowson Street in centre. My house 33 Field Road.

Aerial view in the 1970s of my flattened house, X marks the spot which is now the car park for the Field Road Health Centre.

Chapter 3 - My Neighborhood

I make no excuse for having two pages of illustrations concerning Field Road. I spent the first 21 years of my life living in this Road. The black arrow below indicates the direction that the photograph was taken.

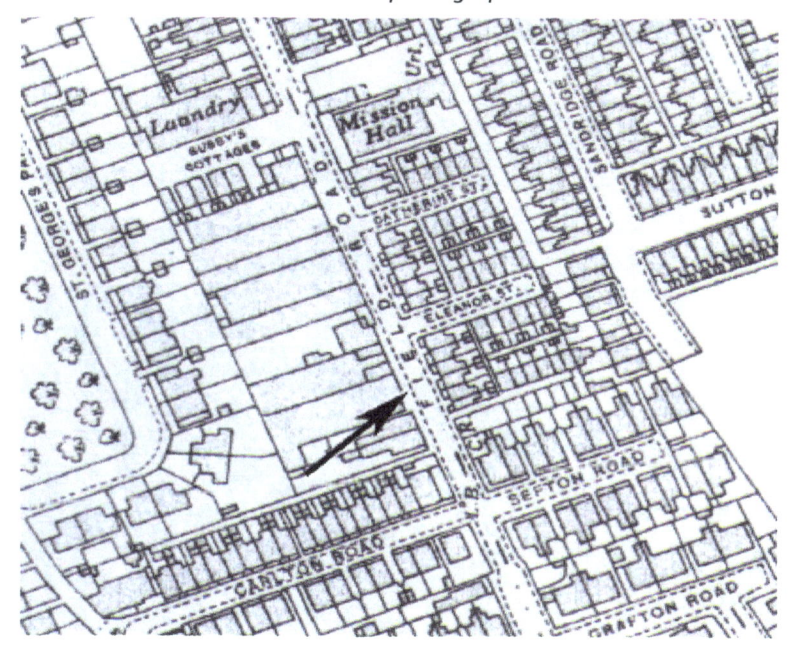

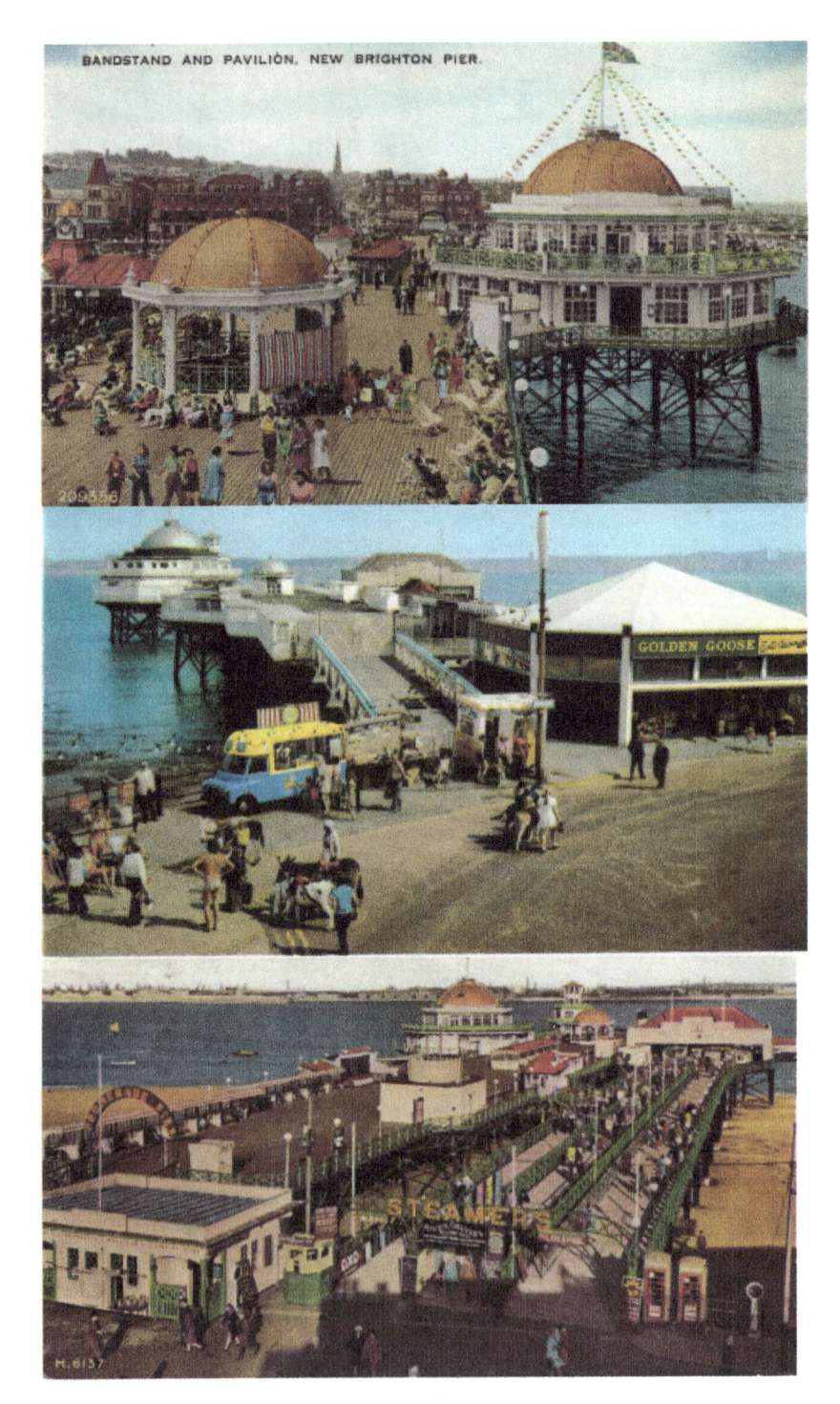

Chapter 3 - New Brighton in the 1960s

Chapter 3 - New Brighton in the 1960s

BOATING POOL AND PROMENADE, NEW BRIGHTON

Chapter 3 - The Tivoli

In January 1978 with a lump in my throat I witnessed the Tivoli being torn down. The very same magnificent structure was completed in Easter 1914 and designed with ornate gold and light-green rococo style mouldings around the balcony and walls, reminiscent of an Edwardian music hall. The outside was dominated by pagoda-shaped pyramids. In those halcyon days of the post-war period, the Tivoli, Tower Theatre, New Brighton Pier, Floral Pavilion and Winter Gardens, produced fantastic shows with the top entertainers of the day. Later in the 60s the Tudor club took up residence in the upstairs of the Tivoli.

Chapter 3 - Birkenhead Market

Birkenhead Market was a wonderland for a little boy going shopping with his mom. You could buy just about anything and all at bargain prices. My mom would smile as she told me about Bob Strong who sold his tonic in all weathers; he would exhibit his muscular torso which was living proof of the its attributions. A short distance away was Mr O'Toole with his thick black mop of hair and bushy moustache; he claimed his product could grow hair on just about anything. Alas they had long gone, to be replaced by another generation of larger than life characters.

The real market was outside where all the 'orators' where located. A truly amazing spectacle was the pottery man who could balance almost a complete dinner service on his arm; his pitch was to reduce the price as he added more plates. In between this class act he would juggle cups and saucers - anything to attract the shoppers attention." Not £5, Not £4, Not even £3! come on folks give me £1 and the lot's yours!" Hands would go up and his assistant would pass out the bargains.

But the star of the show had to be Eli, a bartering Del-boy type, with a fast patter and convincing manner. I could watch him for hours my mom would have to drag me away.

He would start by pulling some items out of a box – crockery, clothing, shoes, rugs- just about anything, and then give a price. With a constant stream of patter he would bring the price lower and lower until someone in the audience would shout " Er y'ar Eli" and then one of his lads would take the money and pass over the goods. If you weren't careful you got sucked up with the auction fever and bought something you really did not need. With his caustic and sometimes grim humour, he attracted larger audiences.

Birkenhead News Wednesday 13 November 1974
The alarm was raised at 8.40pm at Birkenhead market. Night-clubbers in the basement of the market complex were evacuated from the Hamilton Club. The Mersey Tunnel Control Room at the back of the market was also damaged.

News 27.8.77
Today marks the end of an era in the history of Birkenhead's 132-year-old market. Trading will take place for the last time in Hamilton Street before stallholders move into the town's new multi-million pound Grange precinct.

161

Chapter 3 - School Years

Vaughan Road Infants & Junior School
The school was built in 1908 and originally housed separate infant, junior, senior boys and senior girls schools, all housed in an Edwardian building which was designed to be formidable and austere. This is where you do as you are told or else. During the 1950s the school consisted of Vaughan Road Infants & Junior School both located on the ground floor.

New Brighton Secondary Modern was housed on the upper floor. Each school had a separate entrance and head teacher.
I went to Vaughan Road School and can still remember the smell of the floor polish and poster paints. We had a real sense of freedom as children, a rarity nowadays, and were allowed to roam the fairgrounds and Vale Park making our own entertainment. My recollections are somewhat limited and scrambled but here goes. As a pupil, one had no real option but to accept the school and its practices, but that does not stop me from writing about them after the passage of time. We were a scruffy lot, our mums did try their best but the art of playing made contact with the ground and dirt inevitable. Most of the children in my class wore hand-me-downs. I was a posh kid having new shoes and a school uniform that actually fit, but all my shirts always had the name Newton inside, and came via the lady my mum cleaned for in Portland Court. Her son went to a private school and all his clothes were passed down to me.
The day of the week could be calculated by examination of the tide mark on a child's neck or arms. Most only had a bath or good wash once a week. Our reward for good work was to have a star entered into your book. The

Chapter 3 - School Years

Vaughan Road Infants School. Large class of 38.

Roy

Vaughan Road Badge

Recorder Lesson

Typical Classroom

163

Chapter 3 - School Years

top mark was a gold star, then a silver and all the way down to a red star. These were also entered against your name on the house board so that everyone could see your progress.

In the juniors our favourite game was British Bulldog. Two individuals are chosen as bulldogs (after which the game is named). The bulldogs stand in the middle of the playground. All remaining players stand at one end of the school playground (home). The aim of the game is to run from one end of the school yard to the other without being caught by the bulldogs. When a player is caught, they are bounced up and down three times before becoming a bulldog themselves. The winner is the last player who is free, usually the school bully. Because of health and safety laws and regulations this traditional game has now been banned. It was too much fun anyway. Along with conkers and marbles.

I remember Mr Eyre, the headmaster and other teachers - Mr Halfpenny, Mr Smith, Mr Waugh, and Mr Curry.

I remember learning how to play chess at school, which gave me many hours of enjoyment in later life.

In those days polio and TB were a real threat; polio reached epidemic levels in 1947 with nearly 8000 cases. Hospital wards were filled with rows of patients encased in iron lungs, mechanically keeping them alive. David Simon was struck down with polio. It almost killed him, leaving his leg weak on his left side and he was obliged to wear a calliper.

His disability was to shape his school life; his determination, was something I will always remember.

We became good friends in school. His humour and wit carried him through his ordeal. I just wonder what became of him.

We used to spend all our money on football cards found in bubble gum. A thin slice of gum covered in a white powder had the best smell in the world. We would swap our duplicates at school putting the cards into football teams or arranging them in order of our favourite players. Mum would also collect the cards in Typhoo Tea for me.

I had my spud gun confiscated at school, to the relief of my mother who was cheesed off with the numerous holes in her potatoes.

On reflection I had a terrible memory for most things. I rarely forgot anything that had passed by my eyes, but didn't remember any sounds or words that went through my ears, especially spoken by my teachers.

With a pocket full of dried peas as ammunition for my pea shooter, I felt indestructible. Nowadays it would be a Nintendo DS with a fist full of games. How things have changed. And as for the girls I fancied, in most cases it was not reciprocal. We always passed on notes to the girls especially in class when the teacher was not looking. Sue once wrote:

"I think you're really nice!"

I replied "Can I see you after skool" [sic]

But I didn't have the courage to send the note.

Chapter 3 - School Years

I didn't quite know what it meant but it seemed something really good at the time and definitely worth hiding under my bedroom carpet away from my mum.

In our school the boys did not play with the girls. If you did you would be branded a sissy.

I remember having to participate in the Gay Gordon's and actually having to dance with the girls, and the teacher saying:

"It's one, two, three, four, link arms. And away we go" followed by...

"Right hands joined over her shoulder (boy's arm behind her back) and left hands joined in front, walk forward four steps starting on the right foot and move off sharply. Dutton link arms properly!"

The tune seemed to progress to:

Aunty Mary had a Canary up the leg of her draws.

The kids would all join in the vocals to numerous giggles and merriment. "Shut up" and .....

"Its one, two, three". To get the team back into synchronised dancing. Each person was invited to select a partner but this never happened voluntarily so the teacher selected for you. Thus it was the luck of the draw who you got as a partner. I was quite tall so always seemed to be paired off with Judith Briley who was even taller than me.

The teacher had an old 78rpm record on a turntable that defied the concept of centrifugal force with the needle jumping up intermittently, causing a slight interruption to the Kenny Thomson Scottish Dance Band rendition of this popular tune. It was always a mystery to me why we bothered; we always crashed into the couple in front. The teacher got agitated. We normally ended up with lines, and no one was talking to each other. But all was not lost. With the insistence of my mother, I then went on to finalise my dancing prowess at Greenbank Dance Studios.

We all received free milk and sometimes in the winter it was frozen so we put the milk crates near the radiators to defrost.

We had a huge blackboard at the front of the classroom, it was quite a messy operation for the teachers. They were always dusting themselves down from the chalk dust. All the work revolved around this, and we had to make notes using ink pens. Our desks were from the Victorian era with loads of old chewing gum stuck underneath and a multitude of names, dates, love hearts and slogans engraved into the wood. We did reading, writing and arithmetic. - the three Rs - but there were no calculators. You learnt your times table and we had an abacus in the classroom.

The nit nurse came round at frequent intervals (NItty Nora) and if you had an infestation you had your head shaved and stank of DDT.

The teachers demanded respect and got it! The headmaster was a figure of authority and being sent to his office was scary, and would involve physical punishment. It was during this period that I first started to hang around with Rodney Upton and we sat close to each other in our class

Chapter 3 - School Years

room. Looks could be deceptive because Rodney was probably the brightest in the class but the scruffiest looking. I went home with him on several occasions and would chat with his dad, Frank, about coins. Frank Upton was a wiry old customer and I have never seen him without his flat cap and with a large collection of antiques and coins. His home was more like an Aladdin's Cave.

Leaning over during one of our lessons Rodney whispered in my ear "Roy, why don't you come down tomorrow and give me a hand to bait up my lay line. You'll have to get up early". I nodded in agreement. The idea was to lay a line between two poles with hooks attached, usually across a gully, to bag a few plaice. We had to return promptly after the tide receded to gather our catch before the sea gulls devoured the lot!

I now had the difficult task of explaining to my parents why I wanted to get up early. I managed to persuade them, and with a pair of Wellington boots in my bag, off I went to hopefully catch our dinner. Arriving at Rodney's home in Seymour Street, I was welcomed at the door by Frank. "Come in lad, Rodney will be out in a minute. Remember to watch out for the tides. You'll have to a get a move on. The tide is on the way out now as I speak." Violent coughing followed this comment because poor old Frank suffered from asthma.

The Uptons had been a feature down on the beach at New Brighton for many years with their donkeys and beach combing. Frank could be found most days under the pier looking in the pools for coins and other valuables that had been dropped through the walkway by the holiday-makers. With an infinite knowledge of the area and the tides, he had certainly made this venture into a worthwhile occupation. Frank had told me about the rarest penny of them all, and it was my main dream to find a 1933 penny which would have allowed me to retire aged 11.

While we were waiting for the tide to go out, we couldn't resist skimming stones. There's nothing I don't know about stone skimming. I could select a stone that would guarantee five or six bounces off the surface.

At long last we could see the top of the lay line in the distance and the race was on to beat the seagulls. Rodney raced ahead and I followed. Pausing to get my breath, I stepped back and sank! Not just a little sink, but a damn great big sink; past my welly tops, and above my knees. Swearing from the blasphemer's book of basic swear words, quite limited because of my young age, I lost my balance and fell forwards. My legs couldn't move and I had to use my hands to break my fall! So there I was on all fours, covered from head to toe in mud. My wellies were full of mud and sea water. I risked a dodgy move with my left leg and tried to lift it out of the mud. A really bad move! Out my leg came, minus the welly! I fell back and ended up lying on the mud!

By this time Rodney had seen my predicament. I was well and truly stuck, and shaking his head he produced a scornful look,

Chapter 3 - School Years

"Well, there goes the catch!"
As he outstretched his hand to pull me out of my tomb, the mud just kept trying to suck me back in. I got out and had lost one of my wellies in the black gooey mud.
Rodney laughed and said, " Looks like the mud got a trophy."
It was a disaster. I made my way home! Needless to say I was never invited on another fishing expedition. My mother was not best pleased, so it was an early night for me.
My very first date happened in the Junior School when I managed to

pluck up enough courage to ask a slim young lady out. Her dad was Cyril Fletcher who was the owner of the Kentucky Derby, in the Tower Grounds; he also compared a very popular Radio Show. I was invited to their home for tea. I could not understand why I had to use my pocket money to buy the girl a box of Cadbury's Milk Tray - this was at my mother's bequest. It just seemed a total waste of money, and I was not even going to eat the contents. Several times we visited her dad's enterprise; I did manage a few free goes of throwing the balls into the holes. The higher the score, the faster the horse got to the finish line. The venture must have been a success as they had a nice house in Vaughan Road.
Finally, what were those round triangular things made of folded paper with writing on that the girls stuck their fingers into and moved about and asked questions? At this stage in life, the Japanese and Chinese were not clever enough to have invented electronic games. So for the girls it was tops and whips, and hop scotch, with conkers, marbles, and climbing trees for the boys.
I was lucky I did not get introduced to corporal punishment at this early age; I had to wait until Thorp got his hands on me. But David Lawton was not so lucky; on the 31st May 1956 John Dalby, John Ricketts, Jacob Ryan

Chapter 3 - School Years

and David Lawton were all caned for climbing trees in Vale Park out of school hours. Shown below is a copy of the Punishment Book for 1956.

David Lawton could have led a charmed life. He writes:
The head of Vaughan Road School in our day was Mr. Eyres. A Freemason of high order. How I got to know this, is that my father told me, as he was in the Prince Llewellyn lodge at Manor Road. I remember him coming to see my father when he came off his motorbike in the early sixties. I was gobsmacked when my father told me that Mr. Eyres had told him if he knew at the time that my dad was a Mason I would have passed my eleven plus!!!!' Now then, fix or no fix???

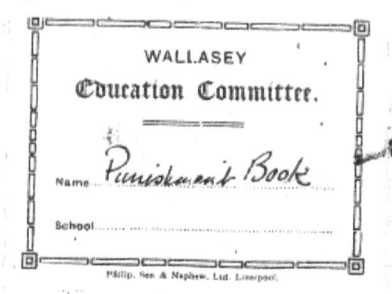

Chapter 3 - School Years

Mr Delamere and the class of Class 4c -1958
Back Row
1. Barry Thompson, 2. Jeffery Robinson, 3. David Symes, 4. Malcolm Andrews, 5. ? 6. ? 7.? 8. Charles Neal.
Middle Row
1. Malcolm Newton, 2.? 3.? 4.?5.? 6. Roy Dutton, 7. ? 8.? 9. Graham Baker, 10. Brian Fox
Front Row
1. Christine Todd, 2. Janet Neal,3. Barbara Whittaker,4. Pat ? 5. Eileen Radstock 6. Judeth Briley, 7. Roberta Smith, 8. ? 9. Sheila Atherton,10. Linda Clows,11. Norma Ball

Our form teacher was Mr Delamere a man of considerable charm, but slightly bereft in the looks department. His large nose took prominence on his face. His rugged complexion owed more to the fondness of alcohol than the pursuit of outdoor leisure activities. Wearing the standard teacher's uniform of the era, a herringbone jacket, leather patches on the elbows, corduroy trousers that resembled an accordion, and brown brogue shoes with their steel tips, you could hear him coming down the corridor a mile away. He always came into school smelling of beer. He either lived next door to a brewery or enjoyed a drop of the amber nectar. His romance with Miss Booker was to be the talk of the school for a term or two. They were engaged whilst I was attending the school. Mr Delamere also collected stamps and encouraged the pupils to bring in their collections. I had been given a fine collection of early Victorian stamps by an uncle. When I took them into school to show Mr Delamere, his eyes lit up.
"Well well well, lots of swaps here, you lucky boy."
He had his swap album with large multicoloured stamps from all sorts of exotic places that not even the geography teacher had heard of, so he picked out my gems with his tweezers and I was invited to select from his swap collection. It was only years later that I was to discover these stamps

were totally worthless.
We were informed that the romance started when Mr Delamere, on entering Miss Booker's class room, found her standing on a chair disconcerted about a mouse that had scurried past her. Our gallant form teacher found a box and with the help of a brush rendered the rodent temporarily unconscious. Both teachers took the rodent to Vale Park during their tea break. Miss Booker's admiration for our gallant Mr Delamere apparently came to light in the park. The romance was born and the subsequent engagement which was announced at morning assembly. Mr Delamere was also an arts teacher, so I am sure that they could spend their married life sketching one another. It was school policy that once they married one of them would have to leave.

In 1963 the senior children moved to other premises and in 1971 the junior and infant children were brought together as a single school with one head teacher.

New Brighton Secondary Modern
If you failed the eleven-plus you moved to new heights in your academic career by moving upstairs to New Brighton Secondary Modern.

Woodwork lessons were carried out at Field Road Technical College, while the metalwork and domestic science activities were performed at Laburnum Road in an old prefab building. The sports field at Withens Lane was used for football, cricket and field events, while the Guinea Gap Baths operated our weekly swimming lessons.

The 1944 Education Act created a system in which children were tested and streamed at the age of eleven. Pupils were allocated to a school according to their performance in the eleven-plus exam; a pass resulted in a grammar school or technical school education and a failure in a secondary modern school education.

I remember sitting the eleven plus exam. We first took the exam called the 'Review' which you had to pass in order to sit for the scholarship. I can remember thinking to myself, I've never done sums like these before, so the inevitable happened; relegation to the second division.

The assembly at the start of the school day set the tone for the day's activities. When all the boys and girls were assembled having marched into the hall in single file, class by class, like the contents of an endless toothpaste tube, the headmaster led the school in a couple of hymns accompanied by Miss Watson on the piano. A classroom was set aside for the individuals that were not of the Christian faith, containing a couple of Jewish students and an Indian lad who was a Parsee, (they apparently have a religious connection with fire.) So this was an automatic no no, on account of the risk to the school. The teachers in the main were all middle class - know more; earn more; live in a nicer area types. They had a job for life and tended to set a low priority for transferring their knowledge to their pupils, sometimes under a full security clampdown, on a need to know basis only. "Dutton, shut up" seemed to ring around my ears. They had mastered the ability to make their specialised subject as uninteresting as possible. I was told many, many times that this "will be the best years of your life" and this was in the days of corporal punishment, bullying, and uninspired teaching. They must have been joking!

It was around this time that my father had become a little disenchanted by my school reports. I had explained that it was very difficult to get A and Bs and that most of us only got a C or a D. The comments, also from the teachers, were not terribly helpful with "Could try harder," "Does not pay attention" etc. In those days parents were never invited to the school to visit the teachers for a progress report. The teachers knew best, and any constructive comments from parents, were just not required. So my father decided something had to be done. An old friend, Charles Draper who lived in Kingsway, in Wallasey, and just happened to be a teacher, was contacted. Each Sunday morning at 11.00am, I would travel down to his home for tuition. Anything I did not understand from school would be explained, together with homework set. This was the catalyst for a remarkable recovery in my intellectual ability. I was even selected to represent Atherton House in the school quiz. Mr and Mrs Draper's house was a new experience for me; full to the gunnels with books but quite sparse in the furniture department. With two sons, one training to be a doctor and the other in the 6th form of a Grammar school, this environment certainly seemed to have paid off.

Our teachers were a mixed bunch; some good, some bad and others just non- descript. Mr Moscroft played rugby and tended to be injured a lot. He limped around the school, frightening pupils with his black eyes. When his mouth did allow words to flow from it, it was usually English literature. I can still recite parts of *The Tempest*, so something must have worked. With a deeply buried sense of humour, he could be encouraged to perform if he had a straight man with him. Henry Owl quite often supplied the necessary dead-pan attitude which I believe came naturally. Using a multitude of complicated words he sounded more like an old time music hall compere.

Mr Stokes, our spectacled music teacher, was a man of quite considerable girth. He wore his hair short, but still had sufficient hair to enhance its appearance with a liberal application of Brylcream which allowed the maximum solar reflections possible. Very smart in appearance, it was if he had stepped straight out of Burtons, the tailor's shop window. Ex army Physical Training Instructor (PTI) and bandsman, on occasions he must

have thought he was back in the military as he was prone to bully his charges. Dave Lawton remembers one particular incident that is engraved in his memory.
Stokes was a bully, he kicked my backside all the way up the stairs to Mr. Thorpe's study, pushed me in and ordered him to cane me till I cried!! This I wouldn't do, and, much to his disgust, (after I had received six of the best) Thorpe sent me to my class. Outside his room was Timmy Jarman waiting for punishment who I winked and grinned at. He had heard it all. Later in the day we had Stokes for music and he tried to humiliate me by saying to the class that he had me beaten till I cried. I stood up and called him a liar and so did Timmy. I thought he was going to kill us, but he walked out and Thorpe came back in and finished off the lesson. Needless to say he never got to me again!!

The photograph above shows Mr Stokes co-ordinating the activities of the school choir. Next to him Dave Lawton, Lennie Hardman, then Allen Green. Top right of the lads is Lennie Smith. Third row down with the open neck shirt is John Ricketts. Next row extreme left is David Allen. Front row with open shirt, second from the girls is Martin Goodwin and in front of him is Tony Betteridge. The other lad at the left of the front row is possibly Donald Speakman.

Dave Lawton was in the Emmanuel Church choir, along with Charlie Neal and Sid Evans. Stokes found out Dave was head boy in the choir and bullied him to take part in the school choir.

The event took place at the Oldershaw School. Allen Green, Lennie Hardman and Dave Lawton sang 'Bambino', then Lennie Smith and Tony Bettrige played harmonicas. The performance was much appreciated and the choir came second in the schools competition.

At the slightest excuse Stokes would play his trumpet. The hairs on the

Chapter 3 - School Years

back of my neck still stand up when I hear *Trumpet Voluntary*. Sometimes the class would accompany him on the recorder, all playing out of tune and in a different key. The delights of the recorder will always stay with me, especially the taste and smell of the Dettol that the instruments had been standing in. Still anything had to be better than the triangle.

Mr Prydderch (Jones the slipper), our physical education (PE) teacher, of Welsh origin, with an accent to suit, had a long forehead and looked like a typical military man; erect, with the obligatory moustache. He had a long body and short legs, and really did not look the part in his white shorts, running around. He told us on more than one occasion.

"That this was a characteristic of a true Welsh miner."

It just a shame he did not stay down the mines. To supplement his physical prowess, his regular use of the plimsoll on people's rear ends had developed into an art form. It was probably a fetish of his, to request the disobedient pupil to go to the changing room and select one of the plimsolls from the school supply. He would then request the culprit to bend over and he would administered the punishment in front of the whole class. To add to the excitement of our cross country runs, he would encourage the laggards to get a move on by the application of the plimsoll across their backsides. He had been known to throw chalk and blackboard dusters at inattentive pupils. A cursory glance out of the window to watch the girls playing netball in their gym knickers could invite an artillery barrage. In all a most unusual character, who would probably be locked up today.

Miss Watson was the girl's Head Mistress. She taught religious education (RE). A middle-aged lady with a well- developed gravity- inflicted bosom, a faint moustache which graced her upper lip and a mole with the obligatory hair growing in the centre situated centrally on her right cheek, she was devoid of all sense of humour or any pretensions of femininity. A portly lady who always seemed to wear drab colours, she would not tolerate any familiarity from the boys towards her girls, any attempt at levity on my part was sharply nipped in the bud. She had a thinly disguised hostility to any of the male gender. She was in charge of the girl's corporal punishment and discipline and as an encore would gladly take the ruler to your knuckles if unruliness or disobedience prevailed. In the playground when the bell rang we all had to line up.

A young Miss Watson

Her specialty was a slap on the back of the legs if your leg was not in line with the others: a charming lady best suited to a position in an SS barracks. One particular event Dave Lawton remembers:

Miss Watson had a twitch at the side of her mouth, Zena Pemberton (sister of Warren Pemberton, drummer in the Undertakers) was pulled out of class by her. Miss Watson cut a comical figure, and her stress level seemed to increase

Chapter 3 - School Years

the frequency of the twitch. Zena had to hold her top lip over her bottom lip with her hand while being told off, to prevent herself from laughing.
"Take your hand away from your mouth at once,
What was that? Don't you dare mumble at me"
So taking her hand away, she burst out laughing along with the whole class. Mrs Watson proceeded to slap the back of her legs. Oh happy days.

Mr Price was deputy headmaster and also taught maths, which to be perfectly honest was not the easiest subject to teach, but I feel his lessons left a lot to be desired. At the time he was having problems with his eyes, and had to undergo some surgery, which I am sure did have a bearing on his teaching.

Miss Beasley, our games and history teacher, had the testosterone of all the adolescent males in the class working overtime. She wore glasses and was well endowed in the top part of her anatomy department. With a soft and intensely erotic voice she would whisper the words in soft tones. She must have been the voice coach for Mae West.

I was in continually tormented by Angus McClean who always came top in the art lesson: I always came second. I could never knock him off his pedestal. One particular painting of an underwater submarine based on *20,000 Leagues under the Sea* had been traced from the cinema advertisement in the *Wallasey News*. Using the only material I could find in the school, namely the Izal medicated toilet tissue, I managed to trace the image onto my drawing paper, then coloured it in: job done!

The art work was given to Miss Booker "Very good Dutton" she said in an enthusiastic voice, only to take a closer look when a whiff of medication drifted under her nose. Having a soft and whispery type of voice she suggested that something was wrong with my masterpiece.

"You were told not to trace your work; it was supposed to be original. Off with you!" Result no marks. I could never understand why such a tissue was used, possibly the smooth and glass texture would discourage children from using too much. On the positive side you can make a kazoo out of a sheet of Izal and a comb, and it could also be used as tracing paper by impoverished artists such as me.

I was the rubber monitor and had the unenviable task of collecting in thirty-two rubbers at the end of the art class. The teacher was first out going to her next lesson, so all the rubbers were thrown at me, bouncing off the walls and ceiling to the great amusement of the other pupils. So as a result I was always late for the following lesson. We were under strict instructions not to run whilst in the school. Nick, our attentive headmaster, would linger in an alcove just like a traffic cop waiting for a speeding motorist. If you were late for the next lesson, you would get detention and lines. A hundred lines "I should not be late for my next lesson". Most small infringements of the rules necessitated lines or detention. But if you were caught red-handed doing something really naughty like smoking or

Chapter 3 - School Years

truancy or being late for school, then it was corporal punishment.
Our headmaster was Mr Thorpe. A strict disciplinarian and a firm believer in corporal punishment for naughty boys!
He was fondly known as Nick (as in the devil, Old Nick). An invitation "to see the headmaster" usually meant six of the best. On entering his study, past the school secretary's office, a knock on the door produced two responses, - Wait or Enter. At one side of the fireplace stood a bookcase with a section to hold his gown and mortar board, and on the other side, a number of canes of varied thicknesses and pliability, each hanging on a separate hook. After a thorough dressing down, he normally ended with:
"This will hurt me more than it hurts you."
I would think, bloody fool how does he work that out.
The choice of hand or backside seemed to depend on his mode.
He then walked around me in his robes like some sort of horrible circling bat, looking me up and down.
"Boy! Raise your hand in front of you."
A suitable cane was selected and he gave it several swishes in the air. Quite often he would position the hand by using the cane as a remote extension of his hand, and once happy that the hand was in the correct position and raising the cane above his head, the necessary punishment was inflicted. The deed had to be witnessed and the punishment entered into a book. I often wondered about the secretary outside; she must have been able to hear the thwack of the cane all day everyday. Was she in sympathy with the poor victim and cringe from every stroke received or did she think they deserved everything they got? She probably just switched off, but an interesting thought all the same. I would try not to give the sadist the satisfaction of a yell or ouch. I just looked away, similar to having an injection. I also saved my tears for on the way back to the class room. It was a measure of pride to show the red marks, and say "It didn't hurt anyway", to my mates and the inquisitive gathering around at lunch time, shaking the hand profusely seemed to remove the tingle.
I am sure some teachers administered cane, slipper or ruler more for their own satisfaction than as an appropriate punishment. What we needed was love and care especially in the pre-teen years, with punishment as a very last resort. I don't think the punishments did me any harm. It certainly helped to instil respect and order into what could be a chaotic upbringing for some individuals. The following is an account of one particular punishment inflicted on Dave Lawton;
I remember when I was being held prostrate over Nick's desk and being held down by Mr.Price (his deputy) looking at his secretary while he caned me. I remember my Mum crying when she saw my backside after a thrashing by him. She was going to go to school to see him over it.

Mr Thorpe

Chapter 3 - School Years

I had to put a stop to that, as it would have ruined my street cred. I deserved all the punishment I received. I did not find him a bully or sadistic. It never did me any harm. In fact looking back it did me some good as it taught me respect.

Not all of the teachers were misfits. We did have some teachers worthy of praise within these pages.

Mrs McCabe was a funny old stick. She looked like Queen Elizabeth the First with her hair and pale white face make-up, black eyeliner and red lips, but that made our history lesson a bit more entertaining. She was very strict but a fair teacher.

But the teacher I remember most vividly belonged to a younger generation - Mr Brian Foster, our metalwork teacher who was a real hard-working professional. He organised the Mountaineering and Touring Club (M.T.C) with trips all over the country including the Peak District, Lake District, and Snowdonia. The group would stay in Youth Hostels. He even organised skiing holidays abroad. He gave me such a love of the outdoors that I have been hooked ever since.

He dedicated many hours of his own time in helping organise school out-

**Headline in the *Wallasey News* dated Saturday 23 April 1960.
Schoolboy mountaineers off to Switzerland**

ings. He was stationed for most of the time at Ladurnum Road, where the girls had their domestic science classes. In those days, half a day was dedicated to swimming, metalwork, woodwork, religious instruction and PE, all of which would be ideal if your vocation in life was a priest living on a remote island. You could build your own church and would not be too concerned if your canoe sunk. No need for languages or anything useful. Anyway back to Mr Foster who taught metalwork one afternoon a week. He filmed many of the school outings, and had parent evenings to show off the 8 mm films. Many photographs were taken. It was a treasure trove

Chapter 3 - School Years

of nostalgia, and I did eventually locate some of the archive.
I went on many different M.T.C trips, and I always seemed to end up

**Headline in the *Wallasey News* Saturday 20th August 1960
New Brighton Secondary Modern School Mountaineering and
Touring Club, with B.J.S.Foster on an expedition to Southern
Ireland. They christened a peak in Macgillycuddy's Reeks.**

injured. My first trip was to North Wales when I managed to slip off a rock whilst in the process of climbing over a fence. My leg got caught on some barbed wire resulting in group leader Bernard Dabner having to take me to the hospital in Mold for 13 stitches. My next disaster could have changed my life forever. We went on a week's Youth Hostelling tour to the Isle of Man. On the third day whilst staying at a hostel in Douglas, I heard a rustle in a tree, looked up and bang! - something hit me in my eye. I panicked and with blood all over my face was taken into the hostel. One of the boys had made a spear with a sharpened end, and had thrown it into the tree to try and dislodge a bird's nest. I was to find out later after three stitches in my eyelid that the tip of the spear had only just missed my eye ball. So returning home with a black eye and a stitched eye lid my father announced:
"You're not going on any more trips with the school."
"But Dad, it was an accident," came my reply.
"That's it. Final. No more trips."
It was to take almost 12 months before I managed to persuade my parents to let me go on a trip to Cornwall on the 4th August 1962. I managed to break the jinks and a good time was had by all.
On Thursday afternoons, the girls of our class would be out of the way taking domestic science (learning the important tasks in life to be like their mums; cooking, ironing and cleaning up after us lazy lot).
Mr Bradshaw was our woodwork teacher. He was firm but fair, with a very

177

Chapter 3 - School Years

dry sense of humour, and was always cracking jokes as well as possessing the art of information transfer.

"Get plennyer beeswax on it lad" was one of his favourite quips.

He explained how to plane the wood and how to use the saw whether it be circular, band or tenon. He respected his pupils and spoke softly and if you misbehaved he had a wonderful sarcasm that would put you in your place without even raising his voice. We made all sorts of mundane objects that were not very useful but took weeks of painstaking work. My final project at school was a wooden jewellery box. The four sides were joined by mortise and tenon joints, and the top and bottom were to be glued in place. I was halfway through eating an apple in class when Bradshaw spotted what I was doing. I was told to stop eating and put the apple down. When it was my turn to glue the top and bottom on my box, he got me to place the half-eaten apple inside. The following week we had to saw the box in half; the idea was that a thin liner would be fitted inside to complete the work of art. My box had a smelly mouldy apple inside, much to the amusement of the other members of the class.

Mr Henderson, our science teacher, was a real star in my eyes. He was very informative and knowledgeable, able to transfer his enthusiasm of his subject to his pupils - a rare attribute in our school. He also operated the after-school science club and he was the one who started my love affair with chemistry sets and making big bangs and smells.

From the Wallasey Message Board; Knowhere Guide, 2008 Dave Baker comments: *I went to Withensfield from 1965 to 1969, Mr, Burton and Mr Burgess were my form teachers. It was in the reign of Harry Burgen and Headmaster Thorpe. My friends at school were, Mike Molden, Les Cotterall, Dave Bird, Phil Robertson, Barry Lavercombe etc.*

With the MTC we went to Ireland cycling from Dublin to Belfast.

Anyone remember Mr Henderson, he swims with his wife at the baths in West Kirby, he is very frail but manages quite a few lengths!

The Guinea Gap baths was the venue of our weekly swimming lesson, the high point of the trip was the cake shop before we got on the bus back to school. There were Chelsea Buns and other sticky things. I always remember my favourite was buying a lump of Wet Nellie or Nelson Cake if you want the posh title. This was a layer of pastry spread with jam then covered with pieces of cake and biscuit and soaked in a sort of custard made with sweet condensed milk. It was just what I needed after an afternoon swim.

On my way to school I always called into the home of Graham Baker, one of my school mates. We would walk down to the school together. In the winter we quite often walked to school in a pea-souper; a lethal mixture of fog, smoke and other pollutants. In the days before central heating, coal was the only way to heat your home and this produced smog which was

Chapter 3 - School Years

part of the British climate which was common in the 50s. Factories were also bellowing out black smoke. Looking down I could not see my feet. The dense fog seemed to blanket out all sound and if you put your finger up your nose it came out black. Mum gave me a scarf to wrap around my face as protection against the fog. The Great Smog of 1952 prompted the Government to introduce the 1956 Clean Air Act which introduced smoke controlled areas, and slowly the atmosphere became breathable again.

I was just fourteen in 1961, had recently become a teenager and was in love for the very first time. The apple of my eye was Penny Watkins, a girl in the same year, but a different class. The way she giggled touched my heart. Her cherry-red lips set my blood boiling and her movement was poetry-in-motion! I would have shared my last Everton mint, done her homework, carried her satchel, and played a tune on my comb with tracing paper; in fact I would have done anything to please this beautiful girl. I wanted to take her out, and walk hand in hand. But this was not to be; she was unapproachable. I was just too young and immature in her eyes. I would like to thank her for allowing a besotted teenager to be in the presence of an angel for those few short years. Our paths were to cross later in life but more on that later.

Mrs McCabe was in charge of the library and I was one of the chosen few appointed as a librarian. This involved wearing a badge of authority which gave you an air of importance. I had been a Milk Monitor in the Junior School so this was definitely a step in the right direction. This had to be the first step in the hierarchy of life. Other equally important tasks included Dinner Monitor, Window Monitor, and Pencil Monitor, responsible for sharpening pencils with a hand-cranked machine. These were all different forms of slave labour: why can't they open the windows themselves?

I was threatened with having my librarian badge removed for answering back. Mrs Gillespie, the dinner lady, had taken offence concerning my remarks about the walking salad or should I say caterpillar on my lettuce. She told Mrs McCabe that I was being cheeky and answering back; every imperfection with school dinners was taken as a personal insult, and who can forget rice pudding, jelly and custard, frogspawn (tapioca pudding) and semolina. If you had some spare pocket money left over, a childhood treat was a *Frozen Jubbly*, an orange drink, made into a huge ice lolly sold in a pyramid shaped carton, which the sweetshop owner had popped in the ice cream freezer, or black jacks and fruit sandwich chews-two for a penny - or penny arrow toffee bars, and wagon wheels (a chocolate coated biscuit) were other favourites. I nearly forgot bazooka Joe bubblegum with a little cartoon strip inside It's a miracle I still have a set of teeth.

The favourite place for a sly smoke was behind the toilet block. A packet of five "Domino" cigarette's cost six pence, or you could buy a single Woodbine for tuppence.

Chapter 3 - School Years

so corporal punishment was probably the only instant solution. Dave Lawton recounts:
Walked up the figure-of-eight and my mate Robin Bettridge fell off the top and landed on one of the cross-members. We were all pissed!! Luckily he only broke a couple of ribs.
Tried to get into the club next to the Travellers one Saturday night and in climbing over the back wall it collapsed and we went down with it. We all had brand new suits on which were a right mess!!! Yes, good old days, blackberry picking at the Red Noses, hedge cutting. Throwing bangers into the whist drives in the church hall with John Ricketts, sulphur bombs into the guides in the wooden hut to get chased by Miss Marsh. Throwing things at the park keeper in Vale Park and walking on the grass so he would chase us and most of all I got caught. I only realised why, when I was told my hair colour gave me away! I think it was a good job I joined the Royal Navy as it quietened me down a lot. Probably saved me from ending up in jail or the likes.
I remember getting the children's roundabout working at the bottom of the Tower grounds by pushing it around, and getting into the tunnel of Billy Mann's miniature railway and messing with his steam engine. Result,

a load of us all got caught and caned by Nick. Instant justice, no police. I shudder to think what would happen nowadays. I would probably have a police record by now.
My school bag had a *Ban the bomb* sign painted on the back; it was my one-man protest against the insanity of the atom bomb. It was bought from the Army and Navy Store in Birkenhead and was my pride and joy. With various other emblems and comments inked on the surface, it was to stand the test of time. The thick canvas bag contained all my school books, well worn and used. It was amazing to see inside the front cover the previous owner's name, some dated back before the war. In my final year I actually went into Mr Thorp's office with my mother for a careers

Chapter 3 - School Years

advice meeting. I was given a reference by the headmaster and told about job vacancies in the area suitable for school leavers. A job had come up in Strothers' record department in Liscard which he thought could be a possible career opportunity if I passed the interview. Luckily for me, my dad had other ideas. I left the school a lot more street-wise, but academically, not much better than when I entered. If I had not been tutored, then I would be making sandcastles now. Numerous governments keep changing the status of schools, Grant Maintained, Academies etc. No one seems to consider the obvious; education depends on the quality of teaching. Its as simple as that.

From an article in the *Wallasey News* dated the 6th April 1963.

The final speech day and prize-giving for New Brighton Secondary Modern took place at the Civic Hall on Tuesday. Its pupils will be transferred to the Liscard Secondary School, and the old building at Vaughan Road will become exclusively a junior school. Mr Thorpe informed the audience that the intake of pupils was falling, and that was the main reason for the school closure. He went on to lament:

"Nearly fifty years ago, on a bright summer's day at the beginning of a new school year, a small boy was taken by his mother to be enrolled by Mr Bardsley, the then headmaster of Vaughan Road School. I was that small boy. Hence, you can well imagine that this speech day and prize distribution, the last major function of its type before the school closes down at the end of this school year is in some ways for me a sad occasion".

I indirectly got a mention by Mr Thorpe in his speech, not about the caning but the fact that "The year 1961-62 had been the most successful year in the history of the school from an academic viewpoint. Fifty-two pupils had been entered for the Wallasey Secondary Schools Certificate of Education and 46 had gained their certificates. Of these, 26 passed in six or more optional subjects, including eight who had passed in nine subjects the maximum number possible. I was in the latter group. On leaving school I was elated with my achievement; the world was now my oyster, nothing could hold me back.

I was to find out a little later that my academic qualifications were just marginally better than a swimming certificate. No one had heard of this certificate so it was back to the drawing board. The newspaper article continues: A highlight of the evening was the excellent singing of a mixed choir of about 50 voices comprising pupils, teachers and parents. They were accompanied by a group of instrumentalists including the school's own recorder players and led by their music master, Mr. J.C. Stokes, on the trumpet. Need I say anymore!

Note: Liscard Secondary Modern was also called Manor Road School then renamed Withensfield Secondary. In 1965 Mr Thorpe was the Headmaster and Mr Burger was Deputy Head.

Chapter 3 - School Years

Another view of the Tower Grounds, showing the side of the Gost Train.

Things my Mum said:
Don't pull funny faces or you'll stick like it.
Fur coat: No knickers! or Mutton dressed as lamb!
Wait till your father gets home!
Do that again, and I'll make you smile on the other side of your face!
If you pick your nose, your head will cave in.
Crusts of bread will make your hair curly.
She has a mouth like the Mersey tunnel.
If you fall off that wall and break your legs, don't come running to me!

Quarry Bowling Green, Rowson Street, New Brighton. Spent many happy hours playing cowboys and Indians. Also on the swings out of shot.

The Big Bang

My introduction to the delights of chemistry came via a Christmas present of a Merit Chemistry Set. On the box it promised a life-changing experience. This I was to discover later may have been a little closer to the truth than I could have ever imagined. Making crystals and stink bombs just whetted my appetite. It was about this time that Mr Henderson started his science club at school, with access to all the schools chemicals and equipment. My fascination with loud bangs and flashes seemed to stem from this time. My birthday was to be a turning point in my endeavours. Mrs Leary-Shaw, the lady my Mum cleaned for in Portland Court, asked my mum what would I like for a present. I ended up giving her a shopping list of chemicals and apparatus I needed. She even went over to Oakes Eddon in Liverpool and purchased the lot. She was a kind lady, who was to be my saviour, although I was not to know it at the time. After experimenting with gunpowder, a much simpler approach was found using sodium chlorate (weed killer). Berriman's the local ironmonger had unlimited quantities of the powder. The long school holiday allowed unlimited access to a potential launch site-namely my back yard, while both my parents were at work. With some eager helpers including Billy Price a few years older than me, Robert Bailey and Alan Jackson, and a couple the younger lads, I had a reliable team of helpers. Mixing the chemicals could be quite scary but it was vital that the chemicals were ground to a fine powder. The team gathered for our first public demonstration. Having mixed equal parts of sugar and weedkiller, a small amount of the mixture was placed on a brick. I then raised a hammer and hit the mixture with as much force as I could muster. Bang! All the pigeons on the roof opposite went into orbit. Billy immediately requested we do it again but with a bigger heap of the chemical. I obliged only this time the bang and force was unbelievable because the

Chapter 3 - The Big Bang

hammer flew out of my hand and bounced off a couple of walls before hitting Billy on the head. The screams were unmerciful as the blood poured from his wound he immediately ran out of the yard holding his handkerchief over the wound doing about 50 miles per hour towards to his house in Carlton Road. At almost the same time a very exited guy that owned the pigeons opposite could be seen standing on his wall with a red face and a look of rage on his face shouting "Which bloody idiot frightened my pigeons?" and waving a fist in our direction. The pigeons had taken off with such speed that numerous feathers and droppings were floating down from high. It was time to exit and regroup.

It had taken well over a week for things to settle down. Luckily Billy had not spilt the beans and the guy with the pigeons had disappeared. The remainder of the team were ready for more excitement. Robert went around to Berriman's for a bag of weedkiller.

Berriman's the ironmongers had a high ceiling and behind the counter the wall had drawers up to the ceiling. The labels showed all types of screws, nuts and nails. Neat racks held punches, bradawls, saws, drills in all sizes, bolts fixed in rows, some fat as thumbs, some thin as wire, and there were tubs of putty, and paint lots of paint - and always a smell of paraffin. The two brothers that owned the Aladdin's cave were dressed in long brown coats and if a few bob crossed their palm, they fetched exactly the thing you wanted. They had just about everything. They had supplied many parts for my first independent means of transport- my home- made go-cart; just a few planks, four wheels, the front ones swivelling. They supplied my weedkiller for some of the biggest bangs Field Road had heard since the Blitz. and the copper tube for my home-made guns.and the broom handle that fitted my tea chest for our first skiffle group. In fact everything that made my dreams into reality came from Berrimans. They worked as a team to locate any obscure part or suggest an alternative. If synchronised ironmongery was an event in the Olympic games, they would have won hands down.

Anyway back to bomb-making. Billy who had a bandage on his head attended anyway. Alan and a couple of the younger fraternity were 'yes men', constantly echoing him and reinforcing his comments. 'Opinion conformity' is what psychologists call it. I had promised the team a real gun this time. My idea was a copper tube hammered over at one end, with a hole drilled to facilitate a fuse, a ball bearing that fitted neatly into the tube on top of the weedkiller and a wad of cotton wool to hold everything in position.

Billy being the eldest took charge of the operation and instructed everyone that after the fuse was lit, we were all to retire to the bunker meaning the outside khazi (toilet). He did not want any recurrence of the last fiasco. The first couple of attempts at lighting the fuse failed, but eventually through sheer persistence the fuse ignited. We ran into the

Chapter 3 - The Big Bang

bunker, Bang! The ball bearing shot out of the tube straight through the back door. If anyone had been passing on the other side, I would be doing a life sentence now. The copper tube took off in the opposite direction bouncing off a couple of walls before it came to rest. Billy was the first out and pronounced the firing a complete success and he then proceeded to pick up the tube, which was red-hot. Another blood-curling yell and the tube was thrown back on the floor, as he legged it off home.

I reverted back to some solo experiments in the back bedroom. Robert and I had set up communications between our two bedrooms by a wire and morse code signalling that went over the roof of Mr and Mrs Rice's house at No 31 and poor old demented Miss Gregory at No 29 all the way to Robert's house at No 27. I think we only added to Miss Gregory problems as she had already accused Robert of stealing all her belongings, so you could add the slates on the roof to that accusation, due to the noises we made trying to get the wire in her gutter. The poor soul was suffering from dementia.

The next logical stage of the operations was a rocket. The types of explosives used to date were ideal for making bombs, but unless you wanted the rocket to blow up on take off, something else was needed. We needed a slower-burning fuel. Back to experimenting with gunpowder. The proportions of the sulphur, charcoal and potassium nitrate were critical along with the mixing process, but at long last the correct formula was found. A suitable aluminium tube was found, courtesy of Mr Foster's metalwork class at school I was able to attach the fins. It was painted the same colour as Blue Streak which had been a British ballistic missile designed in 1955. The launch site was selected with care because it could not be in a built-up area. New Brighton Beach was ideal. It took us about 20 minutes to transport the rocket to the launch site. Billy had declined the offer of igniting the rocket so I was left with the task. The erect rocket really looked the part; the only problem was no cover on the open shore. The fuse was lit, smoke and flames bellowed out of the rear end and the rocket fell on its side and spun around in all directions scattering the team. It was a complete disaster.

Back to the drawing board. I was now experimenting with nitro-type explosives at one stage I managed to burn my hands from the fumes of the nitric acid; they just turned yellow. I was very lucky to get them under a tap quickly. One of my experiments went terribly wrong the house was filled with toxic fumes. My father intervened. The lot was put in the bin chemicals, apparatus, notes - and I was read the riot act.

On reflection it was probably best while we still had a row of terraced houses standing.

I then moved on from the practical aspects of space travel to the theory with the formation of the Wirral Astronomical Society.

Chapter 3 - Buried Treasure

In the last year of school, one of my friends brought in a treasure map. His uncle had given him an old book that was falling apart, and inside it contained this map. My imagination ran wild; I was thinking of Squire Trelawney and Jim Hawkins who found Flint's treasure by using a similar map. Remember the story of *Treasure Island* by Robert Louis Stevenson. All I had to do was organise a suitable swap, and the map was mine. It was not quite that simple and protracted negotiations followed because of another interested party in the name of Fred and the price escalated. But eventually I became its new owner; it took half a dozen American comic books *The Adventures of Superman*, and half a crown to seal the deal. Several pages of hand-written notes accompanied the map, which listed his finds including coins and other artefacts and more importantly the locations. It also included a complicated chart of tides and dates, which to my disappointment was completely out-of-date. My plan was to use my home-made metal detector to find the rest of the missing treasure. His uncle had found the treasure by eyesight alone, so just think what I could find with a metal detector. From the information it was vital that the expedition went out at low tide, in fact a neap tide being the best time to explore the site. The Wirral Astronomical Society had already visited the Institute of Oceanographic Science, so I already had a contact. It only needed a short phone call to find out the most suitable dates and times for our treasure hunt to begin. A neap tide comes twice a month, in the first and third quarters of the moon.
I had waited in anticipation for the day to arrive. My headphones, batteries, large copper coil and electronic circuit were all placed securely inside my rucksack. The pole/ handle had to be carried separately. It could be reassembled when we arrived on the beach. I took my mate Alan with me and he was sworn to secrecy. We did not want Black Dog to turn up. It was early morning when we got off the train. There was a nip in the air; we must have looked a bit strange in our Wellington boots and carrying a broom handle. Our destination was Meols Station, only a few stops away. It was a short walk to the promenade and Dove Point. Checking our map, which was drawn up in the 1860s, things had certainly changed a bit. On planning the trip we had never thought that the map could be out of date. My Sherlock Holmes instinct suddenly came into play.
" I think it was fair to assume that Dove point was to the left of the slipway opposite Newlyn Road". Alan nodded in agreement. We decided to start by walking out into the sand opposite the road, with our assembled metal detector. I tossed a penny coin onto the sand and did a quick test. When the metal detector was tuned normally it produced a dull periodic tone with short bleeps, but on detecting metal the bleeps and tone increased in volume.
"Lets hear it; come on, give me a go," demanded Alan.
Passing over the headphones and then the handle of the contraption, he

Chapter 3 - Buried Treasure

187

Chapter 3 - Buried Treasure

started to wave it around.
"I can't hear anything," was his sarcastic remark.
"You're moving it too fast. Scan slowly from side to side, about an inch off the sand". I said angrily.
"Here, you do it, "was his reply as he passed the equipment back to me.
I did not want to waste any more time; if the tide turned, we will have to return home. A few more adjustments and I was into my rhythm, scanning carefully from left to right as we moved forward. The wet sand was a problem in adjusting the controls. Looking back we could clearly see are tracks so we tried not to repeat the same search area.
"Look! Look! Look, it's over there - the submerged forest,"
and I pointed excitedly as Alan turned in my direction.
"At least we are in the right place Should we dig around the stumps?"
"No. Let's walk around and see if we can spot anything."
It didn't take long before we found a clay pipe; its stem was missing but we had the bowl which was discoloured and had lost its clay white appearance, but it was a start. The next object that Alan spotted was a metal hinge type thing it was encrusted with rust and very brittle. We tried to clean it in a pool but it broke in two.
"Let's take it home. We can mess with it later." I just wanted to stop Alan trying to clean it before it broke into even more pieces.
"No, I want to see what it is."
We now had the thing in four pieces with a bit falling into the puddle, Alan giving up on the cleaning.
"Ok. Here you go, "he said, passing over a hand full of rusty bits.
"Thanks," I replied.
The submerged forest contained a few dozen exposed stumps with dark muddy areas marking others that were not as well defined. The exposed short black stumps each stood in a pool of seawater with small scrimps darting around as we approached. As I stepped into one of the puddles

The Submerged Forest Meols looking towards Hoylake

Chapter 3 - Buried Treasure

particles of light illuminated the tube worms as they darted back into their calcium homes. Most of the sand had changed colour with outcrops of clay clearly visible; the dark shades of brown and black made the place a little mysterious, as if waiting for the monster from the black lagoon to appear. The tide was still going out and the glistening streams connecting some of the pools were now struggling to keep their watery secrets. It was time to try our metal detector. In between the stumps lay deposits of dark mud hiding secrets in their depths, waiting to be tested by an uninvited Wellington boot. It was now or never but trying to scan between the mud pools was difficult. Then!
Bleep, Bleep, Bleep very loud. I threw the trowel down and told Alan where to dig. Only about a foot down and the hole started to fill up with water. I checked the spoils around the hole; no response. I checked the hole again but the water now blocked out the signal.
"Let's dig deeper." It was such a loud signal, there must be something. Another six inches and we came to long twisted roots, which on exposure to the air smelt foul. "Wait! What's that," I said pointing to a long metal object, its outer shape resembling a long flat hook. The roots had been reluctant to let the object loose. This time I took over the archaeological dig lifting it carefully out of its hiding place. I wrapped the encrusted object in some newspaper and placed it in my rucksack. The hole by this time was completely full of water. We continued on our quest amongst the stumps for another hour or so before the cold got the better of use, and the batteries failed on our metal detector. What an adventure. The following day when all the spoils had been cleaned and sorted, our tally was two broken clay pipe stems and accompanying bowl, a rusty key and a silver coin from the reign of Postumus, A.D 268-9 with the reverse totally illegible. The ultimate prize a fibula or roman brooch, which if intact would have had a pin attached. It appeared to be made from some sort of ornate bronze. Numerous bottle tops and unidentified bits of rusty medal were all consigned to the bin.
It was quite some time later that I was to discover the true origins of the map and the notes. In 1863 the Rev A Hume, the Honorary Secretary of the Historic Society of Lancashire and Cheshire, wrote a book entitled *Ancient Meols - An Account of the Antiquities found near Dove Point*. In the spring of 1846 the Rev Hume happened to be in the parsonage of Hoylake, when he noticed various artefacts on a chimney wall .He was to discover later that an old man in the village had found them. The Reverend made his acquaintance and procured the collection. He proceeded to catalogue and study the artefacts, and the result was his book containing the treasure map. On investigation he was to discover that a vast number of artefacts had been discovered in and around the point; between 1817 to 1849, well over 3000 objects had been found. These ranged from gold coins, rings and jewellery, to brooches, amber

Chapter 3 - Buried Treasure

beads, Roman Fibulae (Toga-Pins) pottery, flints, tools, pewter, and copper items. There were more mundane articles - clay pipes, keys, spurs, buckles, combs, nails etc. The finds covered different historic periods dating back to pre-Roman days and up to 1700. The majority of objects found were of Roman origin. The more modern objects are found further westward; certain Saxon coins were found nearly a mile to the west, and on the clay outcrop.

From the present water line we can trace the course of habitation from the eastern side of Dove Point to the village of Hoylake.

At the time of the Domesday Survey, Great Meols appears to have been recently sanded up and it possessed then only about thirty acres of arable land connected with five families mentioned. Meols is called Melas in the Domesday Book. The ancient manor, then held by Robert de Rodelent and said to have stood on Dove Point, has now been washed away.

The coast formerly projected much farther out to sea, indicated by ancient maps, and the fact that a considerable portion of the racecourse has been lost. A lighthouse and ancient house/mansion together with a well have all gone the same way. The stumps were last regularly viewed back in the 60s but have since disappeared under the shifting sands. An occasional neap tide may reveal their whereabouts in the future. The trees were at their largest towards Hoylake and smallest at Leasowe,. They were mainly oak, alder, elm and beech.

The next obvious question is how did all of these objects come to occupy such a relatively small area.

Chapter 3 - Buried Treasure

There are four main theories:
1. Shipwrecks
The idea of having a museum on board a ship has to be discounted. A series of ship wrecks over a long period of time is not feasible. Records indicate a medieval highway around the peninsula seaward of the present coastline.
2. Fluvial Deposit
It has been suggested that these objects of antiquity were originally connected with Chester and they were carried down the River Dee by the force of the tide, and with tidal action arrived off Dove Point. It is very unlikely that Neptune could hide and move these things; the metallic objects are far too heavy.
3. Aquatic Settlement
A popular theory concerns earlier inhabitants erecting their huts over the water, some distance from the land, producing a tidal moat between them and their enemies. Some of the original stumps did appear to have certain symmetry.
4. Destruction of an Ancient Settlement
The finds point to the objects belonging to resident people, and not to mere passers-by. Their houses were probably made from timber.
Of the wearers of the spurs it may be said:-
Their bones are dust,
Their swords are rust,
Their souls are with the saints, we trust.

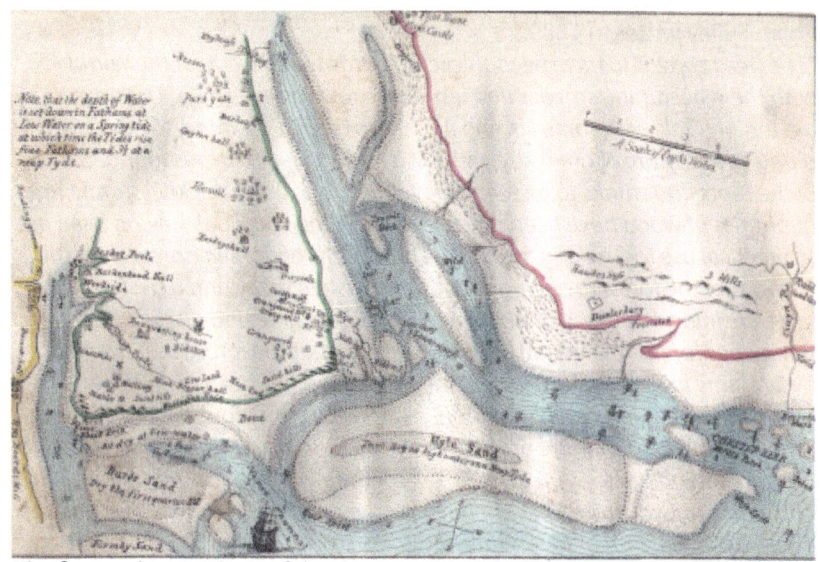

The first authentic chart of the shores around the Wirral was produced by Captain Grenville Collins in 1687. Note the Dee was the primary river.

Chapter 3 - Buried Treasure

The site has probably been occupied by various groups of people going back to pre history. The violent nature of the tides and the vortex effect around the stumps have played havoc with the normal strata, hence the finds are mixed in terms of age.

The earliest mention of the submerged forest occurs in description of Cheshire dated 1615 by William Webb entitled *Kings Vale Royal* in which he calls the forest the 'Meols Stocks'.

In these mosses, especially in the black, are fir-trees found under the ground, in some places six feet deep or more, and in others not one foot; which trees are of surprising length, and straight, having certain small branches like boughs, and roots at one end -as if they had been blown down by the winds; and yet no man can tell that ever any such trees did grow there, nor yet how they should come thither. Some are of the opinion that they have lain there ever since Noah's flood.

The "Noah's flood" theory is probably a non-starter, but we owe a debt of gratitude to the writer from yesteryear for the detailed account of the submerged forest in his day.

In 1828 a visitor to the Wirral wrote:

"This beach at about half tide level, presents a curious and highly interesting spectacle of the remains of a submerged forest. The numerous roots of trees which have not yet been washed away by the sea, or carried off by the neighbouring inhabitants for firewood, are in a very decayed state. The trees seem to have been cut off about 2 feet from the ground after the usual practice in felling timber; and the roots are seen ramifying from their respective stumps in all directions and dipping towards the clay sub soil"

Philip Sulley writes in 1889:

"The trees appear to have been thicker towards the Dee end of the Wirral with them becoming smaller and less dense towards Leasowe. The trees are mainly Oak, with some Fir, and appear to a certain extend, to have been planted. Many are of great size, in 1857 a tree 35 feet long was found. Some of the roots and trunks to be seen at low tide are of great thickness, and large quantities of wood have been taken from here, the black oak having been put to practical use for making furniture. The inroads of the sea are so great that portions of the forest are being constantly washed away and a fresh surface laid bare inland. William banks who was resident here and discovered antiquities for more than half a century, states that the forest, as described by Dr Hume in his book on Ancient Meols in 1863, has been completely destroyed. Yet there is no diminution in the extent, and doubtless this forest called submarine but more properly subterranean, extends for a considerable distance inland. It crops up at the banks of the Wallasey pool along the line of the new railway from Birkenhead Park to the old dock station; and was uncovered by the Great Meols railway station when the large ponds were excavated there".

Chapter 3 - Buried Treasure

A description by E.W Cox in 1895 which states that:
"The remains of circular stone huts, up to two feet below high-water mark, made of wattled wood coated with clay, and the ground was abundantly marked with hoofs of horses with round shoes, and with the foot marks of cattle, pigs and sheep".

From The Romance of Wirral by A.G. Caton.
In 1891 the Spring-tides dislodged some drift sand, and shewed, on what had been the original surface, the foundations of ancient British huts, which had been made of wattled-work coated with clay, and so arranged as to form an irreular village street.
The Roman objects found have been so numerous as to show that there must have been an important Roman station here.
The Saxon objects found show a gradual change of residence, owing to changed physical conditions.
The remains of Norman pottery and numerous goad-spurs show what a highway the woods and sands of this district were for the knights and traders of old.
Articles belonging to comparatively resent times, that is to say the 16th, 17th and 18th centuries, have been found nearer to the present Hoylake, and still farther removed from the site of the early settlements.

SUBMERGED FOREST MEOLS SHORE

193

Wirral Astronomical Society

My fascination with Space resulted in the formation of the Wirral Astronomical Society in 1961. Robert and I and a few friends formed the nucleus of the society and we held our meetings in our homes until the membership increased when we had to find a larger venue. A church hall in Ennerdale Road came to our rescue. Our meetings were held monthly to discuss the observations and activities of the various groups.

With regular guest speakers our meeting were well-attended.

Mr Bellis, a keen member of the Royal Astronomical Society, had been one of the first people to hear the bleeps from the Sputnik, the world's very first artificial satellite which took about 98 minutes to orbit the earth. The launch marked the start of the space race between the US and USSR.

Listening for messages from the stars on home-made tracking equipment are Michael Gray aged 17 and Michael Edwards aged 16.

He recalled that his amateur radio observations were not believed. The authorities took some convincing; they just did not believe him, and it was not until the Russians announced the launch that people started to take notice. The signals continued for 22 days until the transmitter batteries ran out on 26 October 1957. Members of our Society would visit his radio telescope in Bebbington, which was constructed from old Second World War RAF equipment. His aerial array

Studying a map of the stars are (left to right) R. Colquhoun aged 15, Colin Green aged 14, Michael Gannon aged 17, Robert Bailey aged 14 and Jimmy Cairns, aged 16.

(interferometer) formed an important part in receiving the signals from space. His garden was a mass of poles and wires. With unlimited patience he would explain the technicalities of the apparatus. He was a really likable and interesting person with time for the younger generation.

Chapter 3 - Wirral Astronomical Society

Checking the stars from the back garden are (left to right, standing) Joyce Scudder, aged 16 (secretary); Malcolm Read, aged 14 (treasurer), and Martin Pacey, aged 12, with Donna Leigh, aged 15, seated.

Joyce Scudder and Roy Dutton, aged 16 (President of the Wirral Astronomical Society) study a picture of the blast-off of an American rocket.

Another regular visitor was Mr Rawlinson who would talk about UFOs. His strange appearance and over-jealous excitement when taking on the subject made one think he was slightly out of his terrestrial head. He had a habit of repeating any important words, and he would also speak a sentence and then repeat the last word. Numerous photographs depicting UFOs would be displayed and explained normally with the Ash (Mr Paul Ashton) arguing about their authenticity. He was always trying to locate the string attached to the plates.

We arranged visits to places of interest including Bidston Observatory. The Tide Prediction Machine was my favourite. It had numerous wooden gears and the operator would turn a handle which would set the gears in motion. The rotation caused mechanical counters to rotate and the reading was then written down. The process was then repeated using different cogs representing the moon's gravity and numerous other contributing factors. And bingo the tide in the Mersey on some date in the future would be predicted.

Mr Foster, a teacher from New Brighton Secondary Modern, helped with the very first issue of our Bulletin. In those days, this was a complicated process involving a duplicator machine and wax stencils. An interesting article was contributed by Mr Patrick Moore entitled *Volcanoes on the moon* and

195

Chapter 3 - Wirral Astronomical Society

formed the centre piece of the publication.

We managed to attract the attention of the Liverpool Echo which ran an article on our society on 26th April 26th 1963 - a full page. I quote:

"Wallasey Teenagers keep a nightly watch on the heavens."

Most of our regular members were listed by name; details of some of achievements and activities the article attracted even more members. Enter Mr Paul Ashton (The Ash) into our lives, an eccentric Oldershaw scholar with a profound interest in astronomy. He became an enthusiastic member of the group, but was prone to arguing and disagreeing with the majority of the society's decisions.

Half of the members had telescopes of various sizes. My father had won quite a large amount on the horses - his "Canadian Bet" with some rank outsiders had netted him over £300, a small fortune. In fact when he went to get paid out by the bookies they paid him in three instalments over a few days - so it was treats all round! My mother a new coat and yours truly a brand new telescope and tripod from Charles Frank Ltd up in Scotland. It was now the rings of Saturn, moon craters and late nights for me.

The Ashe's 2" refractor fell out of the window while he was observing a lunar occultation. It was quickly repaired with sellotape; unfortunately future results took on a slight bias to the right.

To make satisfactory observations it was important to find a location that was not polluted by light. Our favourite location was the Leasowe Golf Club and the Ash's house conveniently backed on to the same. The rocket drawing produced by G.H Davis in 1932 depicts a moonship that would travel to the moon and it was not far off the mark. Some 37 years later it was to become a reality with the first man landing on the moon. It was also my inspiration for joining the British Interplanetary Association, and dreaming of man's conquest of the stars.

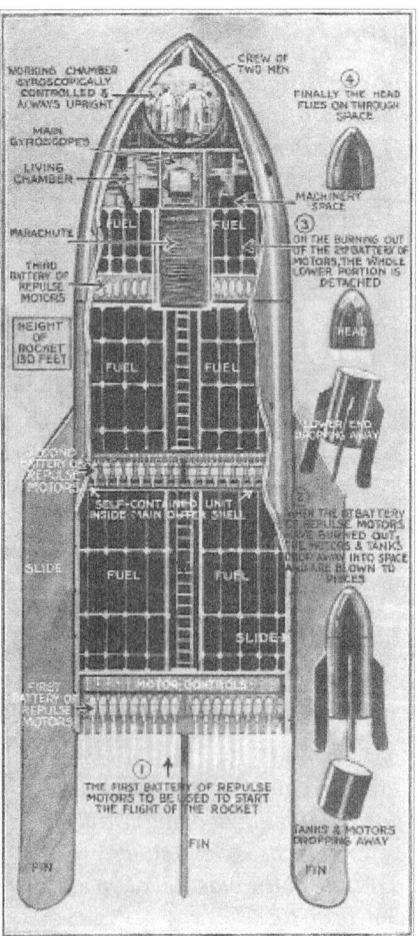

Chapter 3 - Smuggler's Cave

On the 21st September 1963 I paid a visit to the smuggler's cave. It was in aid of a good cause, Wallasey Boys' Club and for a silver sixpence you could venture down a hole in the garden of Mr Norman Kinghams "Rock Villa" in Wellington Road, to explore the subterranean passage which was illuminated only by candle light. It helped create an authentic atmosphere and allowed my imagination to run riot with smugglers and pirates. A combination of a natural cave and man-made arch, it extended to the cliff face where the sea used to come up to, until about 80 years ago. Boats could tie up at the entrance and then the booty was taken into the tunnel and up to the house that is conveniently built on top of the main chamber. Wallasey up to the middle of the eighteenth century was a desperate region. Most of the inhabitants were wreckers and smugglers and would prey upon Liverpool-bound shipping. That part of Wallasey was separated from the rest of Wirral by a tidal pool. Many a fierce fire was lit on the Wirral shore on stormy nights to lure a good ship aground. Some books suggest that the tunnel was linked to an underground cave system under the Palace which was eventually transformed into "The Grotto", where small boats could sail past illuminated caves. There was a rumour that it was even connected to Mother Red Caps almost a mile away.

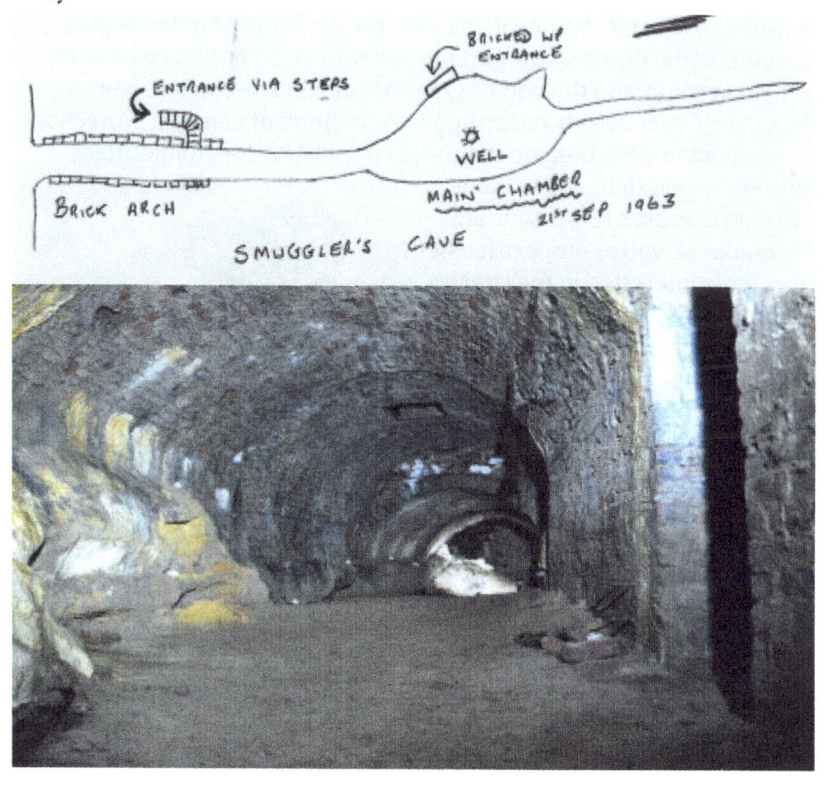

Chapter 3 - Civil Defence

I was to become a Cold War warrior by joining the part-time Civil Defence Corps. After walking around as a teenager with a ban the bomb badge on my lapel, I was now a pillar of society. The call went out for volunteers and I joined. It was my civic duty, or could it be the annual bounty of £5. The Cold War era was a horrible period for humanity; I like many others thought the end was nigh. It was imperative that the authorities rehearse for nuclear Armageddon. The Cuban Missile Crisis in October 1962 had been a close-run thing, and the appearance of the 1964 film *Dr. Strangelove or: How I Learned to Stop Worrying and Love the Bomb* only helped to reinforce the anxiety. Its powerful message, in which Kubrick presents a tragic incident as satire, came out at the height of the paranoia of the nuclear age and the Cold War. The scariest thing about this film was how it make you laugh at the impending apocalyptic ending. By presenting it with humour, it conveys just how much of a farce the nuclear arms race was in real life. At the time we lived in the era of mutual assured destruction. The headquarters of my unit was at the Concert Hall in Manor Road Liscard. With my electrical background I was drafted into the communications section. This involved setting up communications in the field. Joe our instructor had a favourite saying: "Control and Command, are vital for correct decision making".

So with those words ringing in my ears it was off on one of our regular exercises in the Corporation Yard, littered with dead bodies covered in tomato ketchup, and the odd fire. Another of his favourite one-liners was "Duck and Cover" which was a suggested method of personal protection. It was an attempt to prepare the civilian population for atomic attack through staged drills, evacuations, and field exercises. Boy Scouts and Girl guides served as mock casualties. I was more interested in the later as I attempted the tricky manoeuvre of laying the cable around the girls.

At the time the Birkenhead Corporation Control was located in a purpose-built Civil Defence Corps Control Centre beneath the Technical College Theatre (later re-named the Glenda Jackson Theatre. The theatre itself is now closed and a fine set of flats have sprung up on the site. Lets hope they don't disappear into the abyss. I could never understand why the deep air raid shelter built in 1941 under Bidston Hill had not been used.

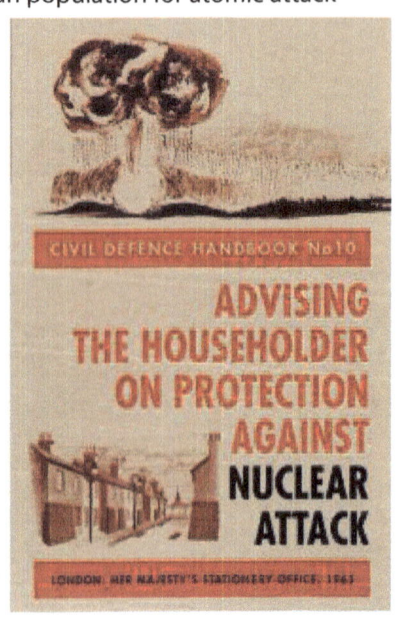

Chapter 3 - New Brighton Tower

The original idea for a spectacular attraction in New Brighton was the construction of the biggest wheel in the world. Eat your heart out, London Eye. We thought of it first! The project was first discussed in 1895 and the drawing below is from a press cutting dated 23 June1896, which announced the scheme for "New Brighton's Graydon Great Wheel and Towers".

The New Brighton Graydon Castle Great Wheel and Tower Company was formed in November 1896 with a capital of £140,000. The prospectus informed *"Of the annual 11 million visitors if only 50 per cent of visitors rode the wheel, a profit of 50 per cent was possible".*

Not all was well. Walter Basset went to court, claiming he had signed an agreement with Graydon on 10 August 1895 which gave him exclusive rights. The case went to litigation and dragged on and on, and eventually the project was axed.

The Tower, with steel girders and of a bricks and mortor construction, eventually became the attraction. Given the changeable nature of the weather, on the Irish sea coast, warmth and fun could only be guaranteed at an indoor entertainments centre.

Maxwell and Tuke designed the New Brighton Tower during 1896 and were able to produce a more expansive and exciting design than Blackpool Tower. New Brighton Tower was bigger in every way, a massive Gothic pile of heroic proportions. Its Tower was 567 ft 6 ins high and 48 ft 9 ins taller than Blackpool Tower. The buildings surrounding its base contained the Grand Tower Theatre, seating over 3,000 people, the ballroom, a billiard saloon, a small menagerie, a restaurant and a winter garden, and all made from sturdy red Ruabon bricks from Wales with fancy terracotta and stone dressings. With an octagonal design and the Tower at its centre, it was a truly a magnificent building. The four corners of the octagon were emphasised by tall pavilions with steeply pitched roofs topped by cupolas. The Ballroom, which accommodated 1,000 couples, was decorated in classical style in white and gold, and featured painted panels of the civic emblems of Lancashire towns. The Grand Tower Theatre was the largest theatre in England; its spectacular interior positioned within the eight legs of the Tower.

With the lack of maintenance during the First World War, the Tower metal structure was demolished between1919 to 1921. The actual Tower Buildings remained until burnt out in 1969.

Chapter 3 - New Brighton Tower

The Waxworks
In the entrance was a giant picture made from tropical butterflies. Entering the display through a curtain, your first delight was a wax work model of Queen Victoria, dressed in a replica black velvet outfit and next to her was an old bath chair with a single front wheel and a steering tiller. Her cheeks were rosy and she looked almost too cheerful, especially as she was mourning Prince Albert.
There were other kings and queens including Henry the Eighth, and some other less interesting figures which I just can't remember.
Then you went down a dark stairway to the chamber of horrors. The first horror to present itself was Sweeney Todd the demon barber of Fleet Street, with a mock-up of his barber shop, and a revolving chair that allowed the customer to be tilted backwards to have his throat cut. The customer was eventually dispatched via a trap door into the cellar.
With copious amounts of red dye covering his white overhaul, flickering oil lamps on an old wooden bench revealing blood-covered razors and combs, it was truly frightening to an eleven year old!
Other bodies could be seen hanging from the walls in various states of painful agony, including a guy on the rack complete with dislocated arms. There was a coffin with iron-maiden spikes complete and a terrified-looking girl on top whom it was about to be closed; there was also a couple of mummies on either side, just for good measure.
On the way out a poor soul sat in a chair with thumbscrews attached; his haunting eyes seems to follow you all the way out.

★ **DODGEMS** EVERYONE ENJOYS THEM
Make sure you try the
FUN ! THRILLS ! SPEED & SKID !! DODGEMS !
★ ★ ★ ★
TRAVEL on the WEIRDEST JOURNEY OF YOUR LIFE !!
★ **THE GHOST TRAIN** SHRIEKS — LAUGHS
SURPRISE—SUSPENSE !
★ ★ ★ ★
You Must Visit Our GREAT SHOW
★ **THE WAXWORKS** Crammed with Interesting
and Exciting Tableaux
GREAT STORIES OF LOVE, CRIME AND ADVENTURE TOLD IN BRILLIANT WAX ARTISTRY and a great CHAMBER OF HORRORS—
one inclusive charge only
★ ★ ★ ★
★ **GIANT AMUSEMENT ARCADE**
(Left of Tower Building Entrance)
★ THE LATEST
IT'S NEW **ROLLO** HAVE A FINE TIME WINNING
GRAND PRIZES !
OVER 150 FUN AND PRIZE MACHINES
Shooting Ranges ! —— Automatic Rifles ! —— Radio Rifles !
Also in the Grounds : Skid — Electric Speedway — Skee Rolls —
Mirror Maze — Crooked House — Autodrome
AMUSEMENT EQUIPMENT COMPANY

Chapter 3 - New Brighton Tower

The Tower burnt down on Saturday the 5th April 1969. Along with the flames went millions of happy memories. Steps were taken to have the charred shell of the Tower demolished.

201

Chapter 3 - New Brighton Tower

New Brighton Tower Grounds
New Brighton in the 60s was very different to the way it is now. The ferry brought an endless stream of day trippers from Liverpool to arrive at the Pier. It was a real seaside resort up there with Blackpool and Southport. Thousands of people from all over the country came by couch to visit the resort whilst some people actually came for their holidays! With a big outdoor fairground, as well as the Indoor Palace, plus numerous amusement arcades scattered along the promenade and up Victoria Road, you could always find a place for your loose change.
New Brighton Baths was the biggest outdoor pool in Europe and with the best pop groups in the world appearing on the Tower, and numerous live entertainment venues in pubs and clubs, music was everywhere - the perfect soundtrack for a youth. It was truly a fantastic place to grow up. My first memory of the ghost train in the Tower Grounds was not of the ride itself; it was of being scared by its haunting exterior! When you walked past the ghost train it was a formidable experience for a little boy. "Look at that!" I said as I pointed at the two large white ghosts which adorned the top of the ride.
"Mom, let's get a move-on. it's scary!"
"Ignore them, Roy. They're not real."

I was reassured momentarily until I heard the train coming; it clanked along the track with a metal on metal scratching noise. There was a twist of smoke in the glow of the phosphorescent zombie heads just as the train hit the doors and descended into the abyss. My mom's smile shines at me in the damp air. I look up at the ghosts, their green angry faces and evil eyes seemingly following me, and it was enough to make me hide behind my mom as we walked briskly past. Phew, that was a close shave!

Chapter 3 - New Brighton Tower

Despite her years I think my mom also found the fake monsters and blaring sound effects alarming. What a pair we make.

The 'Rota' was another unusual ride, you got in, it started revolving, then the floor disappeared from under your feet, and, everyone were stuck to the sides. Can be seen top right in the photograph.

During the long summer months my mom would take me down to Victoria Gardens to watch Punch and Judy. It was never going to be politically correct with the squawking voice. Punch, the hunchback with a hooked nose, his wife Judy, the baby, constable, crocodile and the hangman. It was never a PG rating, but what fun!

Chapter 3 - New Brighton Tower

Talking about things that sway in the wind, a cable lift of sorts was constructed to take people to the top of the tower building. I can remember it was quite a height, in fact they just seemed to be glorified buckets that you could stand in to admire the view. The contraption would not have looked out of place on a building site. It was quite hairy in a breeze and it looked an awful long way down. I remember once seeing the wire come off the wheel and the fire brigade had to rescue the people. Also located in the Tower grounds was a unique Victorian

wooden carousel with the hand- painted horses moving up and down a pole. There was music from an automatic pianola-type organ where reams of folded thick punched card was used to supply the tunes. I was not too keen on an actual ride, but I always stopped to hear it play; the creaking wood took my mind into a magical age of wonder.

But my most enduring memory was of the wall of death! The roar of the dare - devil motor cyclists' engines as they drove their machines around the shaking vertical walls, criss-crossing each other at the very edge was breathtaking. The crowd of onlookers would step back thinking they were about to overshoot, but they always pulled away at the last possible moment. The audience views from the top of the drum, looking down. The riders started at the bottom of the drum, in the centre, and ascended until they gained enough velocity to drive horizontally to the floor.

Chapter 3 - New Brighton Tower

Peter Catchpole and his glamorous assistants took the spectacular ride to new heights. Ingrid who was married to Norman McGonigal was one of the stunt riders. His other assistant was Ursula Brown she would sit on the motorcycle rider's shoulders and defy the laws of gravity. After Ursula split with Peter Catchpole she married the businessman Reginald Brown and later moved to Florida where she met many cinema legends at parties held on Reg's yacht including Frank Sinatra, Bing Crosby, Ava Gardner and Ingrid Bergman. Reg later set up a charter business on the Mediterranean, but it was due to his failing health that they eventually sold up and returned to New Brighton. Peter Catchpole was a real entrepreneur of the old school with involvements in night clubs, rides and other entertainment ventures. One of the many controversies involved a Board of Trade inquiry looking into the dealings of New Brighton Football Club - the directors were accused of asset stripping and Peter who was chairman conveniently left for Australia. In later life Peter went into partnership with Ken Fox operating one of the few surviving wall of death shows until his death in 2002. The original American Indian Motorcycles, which have been used since around the 1930s formed the backbone of the touring company. Peter had a lot of bad luck with many of his projects mysteriously busting into flames but he was a real character. A fatal accident occurred when Leonard Sidney Sutton a coach driver was killed by a female motor cyclist when she lost control and shot out of the Wall of Death in the Tower Grounds. Mrs Zoe Campbell aged 21 of Greenbank Avenue was unable to give evidence at the inquest as she was in hospital with a fractured leg. John Campbell, the rider's husband, said she had been riding for more than ten years and was experienced.

WIZARDS on the WALL

TOWER GARDENS,
—— **New Brighton** ——

YOU MUST SEE
Fearless Fred Farrow
and
Cyclone Billy Bellhouse
THE ENGLISH WIZARDS.
Riding and Stunting on High Power Motor Cycles on an Upright Wall.

A SUPER THRILL
THE AUSTRALIAN PURSUIT RACE.
Two Riders on the Wall at the same time Racing at Terrific Speeds.

CONTINUOUS DEMONSTRATIONS
(Including Sundays)

ADMISSION NOW REDUCED TO
ADULTS 6d. CHILDREN 3d.

Wallasey Printers Ltd., Belle Vue road, Wallasey.

Chapter 3 - New Brighton Tower

*The Wall of Death
Tower Grounds*

Chapter 3 - New Brighton Tower

My girlfriend, Helen. I think she was a long standing shareholder of the New Brighton Tower Company because her ability to spend my money held no bounds. It was "Roy, Roy win me a bracelet!"
After attempting to chuck hoops so they landed flat on the deck around a rectangular block of wood bearing some cheap sparkly bracelet, I suggested a walk along the promenade. My eventual aim hoping to get my wicked way in Vale Park.
"Look! Look, Ducks! I always win!" she said pointing at the stall.
I was never a fan of floating ducks with a hook on top. The idea was to hook the duck out of the water; each duck had a number underneath and the prizes available depended on the points scored. After some fly-fishing we became the new owner of "Kermit the frog" - I needed a puppet like a hole in the head.
"Helen, let's go on the ghost train," I said In anticipation of becoming stranded in the dark in the middle of the ride.
"No, it's too scary" I looked at her in absolute amazement.
"No it's not!" My voice must have echoed my frustration.
 "We're having lots of fun. Let's try the air rifles."
It was once said that displays of skill at shooting through a bent sight and trying to win a cuddly toy for your girlfriend is a rite of passage for many young men. But this young man was a reluctant participant.
I was starting to get a bit closer to a certain no-go area. It was always a good idea to steer well away from the roller skating rink frequented in the main by teddy boys and other tugs more interested in mortal combat than the gentile art of skating. It was a requirement that all and sundry went around the rink in the same direction. However, the signal for a set-to was normally when a group chose to skate in the opposite direction.
The smell of the fair had drifted towards our nostrils, diesel mixed in with candyfloss and deep-fried doughnuts, hot, sticky and greasy with enough sugar to give a whale diabetes. And guess what "I'm hungry; let's buy a doughnut". Then after she had been fed and watered.
"Roy, Roy let's go on the coaster."
The roller coaster was something that the Health and Safety people these days would close down immediately! No futuristic theme, just a very rickety wooden structure with a metal track winding precariously around in a figure of eight. With a good wind behind it, I am sure it could have taken up residence on the pier. I often wondered if the cars were supposed to shudder and clank and give the occupants the feeling they were going to brake in two. And was the structure supposed to sway? It all looked very precarious to me; there was no way in a million years I was going on that thing!
"No, no. The thing's falling apart," was my immediate response! I was really starting to get cheesed off with all of this.

Chapter 3 - New Brighton Tower

It was starting to get past my bedtime and I just knew I was getting absolutely nowhere. I had been dropping hints like mad, so in the end I suggested we both went home. I took her to the bus stop to catch the No 1 to her Seacombe abode.
"When will I see you again?" was her parting comment. "Soon," was my reassuring reply as the bus disappeared into the distance.
Then I mumbled in your dreams!!!
There was also a small zoo that was attached to the back of the Tower. During the summer holidays I went out with Jill, a girl that helped in the Zoo. She used to have to go up and down Victoria Road going round all the greengrocers and bakeries for stale bread and cabbage leaves for the animals. If I arrived early I could get in for free, and help feed the animals. The entrance was through a turnstile in a small log cabin and the zoo was contained in a log stockade, just above the quarry where Tommy Mann's miniature trains operated.
Most of the large cages had been made from old train wagons with steel bars added onto the front. To my mind it was awful place, with the animals being confined to small cages with no chance of any real exercise. I always remember the sad and degrading appearance of the resident tiger which was housed in a small cage about six times its body length and would spend the whole day walking around in the same direction oblivious to anything around him. The birds were luckier as they were housed in a large avery. Jill told me the meerkats had all escaped burrowing out of their enclosure a long time ago. I think they are hoping that they will return. I enquired if there had been any other escapes?
"A peacock escaped the other week. He's since been spotted on windowsills on the Upper Side of the Tower, in what is perhaps a brazen bid to join high society".
The zoo was really on its last legs. After the Tower burnt down what was left of the Zoo become part of the Welsh Mountain Zoo.
Another memory of the Tower grounds was 'The Lakeside' which served beer to anyone not wearing a school uniform. But more about those dens of iniquity later.

Chapter 3 - New Brighton Tower

The roller skating rink frequented in the main by teddy boys and other thugs more interested in mortal combat.

Another of Tommy Mann's enterprises - the kiddies fair in the Tower grounds next to the promenade.

Chapter 3 - New Brighton Tower

The roller coaster showing its rickety wooden construction with a metal track winding precariously around in a figure of eight.

During the long summer months my mom would take me down to Victoria Gardens to watch Punch and Judy.

Chapter 3 - Tommy Mann's Minature Railway

Tommy Mann's Miniature Railway
A special treat was a trip to the Fairy Glen in the Tower grounds. My mom would pay for me to ride on the merry-go-round and then visit the miniature railway.
From the *New Brighton Guide* of 1955;
"The children will love Uncle Tommy's Kiddies Playground on the tower promenade, New Brighton with its real miniature trains running through fairy grottoes. There are rides, helter-skelter, hobby horses, fairy coach wheel and a host of other attractions, specially designed for the safe amusement of children." The railway closed at the end of the 1965 season and later the 'Fairy Glen' was filled in and the whole area grassed over. No one would ever know that a miniature railway ever existed in this tranquil location.

The story of the miniature railways in New Brighton has to be told; it brought enjoyment to thousands of children and adults that travelled on the magical line. It was my first introduction to the delights of steam, which has continued to this day, even though it had been an illusion. There is something magical about an 18" gauge railway which is not much taller than the children travelling on it. It all started in the late 1930s with a 22" gauge engine on a short track. The loco was a Fordson, but by all accounts did not last long. A kind of boxed tractor on wheels did operate along New Brighton Promenade for a time. It was not until

Chapter 3 - Tommy Mann's Minature Railway

after the war that Tommy Mann became a showman He operated the motor boats on the Marine Lake at New Brighton, and expanded his entertainment empire in different directions.

He bought the train and equipment in 1947 and set about installing his new venture in the Tower Pleasure Gardens ready for the 1948 season. The actual site was relatively small so an elaborate fairy glen was created in a disused quarry. With extremely tight curves the circuit proved a bit of a challenge but Tommy was not to be deterred and devised a way to stop the train, *Sentinel*, at certain points. The train travelled parallel with the promenade, then entered a tunnel which contained an illuminated model which was the first stop. Then on entering the cutting it slowed down to view the wishing well and fairies. The *Sentinel* was converted to look like a steam engine with a dummy boiler and bunker. It lasted until 1951 when another loco was obtained. Built by David Curwen Ltd and named *Crompton*, it had been custom-built in less than 5 months. It had an anthracite-burning engine which propelled the loco safely around the sharp bends. The line was described during its peak of development in the August 1952 edition of *Model Maker*. With the new engine came a new carriage, an overbridge and a miniature signal box. The miniature railway closed after 17 years of happy journeys.

Chapter 3 - Tommy Mann's Minature Railway

T.M.E. SPECIALLY REDUCED PRICES AND **T.M.E.**
"ALL-IN" TICKETS FOR CHILDREN'S PARTIES

★ THE CHILDREN WILL LOVE
Uncle Tommy's Kiddies' Playground
on the
TOWER PROMENADE, NEW BRIGHTON
TEA GARDENS   TEA GARDENS

One of the trains leaving for a tour of the Fairy Grotto

with its real miniature trains running through Fairy Grottoes. Rides, Helter-Skelter, Hobby Horses, Fairy Coach Wheel, and a host of other attractions
SPECIALLY DESIGNED FOR THE SAFE AMUSEMENT OF CHILDREN

TEAS   **ANOTHER GREAT ATTRACTION!**   TEAS

THE SUPER MARINE LAKE
CENTRAL PROMENADE

9½ acres of safe boating . . Drive your own Motor Boats
Rowing Boats . . . Paddle Boats
Motor Launch "Majestic" leaves regularly for
Trips Round the Lake
ADMISSION FREE TO LIDO PLATEAU
DECK CHAIRS :: ICES :: REFRESHMENTS
TEAS   TEAS

"All-in" tickets obtainable in advance on Sale or Return Basis
PARTICULARS FROM:
TOMMY MANN'S ENTERPRISES, MARINE LAKE, NEW BRIGHTON
Telephone: Wallasey 1823

SPECIALLY REDUCED PRICES AND
T.M.E.   "ALL-IN" TICKETS FOR CHILDREN'S PARTIES   **T.M.E.**

Chapter 3 - Tommy Mann's Minature Railway

The boating lake, home of Tommy Mann's speedboats, with the Travellers' Rest in the background - a regular haunt of my parents. Tommy Dutton would play the piano in the lounge for the Saturday night singalongs.

Tommy Mann and family in 1947, always the showman he owned the New Brighton Duck, miniature railway, kiddies' fair with the oldest operational ride in the UK, a set of Dobby Horses dating from 1820, and don't forget the speedboats.

214

Chapter 3 - Palace Indoor Fairgrounds

Palace Indoor Fairgrounds
New Brighton's Palace Theatre, opened in 1882, included a covered amusement park, a theatre, a skating rink and an aquarium, and was demolished in 1933. It was replaced by Wilkie's Indoor Palace Fairgrounds. It was only later in life that I was able to savour the Horror House ride, the main part of which went underground and had a habit of breaking down. If you were one of the unlucky riders you could emerge breathless from the steep tunnel up to the exit. I think the master plan had been copied from Disney but without the mechanical problems. It was well advanced for its time. My mom had worked in the underground maze during the war when it was an ammunition factory, later to become the Creep Inn Nightclub. My all-time favourite ride was the Jet Planes which offered the rider a joy stick with up-and-down motion operated by compressed air.

The machine was massive with a diameter of 54 feet, and 12 planes each capable of seating 2 adults or 3 children. The ride operated in an anti-clockwise direction, the hiss when you operated the controls just added to the excitement, as they climbed up to the rafters in the roof.

Chapter 3 - Palace Indoor Fairgrounds

Another of my favorite rides was the Waltzer with its flashing, rotating coloured light, and powerful music.
The idea was you coaxed the girl to accompany you on the ride in the hope that fear would force her into a tight embrace. It was the ride operators that pulled the girls as they jumped from car to car on the moving Waltzer to collect fares and spin the seats around. The beat music was loud and the girls just became intoxicated by the music and motion. How I envied those guys.
The 'New' Palace Amusement Centre on New Brighton Promenade was completed in Whitsun 1939. It was the biggest undercover amusement hall in Europe. During the Second World War, Wilkie helped the war effort by operating a makeshift ammunitions factory situated below the New Palace. My mother worked in the factory filling bullets with cordite. It was piecework and she was paid by the weight of the boxes produced, working shift work day and night. She was probably supplying the ammunition for her husband to fire at the Hun.
Wilkie had the idea of starting his own show and it was not until a couple of years after the war in 1949, his dream was realised when he opened his "W H Wilkie's Mammoth Circus and Zoo" next to the New Palace. In 1954 he fell in love with Suzanne Gendarme, a French trapeze artist working at his circus. They travelled out to South Africa together to look into the possibility of a travelling circus. Later that year they relocated the circus to Durban and from all accounts it took South Africa by storm, featuring top class international artists. Some nine years later the circus site was to find a new tenant - tenpin bowling.

Chapter 3 - Palace Indoor Fairgrounds

Wilkies Waltzer became a magnet for the girls, the fairground lads would ride on the platform to show off, spining the cars around faster and faster, then later, check behind the seats for loose change.

Chapter 3 - Palace Indoor Fairgrounds

WE MEET AGAIN!

From the *Liverpool Echo* of 13th April 1989
Bill Wilkie is to celebrate the 50th birthday of the giant indoor fun centre. When it opened for business at Whitsun in 1939, it was the biggest undercover amusement hall in Europe. On May 12 all the current attractions will be free to dozens of handicapped or underprivileged kids.
Mr Wilkie is trying to trace a group of wartime heroines so they can come too. About 250 women worked in a temporary factory in the building's basement during the war making shells and radar parts. The Creep Inn now occupies the site.
On seeing the article in the *Echo, my mother* made contact and was reunited with a lost friend, Jean Duff, whom she last saw in 1944. The above photograph shows Jean, her husband Joe and my mom, Dorothy, with a wartime photograph. They recalled how wartime singing heroine Vera Lynn visited the factory one night after appearing at the Empire in Liverpool. Dot, whose maiden name was Hammond, used to make bullets while Jean worked on radio parts. Jean said: "We used to come in through the shop at the front and show our passes with our photos because it was all secret war work. The Mayor of Wirral, Councillor Reg Cumpstey, praised Mr Wilkie and his family for supporting New Brighton down the years.

218

Chapter 3 - Tenpin Bowling

A new craze was to sweep the country in the early sixties. Tenpin bowling arrived from America and one of the very first to open was Fairlanes in New Brighton. It was in October 1963 when the swashbuckling Hollywood star, Douglas Fairbanks, with numerous films T*he Mark of Zorro, Robin Hood* and *The Thief of Bagdad* under his belt, arrived for the grand opening. He had been one of my heroes from the silver screen, courageous and bold. It was certainly worth a visit to see my hero……..
"On our part the centre is a calculated gamble", said Mr Fairbanks. "It is the seventh centre we have built in this country. I see your Coat of Arms motto is *'We are bold whilst we are cautious'.*
It's a pity just for this occasion that 'bold' isn't spelt the other way. The Mayor was invited to bowl the first bowl by the manager of the centre, Mr Jack White, who comes to Wallasey from the Fairlanes Centre at Hull. The Riverside Bowl & Lazer Quest is on the same site as the original 1963 bowling centre. The Palace Amusement Centre next door is still owned by the Wilkie family, but the circus site is now the bowling centre.

Gala Grand Opening Programme

FAIR LANES

Wallasey Bowling Centre

SATURDAY, OCTOBER 19th 1963

Bowling's fun at
FAIRLANES

FULL SWING TENPIN BOWLING

TENPIN BOWLING THE FAIRLANES WAY MEANS
★ Free Admission ★ Snackbar and Club Lounge
★ Luxury surroundings ★ Free Nursery Corner
★ Free instruction ★ Well-organised leagues

COST 3/6 per person per game   OPEN Everyday from 3 pm

MARINE PARADE   Telephone: NEW BRIGHTON 1238

Chapter 3 - Wilkie's Circus

I will always remember my first visit to the circus; with three shows on a Saturday, Wilkie's Circus was a popular attraction. Inside the ringmaster would crack his whip, and the clowns would arrive chasing a dwarf around the ring. The head clown had a tall white hat and a painted white face; one of the clowns started to cry with water squiring out from his eyes, which made everyone laugh then his red nose flashed on and off. There were performing sea lions playing tunes on motor horns and lions jumping through hoops, and made to roar. I gave a sigh of relief when the lions were chased down a tunnel out of the circus to be locked back up in their cage. Dogs on seesaws and elephants rising up on their hind legs all added to the fun. Above our heads in the big top, we were thrilled to see the trapeze artists as they caught one another in mid-air, and finally jumping out of the sky into their safety net. And to add even more excitement, there was the spectacle of a tightrope walker as he tiptoed along a thin cable, and returned on a cycle with his beautiful assistant perched on his shoulders. The cheers and gasps from the crowd only heightened the excitement. My dad's new found interest in equestrianism may have had something to do with the scantly clad girl covered in sequins and sporting a gorgeous white plume headdress, riding on a white stallion. What a show!

All the fun of the big top in our own back yard in New Brighton.

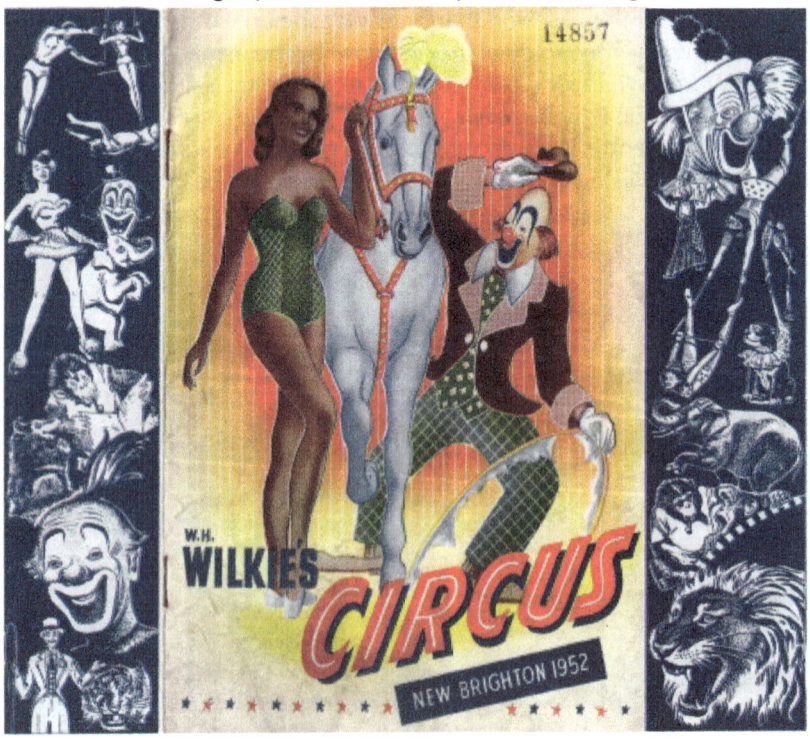

Chapter 3 - Wilkie's Circus

OPENS JULY 4th

W.H. WILKIE'S MAMMOTH CIRCUS

adjoining NEW PALACE, NEW BRIGHTON

A FEAST OF LAUGHTER, FUN AND STUPENDOUS DARE-DEVIL THRILLS!

EUROPE'S GREATEST CLOWNS ★ DARING TRAPEZISTS ★ BEAUTIFUL HORSES ★ ACROBATS ★ THRILLS ON THE HIGH WIRE ★ PERFORMING DOGS ★ JUGGLERS

3000 SEATS
1/6 — 6/-
SPECIAL PRICES FOR CHILDREN.

NEVER MIND the Weather

Chapter 3 - Captain's Pit

One of my favourite haunts was the Captain's Pit. In those days you were not allowed to fish it was illegal, so fishing rods were definitely out of the question. We all used hand lines, and made a little ball of dough out of bread to stick on the hook as bait. There was so much weed in the pond that we had to take a supply of hooks to use when the line got snagged. To prevent illegal fishing was a preoccupation of the park keeper sometimes he hid in the bushes or arrived at top neck speed on his bike. Woe betide you, if you got caught! He didn't seem to grasp the concept of kids and fun. Each night he would lock the gates but we would just jump over the low wall round the park. Another problem that we encountered was a bit of serious courting that was happening most nights in the park shelter. To the lovers engaged in these extracurricular activities a load of giggling boys running around the pond was an undesirable distraction.

My mate Rodrick had a pond in the back of his house in Mount Road, so we were always on the look out for some fish to stock his pond. His uncle lived in a house with a large garden on the corner of Sudworth Road and Mount Road. We would play with his air rifle in the garden, and shoot at targets we set up and anything that moved. It was in the days when gardens were full of sparrows.

Many legends and stories surrounded the Captain's Pit. On the long winter nights, we would sit fishing and the various stories would be told. There was the sea captain who sailed the mighty oceans but managed to get drunk and drown in our very own pond! Some disagree and say, "It was his wife that threw herself into the abyss when she heard the news her husband had been drowned at sea." After this tragedy his or her spirit was said to haunt the pit. Any shadow or untoward splash was put down to ghostly apparitions. It was around this time that someone would get their stories mixed up and regurgitate the tale of *The Pit and the Pendulum*. Rod's dad had told us all about the couple that drowned in the pit, a man named Thomas Howard and his wife Hannah. They were accompanied by

Chapter 3 - Captain's Pit

his brother, a lad just fourteen years old. He had witnessed Thomas jump into the pit as if possessed and when his wife tried to save him, she also drowned. Some say drink was the cause and others he was under a spell. but this story was true - so we were told!

In the pit were some of the largest carp that you could imagine, and we sometimes spotted a large mouth brake the surface of the water. They would lie motionless with just their backs breaking the surface; we always spotted the bubbles and swirls on the surface of the water caused by the sudden movement of the carp. They were massive. The story was that when the aquarium closed down in the Tower, the carp were put into the pit. We fished for smaller game - roach, gudgeon and rudd.

Carp were definitely out of our league! Someone said that they had caught a pike and the toothy predator had taken a slice out of his finger, and he had the sticky plaster to prove it. We found out later it was a lie. I was not to know it at the time but the church next to the Captain's Pit - All Saints Church - would be a feature in my later musical life.

Chapter 4 - My Working Career

This section of the book requires an introduction, and covers my working career. In parallel with my labours, I also engaged in various entrepreneurial activities including renting and renovating property, the rag trade, a pet shop, electronic and instrumentation businesses, followed by engineering and industrial supplies and finally publishing and telecommunications. I did all this with the object of gaining financial independence and freedom from a regular 9-5 job.

I was determined that I was going to be in control of my own destiny. I had watched my father work hard all his life and not make it to the finishing post and I didn't want that to happen to me. My first lucky break was obtaining an electrical engineering apprenticeship with a blue chip company, Tate & Lyle. Then through my studies at technical college, I moved into the field of electronics and instrumentation which at this time was in its infancy.

All the companies in this area that employed me have now shut down. Sunderland Forge, Tate & Lyle, GEC, Cadburys, Champion Sparking Plug Company, Burmah Oil, Bidston Steel. It is as if they never existed but they supplied highly paid jobs and supported many thousands of families.

So before they disappear from people's memories, I have included them here. When I look at the state of our industry to day I am glad I don't have to begin all over again and try to make a living.

We went from a society making things to a society of service industries, compensation lawyers, call centres, and casino banking.

We have moved from a country that gave the world its prosperity through the Industrial Revolution to an inward-looking, politically correct and dysfunctional society. The loss of our strong foothold in manufacturing is a sin for future generations.

We also sold out our industrial heritage - our nuclear industry to the French, our steel industry to the Indians along with Land Rover, and our remaining car manufacturing to American and German companies. The little manufacturing that remains in the UK is mostly owned by foreign companies.

Below are the companies I worked for only one is still in existence.

Sunderland Forge	July 1962 - June 1963
Tate & Lyles	June 1963 - June 1968
T & J Harrison	June 1968 - May 1969
Rewinds & J Windsor	July 1969 - Nov 1969
Cadburys	Dec 1969 - Mar 1973
Associated Octel	Mar 1973 - Sept 1974
GEC Medical	Sept 1974 - Jan 1975
Champion Spark Plugs	Jan 1975 - Sep 1975
Wirral Inst. Services / Instamec	Sep 1975 - July 1985
Instamec Ltd (Costains)	July 1985 - Nov 1987

Chapter 4 - The Sunderland Forge & Engineering Co. Ltd.

My mother worked for Mrs Leary-Shaw in Portland Court, New Brighton, she had cleaned for the lady for many years. Out of sear desperation one day, my mother mentioned the fact that none of my applications for an apprenticeship had come to fruition. Mrs Leary-Shaw told my mother she would have a word with her husband, Jack, and see what they could do. Jack was the chief steward on one of the Empress boats and had many contacts in the shipping business. The result an interview with Mr Smith the Managing Director of the Sunderland Forge, manufacturers of switchboards, generators, alternators, electric winches, and switch gear.

It was a warm sunny day in July. Mom had pressed my suit and starched my white shirt. An impressive tie was found and I was ready to make the trip to Birkenhead. The interview was scheduled for 12:30pm which I figured must have been just before his lunch break. I found the place without any difficulty. A brass nameplate outside displayed the name of the company in Pilgrim Street. A door led up a flight of stairs to a corridor with numerous offices on both sides. It was now that my nerves kicked in. The first door was open and I saw a lady typing away and a sign indicating that this room was the reception. I walked into the room and said "Excuse me, I have an appointment at 12:30pm with Mr Smith." Looking up from her typing she pointed to a chair and said, "Sit down there; I'll tell him you've here." The offices appeared to be quite busy with people coming and going, and guys walking around with rolls of drawings under their arms. After what seemed like hours, I was directed to Mr Smith's office. Still clutching my School Leaving Certificate and a reference from Mr Thorpe, my Headmaster, I knocked and duly entered the room. I was told to sit down and an open-stretched hand took charge of my documents which were then removed from the brown envelope and duly examined. "I see you got an A in medalwork. Are you good with your hands?" was the first question, as he peered over his spectacles. "Yes Sir I enjoy making things" was my timid reply. "You know, you can't start an apprenticeship until you are 16 years old. You'll have to work in the stores and learn the workings of the company, learn about the equipment used and the like." I nodded in agreement. "Well, your reference from the headmaster speaks highly of your attitude and reliability which are some of the attributes required if you wish to work for the Sunderland Forge". He Flicked through my papers and then handed them back with a smile and an acknowledgement that he thought I would be a suitable candidate for employment. "When can you start?", was his next question. I was quite taken aback by the speed of things and gasped and tried to collect my thoughts. "I can start next Monday" came my reply. "Our school holidays start in about a week's time, and that is my official leaving time. "Ok, that's fine."

Chapter 4 - The Sunderland Forge & Engineering Co. Ltd.

"I will get my secretary to type up an offer of employment and we will pop it in the post to you. You will report to Jack in the stores, but this will be detailed in your letter - starting pay, hours and holidays. It will all be outlined." I left the office and was so excited I just cannot remember the trip home. I ran down Field Road to tell my mom the good news. Time soon passed and I was to start my new job. My very first week's wage was £2. 12s 6d. (That's £2.62p in today's decimal money!)

Jack in the stores was quite a firm character and around 50 years old. He was short and had black greasy hair that had been strategically plastered over his bald patch. His moustache had seen better days as it was starting to thin a little, probably due to his nervous habit of playing with it. He wore a brown knee-length coat, and a short pencil was always balanced on his right ear. He had the statue of a store keeper with an attitude to match, a stickler for the correct paperwork and with numerous decades of store keeping under his belt, he knew where every nut and bolt was kept. He seemed to possess a computer memory and he could source most items within a microsecond. He was reluctant to call me by my Christian name, I just had the impression his brain could not hold information unless it was in the form of a six-digit store code. His conversations lacked any full stops and he tended to drawl on a bit. So it was.... lad, do this, or lad, do that etc.

After a while it did start to annoy me but you can get used to anything. It did not take me long to discover that apart from my store duties, I was the general dogsbody around the place. There was a distinct pecking order, and first in was always the general dogsbody. From making the tea to going to the market for the cheese barm (bread) rolls, cheese without margarine, cheese with onion... the combinations were endless. I also had to run to the shops for fags. I was handed over the tea swindle by the previous slave, or should I say tea club. It was my responsibility to collect one shilling off each of the members and from this I was expected to buy the tea and milk. We got the sugar free from next door. At each break time, I was to have a large urn of tea brewing before they came in for their break. It was one such break time that I was relaxing in the 15 minutes allocated time for the brew when I received a belt across the back of my head from an irate welder.

"What's all this shit floating in my cup?" was the exclamation which passed his lips.

"I don't know" was my immediate reply, positioning myself away from any possible repeat belting. Jack came to my rescue.

"Leave the lad alone" On a closer examination of the cup, the guy sat next to the welder chirped in and said "He's been using cheap tea" This seemed to aggravate the welder even more.

"We give you money to buy PG tips, and you've been buying the cheap stuff.

Chapter 4 - The Sunderland Forge & Engineering Co. Ltd.

It took a while for this incidence to subside. I had been told by the previous custodian of the tea swindle that to make some cash out of the operation it was important to buy the good stuff and mix it with "Golden Stream" tea which was half the price - then, bingo you stood to make a few quid. Unfortunately the mixture in the large tea caddy had settled out and was running low when I made the brew. So it was back to the drawing board.

My first visit to Cammell Lairds was a real eye-opener. Everyone was on steroids (piecework) and the whole place hummed with activity, noise and the smell of red lead. No one slacked: if you did, you lost money. The foremen all wore suits with bowler hats; most of the hats were covered with paint and welders' burn marks. It was truly surreal.

It was marvellous to see these massive ships surrounded with planks and scaffolding and cranes that disappeared into the clouds. They were like scales on a massive dinosaur. It was like an ant colony on a massive scale everyone seemed to know their place. Pneumatic hammers pounded on the side of the ships hull, sending echoes in all directions, the shouts of the men, it was all overpowering.

Cammell Lairds was probably just past its peak but with 7,000 people working in the yard, it was busy, even though stiff competition was starting to emerge. The last launching of 1962 took place on the 12th October with the Shell tanker *Oscilla*. Their completed jobs included a submarine *HMS Odin* and *HMS Devonshire*, Britain's very first guided-missile destroyer, *CS Mercury* the very first cable-layer built for Cable and

Wireless, and the *Manx Maid*, the first drive-on drive off car ferry. It had been an exciting year, and these were just a few of the ships built. My head was just spinning trying to take it all in.

"Lad who are you looking for"? Turning around it was one of these bowler hated gentlemen. "I need to go to the electrical stores, I've brought some watertight deck fittings from the Sunderland Forge." Adjusting his bowler, he pointed me in the direction of the stores. I was to make many visits to the yard each as impressive as the last. If I had time I would wander around to see what was being built.

Chapter 4 - The Sunderland Forge & Engineering Co. Ltd.

My job even gave me a direct link to the *RMS Titanic*. After a few weeks in the stores and during a clear out of spares, one of the directors announced that this electric motor was no longer required. It had been held in stock as a spare for the *Titanic*. It had lain forgotten for years under a pile of wooden crates. So the lads pulled it out and I was told to strip all the copper out of the motor and put the material in hessian bags to be sent to Hector Jackson the scrap dealer in Birkenhead. The director had obviously found a rich vein of additional revenue to help support his Bentley and cigar habit. The Sunderland Forge had supplied Harland and Wolf Belfast with all the electric winches used on the *Titanic*, and the motor was a spare for one of the winches. I remember similar winches coming into the workshop for repair; they had asbestos brake pads. An apprentice would take the inspection covers off the brake drum and blow off the asbestos dust which had accumulated on the pads by using an air line, all ready for the engineer to examine the pads. I remember Jack shouting out "Blow that f**kin dust somewhere else not all over the stores" Happy days!

My world was to collapse when after a visit to Lairds, I returned back to the Forge only to find a load of lads all stood around the shop steward, who informed the gathered mass that the business had gone into liquidation and was closing down. I took the sad news home to my parents. My father got the writing pad out along with the envelopes and sat me down to start the process all over again of writing to firms to see if I could get an apprenticeship. The clock had been ticking down because if you were too old you had no chance. My mother duly reported the bad news to Mrs Leary-Shaw. I worked another two weeks before I picked up my final wage packet with holiday pay and my P45. I was very fortunate in being offered an electrical engineering apprenticeship with Tate and Lyle, There were over 300 applicants and time running out, I was very lucky indeed.

228

Chapter 4 - Tate & Lyle Ltd

My first day at Tate and Lyles was memorable. My journey started at 6.30am. On arrival at Seacombe Ferry I joined a busy stream of people disembarking from the buses. After paying the fare I walked down a long floating walkway within a tunnel. It all depended on the tide whether you walked up hill or down.

The ferry boat arrived from Liverpool on time. On instructions from the Captain the powerful engines would be put astern as the water at the rear began to churn white with the force of the propellers. The boat would shudder as the ropes were attached to the massive steel bollards in a well-rehearsed routine. A figure of eight was made around each pair of bollards. Once the boat was tied up securely the gangplank would drop with a loud rattle of chains. I quickly took a seat and waited for the bells to signal our departure. My first view of Liverpool was The Three Graces- the world-famous skyline of Liverpool consisting of the Royal Liver Building, the Cunard Building and the Port of Liverpool Building. Leaving the ferry there was a long walk up the floating gangway and a stroll down the dock road, past the throbbing heart of the city.

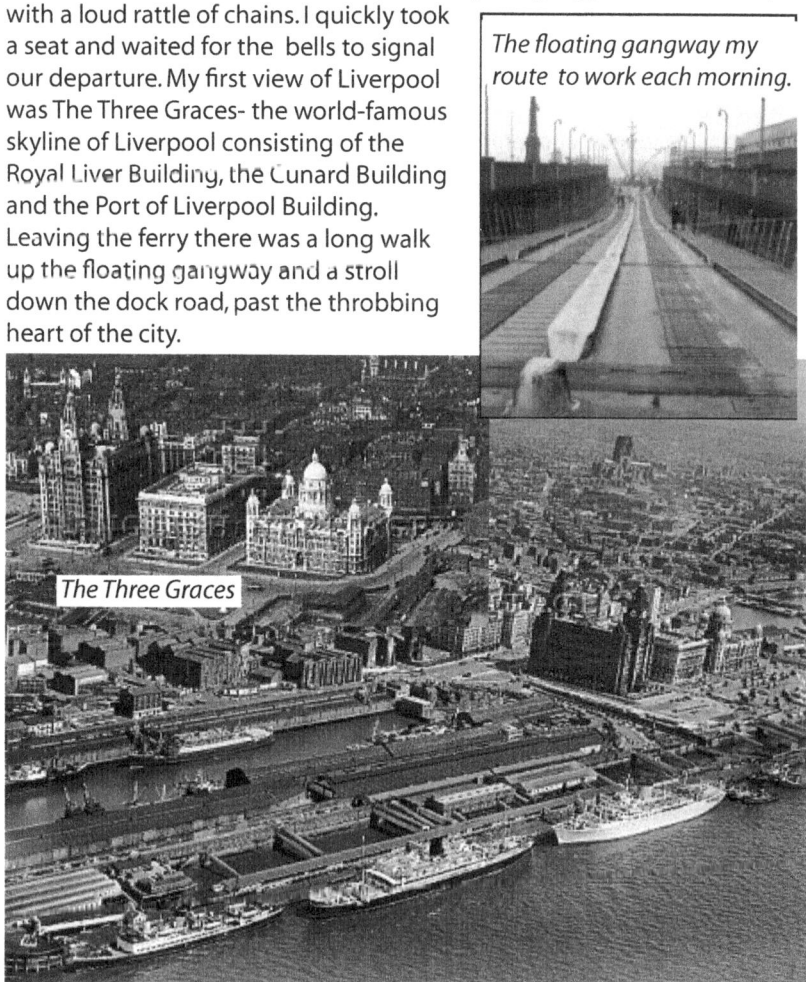

The floating gangway my route to work each morning.

The Three Graces

View of the Pier Head, with the dock road clearly visible. This was the route I took each morning while I was serving my time as an electrical apprentice.

Chapter 4 - Tate & Lyle Ltd

I reported to the gate house on my first morning. The guy sitting inside a small windowed office was the time keeper whose job it was to watch all the workers as they clocked in and out, making sure that no one clocked on anyone else. His blue uniform was immaculate and his ex-military appearance made him look quite a formidable character. I was extremely nervous as I handed in my letter of introduction. Looking me up and down with a totally blank expression, he said,
"Come with me,"
as he handed the document back to me.
"You will be needing this."
A short distance away was a small waiting room where I was told to wait. Eventually I was collected by Mr Harry Moore who was in charge of the Apprentice Workshop. This was followed by a trip to the stores to be kitted out with 2 towels, 2 pairs of overalls, and a pair of safety boots. Then on to the changing room to be given a locker in the apprentice section - there were ten of us in each year, four electrical and six mechanical apprentices, with a couple of process apprentices thrown in for good measure. All apprenticeships lasted the full 5 years. The Apprentice Workshop was on the Fairies site, to the left of this picture. Love Lane! Whoever dreamed up that name should be given an award for stupidity. Smoke and grime covered most of the warehouses around the land-locked refinery with its red-brick walls, worn out and weathered by years of erosion. The Tate & Lyle marble-faced offices and shining aluminium silo towers stood out like a knight in shinning armour, and to many of its workers it was a source of high wages and reliable employment.
A road divided the plant and was used by tankers to ferry their precious raw sugar cargo to be refined.
Tate and Lyle had a fantastic reputation for looking after its apprentices. Each individual participated in a comprehensive training scheme. I was to visit all the different electrical engineering departments on the site. My training started with a month in the engineering stores, to learn about tools and materials. It was while I was in the stores that Burt would send me on worthless errands. Some apprentices managed to take hours, while searching vainly for sky hooks, tartan paint, or a left-handed screwdriver. My next port of call was the apprentice workshop where our master of ceremonies was Mr Harry Moore (Apprentice Supervisor), an old sea dog. He had spent years at sea, engineering himself around the world with

230

Chapter 4 - Tate & Lyle Ltd

Blue Funnel. He took a shine to me and offered sound advice and help in developing my skills.

The workshop's location must have been in the oldest part of the factory; it reminded you of a Charles Dickens' novel. The old warehouse had defiantly seen better days. It was cold, damp and foreboding, and the old cast iron pillars sent shadows across the tiled floor. Each workbench or machine had an enamelled lamp attached to a long flexible arm that could be adjusted. We had to practise filing different metal surfaces accurately so that they fit correctly like a jigsaw puzzle it was a long tedious operation. "Roy, keep your file parallel to the work piece at all times." That still rings in my ears. Next we had to learn how to operate lathes, millers, grinders and other machinery. It was during this time that most apprentices would make pokers and brass stands for their coal fires back home. The photograph below has a funny side. A tour around the factory by several dignitaries had been organised by the company. Just before they stepped into the workshop, Harry told me to turn up the cut on the grinder, the effect being lots of sparks flying from the work piece. Very impressive! This then had the effect of causing the coolant to over heat and produce steam. Now the toilet block was quite a walk from the workshop, so some of the apprentices would urinate in the coolant reservoir at the back of the machine. Our Lord Mayor must have just caught a whiff, judging by his expression. Needless to say they moved off sharply as Harry moved out of sight turning red and shaking his head.

I spent time in the Lift Department, fixing and maintaining the sixty or so

Chapter 4 - Tate & Lyle Ltd

electric lifts around the site. Quite often the faults that were reported were due to the lift being stopped on purpose between floors while the bookie's runner took the bets! I then moved on to the construction department in charge of new installations and projects. One individual who stands out was George, an electrician's mate. He was getting on in years and had been a successful boxer years ago. Looking at his flat nose, cauliflower ears and numerous scars around his eyes you could tell he had been in a few battles. His other claim to fame was his humour. It was at the time when I was playing in a group and had fairly long hair to look the part. "Bloody hell Roy, your hair looks like an explosion in a mattress factory," was a comment from George I will always remember. I had teamed up with Phil an electrician and George for a few months. Interestingly, Phil told me he was cheesed off with this type of work and wanted a change. His dream was to be a social worker and he had been going to night school to study. I often wondered if he ever made the move. With a spell in the electric truck department, and the rewind and electric motor shop, my training was coming along nicely. The power house was to be my next port of call. This was where we generated electricity from the left-over steam used in the process of sugar refining. Sid was the foreman and a bit of a stickler for detail. I had to work nights for a couple of weeks to be shown how to bring our generators on line. We had to synchronise them with the national grid. This was followed by a spell in the Electronic Workshop. In those days we had no semiconductors or transistors everything was operated by massive thermionic valves. We must have had one of the very first check weighers to check the weight of the 2lb bags of sugar as they shot past on a conveyor belt. Its display was cold cathodes revolutionary. I joined an established team of guys including Tony Winrow and Brian Cusak, both of whom lived on the Wirral. Brian was a keen rugby player and would quite often look the worse for wear after a weekend of battling.

Pictured are Tony Winrow, Phil Woods, Ray Gillies, Jimmy Vance, Norman McAlinren, Billy Boyle, Joey Downess, and Brian Cusak. Taken in either 1966 or 1967 at a 'farewell drink' as one of the lads was off to Zambia. Photograph by Ray Gillies

Chapter 4 - Tate & Lyle Ltd

The last 6 months of my apprenticeship was in the drawing office. As you would expect in this era, we had a Porn Club; each member paid in a shilling and you could borrow a magazine, which had been covered in brown paper. Then there was the Premium Bond club, the members having thousands of pounds between them, as each member agreed to share their winnings with the others. We also ran a football Pools syndicate, and there was the Crystal Club snooker team and a quiz team. It is a wonder that anyone had time to produce a drawing.

We took our tea and meal breaks in the main canteen which was in the administration block on the first floor. There were three canteens. The largest was the works' canteen for any of the works personnel. Then there was the Junior Staff canteen, also on the first floor. The last was the Senior Staff Canteen on the second floor. Different groups of workers tended to use different parts of the canteen. The engineering and process apprentices used the tables near the windows that looked out onto the yard and filtration house. The day workers in the centre and the shift workers on the opposite side of the canteen overlooked Burlington Street. For our tea break we had buttered toast and a large mug of tea; most of the lads sprinkled sugar on their toast. Above the canteen were offices, laboratories and also the main drawing office.

The company even supplied the apprentices with a club room. We could use it to do our homework from Technical college and the company even paid for a maths teacher to come in and help us with our homework. His name was Arthur and a few of the lads shared a common interest with him, namely horse racing. So it was not difficult during one of his lessons to change the subject and go into the different odds for different bets.

Lookout point ->

In the nice weather a good sun-bathing spot was on top of the recovery house roof. High up on the corner of the roof was a tall steel construction used as a lookout point in the Second World War, and this was a favourite location for a card school. Importantly the roof had more than one exit, so the chances of getting caught was quite remote. The only regular visitor was the exterminator whose job was to try and catch pigeons. The company tried to keep the numbers down for fear of contamination. The birds would be caught alive using bait inside a wire cage. We used to let them out, so there was no love lost

233

Chapter 4 - Tate & Lyle Ltd

He would dispatch the birds with a flick of the wrist while holding a couple between his fingers and throw them in a sack, before moving off to the next trap.

The two top apprentices from each year judged by their exam results and punctuality were awarded a place at the Outward Bound School, either at Aberdovey, or the Lake District. Fitzpatrick and I came out top boys so off we went.

The rain was pouring down at Penrith Railway Station. I was on my way to the Outward Bound Mountain School at Ullswater. It was Summer 1962, and I was 18 years old, away from home on my own for the first time and my close companion was trepidation. Later I was to hear that this was the ultimate boot camp on the north shore of a lake, set in 18 acres of woodland at the heart of Wordsworth country, and with some of the highest mountains in England.

Ullswater Outward Bound School

A few minutes later I was being loaded onto a Land Rover and then whisked off to the Outward Bound School. There were about 70 other lads there and we were put into the dining hall and split into patrols. Individual adult patrol leaders arrived and then showed each group to their dormitory. After a meal a talk of what life was about and a cup of cocoa, we were all packed off to bed. After a long day I was ready for my bunk bed. In the morning we all had to sign a pledge that we would not smoke or consume any alcohol during the course. I was in Scott Patrol and our dormitory was on the top floor, so twice a week we had a fire escape practice. On the wall outside the window were rings through which the rope was passed through and we abseiled down.

We had to rise at 6am, our kit, beds and dormitory were inspected and marked, and then we had run down to the lake for the morning "cold" dip – we had to jump off the end of the jetty with the instructor wrapped up with his thick jumper and a scarf for good measure. And all this before breakfast! "Come on, lads, get a move on. I want my breakfast. This will wake you up." Then Splash, followed by the fastest exit from the ice cold water that you could imagine!

The next 26 days were the fullest I have ever had in my life. After breakfast, each team took turns to wash up and clean. Then activities for the day rock climbing, knots, hiking, exercises, abseiling, athletics, and patrol expeditions. And to top it all, an assault course, with a 12- foot wall. And if that wasn't enough, there were lectures in the evening.

We even had a night callout to rescue a climber who had fallen and was stranded up a mountain. We had to get this climber onto a stretcher and take him to safety, only to be told he was a member of staff and not really hurt - but it was a good training exercise. This was typical of what was expected of you - total commitment.

I thought how was I going to survive these ordeals?

We had quite a long walk round Goat's Water. Before we arrived with our rock-climbing gear on the buttresses of Dow Crag, our intrepid leader, Campbell Whalley, was above me as I was on the rock face with the necessary three points of contact.

I shouted..."belaying, then belaying now", the climbing signals that we all knew off by heart. Being roped together up a crag was an experience, but don't look down! Campell had not been looking too good at the start of the climb; he had been out on the tiles the night before because one of the other instructors was leaving so they had a quite party. Then, would you believe it, he started to throw up! With four of us all roped together on different parts of the rock face, there was just nowhere to go, but luckily we all wore safety helmets.

My next memory was of canoeing on Ullswater. I was in a two-man canoe and we were learning how to Slalom (zigzag between obstacles). Of course, we ended up with the canoe full of water and it began to sink. Campbell had showed the patrol how to form a life raft using their canoes so we were both rescued, just in time. When I dared put my feet down onto the water bottom, it was only a foot deep! At the end of the second week we split up into four groups and went on a three-day expedition. The route had been pre-planned and took us to the top of Helvellyn. As the mist descended we could not see our hands in front of our faces.

When we eventually descended and reached the road below we were informed by other patrols that the tops had been "Out of Bounds" for the last two days unknown to us! The expeditions were certainly testing making the teaching of compass skills very important.

Then it was the turn of an expedition on your own. With a map and the coordinates for your route noted, and a 20 kg rucksack on your back, off you went. My shelter was to be a bivouac. After a long four-hour walk I came to the halfway point, and it was starting to get dark. I had been told it was a good idea to set up the bivouac on the side of a dry stone wall, one that had traces of sheep hairs. The instructor had informed us sheep are not stupid and know how to stay out of the prevailing wind.

Chapter 4 - Tate & Lyle Ltd

What he neglected to mention was that after I had set up, the stupid sheep decided to come back to its sleeping place.
On the final day we learnt that our team had won the best turned-out dormitory, and came third in the Whitely Shield event. We had a final photograph taken after which we all shook hands and made our way to the train station for the return home. The experience taught me leadership, discipline and respect, and helped maintain my love of the mountains and open spaces.
One of the company directors was a member of the Southport Yacht Club, and he thought it a good idea if we got a team of apprentices together to build a Daily Mirror Class Dingy to introduce them to the delights of sailing. A group of us would stay behind after work and construct the boat from a blueprint and kit of parts. After we made it, we had to make a trailer to tow the boat around. We were even given an old Jeep for the sole use of the apprentices, only to find no one had a driving licence. As apprentices we were all given sixteen one-hour driving lessons and took a driving test as part of our training. If we passed, we were able to use the Apprentices' Jeep, which was, in fact, an old Land Rover.
During our time as apprentices we were required to attend Day Release at one of the local Technical Colleges. It was a long twelve-hour day, as it included a night school session. The courses varied depending on the ability of the apprentice in question. My course was the Electrical Technicians Course; others did National and Higher National courses.

Birkenhead Technical College in Borough Road, I spent 1966-1968 studying for my C&G Electrical Technician's Certificate.

I attended Withens Lane Technical College and then for the last two years Birkenhead Technical College. Glyn Roberts was the Superintendent in charge of the apprentices and he arranged a yearly prize presentation in the form of books or tools. You had to buy the items yourself up to a certain value which depended on the exam results, and bring in the receipt to be reimbursed. I remember my mate, Eddy Wormhole, buying a couple of erotic books including *Lady Chatterley's Lover* and wrapping them up neatly ready for the presentation. He managed to get a handwritten receipt describing his purchase as technical books from a mate in the book shop! The day of the presentation arrived and none other than Mr Tate himself called into the Crystal Club to make the presentations. All our parcels were neatly labelled with our details.

Chapter 4 - Tate & Lyle Ltd

Mr Roberts passed each parcel in turn to Mr Tate who shook hands with each apprentice and said well done. Quite a few of the apprentices were in the know concerning the contents of Eddy's parcel so when it came to his turn, up he went onto the stage accompanied by an unusually loud cheer from the other apprentices with some wag shouting ..."show us your books" to which he scuttled off with a bit more speed. So there you have it -our Managing Director a purveyor of pornography.

Duggy Williams, a life-long communist, had become my mentor in all things political. I was indoctrinated into Engles, Marks and Trotsky during the five years that we travelled together between Liverpool and Seacombe. The ferry boat took office workers to Liverpool and most of them would be sat down all day at their desks. So every day the whole top section of the ferry was full of these chaps walking around in a clockwise direction.

Duggy would call into the paper shop and pick up about 30-40 Daily Worker newspapers to distribute to his friends. It was a type of teenager mental grooming. He would probably have been put on the mental offenders' list by now. He was also a keen yachtsman and had ventured into the blue beyond on numerous occasions. I was totally impressed when he told me his small boat had got him safely to the Isle of Man and back. He was a day fitter, fixing conveyors and machinery in the factory. Duggy was a really pleasant person to talk to, even though I didn't always agree with his politics.

My apprenticeship ran in parallel with the swinging sixties and in my spare time I was a drummer in a pop group. A mate of mine, Peter Ritson who was a fellow electrical apprentice also belonged to a group called "The Riot Squad" but Peter did not complete his apprenticeship as he decided to go off to the south of France with a rock band where they had some success. Bill Ennis was their lead guitarist - the brother of Ray of the "Swinging Blue Jeans". We played several times with them at the Orrell Cricket Club and one event was the Tate & Lyle Annual Apprentices' Dance. Once with "The Ash" as lead singer and another with "The Hud" (John Hudson) and finally with John Moore as the singer. We could never decide on who was the best singer in our group hence all the changes. I remember us opening and warming up the crowd and it went down well. On the last occasion Robert doubled as the cloakroom attendant and made an extra bit of beer money on the side. Eddie Wormhole and I ran the last show but a slight altercation and disagreement concerning the entrance money going towards the alcoholic intake of the organisers meant it would be the last.

Chapter 4 - Tate & Lyle Ltd

And when I made contact with Peter on *Friends United* a couple of years back, he told me he had been living on the Costa Blanca for the past 35 or more years. He still played in a group, and had no regrets.

In the good old days before we were forced by the EU to refine sugar beat, our sugar came from the Caribbean. So the writing was on the wall and on the 22nd April 1981, the Love Lane refinery closed and it was the end of an era.

Demolition of Tate & Lyle Refinery

Chapter 4 - T & J Harrison (Shipping)

It was the policy of Tate and Lyle that on the conclusion of your apprenticeship you had to leave the company to gain experience elsewhere. I had been toying with the idea of going away to sea. Several of my friends had related their experiences in mysterious lands full of dusty maidens and fun - it sounded the place for me. Within walking distance of Tate and Lyle were the offices of T & J Harrison so I decided during my lunch break I would pop down and get an application form. It was a miserable cold overcast day; I had my overhalls on and walked briskly down the dock road hoping to miss the coming shower. On arrival at their offices I walked up to the receptionist and asked if they were taking on electrical staff, and if so could I have an application form. Looking me up and down, she told me to wait there. I looked around and felt a little out of place and I was reluctant to sit down because I was wearing dirty overhalls. So I stood there their like a fish out of water. She asked me my name and proceeded to make a phone call.

"Mr Baker, I have a Mr Roy Dutton at reception inquiring into the possibility of employment in the electrical department".

The short telephone call ended abruptly. She now made eye contact with me as she pointed up the stairs and said in a more friendly voice.,

"Mr Baker's office is at the top of the stairs second on the right."

I knocked on the door and entered expecting to obtain an application form. But some five minutes later after a few questions, I was offered a job subject to a medical. I walked back to Tate's in a daze - what had I done? Did I really want to leave home, friends and family?

The company arranged a private medical which I passed A1. Then I had to go down to the "Pool" for my discharge book. This was a single story building opposite Kingston House, the Seaman's Mission, which backed onto part of the Salthouse Dock. This area is known as Mann Island; after the Sailors' Home closed, the new Shipping Federation or Pool was at Mann Island which has also been demolished.

Not for me the glorious "Queens", or the sleek, modern passenger ships, but, instead, a cargo vessel called the *MV Statesman* which was to take me on a journey into the unknown. We were tasked to travel to the Azores

M.V Tactician

and bring back the crippled *MV Tactician*.

As I struggled up the steep clanking gangway on the *MV Statesman* with my heavy cases, I wondered what on earth I had let myself in for as I viewed the chaos of flying slings of cargo and fork lift trucks - everyone was in a mad hurry to complete the loading. Birkenhead was the loading port. If the lifeblood of the Mersey was the ships, then men were its heart. I struggled over a metal ledge, which I came to know as a *coaming*, part of a watertight door to the ship's accommodation. I made my way past dockers, sprawled along the alleyway, studying newspapers. I located the cabin with the legend above the door - Chief Engineer - and gave a timid knock; I was about to make my introduction and tender my joining letter. A gruff voice barked, "Come In!" and I pushed the door open to find a scowling, grey-headed man, glaring at me, as if incensed by the intrusion. "I assume you have been given your instructions by the Superintendent. Well, you are a passenger until we reach the Azores. We are just awaiting clearance from the Port Authorities then we sail. Good luck!".

A learning curve, so steep as to be almost vertical, was about to hit me between the eyes. I was actually on a ship and about to go to sea!

I was privileged to travel the world and also be paid for it!

As Del Boy put it, "The world was my Lobster!"

I returned to my cabin, unpacked and now, suitably dressed in my officer's uniform, I could go to the saloon for my evening meal. Not for me the engineers' duty mess where they could eat in working clothes, I was on a cruise to the Azores!

After an uneventful trip we arrived at Ponta Delgada in the Azores. It was the Captain's intention to berth the ship as close to the *Tactician* as possible. After our ship was tied up and the gangplank dropped the second mate came in to see me. I was instructed to clear my cabin and report for duty to the Chief Engineer, Mr Norman Thompson on the *Tactician*. On my arrival aboard the stricken vessel, I could not help but notice the numerous cables strung across the deck and a ship's officer arguing with a couple of Portuguese guys; he was having difficulty being understood. "Which cable is this? I've numbered them all so it's impossible to mix them up." I stood for a moment discreetly watching this performance. On seeing my arrival he immediately walked over.

"Hi you must be the relief electrical engineer; come with me and I'll take you to see the chief."

As we walked along the deck the smell of burnt paint and the blackened ventilation shafts underlined the disaster that had struck the ship. Turning to face me and with a look of distain written across his face.

"I'd better introduce myself - I'm Ray, first electrical officer,

I'm trying get these fools to replace the burnt out wiring from the bridge to the engine room, but they don't speak a word of English and I can't understand anything they are saying. And to add to the bloody confusion,

Chapter 4 - T & J Harrison (Shipping)

they've never been on a ship before, let alone wire it up. Did you bring all the drums of cables out with you and the spares I requested?"
Nodding affirmatively, I looked Ray directly in the eye.
"We've got most of your requests and in a couple of cases have an equivalent which should not cause any problems. All the materials are being put shore-side as we speak."
"OK, that's great; let's go and see the chief." Entering the accommodation the acrid smell still persisted. The chief's cabin door was wide open and inside was the second engineer, John Beaton. Both were engaged in an altercation and you could cut the atmosphere with a knife. They did not even notice us waiting.
"Why did you pump the CO_2 into the engine room when my men where unaccounted for?"
The second had a report in his hand and threw it onto the table and said he was not signing it, as it's a load of lies.
The chief was fuming and a red mist had descended on both protagonists; we were still not even noticed.
"Look John, the Super (Superintendant) will arrive any minute and we must all be singing off the same hymn sheet, just calm down and let's talk it through."
"No way," the second replied as he stormed out past both of us.
The chief seemed to regain his composure on seeing us both standing in the doorway.
"Come in, take a seat," he said pointing to a couple of chairs around a conference table. Ray introduced me to the Chief after a few niceties he continued:
"I've scheduled a progress meeting for two o clock; the Supper will be in attendance, and he will want to know the progress, and if we can get back to Liverpool under our own steam. So make sure you can brief him on the progress." With that he immediately stormed out of his office in the direction of the engine room, taking the document with him, no doubt to speak to the second again. We took our leave and walked to the cabin that had been allocated to me.
"I'm sorry it's a bit on the small side; leave your case in here and I'll send in the engineer's boy to give you a hand. Then pointing to the right, he said, "My cabin is the last one at the end of the corridor. When you've got your playsuit on (overhauls) I'll introduce you to the second electrical engineer. I quickly changed and then joined the guys in Ray's cabin.
"Hi, come in. I suppose you were wondering what that was all about in the chiefs cabin?"
Well I'll tell you the true story. It was on the 4th July 1968 and the engine room went up in flames. No 4 generator had caused the problem - a leaking fuel pipe. It was on the fourth's watch and there was only a donkeyman and a cadet down below. When the alarms were sounded,

Chapter 4 - T & J Harrison (Shipping)

the engineers rushed down to try and tackle the fire; John Beaton had tried to couple the fire hose to the hydrant but the remaining generator tripped out and plunged the engine room into total darkness. It was total confusion. Other Engineers tried to enter but were beaten back by the smoke. The fourth engineer, Mr Hughes, had managed to clamber out after shutting down the main engine and was suffering from smoke inhalation and was in a distressed condition. By 22:00hrs the engine room had been totally sealed. The chief engineer Mr Norman Thompson panicked and, without knowing all his engineers had escaped, he flooded the engine compartment with CO_2. It was a deed that could not be forgiven: the forth was unaccounted for and a donkeyman was also missing. Luckily they had all escaped but the chief had not known this when he activated the CO_2.

Captain Skelly had been woken and was on the bridge taking charge of operations but communications to the bridge had been destroyed in the fire so some confusion had occurred with the deck officers under the impression that the fire was in the hold of the ship. The Captain instructed radio officer Frank Lawton to send out an "Urgency" signal to all ships. He decided that an SOS message was not required because the crew could remain on ship, but that was debateable. The Captain had moved all the crew up forward, away from the engine room to prepare to abandon ship. No mains power was available so battery power was used to transmit the message, it read: "Lat 41° 30'N , Long 39° 17'W. Engine room on fire. Position serious." and asked that ships in the vicinity please stand by. The message was picked up and relayed to Land's End Radio. Eventually a tow was accepted from the *Rapallo* which had entered into an agreement with T & J Harrison - every man on board would receive a month's extra salary, with additional remuneration from the owners. Under normal maritime law the cargo would have been divided up amongst the crew of the ship, meaning mega money for all involved, but because the Captain had refused tows from other vessels and waited for a ship now technically chartered to T & J Harrison, the remuneration would be a lot lower. For the next five days *Tactician* sauntered along at 5 knots in *Rapallo's* wake. It did not take long before a Greek deep sea tug *Nisos Chios* arrived on the scene. They tend to hang about like jackals waiting to pounce on their wounded prey, they were hoping that a sudden gale would deprive *Rapallo* of her charge

242

Chapter 4 - T & J Harrison (Shipping)

and give the tug a chance to retrieve her. "Anyway that's the story so far and most of the engineers will never sail with Thompson again. It's a sorrowful state of affairs but we have to concentrate on getting back to Liverpool. Let the company figure out the politics".

I nodded in agreement, but reflected on the fact I may be considered in the same light as the Portuguese electricians as I'd never worked on a ship either!

Later that day I was given the task of checking on the work of one of our Portuguese friends. Looking at the circuit diagram, he managed to connect up most of the circuits incorrectly. I found it easier to do the work myself; it just took too long to explain. Ray arrived and asked how I was getting on? I just shook my head.

"Well, I wouldn't let any of these guys wire up my clothes' line". We both laughed. It took a few days to complete the temporary wiring and clean up the engine room; then we were now ready for sea trials. It had been decided that we would circumnavigate the main island and if all was well, make our move across the Atlantic and home to Liverpool. Everything did go well and to everyone's relief we could start our slow journey home. Luckily for all concerned, the weather was kind and we made it back to Liverpool. *Tactician* was going into dry dock where Campbell and Isherwood could rewire the ship; numerous other contractors were there too as the job was going to be blitzed and worked on around the clock to get it back into service quickly. I took a few days leave and then went on coasting duties. It was a few weeks later that I was given the message to report for duty and rejoin the *Tactician* as the 2nd Electrical Engineering Officer. She was built in 1962 by William Doxford & Sons SB Ltd. Launched 16th of February and completed in the June. She was in a class of her own; she had a Stulcken derrick which could lift a 180 ton - lift big for it's day. Four months after her launch, when arriving in Belize she was caught in a hurricane and rendered invaluable assistance to the stricken inhabitants. In 1968 she suffered an engine room fire. In 1972 yet another fire and explosion disabled her again and she had to put into Walvis Bay for repairs. This time the conflagration killed two men. *Tactician* was renamed *Sea Luck* (not a very apt name) in 1979 for Petralia Navigation Company of Cyprus and moved on yet again the following October becoming *Kero* for Naviera Neptuno S.A. of Callo, Peru. Finally on the 15th of May 1987 she went to the breakers yard in Peru. She had been a very unlucky ship suffering numerous fatalities and accidents - only a few have been recorded here.)

It was a dry typical winter's day when I sauntered up the gangplank, and was amazed at the clean and tidy appearance of the ship. No sign whatsoever of the fire. The ship had been newly painted and gleamed in the winter sun. I had been told to report to Alan Jones, the first electrical engineering officer - my boss!

243

Chapter 4 - T & J Harrison (Shipping)

I was to be the 2nd Electrical Engineering Officer. I first met Alan on the aft crane when he was doing a planned maintenance job. I arrived in full uniform with my newly-stitched braid on the arms showing my rank gleaming in the sunlight.
"Hi. We are going to be working together; have you been to sea before?"
I nodded but thought it would be honest to tell the truth.
"About fifteen days of sea going experience, I'm afraid, just bringing this ship back to port, and a bit of coasting,"
smiling as he looked me up and down
"That must have been fun?"
"Well, it was different, we had to operate shifts around the clock, to bring her back safely. I watched as he completed the job.
In between fixing problems and faults on the ship, we were expected to maintain the equipment. His face looked familiar but I just could not place where I had seen him before.
"OK I'll show you to your cabin; you won't need me to show you around, but I bet it's a lot tidier since you were last on her."
Then it dawned on me, Alan Jones was the very same guy I had seen at the Sunderland Forge in Birkenhead.
The following day we set out on the seven seas - our destination was the Caribbean, Mexico and America. This was to be my first Atlantic crossing and my first Christmas away from family and friends so I was a little sad. As we slipped out of Liverpool I could see New Brighton Tower and pier in the distance. It brought a lump to my throat. We had a large hovercraft on the deck, which was supported by a large wooden construction which hung over both sides of the ship by about 6 feet. It was seated over one of the holds. The chippy was like a mother hen fussing around his construction that supported the massive machine.
My first experience of the Bay of Biscay was about to unfold. I had spent several evenings playing cards with Alan, and the chief steward. It was a golden rule at sea never to play cards for money, so we always played for beer. Our first port of call was to be Montego bay and then Kingston in Jamaica, followed by Tampico and Veracurz in Mexico then across to Galveston on the southern coast of Texas USA. We then travelled up the Mississippi to New Orleans.
The rhythmic pulse of the engines were therapeutic; a gentle roll and slight pitch lulled my body into a false sense of security. All this was to change when the English Channel met the Atlantic Ocean. The Bay of Biscay was to be my nemesis. The first clue should have been a warning. On entering the saloon for my lunch all the condiments had been laid flat on the table.
Each chair had a short chain that could anchor it to the floor to stop them wandering about. The steward had sprinkled water on the tablecloth.

Chapter 4 - T & J Harrison (Shipping)

The sides of the dining tables had been raised with retractable "fiddles" to prevent the plates from dropping off. In really bad weather open spaces could become dangerous, so ropes were strung up between pillars, grab rails and stairwells to help us stay on our feet. In my cabin I had a desk, a day bed and a bunk bed with a sideboard on the outside edge with a lower portion in the middle to let you get in and out - at either end the sides were high enough to prevent you rolling out of bed. Below the bunk was a set of drawers. The idea of the day bed was to enable you to sleep with your overhaul on when you were on call.

I was the first of the engineering officers in the saloon. I was handed the menu the steward must have thought I looked a little puzzled; he said: "We are going into a storm; that combined with the Bay means we are in for some fun." I just shrugged my solders as if I'd seen it all before, but it started to dawn on me that this could be serious. Had I stowed all my stuff away in my cabin? Some of the deck officers arrived along with the old man (the Captain) and took their places on the top table. The middle table was reserved for the engineering staff and the bottom table for cadets and junior engineers. It had been pointed out to me that it was only fairly recently that the grease monkeys (engineers) were allowed to eat in the saloon. I think these guys wanted to return to the age of sail, and could not get used to the idea that the thing was being propelled through the water by an engine, hence our new-found importance. The old man ruled with an iron fist - he was the master, the law, the ultimate authority on the ship. I had been told we were carrying a top secret cargo, which had been deposited in the old man's strongroom.

I got halfway though my meal when the weather started to deteriorate. The steward had to time his walk out of the galley into the saloon and it had to be spot-on to move with the roll of the ship to arrive at the table on the correct side of the officer to serve the food. When the weather was too rough, the cook could not keep the pans on the galley so it was sandwiches and bottled water.

I just could not get used to the weather; I was seasick for days, and the smell of the diesel and the pitching and rolling was a real obstacle to working down in the engine room. At every opportunity I would return to my cabin to lie down but I was told to get out of bed and return to the engine room. Trying to be sick when you had nothing in your stomach is very painful. The second told me *I wasn't on a f**kin cruise and to get your arse down the engine room*. The workload meant I was never allowed to feel sorry for myself and rest. The ship started to pitch violently almost in unison with my stomach. When the propeller (Prop) came out of the water the ship shuddered as the energy was absorbed. The single screw Doxford 8,000 HP engine could travel at a maximum of 16 knots, but in these conditions it was struggling and we were being being propelled backwards.

Chapter 4 - T & J Harrison (Shipping)

We even had several waves land directly on the ship, tons of water landing on the deck made a thundering noise and the odd wave would come down the funnel. At night I had to prop my head between two pillows to prevent banging my head on the metal hull. What I needed was one of those head protectors that boxers use in training. By Sunday afternoon the bad weather was behind us and we were in summer like conditions and could change from our heavy blue wool uniforms into our tropical whites - shorts and short-sleeved shirts with epaulettes and white shoes and socks. With the blue sea meeting the blue sky, the horizon seemed to disappear as we sailed majestically into Kingston harbor in Jamaica.

It was always the norm before the bonded store on board was closed to ask the chief steward if there was likely to be a search and what duty frees could we keep in our cabins whilst in port. His reply was
"In all the years I've been coming here, we've had no problems so book out what ever you want".
The bonded store was locked and sealed before arriving in territorial waters. I had my cabin full of fags and booze, always useful to trade with and also we had planned a couple of parties on the ship. To my absolute amazement as we got closer to the dock, there appeared to be a welcoming committee. A film crew, a military band, bunting and crowds of people all cheering. There was a large rostrum full with dignitaries all observing the scene, and, strategically positioned to the side, a full team of customs, searchers, officers and the like. We found out later that they had come to witness the arrival of the new hovercraft. Needless to say all my loot was confiscated and I also ended up with a fine along with most

Humming Bird

of the crew and officers on the ship.
During the initial sea trials of the British-built D2-002 passenger carrying Hovercraft, the ships officers' were invited for a trip around the harbour, but she ran aground on a sandbank. It was only after a group of volunteers jumped into the sea and pushed the stranded whale off its perch that normal service was resumed. The *Humming Bird*, was to become Jamaica's first hovercraft service across Kingston Harbour, linking Kingston with the Palisadoes International Airport.

Chapter 4 - T & J Harrison (Shipping)

The following day yet another disaster!
One of the derrick ropes had become caught on an overhead lamp. Our third mate Mr Goddard, leaned over to pull the rope away from the lamp and the lamp arm snapped and he fell over 40 ft to the quay below.
He was rushed to hospital in a coma; he was in a serious condition. We eventually sailed without him.
Most of the crew and officers enjoyed Jamaica with some of the ABs overindulging, and a couple forgetting the sailing time. I recall that we flew the Blue Peter flag (sailing within 24 hours). It appeared that the ship's owners had to accept the delay as part of life, but the old man went berserk.
Our next port of call on the 16th December 1968 without actually getting ashore was Montego Bay. When we arrived the largest aircraft carrier in the world, the *SS John F Kennedy* was at anchor.

John F. Kennedy Aircraft carrier

We duly anchored and awaited the arrival of our barges; it was our intention to load the barges with cargo including motor cars. The Boson and a squad of ABs had spent a long time rigging up the derricks with robes and getting everything ready for their arrival. When our friends opposite decided to start a ferry service for Liberty Visits or short visits to Montego Bay, their timing was spot on. As soon as the cargo was about to be put on the barages, the swell from the high powered motor launches used to ferry these guys ashore almost sank the barges. The first mate stopped operations and ran up to the bridge to inform the Captain. Numerous attempts were made to contact the carrier by radio and Addis lamp and even a trip across by our agent, but all to no effect. So we had to arrange to unload the cargo on the opposite side of the ship away from the wake. This took an extra couple of hour's work to the annoyance of the Captain and crew. I did manage during the time to get the third

247

Chapter 4 - T & J Harrison (Shipping)

engineer to take a photograph of me with the beast in the background. I was to find out later that the carrier had sailed from Guantanamo Bay in Cuba. With daily general quarters in operation together with both day and night flight manoeuvres, it was now time for relaxation. It was during the Cold War and America was on high alert. The carrier had a complement 4,950 men, so those launches were very busy. Job completed so we set sail for Veracruz, in Mexico; the short two day trip was uneventful. Lots of flying fish landed on the deck to the annoyance of the crew. They leap out of the water into air where their long, wing-like fins enable them to glide for considerable distances above the water's surface. It's a defence mechanism to evade predators. Our arrival in Veracruz was marked by the appearance of what appeared to be half the Mexican Army. The secret of the Captain's Strongroom was at last disclosed; it contained a massive amount of military arms, from revolvers, rifles to machine guns. We were spirited away from the area while the military loaded several lorries that had pulled up along the quay. We were fortunate in this instance that the customs did not descend on the ship, and needless to say there were no television crews. Veracruz has a blend of cultures, mostly ethnic Spanish and Afro-Cuban; in the late 60s it certainly was a fun place to be. It must have been about 8pm in the evening when we arrived at the Ranchito Club which had been recommended as a place for a good night out. Four of use arrived by taxi along a dirt road a couple of miles from the town centre. We paid the driver and approached the entrance with some apprehension. The building look like a cross between a *Psycho* Bates Motel and an ex-army barracks. The entrance had several large potted ferns that had seen better days. A well worn carpet led the way into the inner sanctum which was very dim but a few lights helped the interlopers to move along a short corridor to a pair of swinging doors. A guy with a Charles Bronson moustache and a look to match stopped us in our tracks, he wanted us to pay an entrance fee, that done, we were in.

Chapter 4 - T & J Harrison (Shipping)

The large dance hall was illuminated by the circular rotating ball throwing moving spectacles of light onto the walls and floor. We moved across to the bar and ordered drinks. Our eyes had now become accustomed to the dull light. Along one wall sat about 40 girls all scantly dressed, chatting and giggling amongst themselves. Each had a number attached to her skimpy outfit. The idea was that if you fancied a girl, you paid the barman a fee (bar fine) for the hire of a room outside and he gestured to the girl who picked up the key and off you went to have your wicked way with her. All the girls had a passport-like booklet that had to be stamped by a doctor every day the girls wanted to work in the bar. If you just wanted a dance, then you gestured to the girl and she would join your company and a lady's drink would be ordered. All very civilized and organized.
Following our night of delight we returned to the ship to find that the cadets' rooms had been requisitioned by the engineers. The cadets' quarters on the ship consisted of two cabins joined by a large study area which was private and ideal for a party. So we joined in the fun of more booze and debauchery.
Then to my amazement it was decided to hide a couple of the girls on the ship for the journey along the coast to Tampico. The following day was a Sunday when the Captain had his Inspection of the ship. I returned to my cabin slightly the worse for wear and in the morning I awoke to see the harbour disappearing in the distance as the engineer's boy knocked and brought in a coffee.
"Morning Roy, do you want me to get you some toast?"
"No, no, I'm fine, but the coffee may help me to sober up!" was my muffled reply. He closed the door gently. It was a tradition on the ship that if the lad looked after you and dhobi (washed) your kit, you gave him a ten shilling note at the end of the trip. I slowly put a towel around my waist and slipped on my flip-flops ready for my morning shower when the door burst open and a red-faced cadet pushed two girls into my cabin.
"Here... it's your turn, you look after them."
"Hang on...hang on a moment!" I spluttered. The girls were giggling and speaking in Spanish and I couldn't understand a word.
The cadet looking very flustered and whispered "The captain's below inspecting our quarters".
The cadet disappeared as fast as Houdini.
I closed the door and the girls made themselves at home and continued giggling and talking. This was serious: if I got caught, it didn't bear thinking about. My career in the merchant navy would grind to an abrupt halt.
The Captain would do the rounds of the ship with the first mate and the chief steward who would take notes. They were on the lookout for dust, dirt, and the general tidiness and appearance of the ships' quarters, so I had to move these girls on. To add to the confusion the taller of the two

Chapter 4 - T & J Harrison (Shipping)

pointing at her mouth indicating she was hungry. All of a sudden a bolt of inspiration hit me between the eyes. I nodded, pointed at my mouth and then the door. I was ready to move them on. I quickly dressed into my whites to the amusement of the girls and off we went. The old man was below my deck, so it was along the corridor to the seamen's quarters and their galley. I opened the door and there was no one inside, so I pointed to the seats and indicated to them to sit down. I shot back out again and back to my cabin ready for the inspection and then a shower. The girls were someone else's problem now. I was to find out later that they had found a couple of admirers that were now looking after them below decks.

The following day we arrived in Tampico. The ship tied up, the gangplank was dropped and almost immediately the ship burst into life with the hatch covers being worked. The girls had departed and things in the accommodation went back to normal. I decided it would be nice to have a meal in the saloon so off I went. I had no sooner sat at the table when I noticed the table had not been laid; strange. I looked at my watch and, yes I was on time. A red-faced steward came out of the galley. "I'm sorry but we don't have any cutlery; it's all been stolen."

It was just at that moment that the Captain accompanied by the chief Steward walked into the saloon.

"What are you telling me? The lot's gone! How could that happen?" shouted the Captain as he took his position on the top table. The chief displayed several empty cutlery boxes.

"Whoever took them must have been here last night. We have only just docked and no one has come on board, so what's going on?" My thought processes went into overdrive - the girls! I stood up and slipped out of the saloon. Walking on to the deck I spotted one of the cadets.

"Have you heard, someone has nicked all the bloody cutlery?" He looked surprised and shrugged his shoulders. " I bet it was those hookers you entertained last night," was my next comment. He started to look a bit concerned. "It's nothing to do with me. I never brought them on board" As I turned to walk away I told him I thought we had best keep our mouths shut. Eventually the captain discovered the truth, but had great difficulty in pointing a finger as the girls had been very busy... not only had the cutlery gone but also some of the seaman's personal possessions - watches, money etc, and they could not report this because of the resulting incrimination. From then onwards we had a night watchman posted on the top of the gangplank so no more darlings could be sneaked on board.

From Mexico we visited Houston and Galveston with my next adventure taking place in New Orleans. Approaching this magical city involved a lot of complicated manoeuvering down the shallows of the Mississippi with the use of tugs and an experienced pilot.

Chapter 4 - T & J Harrison (Shipping)

Engine room Controls

I was on standby for many hours. I had to spend quite a lot of time marking up the ship's manoeuvres by recording the operations of the telegraph manually in a log. This task had been devised to make sure you remained on duty in a specific place so you could be contacted quickly, namely next to the ships controls, during these manoeuvrers.

Bourbon Street in New Orleans was populated by ladies of easy virtue, bars and peep shows. It was here that my love affair with Bacardi was to end. I was pestered by the chippy to give him the keys to the hold. It was my job to make sure all the lighting worked before we docked. I found out later why he was so keen to get hold of the keys - it was to get his hands on some of the Bacardi. The trick was to remove some bottles from the outside of the pallet and smash the remainder with a hammer. It was then assumed that the pallet had been damaged and it went down in the purser's log as breakages. That done, the chippy dropped in two bottles of Bacardi as he returned the keys. What I did not know at the time was he had got a little too ambitious with the scheme, and when the purser with the first mate checked the hold, all hell broke lose. I also decided that it would be a good idea to drink the evidence so with the help of two cadets who were sworn to secrecy, we got some Coke and proceeded to drink the lot. Unfortunately, we all ended up being violently sick but this taught me a lesson, and from that day to this, I just cannot handle any Bacardi. I also decided there would be no more fraternising with the crew.

Chapter 4 - T & J Harrison (Shipping)

Our trip back to Liverpool took just over a week and it was during this time that I discovered Alan's secret. We were down the engine room connecting up some equipment, when with a cable in his hand he turned to me and said," It's a bit dark in here. Is this cable red?" I nodded and then a little later he asked a similar question. I just couldn't believe it! My electrical companion was partially colour-blind. How he could have survived for so long being an electrical engineer when he could not distinguish red, green and brown from one another was absolutely amazing. I arrived back on the Wirral in the middle of a cold and bleak January. After a week's leave I decided to return, to sea; I rejoined the five fathom club and did a spot of coasting, then I rejoined the *Tactician* for another adventure - this time to darkest Africa.

On this trip I was to *cross the line* for the first time (the equator). I tried to keep it a secret but the purser checked my discharge book and figured from the entries I was a 'crossing the line virgin'.

This meant a ceremony! One of the officers dressed up extravagantly as King Neptune; another in a wig and skirt became his Queen. With a court clerk, the surgeon, the barber, and a policeman, the team was complete. Each of the 'virgin' victims were led in one at a time and accused of some deep sea misdemeanour read out by the clerk of the court. King Neptune would then sentence them to be disembowelled then keel hauled and cast to the ocean's depths.

The gathering would then place the victim on a table covered by a sheet and the surgeon would proceed to operate. After a short time, the surgeon revealed the 'innards' in the form of raw sausages or other meat parts from the galley; these were then thrown over the side. Ketchup and jelly now covered the white sheet the whole thing looking a complete bloody mess and the victim was also covered with the slime. The victim would then be strapped into a seat and the Barber would lather up large amounts of different coloured whipped cream before shaving them with a large wooden cut-throat razor. Without warning the victim was then flipped over backwards, head first into a makeshift tarpaulin pool where a couple of assistants would duck them. It was rough and messy for the victims and an unforgettable experience but fun for the drunken audience. After a long shower with a scrubbing brush I eventually recovered.

The Cape of Good Hope is the point at which the Atlantic and Indian Oceans meet and is very near to Cape Town. The weather was very rough, but I had my sea legs so no real problem.

I grew to like South Africa and its weather but with limitations; it made such an impact on me that some 40 years later I decided to make it my home, but more about that later. Our arrival in Durban we were met by a demonstration on the quayside with banners and people sounding horns

Chapter 4 - T & J Harrison (Shipping)

and handing out leaflets. They were protesting against the British blockade of Rhodesia - this was when Ian Smith declared UDI.
After a few hours they dispersed and did not reappear, so it was now safe for our team to go ashore.
The countryside was gorgeous; it was the early days of apartheid with the more draconian pass laws introduced later. The atmosphere between the races was generally not too bad, except for the Zulus who hated the Indians but seemed to like the whites. One of the junior engineers was a half-cast so it was thought best he remained on the ship; it would cause too many problems if he accompanied us to the bars. With different classifications for blacks, coloured and whites, it was all a bit complicated. Different coloured buses for the races, different areas on the beaches, different sections in the cinema, all crazy. Japanese were considered whites because of the trade with their country but most other Asians were considered coloured, a sort of middle ground between the other races. I thought I would have it out with the Afrikaan agent who was sitting in the chief steward's cabin drinking a beer. The Afrikaans were the descendants of the early Dutch settlers whom the British had displaced but who now ruled the country after independence.
"Can you explain the reasons for apartheld? Don't you think that the blacks whose country it is should have a say in things?" Well, that hit a raw nerve! With a certain disdain in his facial expression. "The indigenous population who lived on these lands were all wiped out by the Zulus who were a warring nation. The Dutch arrived in the Cape at the same time as the Zulus came down from the North like a plague of locusts, killing everything in their path" He neglected to answer the question concerning the Afrikaans' approach to the other races. Oddly, in those days there was no television as it was seen as a bad influence and might weaken the ruling party's control of the country; the Dutch Reform Church had an iron grip on the society and government. The highlight of the week was going to the 'bioscope', or cinema, and some people even dressed formally just to view ordinary evening films.
An unheard of event occurred during our stay. All the dock workers went on strike so our stay was prolonged - over two weeks- to the annoyance of the owners. I have two special memories of Durban: one the officers' club in Durban, drinking Brandy Squares (campaign and brandy) whilst eating one of the largest steaks I've ever seen, and the other the continuous noise when the teams of Bantu workers chipped off the old paint from the side of the ship using small sharp hammers. They hung over the side on narrow platforms attached to the hull, then later they repainted the exposed patches. We even had a ship's cat that joined the ship in Liverpool but belonged to no one crew member. She also had a habit of going ashore at every port but always made it back before we sailed.

Chapter 4 - T & J Harrison (Shipping)

With strict quarantine laws in Britain and the U.S, she still managed to dodge the authorities. When you think of the many unsavoury and dangerous parts of the world we visited, it was a miracle that this cat survived.

Our next port of call was to say the least a shock to the nervous system. Lobito Bay in Angola did not have sufficient water to allow large ships to unload close inshore. All the Portuguese colonies in Africa seemed to be engaged in civil war. It all started in 1961 with a rebellion of workers, undergoing forced labour in coffee and cotton plantations in the north: then guerrilla groups got involved and it escalated. So the military were all over the place; the bars were full of soldiers all having a good time in case it was their last! It was really surreal. The local music and dancing provided an animated and exotic atmosphere that mixed well with the mystery of the exotic African pitch-black nights - and the alcohol.

Part of the main beach was surrounded with barbed wire and had been mined. I was told that diamonds sometimes got wash into the sea and the owners of the mines in the hills wanted to protect their interests.

Their was a requirement to have a yellow fever jab otherwise we could not go ashore. The doctor came straight out of the bush, wearing a pith helmet. We lined up in the saloon where the necessary injection was to be done. The AB just in front of me must have moved, because the hypodermic needle, which by this time was probably blunt, had snapped in his arm. The doctor tried to pull it out with his fingernails, but it must have been too slippery. A pair of tweezers was produced from his bag but with little effect. I suggested a pair of pliers and the doctor nodded. Luckily for all concerned this did the trick and I was lucky in being the next with a brand new sharp needle. After this excitement it was down to the chief steward's cabin for a few beers and a game of cards. The unwritten rule on board was that no money changed hands. The stakes were cans of Tenants Larger. After the game we totted up to see who's bar bill the larger went on. The other rule was not to be the last person in the chief stewards cabin because after a few beers he always became a bit gayer than usual. Following on from our previous medical emergency another was to follow. It was during our card game that a black face appeared around the door, carrying a note, which he handed to the chief. Apparently the guy had been hit on the head and had complained of a headache. The chief was the medical authority on board, so he immediately beckoned him in and sat the guy down. Taking this opportunity to study my cards, I did not take much notice of the

Chapter 4 - T & J Harrison (Shipping)

consultation. Then I heard
"That's it, all done you can return back to the deck".
It was only after he stood up that I noticed the sticky plaster on the guy's head.
"But he didn't have a cut," I said.
"I know," said the steward, "but I've stuck an aspirin under the plaster, and he's OK. White man's magic and all that!"
"Christ, what a dump,'"said Bill the stocky fourth engineer as he spat into the filth below. "Tropical paradise my a***."
The sky above was full of black cloud that did nothing to allay the stifling heat. He was the tallest of my companions and had been here before and was our unofficial guide. My other cohort had a wild mop of curly black hair and was a junior engineer, and to his annoyance we always called him Junior. He looked skywards and said "The whole lot's coming down in a minute; just look at all the crap lying around. It will end up a real shit-hole and I've got me best kit on!"
In stark contrast we wore old shorts, tee shirts and flip flops.
'Take a gander at this bloke heading towards us."The policeman on the gate in his ill-fitting uniform was anxious to make our acquaintance . It had been our hope to slip out the dock gates, jump in a taxi to skip the shanty town outside the gates and make it down town.
"He looks like a shoeshine boy to me," said Mac, he of the wild dark hair. The man had a huge toothy smile on his face as he held his hand out to shake hands, "Hey! You fellas need a cab?" he said in broken English.
Bill whispered in my ear, "His brother-in-law probably owns the local taxis and you'll end up in his wife's bordello. Give him a packet of fags and let's escape."
With a quick out flanking manoeuvre we were out of the docks. A short distance down the road, and Junior pointed to a bar. Let's have a drink and order a taxi. Every seafarer knows that being cooped up with other men inside a steel hull for months on end has their drawbacks as well as their compensations. Usually like-minded souls become bound together come hell or high water. You work with them, eat with them, drink with them and of course fall out with them. You get to know your shipmates better in some cases than their wives. The three of us were inseparable- you needed buddies you could rely on. We just could not organize a taxi so we decided to walk into town. It required careful manoeuvring among fragments of the broken sidewalk and heaps of reeking garbage. Crime casts a pall of fear that only ratcheted up the tension, but the couple of drinks we had consumed helped to blank out the concern This once thriving town was reduced to several clusters of cement-block hovels with rusted-scrap tin roofs, held down by stones and patched with plastic sheeting. It was not a place to linger long and with the dark fast approaching, we needed a passing taxi.

Chapter 4 - T & J Harrison (Shipping)

No such luck. Bill looked the most worried of the group. "Come on lads; heads down; let's cover some distance." We eventually arrived in the centre of town which had been affluent once but was now run down; the only maintenance appeared to be on the few bars and clubs dotted around the square. We headed towards the biggest and brightest; the sign had part of its neon lettering missing so to this day I don't know its name. But I can remember a green neon palm tree flashing on and off. It was free to get in and it had a stage down one end with a group playing. The place was full of people dancing, and laughing and enjoying themselves. Language was always a problem, but pointing and gesticulating seemed to do the trick.

Junior went to buy a round of drinks and seemed to take ages. I walked over just as all hell broke loose. As I approached he shot past having been punched. First and foremost it's always best to try and talk your way out of trouble, but no one could understand us. Just as I bent down to pick him up, I too was subjected to a punch in the head. Some quick thinking was required because I could see his lips turning purple and I got scared. I pulled him up onto his feet and he seemed to come around, just as a rain of blows descended on me. I awoke with one eye open and I thought I was in a hospital and swiftly shut it. Where the hell was I?

How did I get here? The mixture of alcohol and pain did nothing to help focus my brain. I was still fully booted and spurred. I risked opening two eyes and realised I was in a police cell and the door had been left open. With shaking hands I pulled myself up and looked around the cell; Junior was in the bunk opposite, bloodied but snoring in a deep sleep. I checked my pockets everything had gone including my watch. Bill was remonstrating with two guards, then spotting me sitting up, Bill walked over.

"Look, this guys are after money to let us out. He says we have to pay for the damage." I must of looked puzzled. What f**kin damage? It was those tugs that gave us a hiding". Bill held his hand out

"Give me what money you have."

"I've been cleaned out," was my reply. Bill sat down next to me.

"We've got to get some cash together or those twats will not release us and the ship sails later today." I got off the bed and with trembling legs staggered over to Junior to take a closer look at him. He was a mess; I tried to wake him but it was no good, he was still out cold. I put my hands in his pockets; nothing! I turned and faced Bill.

We've both been cleaned out. I've already given them all my money and they say it's not enough." I just could not grasp the mess that we had now found ourselves in. We needed to persuade them to let us go.

"Why don't one of use go back to the ship and get the money?" Shaking his head. "I asked him that very question but they said no."

Chapter 4 - T & J Harrison (Shipping)

"Are you sure you are getting through to these guys? Your bits of Spanish and the guards' two-and-half words of English might be leading up the path of no return."

Then would you believe it ...bang, the door on the cell slammed shut! The noise woke Junior up.

"Where are we?" he said as he stared at his blood-stained shirt," I don't remember this". After a few minutes of explanation he hit the ground running. He said he had some money, but it wasn't in his pocket.

"I've got 20 dollars in my shoe for emergencies."

We both stared at each other in amazement,

"This is a bloody emergency," I said.

Bill immediately banged on the door to try and get the guards' attention. The door opened and Bill went to step out holding the 20 dollars, but before he could take a step, the money was snatched from his hand and the door slammed shut again. We must have been in the cell for another couple of hours before anything happened. I think these guys were waiting to see if we came up with some more cash. It must have been when their shift changed because a different guy opened the door and released us. With a gesture to the door and some animated hand movements. We figured he wanted us out of his sight pronto.

We just made it back to the ship before she sailed, with yet another adventure to amaze our shipmates.

Our next port of call was the city of Lourenco Marques, now called Maputo, in Mozambique. Known as LM, it had been a tourist destination with many South Africans trying to escape their moral stranglehold in their country. That was before the Front for the Liberation of Mozambique (Frelimo) started its civil war.

The battle against Portuguese colonial rule started in September 1964. We managed to walk into the conflict with both sides having four years of hostilities under their belt. With a cosmopolitan continental atmosphere, pavement cafes, and the nightclubs which pulsed with action until the early hours, this had been one of Africa's most beautiful and fashionable cities. Its streets were lined with lovely avenues of trees including, palm trees, jacarandas and flame trees. All that was sliding rapidly into the past as thousands of immigrants arrived in the city to escape from the conflict. Litter and filth lay everywhere and major services were mostly non-existent. Signs of the struggle could be seen everywhere with bullet holes and marks on the walls of many buildings. So it was another one of those towns full of military personal, in some instances enjoying their last drink on this planet. The whole place was wild. My concern was the number of firearms in general view, if a fight developed, it was not a case of just getting a bloody nose, there was every chance you could get your head blown off. I was to return again some forty years later when peace finally came but the once beautiful Mozambican city was in terrible disrepair.

Chapter 4 - T & J Harrison (Shipping)

It was a dump; twenty-seven years of civil war fuelled by a lethal mix of oil, diamonds and Cold War enemies left one of Africa's potentially richest countries in a mess.

The final port of call before we returned home was Beira to deliver mail to the Royal Navy who had been running the Beira Patrol which was a blockade of Beira, the main oil terminus for oil into Southern Rhodesia. This began after Mr Smith had declared UDI and upset the British Government and the UN.

Our trip back to Liverpool was a little less exciting. We could not get into Salford Docks in Manchester and we had to anchor out in the Mersey to wait our turn to travel up the canal. In those days the docks were full with ships unloading cargo.

Unbeknownst to me at the time, my life was to take on a totally different meaning. My father had died while I was returning to the UK. The company had told my mother that it was pointless to wire the ship and it would be best to inform me when the ship docked in Manchester. So on my arrival in Salford Docks, my best mate Dave Hepkie was waiting to pass on the devastating news. I decided that my seafaring days were over and I remained on land to help my mom in her time of need.

My father had passed away in Victoria Central Hospital Wallasey on the 30th April 1969. Cause of death was myocardial infarction. At the time he was still working at the Atomic Energy Authority as a Laboratory Assistant.

I was at a bit of a loose end until another mate of mine, Charles Neal, suggested I could get a start with Rewinds and J Windsor. I hated the work in the workshops and eventually escaped to Dunlop in Speke for the annual shut down. It was here that I was to meet a Mr Peter Turnbull, who was just sarting out on his property enterprise. A journey that I was to repeat a few years later. It was while Charles was working for Rewinds that his fortunes were to change dramatically, and this was also to have an impact on my prosperity at a later date. A chance call into Vauxhall's car plant in Ellesmere Port to meet the buyer, Mr Vinnie Jones, had been the catalyst. Passing across some worn welding tips he asked if Rewinds could make replacements. Charles said he would find out; he discovered that Rewinds were not interested. That evening over dinner he showed his uncle Jack who without hesitation said he could make the tips in his workshop at the bottom of the garden, if Charles could supply the copper. Thus, Neal Welding was born.

Chapter 4 - Cadbury

After a couple of successful interviews at Cadburys I was given a start date of 18th December 1969. I was to be employed as an Instrument/electronic technician. Our team consisted of Mr Dave Bradley who was our chargehand and my immediate boss, Michael Davidson and myself. Mr Bob Jones, our telecommunications engineer who was a larger than life character whose main interest in life was weightlifting; he even started the Cadbury Weightlifting and Bodybuilding club. His task was to look after the internal telephone system. The mechanical instrumentation section was handled by Mr Arthur Bromley, who also ran a osteopath and acupuncturist practice in Liscard. To my amazement he also used hypnotism in his work.

Dave and Michael were keen radio hams and during their lunch break, out would come their C B Rigs, then the radio transmitter and receiver would be connected to a complicated aerial array set up on the roof of the machine shop. They would chat to other enthusiasts around the world, or

Entrance to Cadbury, Moreton

send morse code messages. The idea was to try and bounce your signals off the various ionised layers that surrounded the earth and make contact with some distant geek and then exchange calling cards known as QSL cards. We were a happy team and everyone got on very well together. The only bone of contention was the wages; we all knew that our technical abilities warranted a better return. The first to leave was Michael who went on to work for Unilever Research. Then Dave left to work at Burmah Oil in Ellesmere Port and Bob for an undisclosed destination. He tended to be very secretive; probably ended up wire-tapping for MI5. These three vacancies were filled by George Jones, Jimmy Bordley and an apprentice, Joey Smith, so our team was back up to strength again. I was left to run the whole department, taking my instructions directly from Tom Parry, the electrical Foreman. A couple of chargehands Matt Dillion and George Mattews, tried to muscle in on the action, but after I asked a few technical questions, they disappeared back into the electrical department. It was around this time that Jimmy and I teamed up to start a wholesale clothing business. With over two thousand people working in the factory we had a ready-made market. This really took off and the business grew to great heights. We travelled down to Manchester at weekends and bought the goods from manufacturers and wholesalers, both men's and women's clothes. To expand the business we purchased a large J4 van to hold the stock. As with most partnerships, Jimmy and I fell out over the direction of the business so decided to terminate the partnership. My business ventures at the time consisted of a block of flats in Wilton Street, Liscard. I had bought these from the proceeds of sailing the seven seas. But my next venture was to be a total waste of time. It was Arthur Bromley who advised me not to get a business with loads of stock, but get involved in a service industry. Needless to say I took no notice and dived straight into a pet shop business, because of my interest tropical fish, but more about that later.

In those days Instrumentation was still in its infancy and a big concern for the company was ensuring the correct weights of the products leaving the factory. Automatic check weighers had to weigh the product as it zoomed past at an alarming speed, so the electronics had to be sophisticated. The photograph shows ladies checking the weights manually.

Manual weighing before checkweighters

I worked at Cadbury over fourty years ago and the following events are still imprinted on my mind.

Smash Disaster

We had to move a telephone in the Smash production area. Smash was the instant potato that was marketed by Cadbury. Do you remember the adverts on TV, those space potato aliens in their cute metal outfits? We even sold the stuff to Oxfam for their relief programmes until they found out it was virtually useless as it contained no vitamin C, that had all been lost in the production process. So guess what - we added it back in later. Anyway back to the telephone... George and I went along with a long set of ladders to the Smash production area. I was just in the process of setting up the ladders against the wall when there was an almighty explosion and flash and I was blown off my feet; luckily the ladders fell to the ground and missed both of us. My eyebrows, hair and boiler suit were all singed. I looked around in the smoky haze for George; he had also been knocked off his feet and was clearing the dust from his eyes.

" What the hell was that" I said.

George shook his head, the first words from his lips was" Lets get the hell out of here".

Chapter 4 - Cadbury

On the Monday morning a high powered meeting was called. George and I were accompanied into the chief engineer's office with the union convenor, the safety officer, Mr Tom Parry, the Smash Production manager and a couple of other lesser dignitaries.
As the secretary prepared to take minutes at the meeting the convenor said to me
"I'll do the talking"
The Agenda "The Smash Explosion". Mr Wostencroft, the chief engineer said, "We are not here to blame anyone for the incident. We have to discover the exact reasons for the explosion, and make sure that we don't have a repeat of the incident".
It was finally resolved that the explosion was caused by the ladders hitting a hanging florescent light which in the process of falling to earth had caused a spark that had ignited the dust on the top of the light fitting. Up to this time no one had realised how explosive Smash in dust form could be. The outcome was a vigorous weekly campaign of cleaning all the electrical fittings and anywhere else that dust could gather. The whole section had been closed down and the staff sent home until all the safety and cleaning issues had been resolved. Nowadays I would have been on the telephone to a compensation lawyer and taken a few months off work due to shock.

The White Hunter
Fred was the pest exterminator employed in the factory. One of the preoccupations of the white hunter was to keep the wildlife out of the factory. Of special concern were the birds that managed to find their way into A Block. Blue, Marsh, Great and even Coal tits and ordinary sparrows. Because some of these birds were protected, he had to catch them alive and release them back into the wild. The product made in A block was cookies, so any dropping on these delights would probably go unnoticed. Our intrepid hunter could be found most weekends trying to catch the little devils. Once caught, they were held in a cage and transferred to his mate who happened to work on a Crosville Bus. The birds would be taken quite a distance into Wales where they were released, only to return to the factory a few days later. The nuts and ingredients used to produce the cookies were just too much of a temptation. They ringed a few of the offenders and according to the white hunter some had made the return journey over a dozen times. I left Cadburys on the 12th March 1973 for a more lucrative appointment as an Instrument Artificer at Associated Octel.

Burton Foods to close Moreton factory March 2011
Burton Foods has announced plans to close the former Cadbury factory at Moreton on the Wirral, at which it manufactures a range of Cadbury's products under licence. The move will result in the loss of 342 jobs
---

Chapter 4 - Octel

The business at Octel of making additives used in fuels has to be, by its very nature dangerous and toxic. After a short induction course on the safety aspects of such a hazardous environment, I was thrown into the Tel 3 building that made tetraethyl lead or anti-knock used to reduce engine knocking and increase the fuel's octane rating. We had regular monthly medicals if you were found with high concentrations of lead in your blood, you were sent to work on the chloride plant. The primary source of all of these chemicals was salt which was melted at 800 degrees plus to produce sodium and chlorine gas. Strange when you think that from such a life-giving substance can produce two of the most deadly chemicals known to man - sodium and chlorine.

It was here that I was to form my very first instrumentation company in partnership with John Walker. The business was called Electronic and Technical Services. Our first major job was to control the environment in a large greenhouse owned by Peter and Jim Magill on Leasowe Road. They were market gardeners and needed to produce early crops of tomatoes. We got the job because my mate Malcolm Newton was working for the brothers and gave us an introduction. It was also at this time that I was transferred to Octel's instrument workshop with Dick Erdley who worked for Wally Hides, the instrument contractors. We were both doing the same job - modifications to some Honeywell Controls- but he was on twice the hourly rate. I went in to see Tony Hoskins, the Instrument superintendant and asked if I could leave and go and work for Hides but he told me no chance. But it planted a seed in my brain that contracting was the way to go. Basically these two events were to have dramatic effects on my prosperity in later life, even though I was not to know it at the time.

I left the Octel to work for GEC Medical. I had a company car, a monthly salary, an expense account and a promise of quick promotion. The job entailed the commissioning, installation and repair of X-ray equipment around the northwest. Unfortunately, the job did not meet with my expectations as being on the staff meant I was not paid for overtime. Quite often I would get a call out and work late into the evenings and the promised pay rise never materialised so I left after 6 months.

It was now that my business direction was to take a spectacular turn for the better. I went to work at the Champion Sparking Plug Company as an instrument technician I was on shift work so I had more time to set up my own instrument contracting company. From 1968, the Champion Sparking Plug Company operated an automotive components factory on Arrowe Brook Road, employing at one time over 1,000 people. It was closed in 2006 and production transferred to Italy. While working at Champions I sold the Pet Shop business and all its equipment.

It was during this time that my big break came getting the instrument contract for Bidston Steel.

Chapter 4 - Bidston Steel

My introduction to the steel industry was by courtesy of my best friend at the time, Charles Neal. His company, Neal Welding Components, had helped carry out numerous modifications and repairs to the Bidston Steel plant at their workshop in Albion Street. The steel mill had been constructed in record time under the guidance of the chief engineer Mr

Bidston Steel Plant

Michael Stretch (Stretchy). He was a very able and talented engineer with a degree in both mechanical and electrical Engineering.
The first plant manger was Mr Bob Noble, his forceful approach did tend to ruffle a lot of feathers. One of his more spectacular decisions was the idea that the plant would be a sandwich site, meaning the workers would not be allowed to boil a kettle, but must bring in sandwiches and a flask. This was Merseyside and there was no way this was likely to happen. After a short but interesting stay, he was summoned back to head office in Stafford.
I arrived on the scene just after the commissioning stage. The steel plant was divided up into three main parts the arc furnace that reprocessed the scrap metal, the casting machine (caster) that produced 4-inch-square billets and the rolling mill. The mill reheated the billets in a furnace to enable the steel to be rolled into different sizes of reinforcement bars used extensively in the construction industry to reinforce concrete. In fact the very first owner of the plant was British Reinforced Concrete (BRC). The whole plant was of Italian construction; the Arc Furnace had been built by Tagliaferri, and the casting machine by Danieli. The instrumentation on the latter was not quite up to scratch so...enter my company. Stretchy had mentioned the fact to Charles who took me down to the plant in Valley Road. At the time the engineering offices consisted of a group of Portacabins and the administration was carried out in a red brick building opposite. This was the entrance to the site; originally it had been a dockers' club. Now there is a Tesco Superstore on the site; who needs to make things when you can have low paid jobs in a supermarket. I had arranged to meet Charles at the site entrance in Valley Road.

Chapter 4 - Bidston Steel

Crawford, the boss of the operation, had a chauffeur to ferry him around and we passed him in the car park cleaning the company car. Crawford's good friend was Sir Keith Joseph who was Education Minister in Mrs Thatcher's government, so with contacts in high places, how could the operation possibly go wrong.

Crawford was something of an entrepreneur with other business interests including a restaurant in Yorkshire. It fell on his shoulders to get the plant up and running within narrow financial constraints. The owners, British Reinforced Concrete, a subsidiary of Hall Engineering was not a massive company and the investment in Bidston could either break them or propel them into a higher league.

Later Mr Duncan Skidmore was to join the senior management straight from a ladies' garment factory where he had been the M.D. With Roy Mottershead (Mottey), an ex professional footballer whose career had come to a grinding halt because of injury, entrusted to the job of plant manager and with his previous experience of managing a steel mill in Rotherham, the team was almost complete.

Roy brought in Gordon McShannon as chief accountant, a financial wizkid who was later to become the company accountant; this was after the Manchester Steel takeover.

With Kevin McEntaggart employed as works accountant and Mike Bidston as financial accountant, the senior management team, for good or bad, was in place at Bidston Steel and we would float or sink by their efforts. Sandra McShannon and Margaret Goodwin, both wives of the management team, worked in the wages' department.

Arc Furnace

Chapter 4 - Bidston Steel

I had slipped away from my job at Champion Spark to meet up with Charles in the car park at Bidston Steel.
On arrival, the mill was a hive of activity with people rushing all over the place, and there was a huge bang followed by an even louder bang and a massive crackling sound.
"What's that" I said as I nearly jumped out of my skin.
With a chuckle in his voice Charles commented.
"That's the Arch Furnace starting up"
Before we could enter the inner sanction of Stretchy's office, it was

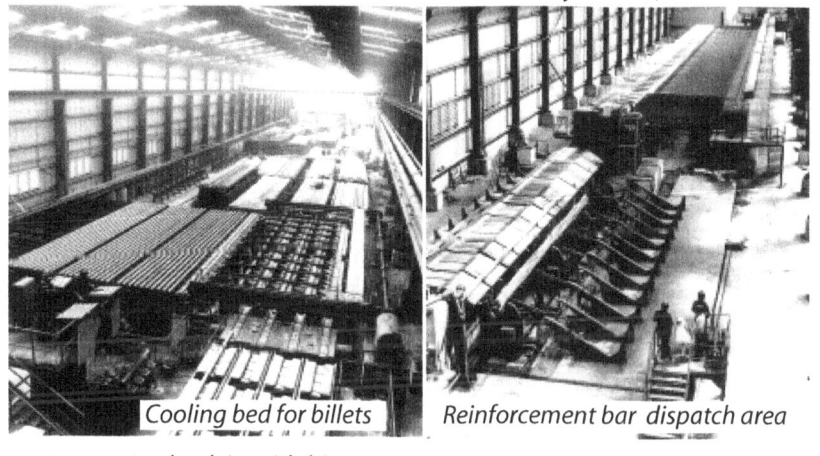

Cooling bed for billets   *Reinforcement bar dispatch area*

customary to check in with his secretary.
Miss Christina Slimming was a delightful creature, with a beautiful well proportioned face and a delightful smile, made all the more mysterious by her donkey jacket, hard hat and green wellies. Very able in her work, she acted as a walking diary and public relations officer for our Chief Engineer.
Mike Stretch was in his early 50s, slim and short in height with blonde hair and piercing blue eyes. He always appeared hyperactive, looking up from a whole raft of drawing.
"Hi, Charles. Have you brought those pump parts back?"
"Yes, they are in my car."
Mike pulled over a chair and sat down. "That's good. Roy Ostle is waiting for them. He's got a couple of fitters ready to fix the pump. These bloody Italian pumps...we'll have to change them!"
Charles used the opportunity to interrupt. "I've brought Roy Dutton the instrument engineer along; he can sort out your problem with the temperature instruments." Mike then looking me up and down , said OK, smiled and leant over his desk and we shook hands.
Mike smiled and looked pleased with the outcome.
He phoned Bob Muirhead to tell him we were here and to show us the problem on the caster.
And that was the start of my involvement with Bidston Steel.

Chapter 4 - Bidston Steel

It was a little later that I first met Mr Roy Ostle, the mechanical supervisor, alias the Bidston Bear or to his friends the "Big O", a man of considerable statue both in size and personality. He was generally always confrontational towards his men scanning the plebs with a hypercritical eye. With small close-set eyes, he distrusted just about everyone. To put everything into context, Roy was Mike's whipping boy; it was his responsibility to make things happen. Because the process of making steel is such a demanding process, there were many problems and brakedowns that had an effect on production; you had to have skin like a rhino to take the flak. Enter Mr Ostle. Also it was the era of the powerful unions. Between 1978 and 1979, Mr Robinson, alias "Red Robo" the communist convener at Longbridge, was behind 523 disputes at the then government-owned British Leyland plant. Our own junior version was Max Ferrier assisted by Mr Brian Anderson who was another thorn in the Big 0's side. All the fitters had been supplied by Site Erection Services (SES). Pat Garry was the linkman with Tommy Breanan, the M.D of the business. Pat was a short stocky guy as tall as he was wide of the Tom Jones School of dress, and he wore the mandatory gold chain and bracelet. Having worked many years in the Gulf, he was not a guy to be messed with. He would certainly have not looked out of place in Al Capone's Mob. When I required labour for a shutdowns or during maintenance at the weekends, a visit to see the Big O was a requirement.

Caster where the steel billets are formed

Every Friday afternoon around lunchtime, Roy would visit Charles' operation in Albion Street for his customary Chinese takeaway, and when appropriate a few glasses of the amber nectar in the Albion hotel.

"You'll be looking like a China-man soon," I commented" He laughed. If only we knew how true this statement would be. While he was in a good mode, I asked

The Big O

266

Chapter 4 - Bidston Steel

"Can I borrow Tony Holmes, your welder." "I have a couple of brackets I need welding on the caster to help get the valves down."
Tony could weld just about anything to anything and would be a useful addition to the team. There was a load of jobs needed doing during the shutdown and I needed the best guys to help; time was money.
"Yes I'll get Alex to sort it"
Alex Woods was one of the foremen under the Big O and likeable and helpful guy. My problem with the Big O was that he always agreed, I think he found saying yes was less hassle than saying no, but quite often nothing happened. Anyway fingers crossed this time. Trevor Walsh was Roy's runner, employed in disguise as a fitter's mate and he was basically at the beck and call of the Big O. Roy had a special section in the stores for parts he had ordered directly for his projects; some wag had planted grass on a couple of his longer running projects. They had become an embarrassment and people started asking questions. So he instructed Trevor to deposit the items in the River Birket. Some future archaeologist on *Time Team* will discover the Pop Eye Multi-jet Jet Bubble Pipe Valve under the layer of Tesco's superstore artefacts and wonder what's been going on here! hence this book.

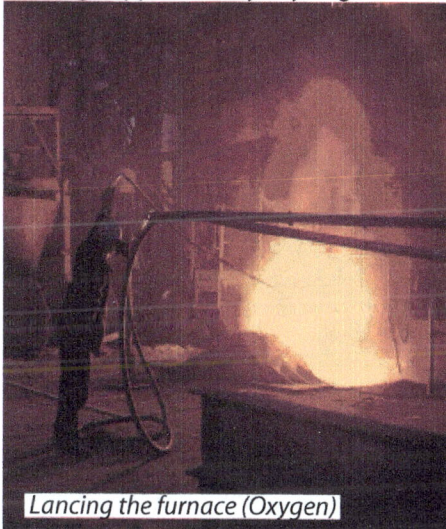

Lancing the furnace (Oxygen)

Graham Andrews and his assistant George Goodwin were in charge of the stores and the buying department. I remember George telling me his office was approximately where the delicatessen was now in Tescos. The stores also had its own personalities; Brian Richards was the foreman, a short guy who wore thick glasses and a moustache - a junior version of the Big O's. When they both got together to discuss various problems, they would both be engaged in synchronised moustache twigging. Brian with his toothbrush moustache was no match for the Big O's Mexican model. A duel would follow, with the Big O promising to remove his stuff from the stores. With Ted Williamson, George Morris, and Eddy, and not forgetting Bernard Brady (Barney), the stores' team was now complete. Working 24/7 you could get almost anything out of the stores.
Eric, the owner of Mersey Fabrications, and Jimmy Hope the manager of J & M profiles, were regular visitors to the site. I would quite often chat with them during the lunch break.

Chapter 4 - Bidston Steel

The steel mill depended heavily on outside contractors.
The Italian engineers tended to be a little superstitious. On the very first melt it was a custom to place coins in the arc furnace along with the very first charge of scrap; this was a good luck gesture to bring wealth and prosperity to the operation. In our case I think the Italians had been a little mean with the cash advance as we will discover later. The main control panel had a red alarm light in the centre. Martin Wyard, an electrical foreman, was in attendance for the first melt along with several Italian engineers. Expectations were high; everyone was waiting in anticipation for the big switch on.
Looking puzzled Martin enquired, "What happens if that red light comes on?"
"Run like fu*k," was the curt reply.
"Why is that?" he queried?
"Because it's not connected to anything!"

Rolling Mill

A party was held in Mike's office on the successful completion of the first melt. Champagne was the order of the day for the engineering staff and a barrel of beer for the workers. Stretchy made a short speech thanking everyone for their efforts with special thanks to Giuseppe, the head of the Italian commissioning team. The party went into full swing with large amounts of alcohol consumed and lots of mutual back slapping. It was a good send off for the Italian team. The Big 0 was the worst for wear and totally drunk; he staggered out of the Portacabin and fell into a drainage ditch. Laying face down and out for the count, someone managed to walk over him. It was during the following day that he went into the fitters' changing room to examine the boots to try and match up the footprints on the back of his donkey jacket. He was absolutely convinced that someone had done it on purpose; he never did find the culprit.
The electrical section was under the command of Mr Peter Black who had worked for Mike Stretch at British Aluminium. A competent and qualified electrical engineer in his late twenties but some would say he lacked experience at this level. Enter Mr Bob Muirehead and Martin Whyard, both employed at the same time as electrical foremen. Bob's practical skills and Martin's organisational ability brought a much-needed balance to the team. It was Martin who set up the stores system with order codes and minimum and maximum stock levels; remember, this was before computers.

Chapter 4 - Bidston Steel

All he had was a Kalamazoo system of index cards. A little later Mr Tony Billiason, and Mr Brian Millar joined the electrical department with Roger Chadwick and John Ravinscroft who follow later. Graham Nixon who was originally working on site for GEC, and eventually joined the electrical department as a project engineer.

All the electricians were employed as contract labour, supplied by Jim Cook (Cookie) of Merseylec. His right-hand man at the time was John Maddocks (Big John). I was to run up against Cookie on numerous occasions; he had a separate Instrument company called Mersey Instrumentation. He was always trying to muscle in on my action. John was later to leave and form his own company M.W.M Electrical, based in the Beaufort Air Sea Equipment factory in Birkenhead.

Douglas Hart was in charge of plant services, which was given the unofficial name of "Parks and Gardens". Doughy a likeable character with a good sense of humour. He had an able-bodied foreman called Mr John McCray and his specialised subject was the operation of the klargester which was basically a septic tank, on legs that digested the sewage. Their biggest responsibility was the numerous beam cranes located around the plant. Billy Marshall, John's chargehand, did most of the actual work along with a couple of fitters. John Revins of Merseyside Lifting Services supplied all the wire robes used on the cranes.

Ladel of molten steel

All the waste gas and dust that was drawn out of the arc furnace was rendered harmless in the cibal plant, another responsibility of Parks and Gardens. The gentleman in charge of the government's health and safety inspectorate was based in Chester and drove past the plant twice a day and could monitor the plant for any infringements as he zoomed past. He was a continuous thorn in our side due to the levels of noise and pollution that the plant generated. Liverpool University was employed to investigate the noise problem and the solution was a massive investment in an acoustic screen some 30ft high and 100yds long to stifle the noise; this cost over a million pounds.

Chapter 4 - Bidston Steel

In the early days I would quite often take drawings down to the local Italian fish and chip shop in Poulton Road to have them translated, using the back of fag packets to draw up modifications. Enter Mr Phillip Beamish a competent draftsman. Mr Arthur Muir was Mike's deputy and later was to take over the roll of chief engineer when Mike left the plant under a cloud. Mike always seemed to be a little aloof and did not suffer fools easily; he tended to hold the senior management in contempt. And I think after he had done the near impossible in making a steel mill on a marsh by the side of the River Birket in record time, his usefulness was questioned.

Mr Cliff Law was the personal manager with Ann Usher working as his assistant. Mr Graham Andrews assisted by George Goodwin was in charge of the purchasing department. One of the perks that I enjoyed whilst at Bidston Steel was the visit to each home game played at Liverpool Football Club. Tommy Brenan had access to a whole row of seats in the main stand, and being a friend of Peter Robinson, the Liverpool Club Secretary, he was able to do a deal for corporate entertainment which was a bit basic in those days without the box. George managed to get Charles and myself an invitation for each home game. We would all sit in a line - the good, the bad and the ugly - with Tommy at one end next a couple of his henchmen, then a few of his contacts at Vauxhalls, and then the Big O, George, Charles and finally myself.

All was not well at Neal Welding. A major disagreement had occurred between the owners and Charles sold out to his brother-in-law Hans. In the meantime, I had formed a supply company called Mersey Industrial Supplies. The idea came about whilst I was in George Godwin's office. The phone rang and it was Graham Exley, MD of Mersey Equipment, asking if their quote for palm chrome gloves had been accepted.

"I'm sorry, Graham, but Arco have come in at a lower price."

George put the phone down and said,

"Every fitter, electrician and production guy get a clean pair of these gloves every day; its about health and safety but they cost a bloody fortune". This interested me.

"What's are the chances of me getting a quote in?"

"Have a go by all means, but they must be chrome-tanned natural leather, and well-made. There are cheap ones out there but they fall apart or split. So I'd need samples and an official quote."

I nodded in agreement chancing my luck.

"What's the best price to date?"

"Well, well, just put it in writing along with the samples," was his reply. But after some persuading,

"OK OK. It has to be under 35p a pair, but we buy them in 1,000's at a time".

It took a while but we found a company called Bathgate in Chester a

Chapter 4 - Bidston Steel

Mr Nish Lenton imported them direct from India but to get a deal we had to buy a container or part-container. So that is how it all began.

We had been operating successfully for about 9 months when I made the offer to Charles of joining the business. It was just getting too much for me to operate part-time. We had a meeting and thrashed out a deal that suited everyone, sealed with handshakes all round. We then bought a shop at 47 Old Chester Road which could also be used as a trade counter, and we had an office upstairs.

Stretchy would hold parties at his home in Pipers Lane in Lower Heswal. All the engineering staff and the bosses of the contracting firms would attend. Mike's wife was a doctor at a teaching hospital in Liverpool. I can always remember bumping into a real skeleton in the passage down to the toilet; it came as a bit of a shock. It was not a plastic version but the real thing. Apparently it came from India - the poor soul had certainly been elevated to a better existence in the afterlife.

I remember standing on the balcony which had a magnificent view over the River Dee, talking to Charley Evans when Alex Woods came up.

"Hi, lads. I think there's too many of you on this balcony; be careful it does not collapse, SES built it".

John Marchant was another of Roy's foreman; he raced motorbikes and was a very likable guy. Stretchy's parties certainly had notoriety: no expenses spared and lavish food.

After such a fun weekend it was back to work again.

Situated opposite the arc furnace was the laboratory that was manned continuously. It was vital that the molten metal was tested through the various production cycles. Mr Jackson was quality control manager in charge of operations. I remember him telling me that they had been approached by Wallasey Council and asked to put a bid in for all the scrap from the demolition of New Brighton Pier. He had to decline the offer because it was made from cast iron, no good for reinforcement bar. It was a sad day for me when they started to remove the pier they removed my childhood memories. Their excuse was it had silted up and anyway the number of passengers had declined.

Quite often I would be called upon to fix various problems associated with the spectrometer which was used to analyze the metal samples. Sometimes they could not draw down a vacuum to allow the spark to ignite. A massive voltage in the order 50,000 volts had to draw an arc from the sample and this was then tested. The metal sample would be taken from the arc furnace at around 1650 degrees centigrade, which in itself was no mean task. The result would come back from the lab then Billy Mainwright, the foreman, would shout out to one of his men... three- and -a half spadefuls of manganese and one of carbon. I always found this amazing as there were seventy tons of molten steel in the arc furnace, so how could he be so precise? Anyway it always seemed to work, because

Chapter 4 - Bidston Steel

the metal came out the other end correct. Measuring the temperature was another difficult operation. A probe on a long tube had to be thrust into the molten metal, and this would be destroyed almost immediately, allowing just enough time for the instrument to record the temperature. The operators were clad from top to bottom in fireproof suits. Each time the furnace doors were opened it was like Dante's Inferno with sparks and flames gusting out. Before the arc furnace could be tilted and the contents poured into its ladle, it had to be lanced, with an oxygen lance, and this was another dangerous operation. Steve Wheeldon was the Casting Manager and one of my tasks was to make sure that the Stordy burners heated up the ladles. The instrumentation could be quite temperamental.

Charles, engineering business went into receivership. I can still remember this as if it was yesterday; Charles called me on the Friday night and told me the news.. "Roy we will have to move quickly on this. The bank has appointed a receiver who will be in the business on Monday morning. I can do a deal with Hans and we should all do well out of this."

I was totally taken aback by the news. It meant Charles was back in charge. What a turn-up for the books - it was eyes down: look in! We had funds within Wirral Industrial Supplies which was the forerunner of Mersey Tool and Welding Supplies, but more importantly we could easily raise money on the strength of the business turnover. Charles took over all the welding component part of the business and Hans continued with the general engineering. We both put our heads together and came up with the new business name of Weldtip Ltd. The arrangement of both businesses working under the same roof did not work, so we decided to buy a factory in Westfield Road which had belonged to Bibby Shipping Line. I wired the whole factory for three-phase supply with the help of Edwin. At the peak we employed 22 people manufacturing welding electrodes and other repetitive engineering components before branching out into general engineering.

It was back to musical chairs at the steel plant. The backroom staff at Bidston consisted of May Whitenbury who was on the reception and later joined the accounts department as a clerk. Dawn who was Brian Millars daughter took over her duties on reception. Mary Dean and Suzanne Cross were members of the typing pool with Sue Bell employed as Duncan Skidmore's secretary. A little more fine-tuning was required at the highest level when Roy Mottershead was promoted to Works' Director, with Peter Marsh from Forge Masters taking over his role. It was around this time that John Stanhope joined the engineering team; he was a good friend of Arthur Muir and arrived on the plant quite out of the blue. His role was to be an assistant to Mr Muir. His engineering ability did leave a lot to be desired, but at least their friendship could be maintained, and Neil Bennett moved across from the production side to IMS.

Chapter 4 - Bidston Steel

It was around this time that we decided to purchase North West Saw Services Ltd, which was originally based on the Tartan Industrial Estate in Hoylake. The reason for our interest was the regular supply of sub-contract work we obtained in the form of grinding printer guillotine blades. A receiver had been appointed and according to Sid, who had been the previous M.D, a bargain could be had. Using the well-tested principle of due diligence, we discovered there was no goodwill in the business, but we decided to have a go.

Sid had taken the business from a profitable operation to a bankrupt business in less than 12 months by leasing cars and other equipment that was not needed. The bank decided it was never going to get its money back so it appointed a receiver. Our offer of £2,200 was duly accepted and included all the equipment associated with the business. We reluctantly retained the employment of Sid, but the two saw doctors were highly skilled in this precise trade and would have to be retained if the business was to continue. Our idea was that we could reduce his overheads by incorporating the business within the premises of Weldtip Ltd. Sid insisted that we required the largest transit van available, his excuse being that the circular saws he sharpened for the Forestry Commission would only fit inside a big van. We took a visit down to the main dealer to organise the necessary lease agreement, when to our amazement Sid insisted on having expensive tinted windows!

"What the hell for," I asked.

"It's to stop people seeing inside; anyway stop it from my salary".

We discovered later that Sid was a member of the Twisted Knot, a Civil War Re-enactment Group. He needed the large transit van to transport his cannon around the country. He had a black powder licence which allowed him to fire blanks. He also slept in the van after the battles. Charles and I had already decided we could not afford his talents any longer, so that was the final straw that broke the camel's back. It had taken a good few months to find out what he was up to. This business turned out to be a disaster for us both and we eventually rented it back.

A takeover was initiated by Manchester Steel; both Bidston and Manchester Steel Mills were classified as mini mills and the idea was to rationalize the product range and reduce costs by amalgamating some management operations. Towards this end, Mr Graham Andrews became group purchasing manager with Gordon McShannon taking up the role of group accountant, both based in Manchester. It became apparent that, due to steel quotas imposed by the European Union to try and reduce capacity in the market and to counter the cheap imports flooding the market, our industry under the stewardship of Mrs Thatcher's government was destined to be annihilated.

Doing what the Luftwaffe could only have dreamed of - destroying our manufacturing base.

Chapter 4 - Bidston Steel

Mrs Thatcher had decided that the future of our nation lay in service industries, washing each other's underpants and selling hamburgers on every street corner.

The very nation that gave the world the Industrial Revolution and helped the progress of mankind no longer needed to make anything.

Enter Elkem, a Norwegian steel company which we all thought was going to be a knight in shining armour and invest in the business; little did we know of the forthcoming break up. The reason for the takeover was that Elkem wanted a foothold within the EU. Elkem, now the new owners of Manchester and Bidston Steel, were given an offer that they could not refuse. A consortium of companies including Allied Steel and Wire, Temple Borough Rolling Mills and Sheerness Steel all owned by BSC and GKN offered the Norwegian company £16 million to close both plants. The unions and local MP's caught wind of the deal and the negotiations went under ground with the outcome that both Manchester and Bidston Steel were taken over by Allied Steel and Wire which just postponed the inevitable closures. The conservative Government had agreed to supply 25 per cent of the funding. Elkem acted in a dishonourable and underhand way. Chris Rynning of Elkem lined up a deal to sell both plants to China at a knock-down price. Now Regional Director of Asia with Elkem, he was awarded a symbolic honorary citizenship of China. In conclusion, we were never allowed to operate on a level playing field as other countries were dumping steel into the UK. Our energy costs were the highest in Europe and unlike other countries, the government's arms length policy had been a disaster. I remember getting the news that the plant was definitely going to close and it was a devastating blow. What was I going to do? I had become very complacent over the past years. Wirral Industrial Supplies, Instamec and Weldtip would be dramatically effected with likely redundancies and closures. Also my stepson Edwin Ingram was in the final year of his instrument apprenticeship on the site and would now find himself out of work. But you know what they say when one door shuts in your face, another opens.

I was still in employed and had a few more weeks until the final *coup de gras;* I thought I could get a good deal out of the remaining 8 months left on my contract. But after a discussion with Mr Brian Miller, I was given a final payment of only one months salary. My priority was to get Edwin sorted; I decided it was too much hassle owning an instrument business; many companies we had worked with had now closed down. I spoke with the owner of Plant Design Services in Wallasey Village and he said he would be able to find me a job but I must update my CV. In those days with no internet or PCs. My new-found agent lined up a job at BNFL as an Instrument engineer on £16 an hour, plus expenses and overtime which in those days was a very good rate.

Chapter 4 - Bidston Steel

Helping Edwin find a job took quite a few phone calls and calling in favours and eventually, after one abortive deal in Southport, I discovered that Associated Octel had just lost an apprentice who was in his final year. A chance in a million - how many apprentices leave in their last year? Edwin was a bright lad and had reached his final year at college and after an initial interview, he was offered the apprenticeship much to the relief of Mercie and myself.

As I write this book, manufacturing is now 17 per cent of national output; the remaining 80 per cent are service industries. The old Bidston Steel Plant is now a Tesco Superstore.

Some twenty years after the plant had closed May Whitenbury organised a Twentieth Anniversary Party. Unfortunately I was not able to attend, but the list that May produced of past employees can be found in the Appendix section.

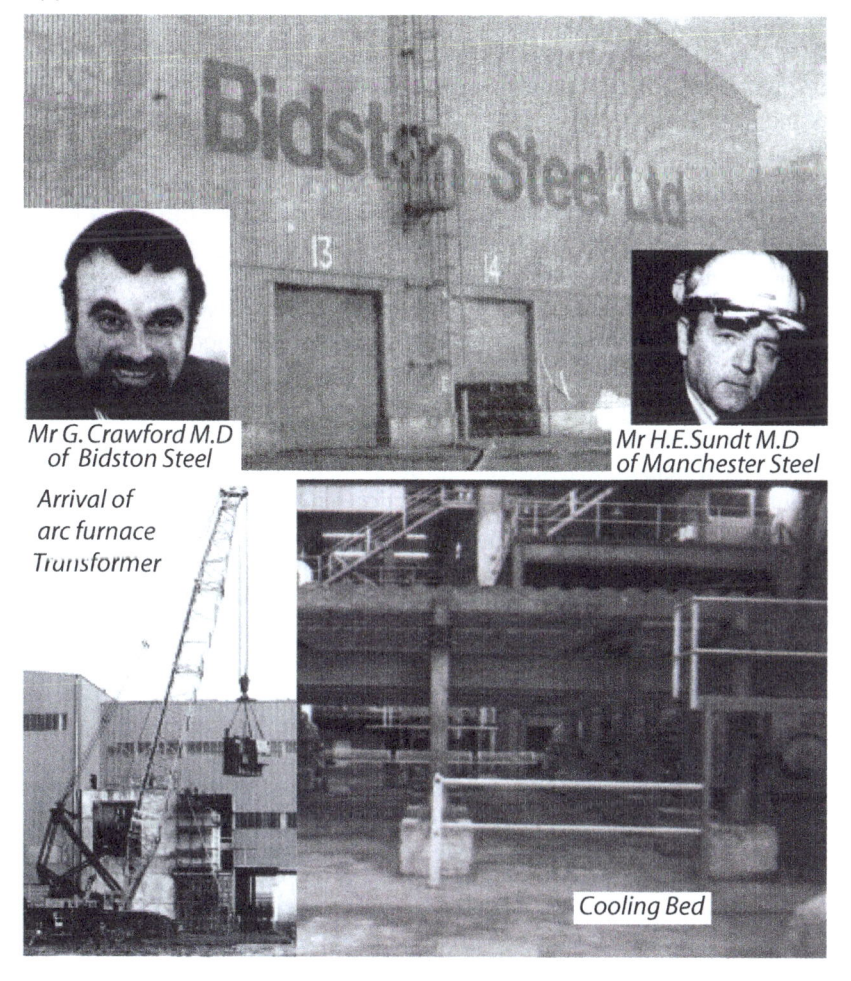

Mr G. Crawford M.D of Bidston Steel

Mr H.E.Sundt M.D of Manchester Steel

Arrival of arc furnace Transformer

Cooling Bed

275

Chapter 4 - Costain

The new door that opened had Costain and BNFL written on the door. The Thermal Oxide Reprocessing Plant (Thorp) was given the go-ahead in 1978 although it did not go into operation until 1994. This is my story of the small part I played in the multi-million pound folly. It was built at Sellafield (formerly known as Windscale). British Nuclear Fuels (BNFL) decided to try and banish the bad memories by changing the plant's name to Sellafield in 1981; but that's another story.

It was a bright and sunny morning when I arrived at the offices of Costain. I reported to reception as instructed in my letter of appointment from Plant Design Services of Wallasey Village. With an agreed hourly rate of £16 an hour under my belt, I was quite happy with my lot, and even though the travelling took an hour in each direction, it was well worth the journey.
I took a seat in reception to await my fate. Looking nervously around, I saw numerous photographs of commissioned chemical plants and in the centre a large portrait of my future leader who was the great-grandson of the founder. Taking a lead from George Orwell's 1984, the sign should of read Big brother is watching you! Instead it read Mr Peter Costain Chief Executive. The receptionist was routinely deflecting telephone calls. Mr Williams will be at Risley all day and Mr James will be in later this afternoon. How did she know where everyone was at any given time? When the next call came, I could see her peering at a sign displayed on the wall next to the main entrance. This had names and two columns showing AM and PM. So this was her secret timetable. I nervously fiddled with my briefcase and looked at my watch. In my briefcase I had a slide rule, scale rule, pencils and a massive rubber for plan B, together with an emergency chocolate bar and a blank note pad. With all this I could rule the world or help build a nuclear reprocessing plant.
Eventually my man arrived and introduction himself.
"Hello. I'm Leo Burns, head of recruitment. You've already had an interview I take it." I nodded in agreement and went on the charm offensive. "It's a nice day to start a new job". He just grunted; he obviously hadn't got a GCSE in the art of conversation. He was a small man in his late 50s with the I've eaten too many free lunches look about him. With a pointed nose and an animated forehead, but his main attribute was the look of total disinterest. The words that flowed from his mouth had very little sincerity. The same words must have been spoken to thirty or forty new recruits each week - arrangement for signing in, car park allocation, starting and finishing times and so on. "You will have to sign the Official Secrets Act and get clearance before you can go anywhere near Risley." He'd done it all before, over and over again, and his mundane voice reinforced this fact. He spoke in paragraphs and I anticipated every full stop so that I could have a mental break. It would have been much easier

Chapter 4 - Costain

if I had been given a printed sheet to read. But no, the laborious routine had to be followed. I was told, I had to attend a short induction course, but before that I was directed towards the stairs and instructed to report to Mr Mike Bailey, Senior Instrument Engineer, on the third floor the end office on the right. I could feel Small Brother watching me as I walked up the stairs; turning round to acknowledge his help, he had vanished. Walking up several flights of stairs to the third floor I came to a long corridor with offices situated on both sides, all occupied by engineers. Mike Bailey's office was the last office before the open-plan drawing office. His office overlooked a labyrinth of drawing boards with several draftsmen beavering away. I knocked on the door and walked in. Mike Bailey was sitting at his desk and he stood up to shake hands. Our eyes met and I saw that he was about the same height as me, of average build with short dark hair. I gathered from our conversation that he was very thoughtful and before allowing words to fall from his lips, each had been processed several times; his words were slow and precise, each sentence to the point and did not contain any surplus information, no repeats, or long pauses. I had to concentrate and make sure my replies were connected to my brain and were not just reflex words. I had to create the correct impression; my problem was my language was adapted to the rough environment working for so long in a factory and having to make things happen instantly. Working with clients at this level of engineering required a more refined approach.

After a short chat I was given a large file and told to read the information and become acquainted with its contents. It was entitled, the Procurement Standards required for instrumentation used on the Thorp Project. I was to work directly for the customer BNFL and take my instruction from Mr Grenville Harrop who was based at Risley, Warrington. Mike stood up quickly and we both walked down the corridor to an office. The sign on the door had been tampered with: I discovered later that the offices played musical chairs - no one seemed to remain long enough to have a proper name plate. Mike knocked on the door and we went in. Sat behind one of the desks was a thin middle-aged gentleman with a rugged oval-shaped face and red cheeks that had been weathered by the elements. Wearing half-rimmed glasses he looked up from his notes.

"Trevor, I've brought Roy Dutton to share an office with you. He will be working at Risley but will need a base over here." Mike quickly left, closed the door behind him and left me standing there wondering what to say. The ice was broken by Trevor, who announced in a thick Glaswegian accent. "Site down, Roy. I'll clear out the desk for you. I hope you don't smoke; this is a none-smoking office, and anyway I hate the stuff." Great, I thought! I was a smoker at the time.

The office had two full-size desks opposite one another with a telephone in the centre. Apart from the chairs under the desks, two other chairs

Chapter 4 - Costain

were positioned beside a bookcase. A filing cabinet was in the corner. On the wall was a large progress chart, like a bar chart on its side with lots of red marks and Post-it notes attached. The blinds had seen better days and hung at 45 degrees in an act of defiance, the string cords all braided and knotted. The office was in need of some tender loving care in the form of a lick of paint. I settled in quickly and found Trevor to be a likeable character, but a man with very fixed ideas that could not be shifted.
One particular incident comes to mind. Trevor was working on a portable decontamination plant for General Electric (GE) over in the States. The idea of the construction was to allow nuclear utilities to apply weak acids to remove deposited radioactivity from equipment. So this task aimed to help clear up the mess that this generation has created for future generations. Very thick metal had to be used to shield the operator from radiation. It was a cold Monday Morning when I arrived in the office only to find Trevor having an irate telephone conversation, with several drawings spread out over both our desks. He appeared very agitated; he must have tried to die his hair over the weekend because instead of the normal reddish tinge, it was now green. He looked a bit like the Green Giant. His Bobby Charlton type hair arrangement was now even more obvious. I settled into my chair opened a draw and took my desk diary out to check on the week's meetings. I could not help but hear the pantomime opposite. The metal slabs had arrived at the profile welders ready to be cut up into different shapes as per the drawings that he had supplied, and these guys were now on the telephone. As he spluttered and shouted, the following one way conversation could be heard.
"What do you mean the sizes are all wrong. Are you looking at the same bloody drawings". Pause.
"The drawings are correct; I checked them myself Aye, Aye, Aye!"
"I don't believe what you are saying!"
"You can't weld two fu*kin pieces together, the integrity won't be maintained!"
"It's just like a bloody jig-saw!"
What have you cut em with?"
"Of course I made an allowance for the cut".
"I can't order any more fuc*kin metal".
"I'll get back!" He slammed the phone down with an even redder face than usual and as he was just about to say something, I interrupted and said, "I'll let you get on with it, Trevor," and quickly exited the office. The conversation was like some sort of black comedy; I had to leave the office before I split my sides.
It transpired later that the slab mill in South Wales had an eighteen month delivery date for the 8" thick plate, and Trevor needed desperately to find another plate or his job was on the line.
When I returned to the office, I waited for him to start the conversation.

Chapter 4 - Costain

"Those bloody idiots have cocked up the job. They had six slabs of metal and all they had to do was cut out the correct shapes with a plasma cutter, no problem. I nodded in agreement.

As to whose fault it was remains to be seen but a week later he was no longer in the office. He had left while I was working at Risley.

I now had the office to myself until a couple of weeks later Dave Pitcher arrived. He was due to start work with the Atomic Energy Authority. I found out later that he was to replace Bob Ainsworth, who could not see eye to eye with the people in charge at the authority. Dave had worked in Saudi Arabia for over 30 years, and had not even seen his children grow up. He had been Senior Instrument Superintendent in charge of all the instrumentation on the Aramco oil fields. The final straw came when he had to visit two of his employees in jail who had been caught by the religious police in the act of distilling Flash - a home-made alcohol. Both had been sentenced to ten lashes and were to be deported after their punishment. He was faced with the dilemma of visiting them in jail to explain that, not only had they lost their jobs, but that this inhuman act was going to be carried out. At the same time his son's body had just been discovered in France; some five years earlier he had been potholing with some colleges when they had become separated in a deep underground passage which had collapsed. Several expeditions had been mounted to try and recover the body without success until quite by accident his body was discovered. All these events seem to put life into perspective for him and he wanted a job closer to home.

Dave was also an authority on fungi and had published several papers on the subject. His return to the UK had triggered different emotions; his wife found it very difficult to adjust after leading separate lives. I think chatting to me brought some relief. Dave was very helpful and his advice and guidance was much appreciated in my early days at Costain. I was to miss his knowledge and invigorating conversation.

Eventually our office manager, Mr Bennett, orchestrated a whole new concept - the open-plan office. During one long holiday weekend all the offices were removed except for Mike's and the open space painted in white, ceilings, walls everything. The drawing boards were white, the drawing we worked on were white, the filing cabinets were white, it was a kind of snow blindness!

With different parts of the project on different floors, it was a client requirement that we kept strict levels of security between each floor. The only permitted communications was through official meetings, and then only on a need -to- know basis. We were told to cover up all the drawings after work because of spy satellites. Two different colour plastic bags were used in the office: yellow bags for top secret stuff, scrap notes and drawings, all to be shredded on the premises, and black bags for old sandwiches, newspapers and non-classified material. So here we were - a

Chapter 4 - Costain

group of engineers, draftsmen, designers all working in an ultra-secure environment and all because it was thought that some other bloody idiot may want to make a similar plant.

As I walked up the stairs I was trying to brush off the dog hairs from all over my suit. I had a meeting at ten o'clock and did not want to look like a dog trainer. I was a member of a car school; three of my fellow engineers took turns to drive the others to work. We all met up at Dave's house in Eastham and from there travelled together to Sharston in Manchester. Dave was the dog lover with two of the moulting variety. Apart from his car reeking of dogs, all the seats were always coved with hairs. I was going to have to change this arrangement. Dave was something of an odd ball. He took clear directions from his wife each morning; she was a professional tarot card reader and could also read tea leaves. This was supposed to give you insight into the situations that are going on in your life, or so he informed us. So each morning Dave would have his cup read and we would quite often quiz him on what she had seen. We frequently teased him by asking dumb questions, but at least it passed the time. Dave worked across the road from our offices, on another top secret project for BNFL.
Grenville Harrop, an engineer of the highest order, was from the Mike Bailey school of etiquette, but spoke with a posh ascent. Grenville had dark curly hair and was tall and thin but had a very pleasant manner. I remember being summoned to Risley, escorted to his office and being told to wait. While I was waiting, the door opened and in walked this scruffy individual; I thought he was the window cleaner. To my amazement he sat down in Grenville's chair and started flicking through some papers on the desk, and all without a word spoken. Shortly afterwards Grenville came in and the window cleaner looked up from his desk. "I'm chairing a meeting this afternoon; have you completed your report?" It turned out this scruffy individual was Doctor Carey, the Chief Engineer.
Grenville must have been satisfied with my work as it was not long before I was given the opportunity to work on the Thorp Project. I think on reflection it was a bit of a trial to see if I was up to scratch. The meaning of life for me now became the *Decontamination Plant*. With its high pressure nitric acid jets, ultrasonic cleaners, and other mysterious processes, we were certainly going to be in for a fun time. When nothing similar has been done before, you are walking on new ground, but watch out for the quicksand - it's called conceptual design, a blank piece of paper, you come up with the ideas then get it scrutinised by the client and marked out of ten. I basically headed up decontamination while they found a suitable staff man to take over. It was the client's requirement that all senior managers were not contractors but employed direct by Costain.

Chapter 4 - Costain

Mike Curtis was my liaison, but he was already heading up the Minor Reagents project; he was a real character quite tall with a full beard and thick glasses, and had quite a crude turn of phrase when any young lady walked past. According to the various rumours in the office, he'd had a nervous breakdown and was found cowering under his desk. Despite that, it goes without question he was a very able engineer. He was rather absent-minded, like Mr Magoo. One alleged incidence occurred on his way into work. He stopped his car at a newsagent and parked in the bus lane, on a double yellow line. The bus duly arrived and parked next to him obstructing part of the road which caused a minor pile-up. By the time Curtis came out of the shop the bus had moved off and he was tutting as he drove off.

We were under pressure so the first couple of weeks were hectic in finding suitable staff. Costains went to great lengths to recruit, even advertising in Canada to attract qualified engineers. Enter Alesky (Ale) a Polish Canadian engineer; it was a bit late in the day for an interview because he had already been given the job. He showed me his CV and his birth certificate which had been issued in Poland during the occupation by the Third Reich; it had a large swastika in the centre and loads of official signatories and really looked the part if you were into collecting World War II memorabilia, but this was the only official document he had that recorded his birth, and it had been accepted by the various authorities so he was stuck with it. We chatted for a while but it became apparent that his experience was strictly limited. I was stuck with him. The next person to join the team was Ian Kid, a really good engineer with loads of experience and confidence. We became great friends later on through our mutual interest in scuba diving.
Dave Ashworth arrived, affectionately known as Farter Ashworth, because of his taste for real ale that he drank in large quantities most evenings in his local hostelry. Most mornings the area had to be evacuated. I had spoken to our planning engineer to ask if an allowance could be factored in to allow for this disruption. Our planning engineer was Joe who was responsible for drawing up plans and presenting schedules of work.
And last but not least Mr Bob Ainsworth who joined a few months later, straight from the Atomic Energy Authority where his straight talking and superior intellect had not been appreciated. Bob was a staff man while everyone else was on contract. His task was to take over from me and head up the team. He was a great guy to work for; he was well travelled and having worked in Nigeria for a fair amount of time, he had an arsenal of amazing anecdotes. We really hit it off. The only problem with each new arrival was that all the same stories were told. The two most noteworthy follow:
Bob worked for Unilever in Lagos. He was in charge of the Electrical and

Chapter 4 - Costain

Instrumentation Department, his immediate boss was the Chief Engineer. The senior management were all white, but Unilever were in the process of transferring the running of the plant to the Nigerians. One of Bob's responsibilities was to order equipment and spares. All the white staff lived in a secure compound close to the factory. The chief engineer's large chest freezer was faulty, so Bob was instructed to order a replacement from the UK. In the meantime Bob shared his freezer with him.

In a secure area inside the docks all the received goods from the UK were held. After a couple of months Bob got confirmation that the freezer had arrived. But before he could claim the item, the newly appointed Nigerian managing director, Mr Wandawanda, had the freezer removed. An irate Bob called the MD and demanded that the freezer be returned immediately, as it belonged to the chief engineer. The response was that it had been taken away by mistake, and that it would be returned.

It took over six weeks to get the chest freezer back, but after a good clean it appeared to be in first class order; all the packing had been removed and it looked as if it had been used. But Bob was relieved and quickly got it up and running in the chief's kitchen. It was some days later that Bob was chatting to one of the Nigerian managers when in conversation he asked if Bob had attended the funeral of the MD's brother.

"Why would I attend the funeral? I didn't know the guy?" said Bob.
"But you supplied the Freezer" replied the manager looking puzzled.
"What bloody Freezer? What do you mean?" was Bob's indignant reply.

Apparently elaborate preparations are required when organising a funeral in Nigeria. All relatives both local and abroad traditionally have to attend the funeral. It can take quite a while so the MD's brother was housed in the freezer while the necessary arrangements were made. It was that very night that as a thank you, the chief invited Bob and his good lady around for a meal. With food prepared from this very freezer, Bob did not have the heart to tell him what had happened to his freezer, and he struggled to eat the food knowing where it had been kept.

The next story was the glass eye and the swimming pool, but I think I'll give it a miss; it's too long. This story would always annoy Mr Ashworth because he wore a glass eye.

A little later the final part of the jigsaw fell into place when Jimmy Boardley joined the team. He had worked on PLC Programmable Logic Controllers for GEC, so he was ideally placed to start work on the logic sequential diagrams. I approached Jimmy when I found out he was in between contracting jobs, and on my recommendation he was given the job. We went back a long way, to the days we both worked in Cadbury.

So with the team complete it was down to some hard work to get our part of the plant designed and ready to be sent out for costing.

Bob

282

Chapter 4 - Costain

The cardinal sin was if you had left out a penetration, which meant a diamond drill job; construction onsite at the time was past the twenty-meter level. The other major problem was a clash with some cables or pipes. It was the task of the model makers on the top floor to review all the modified drawings and make sure that the model of Thorp was kept up-to-date and accurate. I always had difficulty in visualizing the plant in three dimensions by examining a sheet of paper. Luckily my head designer was Donald McPherson (Don McFearful) who was a gifted designer and could spot a clash at 100 yards - very useful to have on any project. His section leader was Wilf Critchly, an unusual individual, and I must admit I was no great fan of his. He was from the 1970's era and school of thought, with a dress sense second to none, but the girls seemed to like it. With his Charles Bronson drooping moustache, he always had a comb in his pocket to tidy up his balding hairstyle and moustache. When he entered the office such tunes as *Staying Alive* and other *Saturday Night Fever* favourites would be hummed. The morning highlight for our section was when the Express Lift engineer's van pulled up and out popped one of the secretaries. It then sped off into the distance. Then Wilf would appear as if by magic, link arms and escort the lady into the office block. We were waiting for the liftman to forget something and return, and that would have made our day.

Apart from the engineers that joined our team, we needed additional designers and draftsmen. Mr Stuart Jackson came to us straight from his adventures in Libya. We seemed to hit it off as we had the same sense of humour and shared similar interests. Mark was the next to join the team, they both sat with their backs against the wall. - quite useful to avoid any backstabbing via our section leader - with another two boards situated in front of them; Don took up one of these locations. Then four large desks pushed together had our complement of four engineers in attendance. A short distance away sat our connection with the twenty-first century- two computer terminals, in those days quite an innovation. In fact we had borrowed the software called ICE (Instruments, Loops & Cables) from ICI. We had to enter cable numbers and instrument loops and the computer digested the information and spat out millions of reports. It was the forrunner of Computer Aided-Design (CAD).

The very first New Year at Costain was a major turning point for me. I had decided to give up smoking. Now was the ideal opportunity because the office was a non-smoking environment, and I was a bit of a pariah standing on the fire escape in all weathers having my fix of nicotine. Every dinner time a group of engineers and designers from our section would go across to Sharston Baths to swim for about 30 minutes. I decided to join them but my first efforts left a lot to be desired. But having given up smoking I quickly managed to build up my stamina to compete with the others. It was around this time that the newspapers

Chapter 4 - Costain

were full of misleading information about AIDs and Jimmy informed me that he was no longer going swimming because he was sure you could catch AIDs from the swimming pool. Jimmy was a keen keep-fit fanatic so this came as a bit of a shock to me, but that paled into insignificance because shortly after that he decided to leave. The embarrassing part of the whole episode was I got him the job and he did not even tell me he was leaving. He just did not turn up for work. Bob gave me some stick because Jim was halfway through the job, and it was going to be difficult for someone else to pick up the pieces. I had no other option than to volunteer to sort it all out while Bob looked for a replacement. So instead of my cosy job of sizing control valves, I was now up to my neck in writing: if, then, else logic statements for the programmers to use in their software. Ian Kidd was the diving master at Northwest Divers, a branch of the British Sub-Aqua Club (BSAC) and I joined the branch in June 1987. They practised in Irlam Swimming Pool because it had a diving board and the water had a depth of 15ft at the deep end, ideal to practise the art of scuba diving. Afterwards we went to Irlam Steel Club for a pint. In those days it would take about a year to obtain the qualification - with lectures given by the training officer, Mike McCullough, together with loads of time in the pool and an exam at the end before you obtained a novice diver qualification. Nowadays PADI do it in a couple of days. Ian had a flat in Eccles, which was full to the gunnels with diving equipment. We always met up at his flat each Thursday, then travelled on to the club, with our cars full of equipment.

My very first and last dive in the UK before I became a warm water diver, was at Devil's Bridge, Kirby Lonsdale in the Lake District. I arrived on a cold and bleak day as the River Lune's icy water was flashing over slippery rocks, glistening ripples in the winter light majestically flowing from the fells above, then onwards with a sweeping curve past the church and town above. We were there to practise drift dives.

The Devil's Bridge is composed of three beautiful fluted arches. It gets its name because of an old legend that tells us that it was build by His Satanic Majesty!

The site has loads and loads of atmosphere, and with the ancient bridge as the backdrop it could have belonged in a scene from a horror film. The pebbled sides of the river made the entry difficult. I had borrowed my gear from Ian except for my mask, snorkel, weight belt, fins, gloves, and hood. I was using my two-piece waterski wetsuit with its 3mm of neoprene, which was about half the thickness the others were wearing. It was so cold I had great difficulty in getting my gloves on with my fingertips going blue. Eventually all fitted up I staggered into the depths, the water was raging on the opposite side. I walked in until I was up to my waist. I then dived in and started finning along. Unfortunately my stab jacket was empty of air and I quickly descended into a deep gully. The

Chapter 4 - Costain

water visibility was very poor. As I went deeper into this hole it became pitch black. The gully was full of mud and decomposing leaves. I was now totally disorientated and it felt as if I had descended into the bowls of hell itself. Luckily I soon stabilised my position by bleeding air into my stab jacket. In our training we had been acquainted with total darkness; with blacked out face mask I had fumbled around at the bottom of Irlam baths so luckily this did not come as a total shock. It was now that the intensity of the cold hit me; every time I moved my arm the ice-cold water shot up my arm and any movement was acting like a pump. I had now drifted downstream in the current and the water was now a thick peaty brown. Suddenly I felt a tug on my fin and my buddy had located me in the dark. He had a torch, but this made very little difference as we swam together and made our way closer to the surface. After about 20 minutes of groping in the dark cold water I decided to call it a day. I quickly got out of the water and changed. I put the heater on in the car and managed to get the circulation going. I then decided to find the other members of the group. Standing on the bridge I glanced around looking for bubbles and activity in the water below. Then one of the ducks suddenly disappeared! Was I seeing things? Then the surface of the water rippled and out shot the duck like an Exocet missile. It was one of Kevin's party tricks; he swam under the duck and pulled it down into the water then let it go! I had decided that this was my final UK dive; maybe I should have worn the correct gear and given it another try. I was lucky that I could travel overseas to continue with my sport - there is no comparison when diving in a tropical paradise.

My opposite number in BNFL was Geoff Holbrook, a young and talented engineer who always attended meetings with mechanic's hands - ground in engine oil with the odd black finger nail were an engine block had wrestled free and landed on the protruding piece of flesh.

You guessed it - his hobby was repairing classic cars. What you can do with a can of WD40 and a lump hammer was truly amazing. When I visited Risley, the security was very strict; I had to obtain a pass and meet my contact in the reception at Hinton House before I was allowed into the building. Until 2003 BNFL headquarters were based at Risley, near Warrington, but they have now moved to Daresbury Park Industrial Estate also in Warrington.

Some unusual activities carried out by our section, included a massive probability study by our latest recruit to the team, Mr Bob Dillon, a young enthusiastic graduate from Salford University who had to figure out when different things would fail. For example it would take 16.5 years for this valve to fail, and so on. There was always some clever Dick ask the 1,000 dollar question...*Starting from when? Now!*

We even had people looking into possible seismic events, adverse flooding conditions. What would happen if an aeroplane should

Chapter 4 - Costain

crash into the Thorp building; ironically, after 9/11, it was not such an outlandish thought. Our seismological reinforced concrete building had eight-meter thick walls full of lead shot to stop the radiation getting out and the aeroplanes from getting in. I just wonder if English Heritage will be interested in the place in a couple of hundred years.

We had meetings about meetings. All the meetings were recorded and before we started a microphone was passed around and each person would introduce themselves. When it was passed to me I said "Roy Dutton Costain's E & I D O, (Electrical and Instrumentation Drawing Office). This helped the secretaries when writing the minutes. Apparently the tapes were retained for prosperity, a bit like the Watergate tapes, but less interesting. The reason was to be able to trace back any problem to the person who had proposed it in the first place. Most of the important discussions took place outside the room around the coffee machine. My remit was to pay special attention at the meetings and zero in on any changes from the basic design using our Engineering Flow Diagrams (EFD's) so that I could produce a variation order that could be fired into BNFL as an increase in man-hours. Thorp was quite often referred to as a Shit Generator because someone had calculated it creates over 150 times the volume of waste, admittedly less toxic.

Oh happy days, travel expenses, and early finishes. And in the pub every Friday dinner time: you could also get a real pint of Boddingtons ale in the RAF club opposite Costain's offices.

Ian Millington was our immediate boss a nice guy, inoffensive, who would just let you get on with the job. He also lived on the Wirral and I gave him a lift a couple of times.

The wind of change was blowing through our industry or should I say a plume of radioactive fallout. The Chernobyl disaster raised concerns about the safety of the Soviet nuclear power industry as well as nuclear power plants in general. The disaster occurred on 26 April 1986, and was to have an influence on the design of Thorp. It took a while for the implications to trickle down to our work. The inspectorate insisted on more stringent safeguards which had a massive impact on our design with more major changes coming through at regular intervals. It was shortly after this kerfuffle that the drawing office settled back into its regular routine. An ABA elimination contest had just taken place between Malcolm, one of our section leaders, and the smallest engineer on minor reagents. He was apparently totally fed up with Malcolm being on his back all the time, so he delivered a left hook that floored our leader. A

286

Chapter 4 - Costain

Christmas party held in December 1987. Stuart standing behind me, using his fingers to make horns appear. On my right Dave Wood with the beard. At the table in the white shirt Ian Millington. With Don McPherson moustache and striped jumper, with half an Ian Kidd standing next to him.

Bob's leaving party with Pat the strip-o-gram on his lap just before we left the pub for a cultural evening in Beranard Manning's club. Luckily I don't think Bob's wife saw the photographs!

Chapter 4 - Costain

Bob listening to a speech being delivered by our strip-o-gram Pat Acton who was later to become Stuart's wife, Mrs Patrica Jackson, but we did not know it then. Bob was emigrating to, Queensland, Australia I visited them in 1995.

Me taking a photograph of the photographer, with the back of Wilf's head and half a Don McPherson. Strange how fashions change; we all had Sadam Hussain-type moustaches, and you know what happened to him!

Chapter 4 - Costain

complaint was duly recorded, and our office manager, who also doubled up as head of security, was given the task to investigate. He walked around with his clipboard and interviewed the people in the vicinity. Of the thirty-plus staff on the section, not one had seen anything. It was a couple of weeks later that by mutual agreement the engineer left - and Malcolm was not invited to the farewell party. Our intrepid section leader who had only been in the job a couple of months just returned to his normal ways, but I think he had learnt an important lesson. Malcolm had a low partition behind his desk and plastered on the surface were pictures of his children and pictures that they had drawn; you know the usual stuff a tree with wheels, a face in a flower, and then mysteriously a caricature of Malcolm showing him on the receiving end of a left hook. It was certainly going to take a while for this event to die down.

This brings me nicely to one of the highlights of the year *The silly shirt competition* affectionately known as the *Load of Shirt Extravagance*. This annual event was enjoyed by all and sundry. Most folk could find a bright and outrageous shirt in the depths of their wardrobe and fines were imposed on those who didn't wear them! It was also a concession to allow some people to wear sun glasses. A worthwhile cause would benefit from our antics.

That summer I took the family and my mum to Tenerife and we stayed in the resort of Los Americas. We had only been there a couple of days, when to my astonishment I bumped into Grenville Harrop. He introduced me to his son and father, and would you believe they were all called Grenville. We had a chat and I offered to buy him a drink.

Another two engineers deserve a mention in this work - Dave Lawton had worked in Indonesia on oil rigs. He told me that both his children could speak *bahasa,* the local language, which they had learnt from the maid, and he was always telling them to stop chatting to each other and speak English. He got a good deal out there: he had a spectacular mansion on the beach, a gardener and maid, schooling for the kids at an International School and a huge salary. He was trying to get a similar deal via his agent. He had a really good sense of humour, and could see the funny side of almost everything.

The other worthy of mention is Dave Wood. He was the outdoor type and he was certainly into the *Good Life* with an old Land Rover, a smallholding with lots of hens and a couple of pigs. He always came to work dressed as a county squire. It was his influence that encouraged me to go on a 7-week holiday to America. We quite often chatted as we both worked in the same office. He had just returned from a holiday in the States, and brought back lots of photographs and literature on Las Vegas, Grand Canyon, Los Angeles and Disneyworld. He really inspired me with his stories and adventures. My own trip was to be a life-changing experience, and planted the idea in my brain to form a telecom company.

Chapter 4 - Costain

A couple of weeks later Bob Ainsworth decided to emigrate to Australia because his wife had been given an offer she could not refuse. She was a stenographer or court reporter and by all accounts could type up to 200 words a minute. With the crime rate increasing dramatically down under, there was a demand for these ladies of skill to take up the gauntlet. So it was off to Queensland in Australia, and Bobs wife was to join the circuit judge on his travels. But before he went we had to organise a big send off. We decided to arrange to meet in a pub, then book an erotic dancer, and then all move off for a cultural evening at Bernard Manning's Club. The day came and we had taken over a corner in the pub. Then in came Pat the erotic dancer; she proceeded to strip off to her underwear and sit on Bob's lap, covering him with lipstick from the numerous kisses planted on this face. Photographs were taken and a good time was had by all.
But unbeknownst to me, Stuart had chatted Pat up and swapped telephone numbers. This was to lead to a happy marriage in September 1989 with the very first wedding to take place at the Novatel in Worsley, Manchester. I have enclosed three photographs of Bob's leaving party.

We were now starting to come to the end of the design phase of the project and because of my in-depth knowledge of the plant, I knew I would be offered a job on the commissioning team at Sellafield. Most of the engineers were camped out at Cockermouth, and were sharing caravans so that they could maximise on their hotel expenses. There was no way I was living like a gypsy so it made me more determined to get Plan B up and running. Our telecommunications company was born and D.J Communications was formed in October 1987 with myself and Mr Stuart Jackson, and was to become a very lucrative business with a turnover of 1 million plus in less than 12 months.

Our offices above the Shops in Oldham Street.

Chapter 5 - Pop Groups

VALE PARK ARENA
3 p.m. & 6.30 p.m.
Weekdays throughout the Summer Season
Ninth Consecutive Season of
Norman Trafford's Entertaining Children's Show
"JOYTIME"
NORMAN TRAFFORD   FREDDIE RAYNOR
MARK STRONG   DOROTHY CARR
TALENT CONTESTS IN AGE GROUPS
at each performance.   Weekly finals 6.30 Friday
AFTERNOON COMPETITIONS
Sat.—"JOYTIME PRINCESS."   Tues.—FANCY DRESS
Mon.—FANCY HATS.   Thurs.—"PETS."
DECK CHAIRS IN ENCLOSURE 9d.   CHILDREN 6d.   CAFE & ICES

Joytime ran for over 40 years in Vale Park, New Brighton and was started by Norman Trafford and his wife, Dorothy Carr (better known as Aunty Dorothy and Uncle Norman).

J is for joytime all happy and gay
O is for our friends we meet everyday
Y is for you and it's your show. You know
T is for Trafford the boss of the show
I is for interval, Ice cream and tea
M is for music we must have melody
E is for everyone to have a good time and that's how you spell
JOYTIME.

One of the main features of the show was the talent contest, children would sing while Uncle Norman "tickled the ivories" on the piano.

Chapter 5 - Pop Groups

Our introduction to the big time came via Joytime. We entered our Skiffle group and won a couple of rounds. Auntie Dorothy and uncle Norman did a fantastic job; they had the patience of saints. Uncle Norman would try and produce an accompliment even though the singer was out of tune and had forgotten the words, swivelling around on his chair and nodding his head in time. They always had smiles on their faces and were wonderful with us all. We took our failure to reach the finals in our stride, and a little later formed our first real group.

I wanted to play drums but my father would not sign the hire purchase agreement. He told me never to borrow money off anyone.
"You must save up your wages and then buy the set".
So I bought the drum kit a piece at a time until eventually I became the proud owner of a full Olympic Drum Kit.

We formed a group called The Exits, later changed to Faze Five. We could never make up our minds as to who the best singer was is it - Paul Ashton, John Hudson or John Moore. They all vied for the position. We had different guitarists, including Chris Middlemiss on bass but Robert and I remained the core members for the duration. The big attraction was the girls that followed you around.

To find a suitable place to practise was never easy. We practised in the cellars of Mr Norman Kingham's house in Wellington Road, then a little later in All Saints Church next to the Captain's Pit, which was to become our regular practice venue. We played each thursday during the Youth Club meeting. Our play list included many of the hits at the time and we had a leaning towards rhythm and blues having been inspired by attending a few all-nighters at the Cavern Club with the likes of Muddy Waters, John Lee Hooker, and Jimmy Read in attendance.

Our possible move into the big time came when we joined forces with the Outcasts. Robert and myself were invited to join the Clare brothers, Bill (Mash) and Ray (Fud). We practised with them and tried to create our own unique sound. They wanted us to tour with them, but we decided it was not worth packing our jobs in for the chance of hitting the big time.

In the very first edition of the *Sun* daily newspaper, Peter Catchpole who managed the Outcasts, successfully got coverage in the newspaper. They set up their gear in a cave on Hibre Island, a bird sanctuary in the estuary of the River Dee. One of Mr Catchpole's publicity stunts or at least that's what Fud told us later. There were no facilities and I wouldn't want to lug all of that equipment across the sands.

The Outcasts

Chapter 5 - Pop Groups

We took some promotional photographs in the back of 33 Field Road. The name of the group had to change for obvious reasons. At the time I was a mod. Below a practice session at The All Saints Church in Hose Side Road, Wallasey.
The line up was Robert Bailey lead guitar, Christopher Middlemiss bass guitar. Michael Gannon rhythm and John Moore singer. We entertained the audience at the Youth Club. I fell out with the vicar, because I had to screw a bradawl into the floor to stop the bass drum moving forward when I gave it a bang with the foot pedal. He did not like the idea of holes in the stage.

Chapter 5 - Pop Groups

Bass Guitarist Christopher Middlemiss. Playing lead guitar Robert Bailey. And Michael Gannon on Rhythm. I was playing the maracas hand can be seen on the left of the photo, no drums too noisy. Singer The Ash (Paul Ashton). This group practice was in my uncle Frank's house in Torrington Road, Liscard.

Robert and me outside Taffy's house: he was the road manager. This was the very same van that burst open its doors going around the roundabout in Liscard. And to my horror the bass drum fell out the back.

Chapter 5 - Pop Groups

It was a nice warm evening when Robert and I went down Rowson Street to attend the Marathon Floodlit Beat Festival. It was not long before we joined a mass of people all making their way to the Rakers' Football Ground.

Mr Bob Wooler was the host of the show and introduced some of the top groups from the Mersey Sound. It was May 1964 and a fantastic gig.

295

Chapter 5 - Pop Groups

On a Saturday evening walking down Victoria Road all the Teddy boys would meet outside the Empress Club, waiting for the doors to open. I would cross the road to stay well away from the noisy gathering, only chancing the occasional fleeting look. It was eyes down; there was no way I wanted to make any eye contact with these guys. I was always fascinated by the clothes and shoes they wore, but that was all. Teds were hard men, and always looking for trouble. They sewed razor blades behind their lapels as a deterrent if they were grabbed, and this was often a prelude to the notorious Kirby kiss (head butt). Knuckledusters and flick knives were the weapons of choice, with the odd bicycle chain thrown in for good measure.

I remember my parents being horrified by Teddy boys with their beetle-crusher shoes, drainpipe trousers, fluorescent pink socks and DA (duck's ar*e) haircuts, and the girls with beehive hairdo's, frilly white blouses, huge circular skirts with paper nylon hooped petticoats and kitten-heeled shoes; stockings and suspenders completed the look. My dad would say: "A spell of National Service would sort, that lot out!"

In those days we jived to the rock'n'roll of Tommy Steele, Eddie Cochrane, Bill Haley and his Comets and Buddy Holly. I remember vaguely the death of James Dean though it didn't mean much to me at the time; then Buddy Holly and Eddie Cochrane. It seemed every time I bought their record, the artist died. The baby boom resulted in millions of teenagers being out and about in the 1960s. It was all happening. Dance crazes like the Twist: John F. Kenney's *Ask not what your country can do for you...* speech; the Beatles; the Vietnam War; protesting; Woodstock; shorts skirts and girls, girls, girls. What a time for your testosterone levels to peak. It was on with my Beetle jacket and winkle picker shoes, and off with the boiler suit. When the boots got wet the ends would start to turn up, like a court jester's slipper. The secret was to stuff newspaper into the ends.

Winkle pickers

My very first experience of the club scene was a visit to the Witch's Cauldron; it was here that I was to lose my best mate Graham. The cellar club was close to the Victoria Hotel and only a ten-minute walk from my house. It was a junior version of the Cavern Club. With the steep stairs winding down to the dungeon, it was cold and damp but later the heat generated by all the bodies made the place sauna-like with condensation mixed with sweat running down the walls. Graham and I had probably visited the place half a dozen times, when a bolt from the sky struck.

Graham who lived in the next road, knocked on my door and shouted: "Aren't you ready yet"

I looked at my watch. I was late.

Chapter 5 - Pop Groups

I shouted that I was washed and just needed to get my kit on. Graham came up to my bedroom and sat on the bed while I got ready. My Beatle jacket was in the wardrobe in my parent's bedroom - the only room big enough to house a wardrobe. In no time I was ready and then it was off out for the evening's entertainment. It was going to be another night in the Witche's Cauldron. We paid our entrance fee and down we went the group were just tuning up. The Vampires were the resident band and Dave was the lead singer. I walked over to Dave and had a quick chat. We had just started our own group so I was picking his brains on the music business. I went back to our usual wall opposite the staircase; this was a good vantage point to see the girls coming down. You can imagine some of our comments!

The downstairs section of the club was a bit like a maze with lots of dark secluded places where you could take the opposite sex and have a snog. The music was raw, with three chord rifts, and loud, and it electrified your soul. Some of the groups used a fuzzbox, that distorted the chords. The riffs got hard and long a fuzzbox stopped the speakers from turning inside out. The sound bounced off the walls and your very bones vibrated to the beat. It was the repetitive beat that contained all the frustration of our generation.

Freddie Scanes ran the Witche's Cauldron; he was an ex-milkman. He couldn't do both - getting up at 4:00am to deliver milk and running the club at night until the early hours. So the milk round was jettisoned and he concentrated on running clubs and managing groups. The club only sold Coke and other fizzy drinks so we would sneak over the road to the Victoria Hotel to try and get a pint or two before we went into the Witch's.

I was quite tall for my age so I was generally pushed forward to get the drinks while the others took a low profile.

It was about this time that two blond girls arrived. Graham gave me a nudge and said :"Lets dance with these two."

This was in the days when the girls danced around their handbags placed on the floor, similar to the Highland Fling but without the swords.

Graham went on to marry one of the girls; they were only 18 years old when they tied the knot.

He worked at the Maganeese Bronze as a plumber until it closed down.

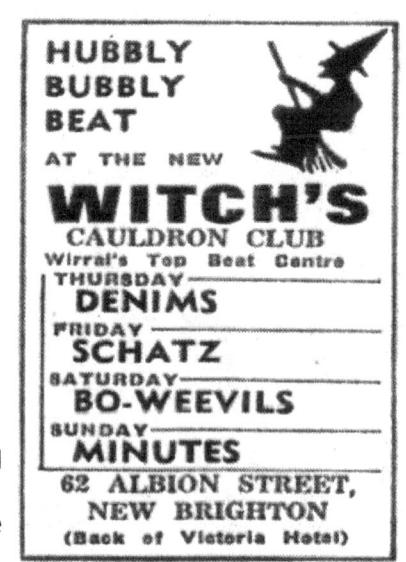

HUBBLY BUBBLY BEAT
AT THE NEW
WITCH'S CAULDRON CLUB
Wirral's Top Beat Centre
THURSDAY
DENIMS
FRIDAY
SCHATZ
SATURDAY
BO-WEEVILS
SUNDAY
MINUTES
62 ALBION STREET,
NEW BRIGHTON
(Back of Victoria Hotel)

Chapter 5 - Pop Groups

Hilda Lewis, (centre) with some of her regulars in the bar of the "Little Brighton Inn".

The next watering hole that had a big impact on my drinking habit was the *Little Brighton* (The Ginny). This was my local and only a short walk from were I lived in Field Road. It was here that I would meet up with all my mates. The pub was run by Mr and Mrs Lewis. The glum faces above were not typical of the place. We always had lots of fun in the pub. Most days we played cards in the middle room and the law according to Mrs Lewis only allowed for small wagers. We had a system of placing all the notes under a large ash tray in the centre of the card table with the coins actually in the tray. Some of the players I remember included the McGonigal brothers, Steve Wickham and Jimmy Crooks. Playing with the brothers was always a problem especially if we were playing three card brag. If they had a blind bet they would eventually get us out of the betting. And I am sure that they split the cash between them but we could never prove it. Some people actually lost their wages in the games, but I even won a car! It was a bit of a wreck and in those days there was no MOT; the police were only interested in motorists if there had been an accident. After I won the old Wolseley, some of the lads wanted a lift to New Brighton and the car was full so they stood on the running boards which fell off. A few weeks later the spring hangers collapsed as I was negotiating a roundabout on the Prom. The motor ground to an abrupt halt. I even had to pay the scrap metal dealer to take it away. After a few beers and playing cards we normally went to the *Tavern* on a Friday, or down New Brighton. If we had not "bagged off" (found a female companion) then it was off to the Transport Club to play pool and more cards.

298

Chapter 5 - Pop Groups

George Glover and me at a dance held at Withen's Lane Technical College. We both wore jackets with velvet collars and George had a frilly shirt and tartan trousers. My contribution to fashion was a pencil thin tie with stud through the collar - all the rage in 1965. How times change!

Chapter 5 - Clubs & Pubs

Davy Jones' Locker, Egremont Ferry
I quite often went with some of my mates to *Davy Jones' Locker*, the only problem was you could be at the mercy of the elements.
Before its demolition in 1983, the buildings at the entrance to Egremont Pier served as a boat yard, the base for a motorboat club and also the infamous *Davy Jones Locker* club. Ray Wood was the manager and he later became Wirral Council's tourism manager. The club had a reputation for being a bit scruffy but had good beer, good music and 'flexible' opening hours, with stay behinds for the regulars. It was previously called the Navy Club.

Tudor Club
The *Tudor Club* was in the old Tivoli Building up a flight of stairs. The cloakroom was at the top of the stairs and I think there was a roulette table in the back room. With two bars, it was a popular club with singles on a Friday and couples on the Saturday. Most weekends there were live groups and a Disk Jockey. Steven Sharp and two other guys owned the Tudor Club. The entrance was at the bottom of Egerton Street.
My mates Jimmy the Board and Tony Halewood were on the door of this club with Peter Pears (Mr Merseyside at the time). It went the way of a lot of clubs in those days and burnt down about 1973.

The Starboard Light club
This club was above Geoffrey's Car Sales which was on the corner of Ewart Street and Hamilton Street. It had an illuminated dance floor made of different coloured glass squares which would break from time to time. They used to have printed signs on the walls saying, "When the floor is full, kindly use the ashtrays provided!"
The stairs to the entrance were very steep to a peep-hole door at the top - no area to stand while you waited; just the top step!
It was very popular with the sea-going community. Later in the 70s, it became the *Cabin Club*.

Riverside
Part of New Brighton baths complex, opposite the sea-wall, the *Riverside Night Club* had a mezzanine floor and you could look down onto the dance floor. They used to run Saturday Night Dinner Dances.

Empress Club

Up a long flight of stairs and popular with Teddy boys in the 50s and then the motor bike fraternity (rockers), this was a club for serious head-bangers. It was run by two brothers Billy & Jack Magee.

If you wore anything white it would show up brilliant white, but the UV lights also illuminated your dandruff, more like an Omo advert!!

In the early 70s some of my mates operated the early exit strategy at the club with Jimmy the Board, Tony Hailwood and Dennis Gooding on the door most Friday nights. Some weeks, Mick O'Reilly would help out. The Empress Motorcycle Club of Egg-Run fame was formed by a group of friends who regularly frequented the Friday Rock Nights at the Empress Ballroom, Victoria Road. Photograph shows entrance next to the snack bar.

Crackers Club

This was the haunt of freight pilots and other dangerous characters of various alien races – some of the women were from the Dark Side, and the aliens were better-looking!! It was like a scene from the Star Wars Bar. But the music was good, though I remember having to walk some distance away from the place to get a taxi as the drivers were reluctant to pick up from there. The local thugs and petty criminal fraternity seemed to use it as an HQ. It had a very bad reputation. The entrance in Egerton Street, was up a flight of narrow steps. Some people commented on the fact you had to be crackers to go there, so it was aptly named.

Chapter 5 - Clubs & Pubs

The Grand
Another of my favourite haunts was the *Spanish Bar* located in the basement of the Grand Hotel. It was a good starting point, to meet up with your mates and visit the clubs in New Brighton.
I remember the main beer was Double Diamond on draft. The entrance was via an imposing set of stairs. The ground floor was a night club of shorts. With traditional jazz on a Sunday afternoon in the *Spanish Bar* and the resident band was the Original Panama Jazz Band (a Wallasey band).
I think that the beginning of the end occurred when the previous enterprising owners placed two large green-painted Statue of Liberty models next to the entrance. The building was eventually demolished in 2006, and is now a car park waiting for an enterprising developer.

The Belgravia Hotel
Situated in Wellington Road, this place was always getting raided by the police due to stay-behinds. Used mostly by "night people" drinking in the residents bar. Occasionally there was live music. Now converted into flats.

Tavern Club
Owned by Jim McCullock in Magazine Lane, this single-story building, originally St James School, had a large car park at the rear. It was one of my regular haunts. I also used Jim's weight lifting Club in Liscard. Eventually Jim bought the *Old Nags head* in Rake Lane and sold real ale.

Late Extra
This New Brighton nightclub introduced the first topless barmaid in the Wirral. Run by Ted Geary and John Brindle, it was good for a late night drink but a bit pricey.

The Creep Inn
This was established in the cellars below the indoor fairground. (The Palace), run by Vera and her husband. It had been an ammunition factory during the war and my mom had worked there. The name Creep Inn a play on its creepy underground location. Recently a planning application went in to open the tunnels under Wilkies Arcade, which would employ actors a New Brighton Dungeon?

Chapter 5 - Clubs & Pubs

Grandma's
This was a great club to visit until it also burnt down. The owner was a Mr Peter Catchpole a Cockney bloke, New Brighton businessman and ex-Wall of Death stunt rider. He had a lot of bad luck with things burning down. The club was in Grosvenor Road, on the site of the old Tick Tock Cafe. In its heyday many of the top Merseyside groups appeared there.

Penny Farthing
Owned by Arthur and Danny located next to the Golden Guinea, you could sit out on a small balcony in the summer with your pint. My mate Charles had his wedding reception at the Penny, much to the annoyance of the brides' mother. Greg Wilson was the regular D.J in the 70s.

Golden Guinea
Originally called the *Kraal* when opened In 1961, this was owned by John Barrymore Stanley who also owned the Weavers' Cafe on Victoria Rd.
It has now been sold to Weatherspoons.
In a newspaper article in the *Wallasey News* dated February 1982, it remarked that the club had just celebrated its 21st birthday.
The club was very popular and if you were not a member it was quite difficult to get in after 11 o'clock.

The Haig Club
The club started as a dance venue in Haig Hall in the 1950s owned by Joe Barnes and Rosa Heyward. It later became a theatre club where people like Jimmy Dainty and Roy Castle performed before hitting the big time. Situated in Haigh Avenue off Sandbrooke Lane, Moreton, there were snooker tables in the room upstairs as well as the usual dance floor.
I saw Roy Castle and Freddy Star and a spectacular hypnotist called Ted Heath.

Melody inn Club
At the corner of Grove Road, on the first floor of what was originally the Grove Hotel, the *Melody Inn Club* was owned by Jackson Earle who ran the Melody Inn Shows at the Floral Pavilion. The ground floor was occupied by one of Reece's cake shops, famous for their chocolate éclairs. The club was damaged by a fire and had to be demolished.

Rock Point (Tower Grounds) also Lakeside.
I had my first underage pint here! They served beer to anyone not wearing a school uniform. It had seen better days even when I used to visit the place.

Chapter 5 - Clubs & Pubs

THE NEW WITCH'S CAULDRON CLUB
62 Albion Street,
New Brighton
(Back Hotel Victoria)
Tel. NEW 5849.

SATURDAY
BOBBY AND THE BATCHELORS

SUNDAY
SAVVA AND THE DEMOCRATS

MON., TUES., AND WED.
AUDITION GROUPS & RECORDS
Your D.J., ROY FERN.

"RAKERS' RETURN"
New Brighton A.F.C's Luxury Social Club
TOWER FOOTBALL GROUND. NEW 5982.
Under new jurisdiction. Full Variety Shows Saturdays and Sundays.
TONIGHT—MOUNT ROYAL GROUP.

SATURDAY, August 16th—
JUNIOR JOHNSON (dynamic comedy, vocal/guitar)
CURLEY CARTER (top Blackpool comedian)
ANNE VIVIAN (glamorous vocal entertainer).

SUNDAY, August 17th—
MICKY MORAN (outstanding musical/vocalist)
The girl to keep you alive.
SID DOOLEY (guitar / vocalist).
FRIDAY, August 22nd—DRAG NIGHT.

FORTHCOMING ATTRACTIONS
Friday, August 29th—THE HORROR SHOW. First time on Merseyside.
Fabulous entertainment.
Friday, September 5th—BACHELOR NIGHT.
Friday, September 12th—THE KRISS CHRIGHTEN PROFESSIONAL
OLDE TYME MUSIC HALL CAST.

Paul Ashton (The Ash)   Dave Hepkie   Roy Dutton
Photograph taken in the Grand (Spanish Bar)

FIRST EVER FABULOUSLY EXCITING

ALL NITE BEAT BOAT

Starring these Top Groups

★ THE CLAYTON SQUARES   ★ EARL PRESTON'S REALMS
★ THE HIDEAWAYS   ★ ST. LOUIS CHECKS
★ THE ROAD RUNNERS   ★ AMOS BONNEY & THE TTs

and Special Guest Stars

THE SENSATIONAL MEASLES

MIDNIGHT EASTER SUNDAY, 18th APRIL, 1965
IMPORTANT! SEE OVERLEAF   Nº 1743

Chapter 5 - Clubs & Pubs

NEW BRIGHTON TOWER — *The PLAYGROUND OF THE NORTH — Enjoy Yourself!*

NEW BRIGHTON TOWER CO. LTD.

AMUSEMENT PARK NOW OPEN
until 10.30 nightly — Bright Lights Galore!

TO-NIGHT! TO-NIGHT! TO-NIGHT!

New Brighton Tower Co, Ltd. presents All Star International

WRESTLING

Doors open 7 p.m.   Commence 8 p.m.

SENSATIONAL HEAVYWEIGHT CONTEST

KING KONG
Hollywood, U.S.A. The monster of the mat, 6' 6", 23 stone

VERSUS

HENRI DOLAN
FRANCE. Sensational mat star.

PAT CURRY	STOKER BROOKS
(CANADA) Tough Lumberjack	(ROYAL NAVY)
v.	v.
IRON MAN McKENZIE	PEDRO THE GIPSY
(SCOTLAND)	(No Fixed Abode)

TERRIFIC MAIN SUPPORTING CONTEST

PIET VON SLABBERT
Light/heavyweight Champion of South Africa.

VERSUS

DUNCAN McROBERT
Scotland. A certain future champion.

BODY 3/6 & 5/-.   RINGSIDE 7/6

Book at the Tower Booking Office ('phone 6176) and at Ushers Travel Service, Wallasey and Birkenhead.
YOU MAY NOW OBTAIN A PERMANENT BOOKING ON YOUR FAVOURITE RINGSIDE SEAT.—Contact the Manager for details.

TOWER BALLROOM
PRESENTS

ROLLING STONES
Plus 12 Top Groups in Rael Brook Contest Final on Monday August 10th, 1964. 7.30 to 11.30 p.m. TICKETS 8/6

TOWER AMUSEMENTS • BALLROOM
CATERING AND LICENSING BARS FOR YOUR ENJOYMENT.
YOU'RE ALWAYS WELCOME AT THE TOWER

Chapter 5 - Clubs & Pubs

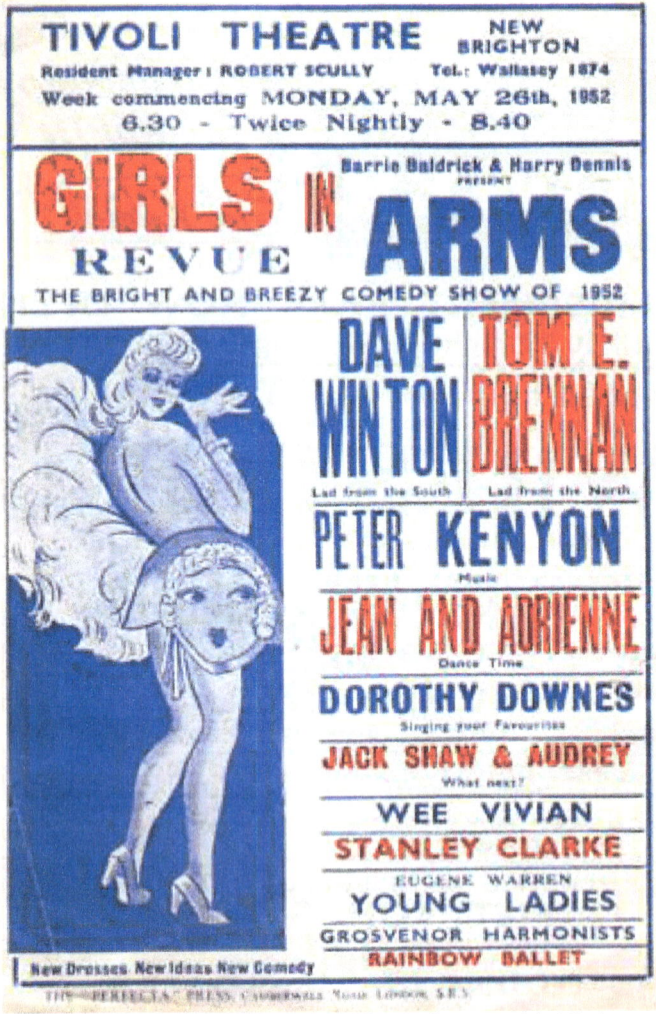

The Tivoli Theatre was opened on the 6th April 1914 with Lily Langtry topping the bill. The theatre catered for all tastes, there was a good sprinkling of concerts, plays and even ballet. Many star turns appeared including Winifred Atwell at the piano, Charlie Chester, Wilson Keppel and Betty. It even helped launch some showbiz careers including Frankie Vaughan and Ken Dodd. I remember looking at the risqué posters outside and trying to sneak a view of the girls with a couple of my classmates, and being chased by the doorman. The big attraction were the ladies wearing very little as they posed around Greek urns; the lights had to be dimmed every time they moved. In later life I would visit the Tudor club above the Tivoli Theatre. It was all to come to an end following a fire the property was demolished in 1976.

Chapter 5 - Clubs & Pubs

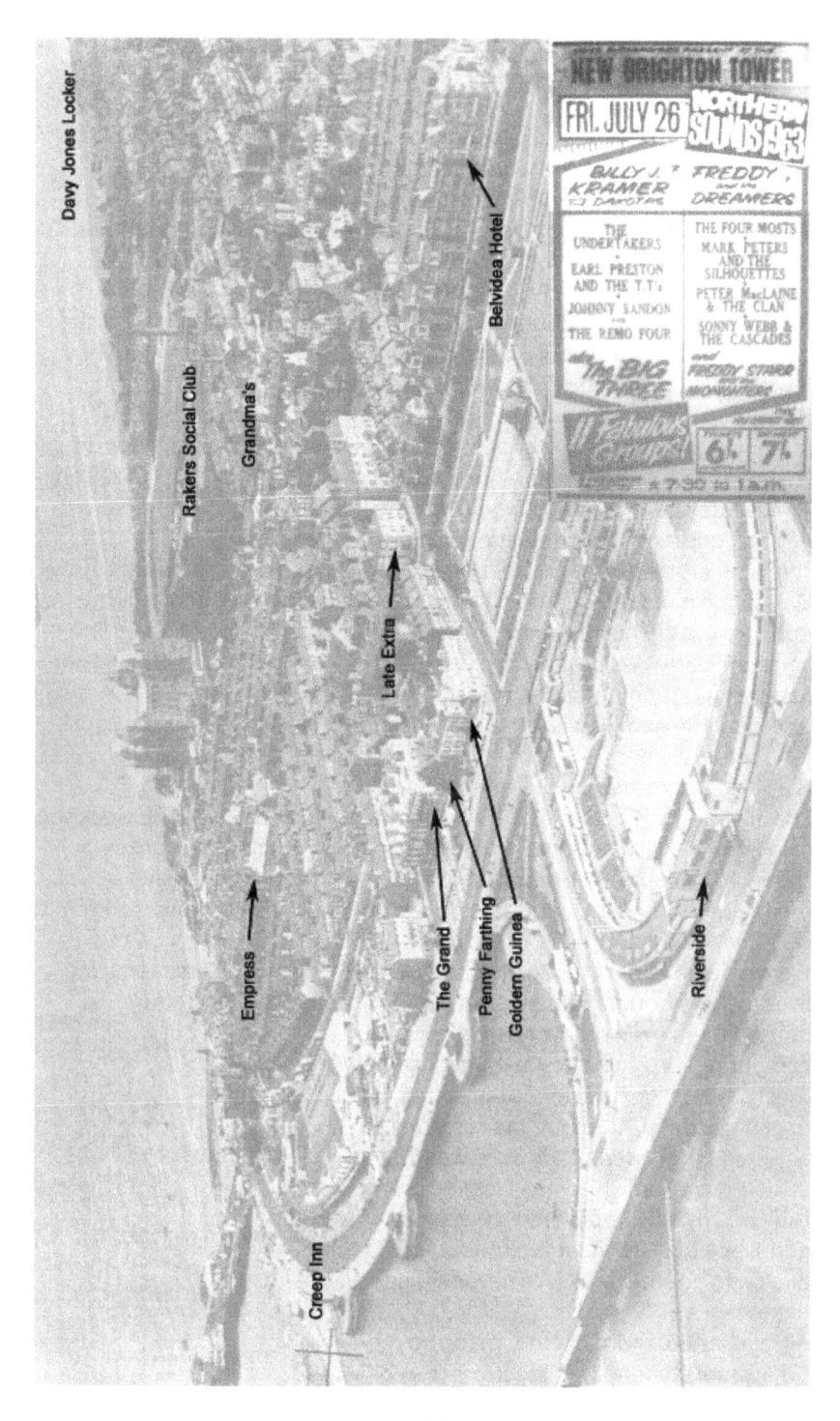

307

Chapter 5 - Buy a Pet

Ever since I was a young child I have always had this entrepreneurial spirit. Some enterprises have worked, while others did not. My Uncle Joe encouraged me to sell my plaster-cast models, which I had painted. Because I could not get the air out of the mould, some of the models only had half a head. Uncle Joe would say:
"Just charge half the amount, a halfpenny instead of a penny."
They say never let a hobby become your business, but I totally ignored this rule. So I ended up with a pet shop selling tropical fish. We even imported them from the Far East via Manchester Airport. I was still working full time at Cadbury's. I had a lady running the shop for me; she was not the brightest soul on the planet, but very willing. I remember a few amusing incidents which I will share with you.
I would call into the shop every day to check how things were going. I remember one telephone conversation which went something like this:
"Hi Roy. A lady has been into the shop this morning and wants to sell an African grey parrott. I told her you may be interested."
My first question "So why is she selling it?"
"Well the problem is her husband died some 6 months ago, and she now lives in the house alone. The bird imitates the wife's voice and calls the dog into the kitchen by name: "Here Rex!" Then in the dead husband's voice the parrot yells... Bad dog! Get out ! Its driving her mad!" The parrot had the dog running back and forth.
Another little gem of wisdom... I overheard her say while catching some fish for a customer:
"It is best for the fish if you keep it in water."
She always made a note of the wildlife that she sold. I noted one week she sold eight hermit crabs; the problem was I only bought half a dozen. So she must have sold two empty shells. We had one complaint later from a marine tank enthusiast who said he had spent hours watching the hermit crab and it definitely had not moved.
We where quite new to the pet shop business, one of the first items of live stock we bought was a dozen gerbils. As a temporary measure we housed them in an old wooden bird cage, and during the night they managed to chew their way out. We had terrific difficulties trying to capture them. As one of the customers adjusted his glasses, he inquired was that an upside-down catfish? When I looked in the fish tank myself I discovered it was a drowned gerbil. So I quickly changing the subject, I took him on to another tank. We never did find all the escapees.
All in all, another project that made no money but was lots of fun.

Chapter 5 - Richard & Jenny

Business was kind to me I was able to move to a much larger house in Moreton. Mercie had three children from a previous marriage, Edwin, Sonia and Denice. We decided after a while it would be nice to start our own family.

Richard was born on the 23rd October 1980 and Jenny on the 5th February 1984 . Both my children went to University and have worthwhile careers. Richard and Jenny are married and Richard and Emma have a little boy called William.

Jenny, 6 years old and Richard 9 years old. School Photo Kingsmead.

Richard centre in the Kingsmead School production of Oliver

Photograph taken in Disney World, U.S.A August 1989.

309

Chapter 5 - Liverpool Trophy Room in Early 1980s

Photographs taken in Liverpool FC Trophy Room. European Cup, League Cup and the Milk Cup. In the good old days when we won everything.

Roy in front of the trophy cabinet

Charles Neal on the left and George Goodwin on the right. In the days when Sadam Hussein moustaches were all the rage.

Strange Goings on

During the preparation of this book an amazing coincidence occurred. I was just in the process of scanning a newspaper article concerning The Wirral Astronomical Society into my computer for my book when there was a knock on the door. A man had come to collect my faulty lawnmower. I starred at him and said I know you from somewhere; he said that my face looked familiar too. After a few questions it transpired that we had both attended New Brighton Secondary Modern but he had been a couple of years below me.

So I left it at that, and returned to my computer... but there he was in the photograph on the screen taken from the article in the Echo. It was Colin Green in the photograph with other members of the Wirral Astronomical Society! So I phoned him and we had a good old natter and caught up on events. What are the chances of that happening? Absolutely amazing. He went on to tell me he played the drums and had played in the Undertakers for a spell. He also knew Gazzer out of Gaz and the Groovers, a mutual friend. Using his pop connections he organised outside catering at various pop concerts up and down the country - as well as repairing lawnmowers.

Colin Green in centre

Another amazing coincidence was on Wednesday the 5th December, the day that Virgin inadvertently switched off our internet connection without informing us. They said it was something to do with an upgrade whatever that meant! I spent part of the morning writing a section on the Wormhole Cave in New Brighton, for my book. When the internet came back on, I logged into Facebook and took a look at New Brighton Memories, a group I set up some nine months earlier. And there in front of my very eyes was a picture of Mr Norman Kingham showing some schoolboys around the very caves that I had been writing about.

I am not one for the paranormal, and I really do not have any explanation for the above. But during the course of writing this book there have been several similar coincidental happenings.

Chapter 5 - Mountaineering & Touring Club

Mr Brian Foster M.T.C

Elsewhere in this book are references to Mr Foster and I have dedicated a couple of pages in my book to his achievements. I did try to enter the same on Wikipedia, but according to them; *it did not meet our notability guidelines* whatever that means.

From the *Wallasey News* May 1988

Old boys' tribute to Brian

Old boy members of an outdoor pursuits club are paying tribute to the group's founder and leader who was buried last week. Now there is talk of a reunion to remember his outstanding contribution to the community. Schoolteacher Brian Foster started arranging outings back in 1954 after talking to Saturday morning art students at Wallasey's Art College in Central Park. They were so successful they became regular events and soon pupils from New Brighton Secondary Modern School in Vaughan Road were appealing to join in with the activities of the Mountaineering and Touring Club.

So began the run of a boy's organisation, which was to span more than a quarter century allowing thousands of youngsters to develop new skills and acquire new experiences. Mr Foster established a unique organisational structure - members as young as 11, elected their own committee which would point the club's direction, while he, the president, was responsible for the practical arrangements and behind-the-scenes work. The group, which began by making wooden gliders and flying them from Moel Famau in North Wales, aimed to take members on one day-long hike or outing each month to venues in North Wales, the Lakes, Lancashire and Cheshire.

And every school holiday would see a residential activity of some kind; a few days walking along Hadrian's Wall, walking in the Peak district, or a long summer hostelling holiday in the Isle of Man or on the Cornish Riviera, climbing in the Swiss Alps or cycling in Ireland.

And the MTC became famous too for its skiing visits to the continent and Scotland, with members competing for trophies for the most proficient skier. The group also catered for railway enthusiasts - going on working trips to the narrow gauge Isle of Man steam railway and through building model layouts of two steam-operated lines.

Mr Foster - affectionately known as "Foz" to colleagues and pupils alike - organised the club from his home in Paighton Road, Wallasey, while teaching at various schools in the town - eventually retiring from Withensfield Middle School in 1982.

Former chairman Stephen Sharp, now 38, said this week; "Brian was responsible for encouraging responsibility and self-discipline in club members and he could always spot a boy's potential and would find ways of drawing it out.

He introduced many of us to the joys of the countryside - God's cathedral

Chapter 5 - Mountaineering & Touring Club

he once called it - and taught how to interpret the weather and many of nature's other features.

And the group's last chairman Andy Ball said this week: "For many club members MTC outings were their first real excursion into the countryside and really opened their eyes to the wider world outside Wallasey. It was very valuable experience and many of today's children are enjoying the open-air through parents who got their first love for rural Britain through the club.

Brian put in hour upon hour of painstaking planning and organisation to ensure that everything would run smoothly for the members. It is a great shame his contribution to several generations of Wallaseyians was never officially recognised.

In a final tribute, past members of the group clubbed together and arranged for a black and yellow wreath in the shape of the club badge.

Chapter 5 - Mountineering & Touring Club

M.T.C Switzerland Holiday

314

Chapter 5 - Family photographs

The book covers a period in my life up to October 1987 when I left Costains. My business career was to reach new heights financially with the formation of D.J Communications in partnership with Mr Stuart Jackson. I hope to continue this autobiography at a later date with an additional volume.

My wife Lanie wanted me to put some of our family photographs within the pages. This is slightly out of context because we did not marry until 2000. In 2003 we went to live in South Africa and bought a house on Millionaires Row in Amazimtoti, outside Durban. And on the 27th November 2001 Adam Dutton was born.

Chapter 5 - Family photographs

South America 2005 Brazil & Peru Inca Trail

Appendices

Appendix 1 - Mom's Poems — p 318
Appendix 2 - Passenger List — p 319
Appendix 3 - Field Road occupants 1960 — p 320
Appendix 4 - Family Tree 1647 -1840 — p 322
Appendix 5 - Bidston Steel Staff — p 323
Appendix 6 - Companies owned by Author — p 326
Appendix 7 - Maps — p 327
Appendix 8 - Arial Photograph New Brighton — p 330
Appendix 9 - Liscard Shopping 1898 — p 332
Appendix 10 - Wallasey Schools — p 334
Bibliography — p 335

Appendix 1 - Moms Poems

Moms Poems
It was only after my mother died that I found in her belongings a collection of poems that she had composed.

Dreams Unrealised
When I and the world were both very young.
There were so many things that had to be done.
And now that - I'm old and my life nearly gone.
There are so many things I haven't done.
I cry for the tears that I never cried.
For the pain and sorrow I hid deep inside.
I cry for the smiles that I didn't smile.
And I cry for the sleep that will come in a while.
The sleep without dreams that will take me away
From the life I lived in a poor sort of way.
I am not ready just yet to be gone - For there's are so many things that I haven't done.

Mother
If you have a mother look after her as you should.
For all the love she gives you from the cradle to the adulthood.
We all take her for granted and never say we care.
So from now on remember, and don't mention her grey hair.
As we all get older and much wiser too.
Just tell her that you're grateful for all the things she does for you.
If like me you miss her.
And would give the world to say.
Hello Mom - I do love you.

Love
How can I tell you of this feeling in my heart.
This longing and yearning whenever we're apart.
I bless the day I met you all those many years ago.
And you know how much I love you, though I may not tell you so.
I couldn't live without you, I wouldn't even try.
For the days with you get better as the years roll on by.

Michelle
To Dear Michelle, all my love Grandma.
When this you see, pray think of me.
The many miles, we distant be.
Although we are a great way apart.
I wish you well, with all my heart.

Appendix 2 - Passenger List

MANIFEST OF ALIEN PASSENGERS

Applying for Admission to the United States Under the Act of December 28, 1945, and of Accompanying United States Citizen Children

S.S. U.S.A.T. PRESIDENT TYLER   Arriving at port of NEW YORK, N.Y.

Line No.	Name	Age	Application No.
1	BARE, Emma	19	W 24516
2	BOYDSTON, Dorothy	20	W 24202
3	BURKE, Olwyn Nancy	21	W 4666
4	CARTER, Olive	19	W 24204
5	CLARK, Christian Melba	20	W 45523
6	COOPER, Doreen May	21	W 45526
7	DEER, Kathleen	20	W 2570
8	EARL, Phillis King	37	W 24205
9	HAMOE, Joyce E.	25	W 24221
10	HARRIS, Ada Emily	34	W 45522
11	JONES, Alexandra Eva Jessie	21	W 24201
12	KISHBAUGH, Jean Hazel Anne	17	W 32383
13	LANTZ, Marion	30	W 2571
14	~~IRBY, Ocyl May~~	~~21~~	~~W 24494~~
15	LOUNSHIRE, Sarah	19	W 2577
16	MELONE, Hazel B.	17	W 4665
17	MENEFEE, Joyce	18	W 2569
18	MOCHINAL, Joan	19	W 24493
19	MYERS, Marian	21	W 4667
20	SALMONS, Kathleen B.	18	W 24220
21	SHANK, Lucy Irene	22	W 24219
22	STERN, Olga Ray	29	W 45525
23	THOMAS, Joan	18	W 24222
24	ZIMMERMAN, Ethel	18	W 2572

332

23 aliens

Joyce probably left on the President Tyler a transport ship assigned to carry military dependents. See above Manifest (Passenger No 17.)
She is also shown on the Manifest of the "Goethals" group 66-C. number 25.
Approx. sailing date 3rd October 1946.
Joyce sent the following telegram by Western Union :
"Travelling by train from Brooklyn to Lincoln, Nebraska arrive 22th Oct "
Telegram dated the 20th October 1946

319

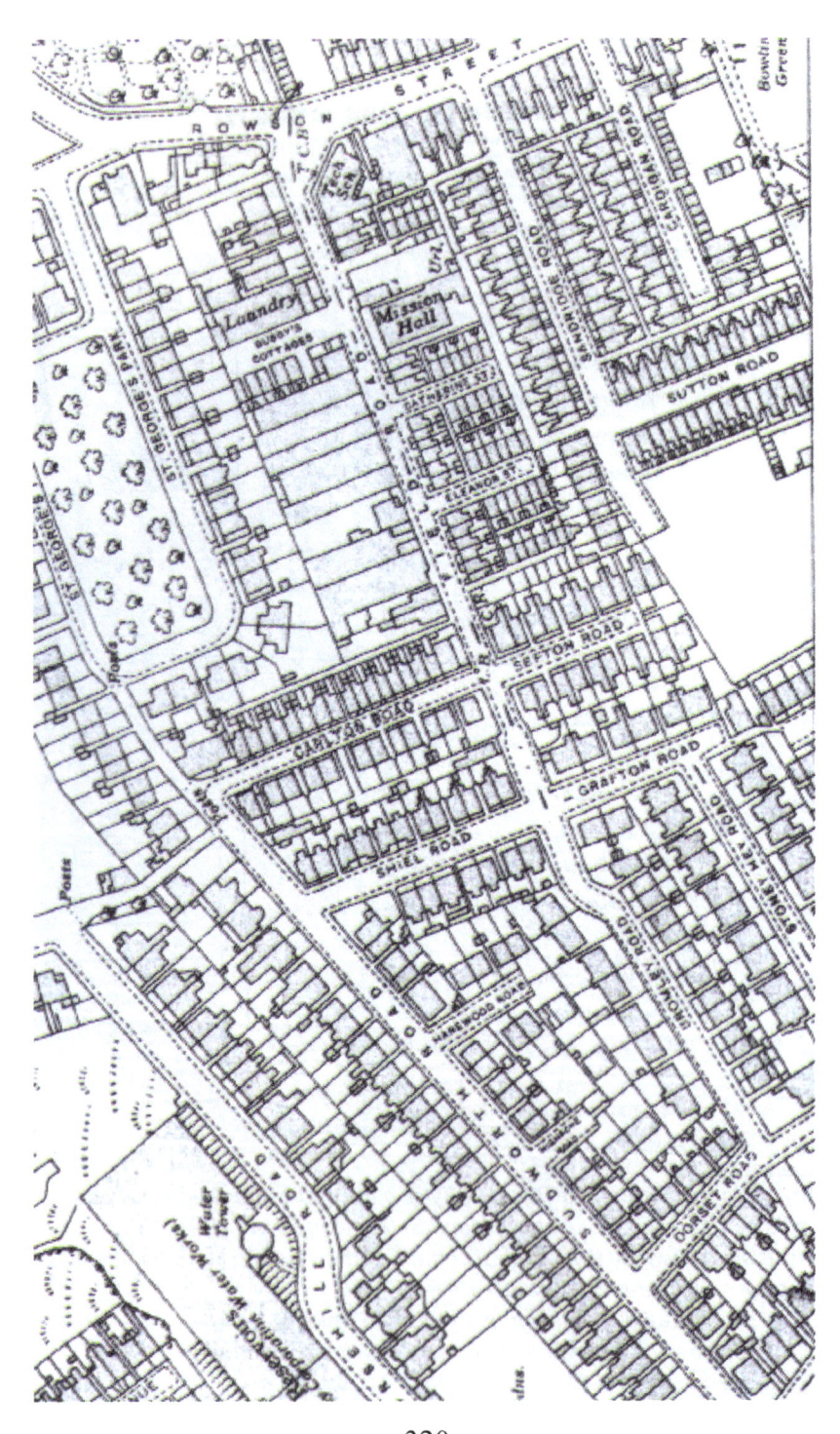

Appendix 3 - Field Road occupants 1960

Appendix 3 - Field Road occupants 1960

Occupants of Field Road & Area - From Kelly's Directory 1960	Eleanor Street	Right Side Field Road
	Left Side	4 Cragg John
	1 Staples Jn	6 Edwards George
Left Side Field Road	3 Kendrick Gordon	6 Joinson Kenneth
Technical School	5 Birkett Jn. W	8 Kophamel F.L
7 Blackburn Percvl. Sidney	7 McEwan Alex	12 Virginia Steam Laundry Ltd
9 Rawlings Jsph. T	9 Kenna Miss K	**Busby's Cottages**
11 Gough Wm	11 Davey Jn	Kenna John & Sons funeral directors
Corporation Yard	Right Side	
15 Nicholls Miss M.J. shopkpr.	2 Leyland Jas	30 Quarry Plant Hire Service
	4 Garnett Mrs. E	
17 Chocolate Cup Co. Ltd.	6 Jackson Jn. Philip	32 Freeman Cyril.
19 Jones Lloyd	8 Plant Thos	34 Salesmaster shopfittings
21 Raystop Geo.	10 Plnk Fredk	
23 Hayes Geo. Fredrick	12 Johnson Wm	36 Pickfords, Removals
Catherine Street		40 Barnes Walter
25 Williams Hugh	**Catherine Street**	40 Walton William shopkeeper
27 Midwood Fred. Wm	Left Side	
29 Gregory Miss Mary	1 Hayes Geo. Fredrick	42 Rushforth Fras. R
31 Rice Alfred.	3 McCarthy David J	46 Oliver Jas Herman
33 Dutton Alfred. R	5 Murry Wm. J	48 Thompson Mrs. G
35 Jones Thomas	7 Glover Mrs M	
Eleanor Street	9 Pumford Frank	**Busby's Cottages**
37 Jones Mrs Mary	11 Harris Mrs D	3 Williams Alfred
39 Munifold Thomas	13 Bower Arth	5 Ball Ernest Hy
41 Howe Thomas.	Right Side	7 Dodson Mrs Eva
43 Hoyland Mrs Louisa	12 Smith Leslie	9 Ball Mrs Minnie
45 Fisher Regnld. C	10 Edwards David	11 Smith Samuel
47 Jenkins Edward	8 Vernon Mrs. Isobel	14 Stowell-Smith Mrs. M
Constantine Terrace	6 Evans Rt.	
1 Cosgrove Joseph	4 Garnett George	
2 Coathupe Mrs Elizabeth	2 Edwards George	
3 Duffy Mrs Elizabeth		
4 Searle William		
5 Morris John		
6 Davies Mrs. J		

321

Appendix 4 - Family Tree 1647 -1840

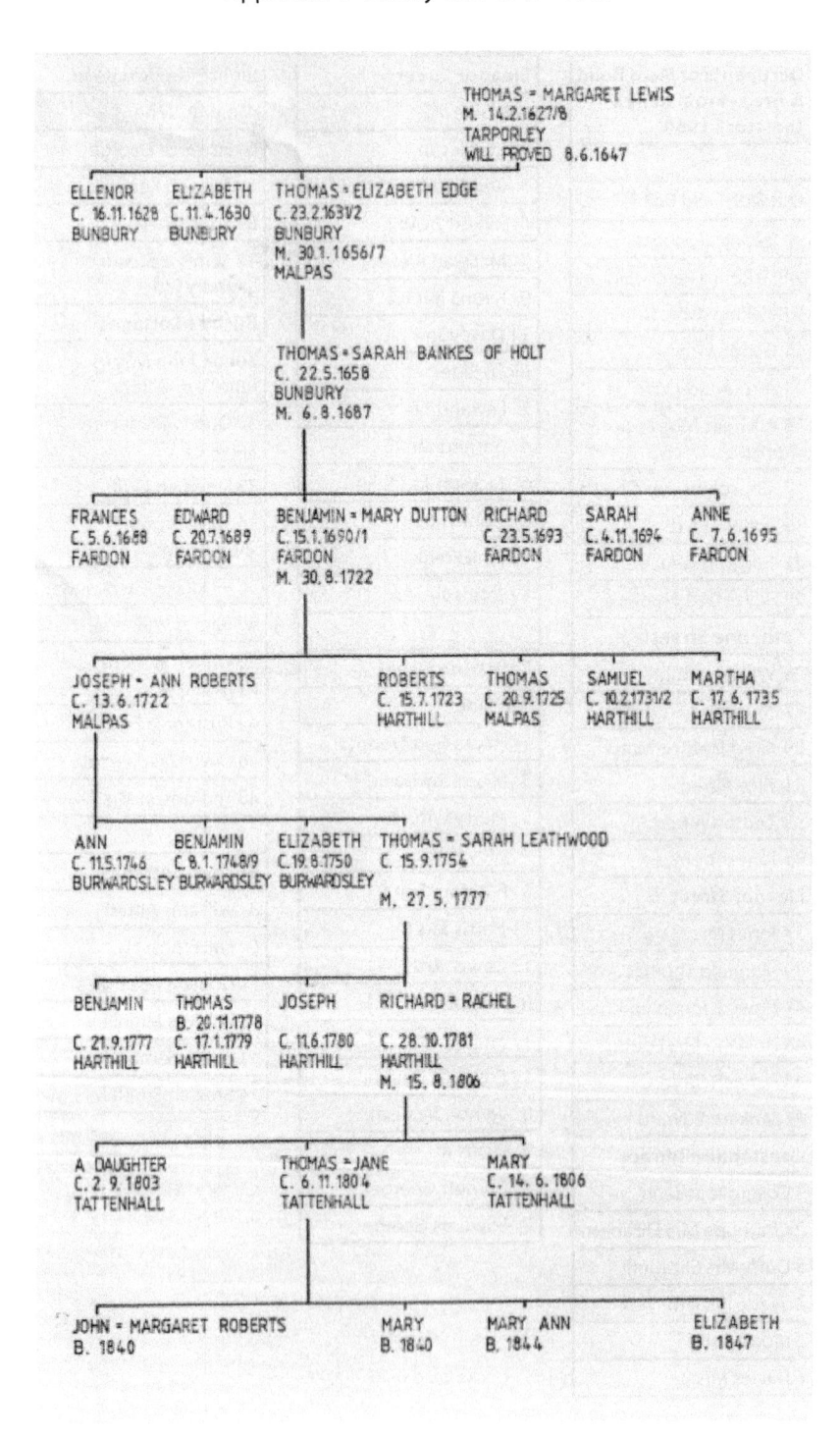

```
                                    THOMAS = MARGARET LEWIS
                                    M. 14.2.1627/8
                                    TARPORLEY
                                    WILL PROVED 8.6.1647

ELLENOR         ELIZABETH       THOMAS = ELIZABETH EDGE
C. 16.11.1628   C. 11.4.1630    C. 23.2.1631/2
BUNBURY         BUNBURY         BUNBURY
                                M. 30.1.1656/7
                                MALPAS

                                THOMAS = SARAH BANKES OF HOLT
                                C. 22.5.1658
                                BUNBURY
                                M. 6.8.1687

FRANCES      EDWARD       BENJAMIN = MARY DUTTON   RICHARD        SARAH          ANNE
C. 5.6.1688  C. 20.7.1689 C. 15.1.1690/1            C. 23.5.1693   C. 4.11.1694   C. 7.6.1695
FARDON       FARDON       FARDON                    FARDON         FARDON         FARDON
                          M. 30.8.1722

JOSEPH = ANN ROBERTS                ROBERTS        THOMAS         SAMUEL          MARTHA
C. 13.6.1722                        C. 15.7.1723   C. 20.9.1725   C. 10.2.1731/2  C. 17.6.1735
MALPAS                              HARTHILL       MALPAS         HARTHILL        HARTHILL

ANN            BENJAMIN       ELIZABETH     THOMAS = SARAH LEATHWOOD
C. 11.5.1746   C. 8.1.1748/9  C. 19.8.1750  C. 15.9.1754
BURWARDSLEY    BURWARDSLEY    BURWARDSLEY
                                            M. 27.5.1777

BENJAMIN      THOMAS         JOSEPH        RICHARD = RACHEL
              B. 20.11.1778
C. 21.9.1777  C. 17.1.1779   C. 11.6.1780  C. 28.10.1781
HARTHILL      HARTHILL       HARTHILL      HARTHILL
                                           M. 15.8.1806

A DAUGHTER         THOMAS = JANE       MARY
C. 2.9.1803        C. 6.11.1804        C. 14.6.1806
TATTENHALL         TATTENHALL          TATTENHALL

JOHN = MARGARET ROBERTS       MARY         MARY ANN           ELIZABETH
B. 1840                       B. 1840      B. 1844            B. 1847
```

322

Appendix 5 - Bidston Steel Staff

FORENAME	SURNAME	AREA
STEVE	WALKER	?
MIKE	CLARKE	B/L
JOHN	FOXLEY	B/L
DAVE	MCWHINNIE	B/L
MICK	ROBINSON	B/L
JIMMY	SOUTHALL	B/L
JIM?	QUIGLEY	B/L?
DAVE	CROSS	B/L
GORDON	ALMOND	CASTER
JOHN	BERRY	CASTER
RON	CARPENTER	CASTER
PETER	DAVIES	CASTER
RAY	DAVIES	CASTER
BILLY	DEAKIN	CASTER
JACK	DOBBINS	CASTER
FRANK	DRIVER	CASTER
JIMMY	DUCKERS	CASTER
BILLY	DUCKERS	CASTER
BERNIE	DUCKERS	CASTER
HOWIE	EDWARDS	CASTER
HARRY	FOWLER	CASTER
PAUL	GRIFFITHS	CASTER
VINNIE	HALL	CASTER
MARTIN	HUBBARD	CASTER
PETER	KENNEDY	CASTER
MIKE	KILBANE	CASTER
BRIAN	MALLION	CASTER
CHRIS	MCCARTHY	CASTER
STEVE	OLOUGHLIN	CASTER
JIMMY	OLOUGHLIN	CASTER
RON	PARRINGTON	CASTER
BILLY	SHAW	CASTER
BILLY	SMART	CASTER
GEOFF	SMITH	CASTER
GEORGE	STONES	CASTER
JIMMY	TAYLOR	CASTER
ROY	THIIS	CASTER
LES	THOMLINSON	CASTER
DAVE	USHER	CASTER
PETER	WARD	CASTER
STEVE	WHELAN	CASTER
PAUL	WHELAN	CASTER
STEVE	WILLIAMS	CASTER
CARL	YATES	CASTER
BOB	EDWARDS	CASTER
JOHN	BROCKLEBANK	CASTER
BRIAN	BURKE	CASTER
DAVE	ELLIOTT	CASTER
BRIAN	JONES	CASTER
MIKE	DAVIES	CD
HARRY	FLEMMING	CD
TOMMY	LENNOX	CD
DAVE	LENNOX	CD
PETER	LYNCH	CD
DAVE	MALLION	CD
NEV	PARRY	CD
SAMMY	SYKES	CD
PHYLLIS		CLEANER
NORMAN	FEELEY	ELEC
GERRY	MCDONALD	ELEC
MICK	ROBINSON	ELEC
JIMMY	ROBINSON	ELEC
BOB	MUIRHEAD	ELEC
GRAHAM	NIXON	ELEC
JOHN	RAVENSCROFT	ELEC
STEVE	AMBLETT	IMS
PAULINE	HEATH	IMS
RAY	LAWTON	IMS
PHIL	NICHOLSON	IMS
REG	NICHOLSON	IMS
GRAHAM	ROBINSON	IMS
HARRY	SWINDLEHURST	IMS
MALLY	THOMPSON	IMS

323

Appendix 5 - Bidston Steel Staff

PETER	TRAYNOR	IMS	LARRY	COOPER	RM
RONNIE	WHITTENBURY	IMS	ALAN	COX	RM
ALAN	WHITTENBURY	IMS	REG	DAVIES	RM
ALAN	JACKSON	LAB	BERNIE	DUNN	RM
BOB	WALKER	LAB	MORGAN	HAWES	RM
BRIAN	ANDERSON	MECH	BOB	JONES	RM
PETER	BARNES	MECH	PAUL	KITCHEN	RM
EDDIE	BURKE	MECH	JIM	LAWSON	RM
FREDDIE	CHAPMAN	MECH	ROGER	LEIGHTON	RM
GEORGE	CORNER	MECH	KENNY	MCKENNA	RM
FRANK	COX	MECH	BILLY	NEW	RM
BARRY	DICKENSON	MECH	EDDIE	REID	RM
VAUGHAN	EVANS	MECH	GRAHAM	RUHE	RM
FRANK	GALE	MECH	JIMMY	SMALL	RM
PAT	HAWES	MECH	HARRY	SMITH	RM
JOHN	HORROCKS	MECH	JIMMY	TAYLOR	RM
ROY	LEWIS	MECH	REG	THOMPSON	RM
BARNY	MURPHY	MECH	CYRIL	WOODS	RM
PAUL	SHAW	MECH	GERRY	COOPER	RM
ROBERT	SMITH	MECH	KEN	GORE	RM
ALAN	STRICKLAND	MECH	KEN	MELLING	RM
CHARLIE	EVANS	MECH	ALAN	OXLEY	RM
MAX	FERRIER	MECH	ALAN	TEANBY	RM
ALAN	GILBERTSON	MECH	JOHN	SUMNER	SCRAP
PETE/SAM	GILLILAND	MECH	LES	CORNISH	SEC
DOUG	HART	MECH	HARRY	DOYLE	SEC
JOHN	MARSDEN	MECH	STEVE	GRUNDY	SEC
JOHN	MCCRAE	MECH	TOMMY	HESKETH	SEC
TOMMY	FORD	MISC	HARRY	NESBITT	SEC
BILL	PLACE	MISC	BRIAN	TOMLINSON	SEC
JIMMY	ANDREWS	RM	DAVY	ARMOUR	SP
KEITH	ARMITAGE	RM	CARL	CONROY	SP
MANNY	BARREIRO	RM	STEVE	CONROY	SP
ALAN	BARRETT	RM	BOB	DEVON	SP
BERNARD	BRADY	RM	JOHN	EDWARDS	SP
FRANK	CALEY	RM	KENNY	EDWARDS	SP
BOB	CARSON	RM	ALAN	JONES	SP

Appendix 5 - Bidston Steel Staff

GEORGE	JONES	SP	JACKY	TILDSLEY	STAFF
CHRIS	LAWLER	SP	LINDA	TIPPING	STAFF
GERRY	LAWLER	SP	JAN	USHER	STAFF
JIMMY SNR	OLOUGHLIN	SP	ANN	USHER	STAFF
STEVE	PICKSTOCK	SP	STEVIE	WHEELDON	STAFF
LENNIE	PICKSTOCK	SP	MAY	WHITTENBURY	STAFF
LAURIE	WHITTINGHAM	SP	KEITH	WILDING	STAFF
BRIAN	DAVIES	SP	KATHY	YATES	STAFF
GRAHAM	HUTCHINSON	SP	GORDON	LYTHYGOE	STORES
BILL	MAINWARING	SP	BILLY	MORRIS	STORES
STEVE	WARD	SP	EDDIE	REID SNR	STORES
ALAN	APPLEARD	STAFF	TED	WILLIAMSON	STORES
SUE	BELL	STAFF	EDDIE	MURPHY	STORES?
NELL	BONIFACE	STAFF	TOMMY	JOHNSON	TEST
CATHY	BRADY	STAFF	BRIAN	JONES	TEST
MAUREEN	CALEY	STAFF	DAVID	JACKSON	TESTER
MARY	DEAN	STAFF	PHIL	BEAMISH	TESTING
JACKIE	DOBBINS?	STAFF	GERRY	WILSON	TESTING
JOHN	FOGG	STAFF	NEIL	BENNETT	TRANS
GEORGE	GOODWIN	STAFF	PAT	O BRIAN	WEIGH
IAN	GORE	STAFF	GERRY	YEARDSLY	WELDER
MARIE	HENDERSON	STAFF	EDDIE	FITZSIMMONS	WTP
STUART	JACKSON	STAFF	PERCY	HEGGARTY	WTP
LESLEY	KELLY	STAFF	EDDIE	MEHERJI	WTP
PAT	LANGTON	STAFF	JIM	SHERLOCK	WTP
CLIFF	LAW	STAFF			
DAWN	LEWIS	STAFF			
KEITH	MC ARTHUR	STAFF			
SUE	MC CARTHY	STAFF			
KEVIN	MCINTAGGART	STAFF			
GORDON	MCSHANNON	STAFF			
ROY	MOTTERSHEAD	STAFF			
ARTHUR	MUIR	STAFF			
CAROLE	ONEILL	STAFF			
DUNCAN	SKIDMORE	STAFF			
CHRISSIE	SLIMMING	STAFF			
GEOFF	TAYLOR	STAFF			

Appendix 6 - Companies owned by the author

Owner of Buy-a-Pet	Oct 1971 - Nov 1974
Partner Electronic Technical Services	Jan 1974 - Jun 1975
Owner Wirral Instrument Services	Sep 1975 - Aug 1976
Owner Instamec	Aug 1976 - Aug 1985
Partner Mersey Industrial Supplies	Nov 1981 - Nov 1986
Director Weldtip Ltd	Jun 1982 - Dec 1985
Partner Mersey Tool and Welding Supplies.	Jan 1984 - Apr 1987
Director Northwest Saw Services Ltd	Sep 1984 - Apr 1985
M.D. Instamec Ltd (Costains)	Sep 1985 - Nov 1987
Partner D. J Communications	Oct. 1987 - Nov 1996
Director D.J.Comms Ltd	Oct. 1989 - Jan 1992
Director Anchor Recruitment	Nov 1989 - Jan 1992
Director Winner Publications Ltd	Dec 1990 - Apr 1992
Director Linkstar Ltd	Oct 1991 - Oct 1992
Owner Tyrell Industrial Supplies	July 1992 - Aug 1996
Partner D.J Leisure the *City Pub*	July 1995 - Mar 2000
Managing Director of Infodial ltd.	Jan 1996 - Current

Electronic Technical Services was formed by John Walker and myself. Our first job involved humidity and temperature controls in half an acre of greenhouse on Leasowe Road owned by the Magill brothers. My link with the horticultural industry continued when I formed my next company, Wirral Instrument Services. Our pioneering development of equipment to control the nutrient film technique used in the growing of products without soil was revolutionary at the time. Probably the biggest catalyst for my entrepreneurial skills was the time I was involved in the instrumentation of a steel mill at Bidston.

In the process of buying some office space in Oldham Street in Manchester, we ended up owning the *City Pub*. This experience took me on an adventure into the darkest corners of humanity, meeting many Charles Dickens type characters on the way. This was the time when organised crime had a stranglehold on the city. I am just putting the finishing touches to my book on the subject 'A tale of two Cities'.

My current business is involved in the telecommunications industry and publishing.

With four books already published in the Forgotten Hero series on early Victorian military campaigns.

Appendix 7 - Map 1611

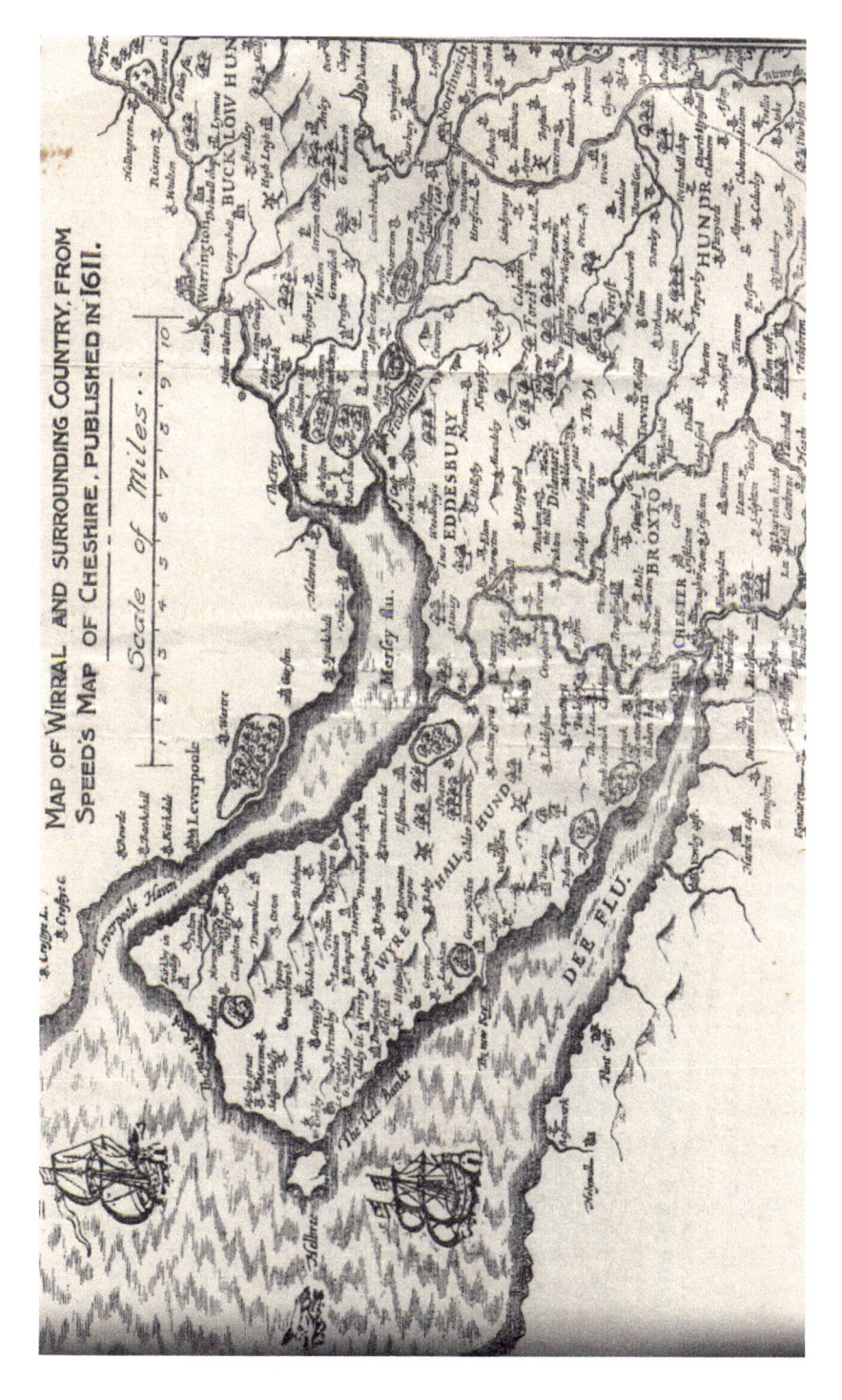

Appendix 7 - Map 1909

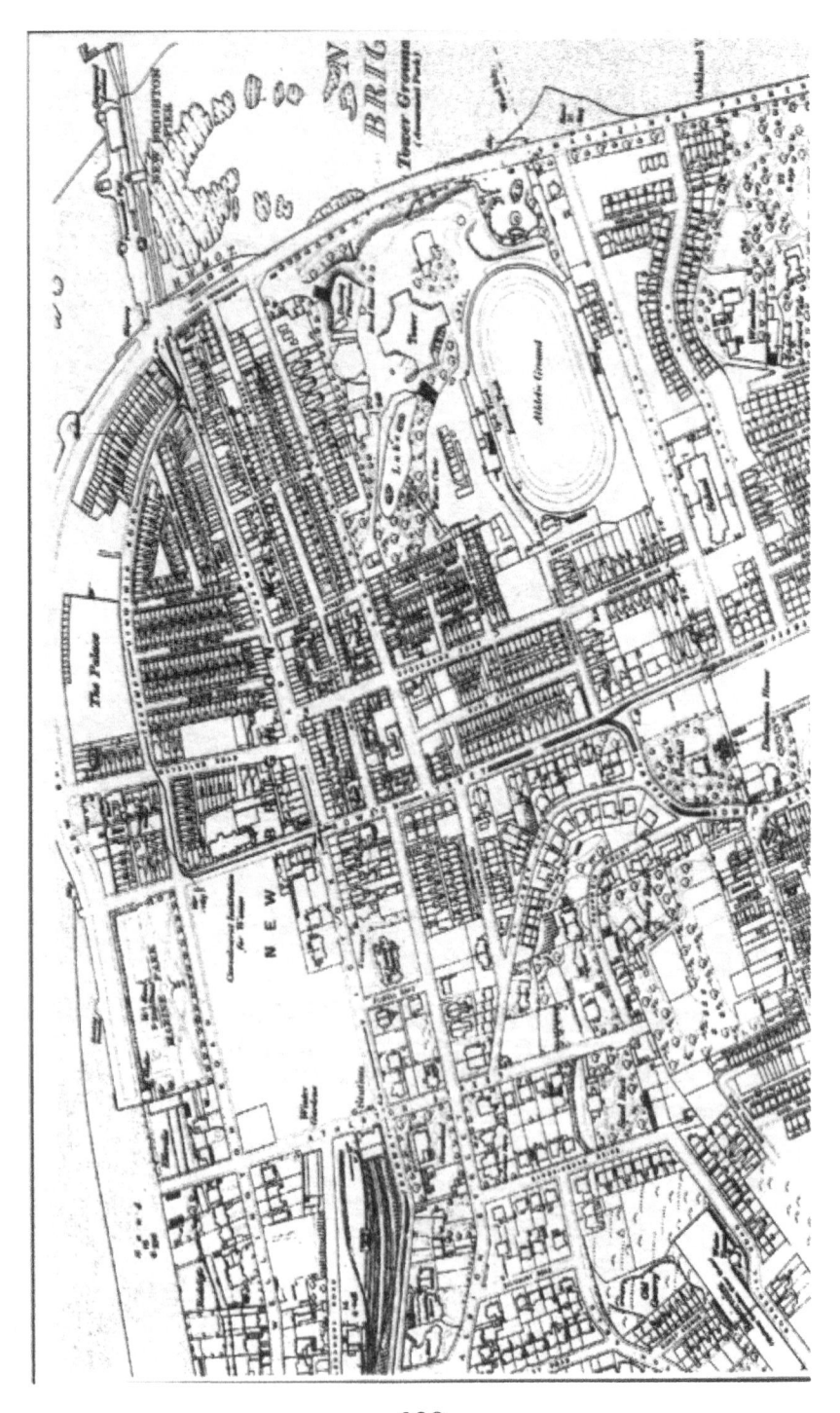

Appendix 7 - Map 1877

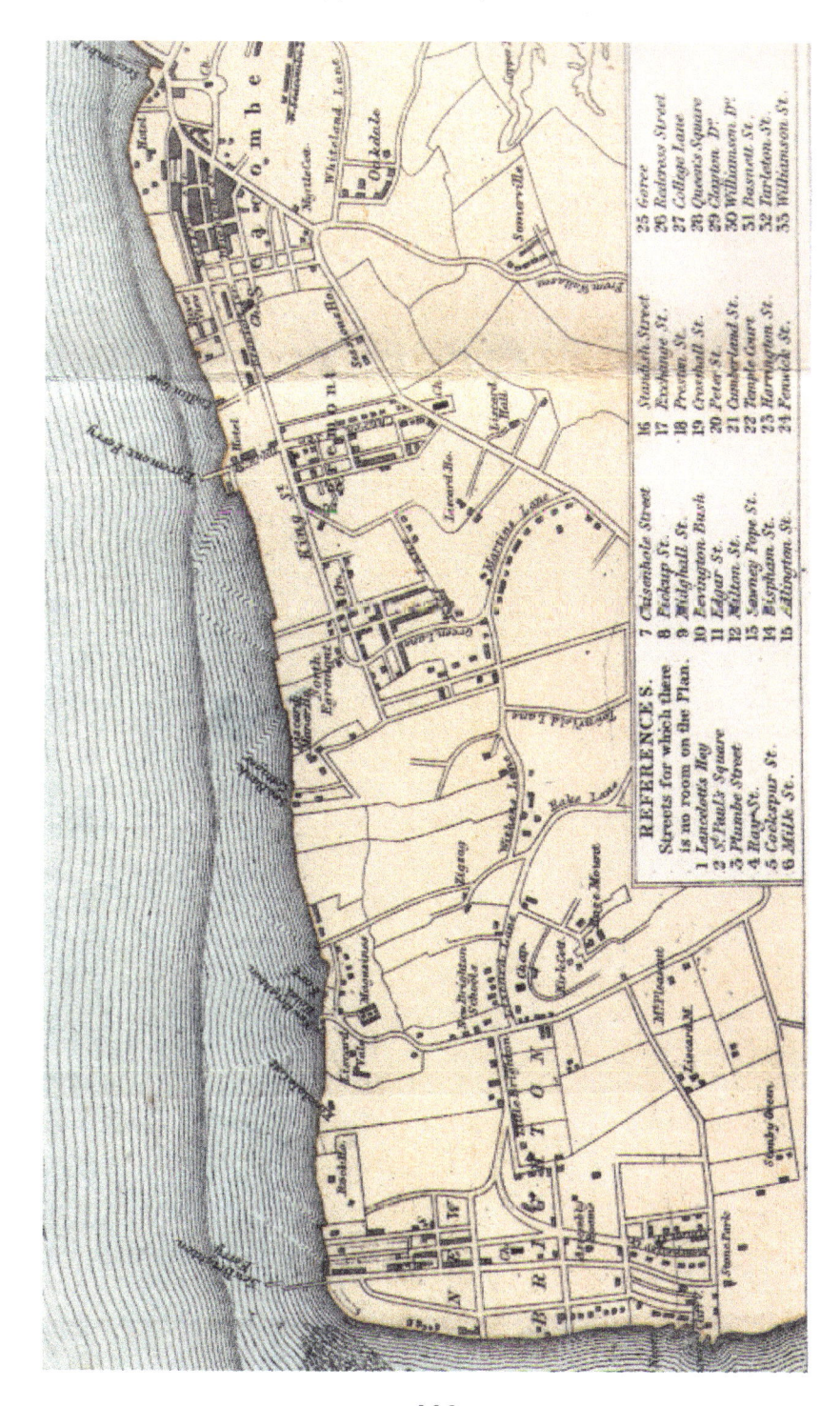

REFERENCES.
Streets for which there is no room on the Plan.

1. Lancelotts Hey
2. St Paul's Square
3. Plumbe Street
4. Bay St.
5. Cockspur St.
6. Milk St.
7. Caisenhole Street
8. Pickup St.
9. Midghall St.
10. Lovington Bush
11. Edgar St.
12. Milton St.
13. Sawney Pope St.
14. Bispham St.
15. Atlington St.
16. Standish Street
17. Exchange St.
18. Preson St.
19. Crosshall St.
20. Peter St.
21. Cumberland St.
22. Temple Court
23. Harrington St.
24. Fenwick St.
25. Gore
26. Redcross Street
27. College Lane
28. Queens Square
29. Clayton Dr
30. Williamson Dr
31. Basnett St.
32. Tarleton St.
33. Williamson St.

Appendix 8 - Arial Photograph New Brighton

Appendix 8 - Arial Photograph New Brighton

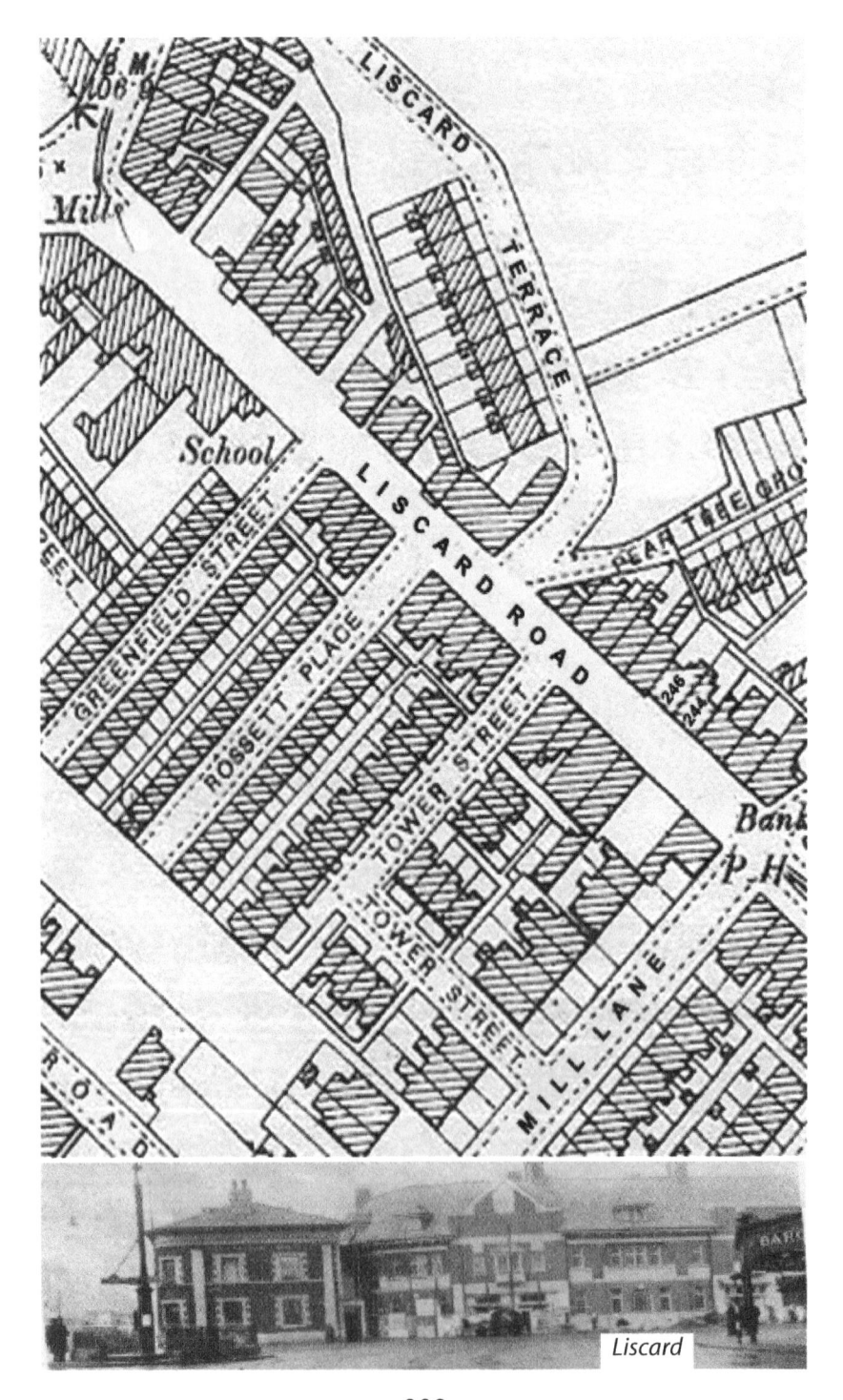

Appendix 9 - Liscard Shopping 1898

Liscard

Appendix 9 - Liscard Shopping 1898

Mill Lane
259 The Tower Hotel Henry Orme
263 Frederick Lewis Pawnbrokers
265 Fred Wells Cycle Maker
267 Queen's Hall
269 Murray R. & Sons Fishmongers
271 Wallasey Laundry Co. George E. Goodwin proprietor

Tower Street
273 James Broadbent Baker & Flour Dealer
275 Joe S Boulton Chemist
277 John Bushell Butcher
279 James Low Painter & Plumber
281 Evan Lloyd Draper

Rossett Place
283 Richard S. Edwards Grocer
285 Ellen Hilliard China Dealer
287 Annie Mullineux Stationers
289 Frederick Gell Pork Butcher

Greenfield Street
St. Mary's Schools Girls
295 Michael T. Graveson Provision Merchant
297 William Patterson Boot Dealer
299 Clare & Co. Corn Merchants

Westminster Road
236 North & South Wales Bank
238-240 Charles Fry Pawnbrokers
242 John Bleakley Painter & Plumber
244 John Dutton Milk Dealer
246 Henry Culverwell Greengrocer
248 James Edwin Pilkington Ironmonger
250 Edward Peirce - Newsagent
273 James Broadbent Baker & Flour Dealer
252 William Warner Watchmaker
254 John D. Smith Baker & Flour Dealer
256 Edward Peirce Hairdresser
258 Kate Barnett Tobacconist
260 John Braithwaite Fruitier

Liscard Terrace
262 Aspinal & Lockley Coach Builders
264 Mathew Ellaby / John Cooil Sadlers
268 Henry Dodd Butcher
272 James Warner Draper
274 J & L Lacy Bread & Flour Dealers

Field Cottages Tower Street
276   Joseph H. Wall Fruitier & Greengrocer
278   Thomas Q. Gick Tailor & Outfitter
280   Bertram Furness Post Office
282   Charles Emery Greengrocer
284   John Howell Confectioner
286   Edwin Harrop Book Keeper
288   John Harrop Coal Merchant
290   John Avery Hairdresser
292   John Taylor Butcher
294   James A. Hodgson Fishmonger & Poulterer
296   Mrs C. T. Drewe Stationer

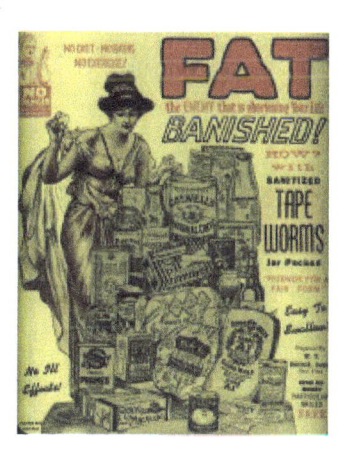

Schools in the Borough of Wallasey 1911

New Brighton | **Pupils**
Vaughan Road (Corporation) | 700
Vaughan Road Higher Elementary (Corporation) | 400
St James' School Egerton Street (C of E) | 300
S.S Peter and Paul's (RC) | 167
Rocks School, Magazine Lane (C of E) | 322

Upper Brighton
Rake Lane (Corporation) | 423

Liscard
Manor Road (Corporation) | 1,153
St Mary's (C. of E.) | 743
St Alban's (R.C) | 420

Seacombe
Riverside (Corporation) | 1,338
Somerville (Corporation) | 1,174
St Paul's (C of E) | 663
St. Joseph's (RC) | 640
Seacombe Wesleyan | 448

Poulton
(Corporation) | 1,000

Wallasey
St. George's Road (Corporation) | 1,000

In 1839 the first elementary school was opened in Liscard under the auspices of the National Society opposite Central Hospital in Liscard Road, and connected with St John's Parish Church until 1894. In that year the school transferred to St Mary's Church.

St Mary's Church in Withens Lane had been built in 1877; before this date services had been held in the Liscard Church Mission where a day school for boys was started in January 1874, called Liscard Church Mission School.

In 1861 there were 10 schools in Wallaey of which six were National Schools each attached to a parish church.

(1) St Hilary's Boys' School, Wallasey Road.
(2) St Paul's School, Seacombe, founded about 1848 and rebuilt in 1867.
(3) St Alban's in Liscard was founded in 1842 and rebuilt in 1861.
(4) St James's, Magazine Lane, New Brighton, built in 1847.
(5) Seacombe Wesleyan School in Brighton Street, opposite the Town Hall, started 1856.
(6) Welsh Calvinistic Methodists School at the corner of Victoria Road (Now Borough Road) opened in 1857-8

Poulton Infants' School, Limelikn Lane, founded in 1848
Manor Road School built in 1903 It became Liscard Secondary Modern.

Ref: Wirral Archive

Bibliography

In writing this account of my family history and my own indulgence in the form of an Autobiography. Reference has been made to many earlier works among which the following deserve special mention:

Harthill Register 1730-98. Baptisms 1781
Malpas Register Baptisms 1728-05 (Published Version)
Burwardsley Baptisms 1750
Malpas Marriages 1725-2 (published Version)
Farndon Baptisms 1692-6, 1691-65
The Memories of Wallasey. The Original Wallasey Fire Brigade - Bertram Furniss 1934.
Minutes of the Wallasey Local Board April 1890-March 1891
Wallasey News 1st April 1977 Looking Back with Ian Roth
Landmarks of Old Wallasey Village 1859 - Thomas Westcott
Liverpool's Children in the second World War - Pamela Russell
The Rise and Progress of Wallasey 1974 - Woods & Brown
Ancient Meols 1863 - The Rev. A. Hume.
New Brighton Holiday Guide. Wallasey Corporation 1949, 1958, 1960, 1970
Wallasey Old and New 1899-1949 Pictorial Souvenir - Wallasey News
The Inviting Shore. A Social History of New Brighton - Anthony M. Miller
The Wirral Journal. Various issues published by Kenneth Burnley.
Ordnance Survey Maps Cheshire Sheet 1898 - The Godfrey Edition.
Life at Lairds. Memories of Working Shipyard Men 1992 - David Roberts
Yesterday's Wallasey & New Brighton 2008 - Ian Boumphrey
The Romance of Wirral 1946 - A.G Caton
Wallasey Now & Then 2010 - Wallasey group Family History Society
Almost an Island The Story of Wallasey 1990 - Noel E. Smith.
A Chat about Leasowe Castle 1924 - Thomas S. Ling
Various Kelly's and Gore's Directories of Liverpool and Suburbs.
Limited Excursion to Liverpool & New Brighton by the Midland and Cheshire Lines Railways 1904
Acts of Parliament and provisional orders relating to Wallasey, 1809 - 1899.
101 Views of Edwardian Liverpool & New Brighton 1972 - Trevor lloyd-Jones.
The End of a Liverpool Landmark 1985 - J.A Watson
Hopps around Wallasey 2010 - Colin Simpson

The end of New Brighton Tower 5.4.1969

Index

A
Ainsworth, Bob 279, 282, 287, 288
Allen, Dave 172
Anderson, Brian 266
Andrews, Graham 267, 270, 273
Andrews, Malcolm 169
Artell, Gerald 55
Ashton, Paul 195, 196, 292, 294
Ashworth, Dave 281
Ashworth, Eric 75
Ashworth, Harry 75
Atherton, James 18

B
Bailey, Mike 277, 280
Bailey, Robert 2, 135, 183, 194, 151, 293
Baker, Dave 178
Baker, Graham 169, 178
Baker, Mary 5
Bale, Stewart 2
Ball, Andy 313
Ball, Delma 85, 141
Ball, Ernest 85, 321
Ball, Norma 85, 141, 169
Ball, Polly 85
Ball, T.P 23
Barnes, Joe 303
Basset, Walter 199
Bate, J.C Mr 34, 42
Beasley, Miss 174
Bellis, Mr 194
Bennett, Mr 279
Billiason, Tony 269
Bird, Bob 2
Bird, Carla 2
Bird, Eleanor 51
Bird, Nathan 51
Bird, William 51
Birnie, James 55
Black, Peter 268
Bleakley, John 39
Bond, Mary Ann 96
Boode, Lewis William 25
Booker, Miss 169, 170, 174
Bordley, Jimmy 259
Bradley, Dave 259
Bradshaw, Mr 151
Brady, Bernard 267
Brady, John 51

Brammall, Joseph Garside 98, 104
Brammall, Lawrence 104
Breanan, Tommy 266
Brindle, John 302
Bromley, Arthur 259
Brown, J. Calvin 35
Brown, Reginald 205
Brown, Ursula 205
Buckley, Elizabeth 60
Burns, John 97
Burns, Leo 276

C
Cairns, Jimmy 194
Campbell, John 205
Campbell, Zoe 205
Captain Thomas 19
Carey, Doctor 280
Carol Dodds 81
Carr, Dorothy 291
Carson, Robert 39
Carter, Harry 51
Carter, Nick 78
Catchpole, Peter 205, 292, 303
Caton, A.G. 193
Chadwick, Roger 269
Clare, Billy 292
Clare, Juna 115
Clare, Ray 292
Clark, Ken 2
Clewett, Lucy 91
Collins, Captain Grenville 191
Colquhoun, Robert 194
Cook, Jim 269
Cooke, Doris 51
Corbett, David 55
Costain, Peter 276
Cotterall, Norman 75
Courtman, Henrietta 121
Courtman, John 121
Cox, Doreen 142, 155
Cox, E.W 193
Cox, Frank 94, 142, 155
Craig, Eleanor 91
Craig, Norah 91
Crawford, G 264, 275
Crippen, Dr Hawley Harvey 44
Critchly, Wilf 283
Crooks, Jimmy 298

Index

Cross, Suzanne 272
Cust, Lady 25
Cust, Sir Edward 25
Cumpstey, Reg 218
Curry. Mr 164
Curtis, Mike 281
Cusak, Brian , 232

D

Dabner, Bernard 177
Davidson, Michael 259
Davies, Ald. P.G. 113
Davies, Davies 119, 120
Davies, Dr Seymour Whitney 42
Davies, Esther 96
Davis, Ann 110
Davis, G.H 196
Dawkins, Mr 23
de Rodelent, Robert 190
Dean, Iris M 70, 71
Dean, Ivy 49, 71
Dean J.A Mrs 54
Dean, Joseph Arthur 60, 70
Dean, John 85
Dean, Mary 272
Dean, Roderick J 80, 81
Dean, Ronald James 80, 81
Dean, R Mrs 54
Delamere, Mr 169, 170
Dew, Walter 45
Dillion, Matt 259
Dillon, Bob 285
Dodd, Henry 85, 333
Dodds, Miss Carol 81
Donald McPherson, 283
Downes & Roberts 41
Dr. Guthrie 21
Draper, Charles 171
Duff, Jean 218
Dutton, Adam 315
Dutton, Albert E. 69
Dutton, Alfred Rhayader 49, 50, 54, 71, 77, 82, 84, 85, 106, 138
Dutton, Alice 76
Dutton, Benjamin 7, 9
Dutton, Dorothy Glady 3, 4, 50, 86, 94, 95, 97, 99, 100, 103, 106, 111, 112, 123, 124, 144, 218
Dutton, Edith Maud 53, 80, 81

Dutton, Edward Robert (Ted) 5, 40, 52, 53, 58, 70, 72, 73
Dutton, Edward Walter 58
Dutton, Elizabeth 5, 6, 36, 70
Dutton, Elsie 55
Dutton, Emily 3, 53, 60, 70, 71
Dutton, Emily Elizabeth 67
Dutton, Frank 65, 66
Dutton, Fred 78
Dutton, Gary 2, 69
Dutton, George Edward 55, 56
Dutton, Gladys M 72
Dutton, Gwen 55
Dutton, Hannah. 66, 67
Dutton, Harriet 3, 51
Dutton, Inspector 34, 35
Dutton, James 47, 52, 65
Dutton, James Herbert 64, 65, 66, 67
Dutton, Jean 66
Dutton, Jennifer 103, 309
Dutton, Joan S 72
Dutton, John (b1841) 5, 6, 36, 37, 39, 40, 41, 42, 67
Dutton, John (b1869) 55, 56, 69
Dutton, Lanie 315
Dutton, Mabel 66
Dutton, Margaret 3, 5, 6, 37, 39, 41, 42, 47, 48, 49, 52, 54, 67
Dutton, Mary 3, 5, 36, 47, 49, 52
Dutton, Mary Ann 6
Dutton, Mary E 55
Dutton, Millicent Beatrice 55, 67
Dutton, Norman Eric 72, 75
Dutton, Peter 9
Dutton, Richard (b1781) 6
Dutton, Richard 103, 309
Dutton, Roy 4, 79, 103, 169, 195, 239, 265, 277, 286
Dutton, Sarah 50, 51, 67, 96,
Dutton, Sidney J 72
Dutton, Sheila 76
Dutton, Thomas (b1867) 3, 40, 47, 49, 52, 53, 54, 67, 70, 82, 84, 138
Dutton, Thomas (b1806) 5, 6, 9
Dutton, Thomas Fredrick 78
Dutton, Walter 40
Dutton, William 60, 61, 62, 65
Dutton, William R 55, 69

337

Index

E
Earle, Jackson 303
Edge, Elizabeth 9
Edwards, Michael 194
Eleanor 91
Elliott, Keith 78
Ellis, Arthur 34
Elmore, Belle 44
Ennis, Bill , 237
Erdley, Dick 262
Evans, Charley , 271
Evans, E.T 41
Evans, Nancy 93
Evans, Norman 93
Evans, Taffy 294
Exley, Graham 270
Eyre, Mr 164

F
F.A.Small 34
Fairbanks, Douglas 219
Faulkner, William 51
Fellows, John 39
Ferrier, Max 266
Fielding, Jack 43
Fletcher, Cyril 167
Foster, Brian 2, 94, 176, 312
Fowell, Rev. Richard Drake 22
Fox, Ken 205
Frank, Charles 196
Fred T. Cummins 34
Ferman, Mary 9
Fry, Charles 45

G
Gannon, Michael 194, 293, 294
Garrant, John 22
Garry, Pat 266
Geary, Ted 302
Gibbons, Harold 24, 39, 43, 59
Gibbons, James 43
Glover, Bill 153
Glover, George 299
Glover, Maggie 135
Gooding, Dennis 301
Goodwin, George 267, 270, 310
Goodwin, Margaret 264
Goodwin, Martin 172
Graveson 41
Gray, Michael 194

Green, Colin 194, 311
Griffin, John W 43
Griffiths, William H 71

H
Halewood, Abraham 39
Halewood, Tony 300
Halfpenny, Mr 164
Hammond, Derek 85, 106
Hammond, Dorothy Glady(See Dutton)
Hammond, Emily Mary Ann 96, 97, 100
Hammond, George William 96, 99, 100
Hammond, Grace (Eve) 3, 21, 98, 104, 119, 123, 128, 129
Hammond, Jessie 96, 101
Hammond, Joyce (Menefee) 3, 98, 99, 102, 103, 104, 105, 106, 107, 108, 109, 110, 111, 112, 113, 125, 195, 319
Hammond, Julia 3, 96, 97, 98, 99, 101
Hammond, Lucy Elizabeth 97, 100
Hammond, Margorie 100
Hammond, Peter 3, 96
Hammond, Ronald 100, 102
Hammond, Sarah 96
Hammond, Sidney 86, 106
Hammonds, Emily Mary Ann 96
Handley, Tommy 14
Harriet Roberts 6
Harrop, Grenville 277, 280, 289
Harry Keenan 39, 41,
Hart, Douglas 269
Hepkie David 2, 258, 304
Heyward, Rosa 303
Hicks, Elizabeth 55
Hill, Steven 78
Holbrook, Geoff 285
Holmes, Tony 267
Hope, Jimmy 267
Howard, Thomas 222
Howarth, John 39
Hudson, John , 237, 292
Hughes, Joseph William 49
Hughes, Mary 47, 49, 53, 53, 242
Hulme, Phoebe 122
Hulme, Robert 122
Humberstone, Frances M. 82
Humphreys, Ben 51
Hunt, J 17

Index

I
Ingram, Edwin 274
Inman, William 25
Inspector Dutton 3, 34, 35
Irish, Edward 49

J
Jackson, Alan 183, 151
Jackson, Mr 271
Jackson, Pat 287, 288, 290
Jackson, Robin 79
Jackson, Stuart 283, 288, 290, 315
Jackson, Vinnie 258
James Leather 39
James Roberts 6
Jane Dutton 5, 6
John Bleakley 39, 333
John Fellowes, 39
John Nicholls 42, 52, 53
John Pemberton 39
Jolly, Harry 75
Jones, Alan 243, 244
Jones, Billy 139
Jones, Bob 259
Jones, Brian 259
Jones, James 51
Jones, Lillian 140
Jones, Tommy 139
Joseph, Sir Keith 264
Joseph, Dutton 6
Joyce, Thomas 38
Jump, Audrey 119, 120

K
Keenan, Harry 41
Kelly, Agnes 55
Kidd, Ian 284, 287
Kingham, Norman 292, 311
Kirkland, Juna Clare 115
Kitson, Captain 20
Koltuniak, Moe 2

L
Langley, Mr 23
Law, Cliff 270
Lawton, Dave 167, 168, 172, 173, 175, 180
Lawton, Frank 242
Lea, James 39
Leary-Shaw, Mrs 111, 183, 225, 228
Leather, James Captain 39, 40

Ledsham, William 38
Leigh, Donna 195
Le Neve, Ethel Clara 44
Lenton, Nish 271
Lever, William Hesketh 11
Lewis, Hilda 298
Littledale, Harold 24, 59

M
Magee, Jack 301
Mainwright, Billy 271
Mann, Billy 180
Marchant, John 271
Margaret Roberts 5, 6, 36
Marsh, John 272
Marsh, Miss , 180
Marshall, Billy 269
Mattews, George 259
McCabe, Mrs 176, 179
McClean, Angus 174
McCray, John 269
McCullock, Jim 302
McCullock, Tom 79
McCullough, Mike 284
McEntaggart, Kevin 264
McGonigal, Norman 205
McPherson, Donald 283
McShannane, Gordon 264
McShannon, Sandra 264
Menefee, Barry R 115
Menefee, Denice Maureen 115
Menefee, Gillian Michelle 115
Menefee, Jennifer Joyce 115
Menefee, Keith 106
Menefee, Laurie Kathlene 115
Menefee, Raymond Anthony 115
Menefee, Shirley Norton 115
Middlemiss, Chris 2, 292
Millar, Brian 269
Millar, Dawn 272
Millington, Ian 286, 287
Moore, Harry 230
Moore, John 237, 292, 293
Moore, Patrick 195
Morris, George 267
Moscroft, Mr 171
Mottershead, Roy 264, 272
Muir, Arthur , 270, 272
Muirehead, Bob 268

Index

N
Neal, Charles 43, 169, 258, 263, 265, 266, 270, 271, 272, 273, 303, 310
Nesbitt, Major D.A.S. 42
Newton, James 102, 106
Newton, Malcolm 169, 262
Nicholls, John 42, 52, 53, 54, 321
Nixon, Graham 269
Noble, Bob 263

O
O'Neill, Dorothy 71
O'Neill, James A. 71
O'Reilly, Mick 301
Ostle, Roy 265, 266
Owens, Bill 81
Owl, Henry 171

P
Parry, Mrs 79
Parsons, Mrs J.W. 81
Peacock, William 16
Pears, Maureen 2
Pears, Peter 300
Pemberton, Zena 173
Pickles, Stanley 81
Piper, family 57
Piper, Magaret 57
Pitcher, Dave 279
Price, Billy 183
Price, George 34
Price, Mr 174
Prydderch, Mr 173
Pugh, Martin 2

R
Ravinscroft, John 269
Rawlinson, Mr 195
Read, Malcolm 195
Rev. R. Ellwood 42
Revins, John 269
Rice, Betty 106
Rice, Margery 106
Richards, Brian 267
Ricketts, John 167, 172, 180
Riley, Margaret 34
Ritson, Peter , 237
Roach, Damon 115, 117
Roberts, Ann 6, 36
Roberts, Edward 5, 6, 36

Roberts, Harriet 6
Roberts, James 6
Roberts, John 53
Roberts, Margaret 6
Roberts, Mrs 38
Robinson, Peter , 270
Rynning, Chris , 274

S
Sacca, Bradley Lynn 115
Samples, Alice 58
Samuel Fleet, 5
Sarah Bankes 9
Scudder, Joyce 195
Seymour Whitney Davis 42
Sharp, Stephen 312
Sharp, Steven 2, 300
Sherlock, Margaret 69
Shone 39, 40
Simon, David 164
Skelly, Captain 242
Skidmore, Duncan 264, 272
Small, F.A 34
Smith, Albert 24
Smith, Joey 259
Smith, Lennie 172
Smith, Mr 164, 225, 258
Spalding, Albert 55
Spragg, William 37
Stanhope, John 272
Stanley, John Barrymore 303
Stokes, Mr 171, 172
Stretch, Michael 263
Sumerville Thomas 39
Sundt, H.E. 275

Sutton, Leonard Sidney 205
Sutton, Phyllis 75

T
Taafel, Rev. Frank O. 113
Thomas Espinal Espin, 26
Thomas Joyce 38
Thomas Somerville 39
Thompson, Norman , 240, 242
Thorpe, Mr 172
Tobin, Sir John 59
Trafford, Norman 291
Turnbull, Peter 79
Turner, Mr 23

Index

U
Upton, Frank 166
Upton, Rodney 165, 166, 167

V
Vyner, Mr 24

W
Walker, John 262
Wall, Mable 60
Ward, Betty 155
Ward, Walter 155
Watson, Miss 170
Waugh, Mr 164
Webster, William , 38
Westcott, Thomas 38, 335
Whalley, Campbell , 235
White, Jack 219
Whitenbury, May 272
Wickham, Bob 298
Wickham, Steve 298
Wilkie, W H 216
Wilkinson, David 50
Wilkinson, Sarah Ann 67
Williams, Duggy 237
Williamson, Ted 267
Wilson, Greg 303
Winder, Elizabeth 55
Winrow, Tony , 232
Wivell. Mrs 129
Wood, Alex 267, 271
Wood, Dave 287
Wood, Ray 300
Woodroffe, C.J 42
Woods, Phil 232
Wooler, Bob 295
Wormhole, Eddy 236
Wostencroft, Mr 261
Wray, Emily 60
Wyard, Martin 268

Y
Yoxall, Robert C. 95
Yoxall, Theresa 95

Z
Zenger, Gary 115, 118

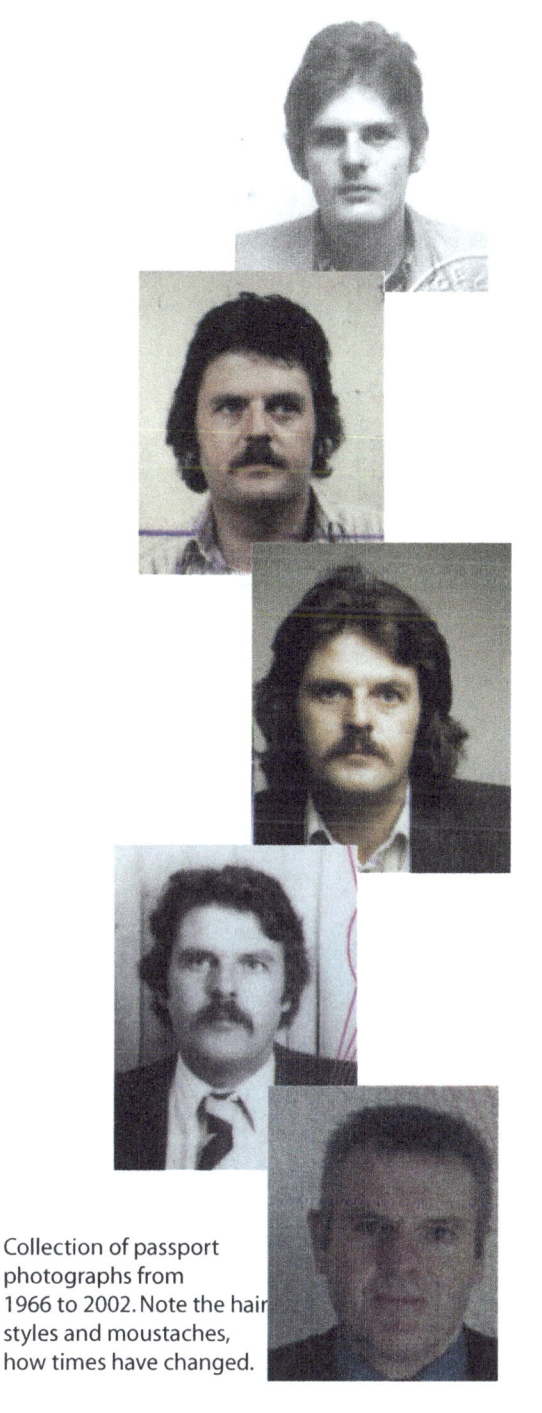

Collection of passport photographs from 1966 to 2002. Note the hair styles and moustaches, how times have changed.

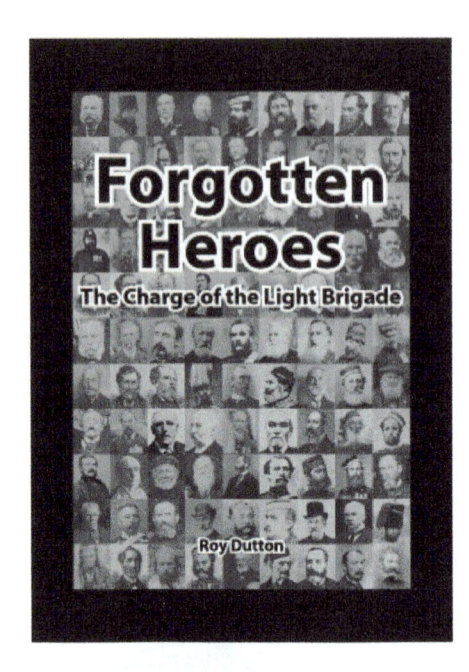

First in the series of Forgotten Heroes, The Charge of the Light Brigade. The book contains first hand accounts of the men who took part in the heroic and tragic Charge at the Battle of Balaclava on the 25th October 1854.
Set within an unrelenting and cruel military campaign, where many would perish, unravelling the myths to find many of the missing Chargers was a massive undertaking.

This book is about the ordinary people that made an Empire and gave the World a Legacy.

**(ISBN: 0955655401) 420 pages. Hardback.
(800 b/w photos, illustrations & tables)**

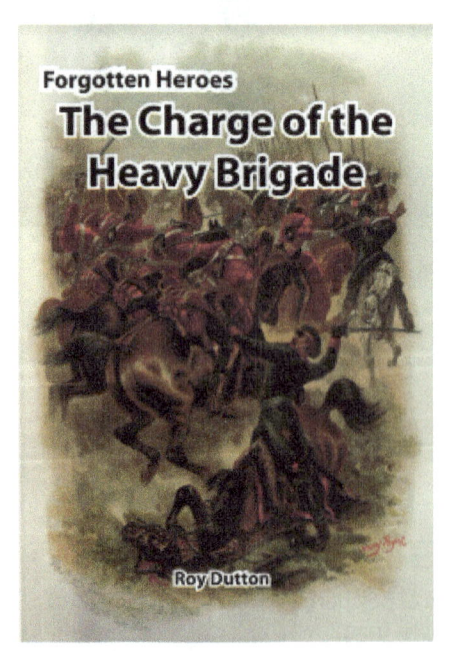

The Charge of the Heavy Brigade at Balaclava on the 25th October 1854, is one of the most neglected events in the annals of British military history. Against all odds they attacked a Russian force which outnumbered them 5:1.
On the day in question the Heavy Brigade were involved in two separate charges. The first was the successful charge of the Brigade on the advancing Russian cavalry, who were intent on capturing the over crowded port of Balaclava, the main supply point for the British army.
The second was in support of the Light Brigade on their unsuccessful attack on the Russian artillery.

To date no book has ever been written on the subject. With over 1300 men listed, with numerous biographical details A truly inspirational undertaking.

**(ISBN: 0955655425) 375 pages. Hardback.
(600 b/w photos, illustrations & tables)
First Edition**

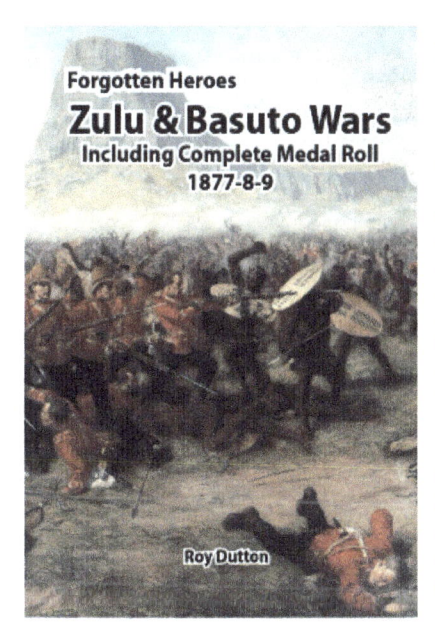

Forgotten Heroes, Zulu & Basuto Wars.
Including Complete Medal Roll
1877-8-9

A work of reference, with details of the Colonial and Imperial forces engaged in the Zulu and Basuto Wars between 1877 to 1879. Over 26,600 men are listed with medal entitlement, casualty lists and troop deployments together with numerous biographical details.
An invaluable guide for both medal collectors and historians. These men at great personal sacrifice helped to build an Empire, on which the sun would never set.

(ISBN: 0955655449) 465 pages.
Hardback.
(200+ b/w photos, illustrations & tables)
First Edition

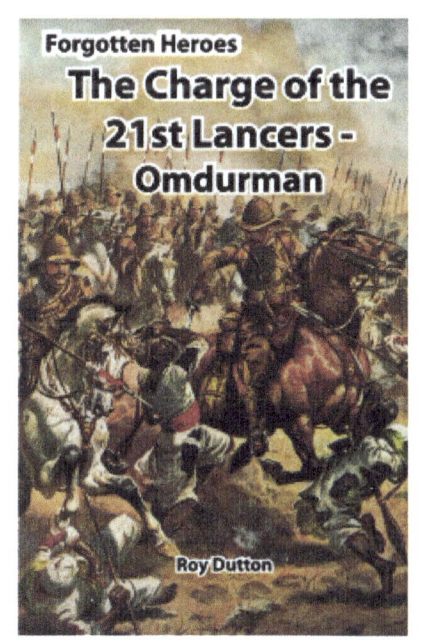

Forgotten Heroes, The charge of the 21st Lancers - Omdurman

The charge of the 21st Lancers at Omdurman on the 2nd September 1898, will go down in the annals of British military history. It is now generally accepted that this was the last true cavalry charge against a standing enemy. With 21 dead and 71 wounded and three Victoria crosses awarded, the 2,500 dervishes were driven from the path of General Kitchener's advance.   With biographical details of all who took part, first hand accounts, medal details, maps, uniforms and numerous photographs. An invaluable guide for both medal collectors and historians.
Includes Medal Roll

(ISBN: 0955655456) 423 pages.
Hardback.
(500+ b/w photos, illustrations & tables)
First Edition